KU-611-010

Contents

Margaret Coventry

The Essence of Prayer

METROPOLITAN ANTHONY
OF SOUROZH

The Essence of Prayer

Living Prayer
School for Prayer
God and Man (with Marghanita Laski)
Courage to Pray (with Georges LeFebvre)

Darton, Longman and Todd
London

This collected edition first published in 1986 by
Darton, Longman and Todd Ltd
89 Lillie Road, London SW6 1UD

Reprinted 1989

Living Prayer: first published in 1966 by
Darton, Longman and Todd Ltd
© Archbishop Anthony Bloom 1966

School for Prayer: first published in 1970 by
Darton, Longman and Todd Ltd
© 1970 Anthony Bloom

God and Man: first published in 1971 by
Darton, Longman and Todd Ltd
© 1971 Anthony Bloom

Courage to Pray: first published in English in 1973 by
Darton, Longman and Todd Ltd
Originally published in France as *La Prière* by
Maison Mame, Paris
This translation © 1973 by Darton, Longman and Todd Ltd

This collected edition © 1986 Darton, Longman and Todd Ltd

ISBN 0 232 51698 7

British Library Cataloguing in Publication Data
Bloom, Anthony
   The essence of prayer.
   1.   Prayer
   I.   Title
   248.3'2   BV210.2

   ISBN 0 232 51698 7

Printed and bound in Great Britain by
Anchor Press Ltd, Tiptree, Essex

Publisher's Note

Ever since *Living Prayer* was first published in 1966 Metropolitan Anthony of Sourozh has been widely recognised as a major spiritual writer. That first book was followed by *School for Prayer* in 1970, *God and Man* (with Marghanita Laski) in 1971 and *Courage to Pray* (with Georges Lefebvre) in 1973. Here the reader will find all four of the classic works gathered together in one volume. It is hoped that this will help the reader familiar with Metropolitan Anthony's writings to assess his achievement to date, while for those coming new to the texts it will provide a unique and substantial work on the spiritual life.

Some biographical details about the author may be welcome, and the reader can supplement these by reading the interview with Timothy Wilson which appears on p.ix-xxii.

Metropolitan Anthony of Sourozh was born in Lausanne, 19 June, 1914. His childhood was spent in Russia and Persia, his father being a member of the Russian Imperial Diplomatic Corps. His mother was the sister of Alexander Scriabin the composer. The family had to leave Persia during the Revolution and came to Paris where Archbishop Anthony was educated, graduating in Physics, Chemistry, and Biology, and taking his doctorate in Medicine, at the University of Paris. During World War II he served as an officer in the French Army until the fall of France and then worked as a surgeon in one of the Paris hospitals and also took part in the Resistance. In 1943 he professed monastic vows while practising as a physician in Paris. In 1948 he was ordained to the priesthood and in 1949 came to England as Orthodox Chaplain to the Fellowship of St Alban and St Sergius; and in 1950 was appointed Vicar of the Russian Patriarchal Parish in London. In 1958 he was consecrated Bishop, and Archbishop in 1962, in charge of the Russian Church in Great Britain and Ireland. In 1963 he was also appointed Exarch to the Patriarch of Moscow in Western Europe, and in 1966 raised to the rank of Metropolitan. He takes an active part in inter-Church and ecumenical work, and was a member of the Russian Church delegation to the World Council of Churches in New Delhi in 1961 and in Geneva in 1966. He is the holder of many awards and honours for his work in spreading the Christian gospel.

INTERVIEW WITH ARCHBISHOP ANTHONY BLOOM*

by

Timothy Wilson

T.W.: Were you born in Russia?

Bloom: I was born in Switzerland in fact, because my father was a diplomat and happened to be there when I was born. But we returned to Russia just before the First World War.

T.W.: What happened after that?

Bloom: My father went to serve in the Orient, in Persia, and that's where I spent the second part of my childhood.

T.W.: What happened to your family after the Russian Revolution?

Bloom: We crossed the north of Persia on horseback and in horse-driven carts, then over the mountains of Khurdistan, then down the Tigris and the Euphrates in a barge. We ended up in a small English boat going to India and from there we got a boat going towards Southampton. I say 'towards' because in fact we never arrived. Just as we were setting off we were told that the boat was far too old to weather any storm so I was full of hopes – that I would end up as a kind of Robinson Crusoe marooned on a desert island. I could never understand how my mother could be so unromantic as to hope for good weather, but anyhow God happened to be on the side of the grown-ups and in the end we landed safely at Gibraltar. But the boat couldn't go any further. So part of our luggage went on to Southampton – we got it back about fourteen years later and had to pay a pound for customs. Meanwhile we travelled through Spain,

*This interview first appeared in *School for Prayer* and is here reproduced as an introduction to *The Essence of Prayer*.

France, Austria and then into Yugoslavia. Eventually we came back to Austria where I went to school for a while, then back into France in 1923. And we finally settled there for the next twenty-seven years or so.

T.W.: This is a very exciting and romantic childhood. But what happened to your father? What sort of job did he do?

Bloom: Of course, he had left the diplomatic service and he decided to make a complete end to the past. He decided to take upon himself responsibility for all the tragic developments which had taken place in Russia and so he became, by choice, an unskilled workman. He worked on the railways, in factories, and did that kind of work until his health gave way. Then he turned to clerical work. But he never tried to readjust himself to the old standards, because he felt that the past was the past and one should take responsibility for all that had happened in Russia.

T.W.: Your father sounds to have been an extraordinary man. Can you remember very much about him?

Bloom: I remember a certain number of his phrases. In fact there are two things he said which impressed me and have stayed with me all my life. One is about life. I remember he said to me after a holiday, 'I worried about you' and I said, 'Did you think I'd had an accident?' He said, 'That would have meant nothing, even if you had been killed. I thought you had lost your integrity.' Then on another occasion he said to me, 'Always remember that whether you are alive or dead matters nothing. What matters is what you live for and what you are prepared to die for.' These things were the background of my early education and show the sense of life that I got from him.

T.W.: What happened about your own education during this period?

Bloom: After going to school in the normal way, I began to work when I was twelve – giving lessons to children who were younger than me so that I could pay for the books that I needed at school.

T.W.: What did you teach?

Bloom: Arithmetic and anything which I already knew and they didn't. Later on I taught latin which I knew very well and managed to pay my way through university by working in this way. I would give three or four hours of lessons every evening, teaching physics, chemistry and latin and this gave me enough money to live off while I was studying.

T.W.: It must have been a very hard life.

Bloom: Yes, it meant that I couldn't do any of my own work on week-day evenings and so I had to cram it all into the weekends, which often meant working all through the night. I used to go to bed at eight in the morning and sleep until midday, then start working again. It nearly finished me, but at least it enabled me to carry on with my studies.

T.W.: Were you studying medicine at this time?

Bloom: After secondary school where I read classics, I went to the School of Science at the Sorbonne and studied physics, chemistry and biology. After graduating (from there) I went to medical school where I finished in 1939 just as the war broke out.

T.W.: So you were qualified as a doctor in 1939?

Bloom: Yes. But then I was called up, in September 1939, and I became involved in the war in two ways – at the beginning and the end I was in the French army doing surgery and during the middle part of the war I was in the French resistance.

T.W.: You were working in a French hospital during the German occupation?

Bloom: I worked for some time in the hospital, but at a certain moment it became risky because I had joined the resistance and we had been doing resistance work there. So I left and taught in a school for a while.

T.W.: You were never caught.

Bloom: No, I'm afraid I never managed to be a hero even in that way.

T.W.: What was your nationality?

Bloom: Up until 1937 I was stateless, but in 1937 I applied for French nationality and I have kept it right until now. So technically I am French, but I belong to that generation which is Russian at heart. By education, culture and so on I can't feel that I belong completely to one side or the other. In Russia I feel Russian because it's my language, it's my country – yet I don't belong to it because I am an émigré. Abroad I am much too Russian to be able to melt completely into the milieu around me.

T.W.: When did you become a Christian? Was there any particular turning point?

Bloom: It came in several stages. Up to my middle teens I was an unbeliever and very aggressively anti-church. I knew no God, I wasn't interested and hated everything that connected with the idea of God.

T.W.: In spite of your father?

Bloom: Yes, because up to the age of 15 life had been very hard, we had no common roof and I was at boarding school which was rough and violent. All the members of my family lived in different corners of Paris. It was only when I was about 14 that we all gathered under a common roof and that was real happiness and bliss – it is odd to think that in a suburban house in Paris one could discover perfect happiness but it was so. This was the first time that we had had a home since the revolution. But before that I ought to say that I had met something which puzzled me a great deal. I was sent to a boy's summer camp when I was about eleven years old and there I met a priest who must have been about thirty. Something about him struck me – he had love to spare for everyone and his love wasn't conditioned by whether we were good and it never changed when we were bad. It was an unconditional ability to love. I had never met this in my life before. I had been loved at home, but I found it natural. I had friends too and that was natural, but I had never met this kind of love. At the time I didn't trace it to anything, I just found this man extremely puzzling and extremely lovable. Only years later, when I had already discovered the Gospel, did it occur to me that he loved with a love that was beyond him. He shared out divine love to us, or if you prefer, his human love was of such depth and had such scope and scale that he could include all of us, either through joy or pain, but still within one love. This experience I think was the first deep spiritual experience I had.

T.W.: What happened after this?

Bloom: Nothing. I went back to boarding school and everything went on as before until we all found ourselves under the same roof. When I found myself confronted with perfect happiness, a quite unexpected thing happened. I suddenly discovered that if happiness is aimless, it's unbearable. I could not accept aimless happiness. Hardships and suffering had to be overcome, there was always something beyond them. But because it had no further meaning and because I believed in nothing, happiness seemed to be stale. So I decided I would give myself a year to see whether life had any meaning. If in the course of that year I could not find any meaning, I decided I would not live, I would commit suicide.

T.W.: How did you get out of this aimless happiness?

Bloom: I began to look for a meaning in life other than what I could find through purposefulness. Studying and making oneself useful for life didn't convince me at all. All my life up to now had been concentrated on immediate goals, and suddenly these became empty. I felt something immensely dramatic inside myself, and everything around me seemed small and meaningless.

Months passed and no meaning appeared on the horizon. One day – it was during Lent, and I was then a member of one of the Russian youth organisations in Paris – one of the leaders came up to me and said, 'We have invited a priest to talk to you, come.' I answered with violent indignation that I would not. I had no use for the Church. I did not believe in God. I did not want to waste any of my time. The leader was subtle – he explained that everyone who belonged to my group had reacted in exactly the same way, and if no one came we would all be put to shame because the priest had come and we would be disgraced if no one attended his talk. 'Don't listen' the leader said, 'I don't care, but just sit and be a physical presence.' That much loyalty I was prepared to give to my youth organisation, so I sat through the lecture. I didn't intend to listen. But my ears pricked up. I became more and more indignant. I saw a vision of Christ and Christianity that was profoundly repulsive to me. When the lecture was over I hurried home in order to check the truth of what he had been saying. I asked my mother whether she had a book of the Gospel, because I wanted to know whether the Gospel would support the monstrous impression I had derived from his talk. I expected nothing good from my reading, so I counted the chapters of the four Gospels to be sure I read the shortest, not to waste time unnecessarily. I started to read St. Mark's Gospel.

While I was reading the beginning of St. Mark's Gospel, before I reached the third chapter, I suddenly became aware that on the other side of my desk there was a presence. And the certainty was so strong that it was Christ standing there that it has never left me. This was the real turning point. Because Christ was alive and I had been in his presence I could say with certainty that what the Gospel said about the crucifixion of the prophet of Galilee was true, and the centurion was right when he said, 'Truly he is the Son of God'. It was in the light of the Resurrection that I could read with certainty the story of the Gospel, knowing that everything was true in it because the impossible event of the Resurrection was to me more certain than any event of history. History I had to believe, the Resurrection I knew for a fact. I did not discover, as you see, the Gospel beginning with its first message of the Annunciation, and it did not unfold for me as a story which one can believe or disbelieve. It began as an event that left all problems of disbelief behind because it was a direct and personal experience.

T.W.: And this conviction has stayed with you all through your life? There have been no times when you have doubted your faith?

Bloom: I became absolutely certain within myself that Christ is alive and that certain things existed. I didn't have all the answers, but having touched that experience, I was certain that ahead of me there were answers, visions, possibilities. This is what I mean by faith – not doubting in the sense of being in confusion and perplexity, but doubting in order to discover the reality of the life, the kind of doubt that makes you want to question and discover more, that makes you want to explore.

T.W.: When did you become ordained?

Bloom: I was ordained in 1948 but before that I took monastic vows. This was done secretly because it was incompatible to openly profess monastic vows and also to be a physician. So I lived a sort of monastic life under the cover of my medical work, trying to be inwardly faithful to stability, to poverty, to chastity, to obedience, but expressing all these things in my medical situation – whether in the war, or afterwards during peace time when I became a general practitioner. Then when I became a priest the fact that I had taken vows came out into the open. Nowadays we lack priests to such an extent that none of my generation who became monks with the intention of leading a secluded or retiring life was given a chance to do it. We were all called by our bishops and sent out into pastoral work.

T.W.: You are still a monk . . .

Bloom: Yes.

T.W.: But you are, so to speak, living in the market place.

Bloom: I don't think living in the market place is any different from living in the wilderness. To be poor financially is in a way much easier than to be poor inwardly, to have no attachments. This is very difficult to learn and something which happens gradually, from year to year. You really learn to value things, to look at people and see the radiant beauty which they possess – without the desire to possess them. To pluck a flower means to take possession of it, and it also means to kill it. The vow of poverty makes me appreciate things much more. But first of all one must learn to be free within oneself. There are moments when you must physically absent yourself in order to learn what it means for something or somebody to exist in their own right and not just as a mirror of your own emotions.

So often when we say 'I love you' we say it with a huge 'I' and a small 'you'. We use love as a conjunction instead of it being a verb implying action. It's no good just gazing out into open space hoping to see the Lord; instead we have to look closely at our neighbour, someone whom God has willed into existence, someone whom God has died for. Everyone we meet has a right to exist, because he has value in himself, and we are not used to this. The acceptance of otherness is a danger to us, it threatens us. To recognise the other's right to be himself might mean recognising his right to kill me. But if we set a limit to his right to exist, it's no right at all. Love is difficult. Christ was crucified because he taught a kind of love which is a terror for men, a love which demands total surrender: it spells death.

T.W.: What do you mean by that?

Bloom: If we turn to God and come face to face with him, we must be prepared to pay the cost. If we are not prepared to pay the cost, we must walk through life being a beggar, hoping someone else will pay. But if we turn to God we discover that life is deep, vast and immensely worth living.

T.W.: Can we go back to the time when you were secretly a monk and also a doctor. What did you learn from this experience?

Bloom: I will give you one practical example. In the hospital where I was working as a war surgeon, a German came in once with one finger smashed by a bullet. The head surgeon came round and looked at the finger and said 'Take it off'. That was a very quick and easy decision – it would take only five minutes to do. Then the German said, 'Is there anyone here who can speak German?' I spoke with the man and discovered that he was a watchmaker and if his finger was removed he would probably never be able to work again. So we spent five weeks treating his smashed finger and he was able to leave the hospital with five fingers instead of only four. From this I learnt that the fact that he was a watchmaker was as important as anything else. I would say that I learnt to put human concerns first. Then one began to pray – a stable prayer, standing before God, face to face, and simply being with God.

T.W.: Then after being ordained you came to Britain?

Bloom: I came to Britain at the end of January 1949 to be chaplain of the Anglican-Orthodox fellowship of St Alban and Sergius, which may sound rather daring considering that I knew not a word of English at that time.

T.W.: I don't suppose it took you very long to learn English.

Bloom: To learn the sort of basic English that allowed me to communicate – and to communicate also a great deal of fun and laughter at my expense – that didn't take long.

T.W.: Do you find any difficulty in communicating now? After all, the Christian faith is not something which people can easily or readily understand.

Bloom: I don't find it a problem. What I aim at is to live within a situation and to be totally engrossed in it and yet free from involvement. The basic thing is that I never ask myself what the result of any action will be – that is God's concern. The only question I keep asking myself in life is: what should I do at this particular moment? What should I say? All you can do is to be at every single moment as true as you can with all the power in your being – and then leave it to God to use you, even despite yourself.

Whenever I speak I speak with all the conviction and belief which is in me. I stake my life on what I am saying. It's not the words themselves that are important but reaching down to the level of people's convictions. This is the basis of communication, this is where we really meet one another. If people want to ridicule me, that's fine; but if it produces a spark in them and we can talk, then it means we are really talking about something which concerns us deeply.

T.W.: Do you find that the surface culture of the modern English way of life makes it difficult to communicate the Gospel?

Bloom: Yes, because the Gospel must reach not only the intellect but the whole being. English people often say, 'That's interesting, let's talk about it, let's explore it as an idea,' but actually do nothing about it. To meet God means to enter into the 'cave of a tiger' – it is not a pussy cat you meet

– it's a tiger. The realm of God is dangerous. You must enter into it and not just seek information about it.

T.W.: Was there anything in particular which struck you about England when you came here?

Bloom: When I arrived in England I was appalled at the British attitude to death. To die seemed to be almost an act of indecency – if you had fallen so low as to die, then there were special people who would come, undertakers, to pack and wrap you up for the funeral. Then two weeks or so later there is a nice memorial service in which one sublimates one's feelings into a kind of spiritual realm. Then I remember that I went to preach at the University Church in Cambridge on the subject of death and a priest there told me he had never seen a dead person. Why is there this morbid attitude to death? In a natural way one does not get rid of people through the back door! If death is nothing but defeat, the end of life, it is not pleasant for the family to look and think it will happen to them soon. Of course, if you have a wrong attitude to death, it becomes more and more horrible and frightening. I remember another incident. An old lady died and the family telephoned me and asked me to come because I was a friend. I arrived but could see no sign of the children. I asked why they weren't there, because in the Orthodox Church the children always go to the dead person and the coffin is left open. The mother said, 'They will be terrified, they know what death is.' It turned out that quite recently the children had seen a dead rabbit which had been crushed by a car, and the parents thought they would be frightened if they saw granny. I asked if the children could come in, otherwise, I said to the parents, they might always have this frightened attitude to death. Eventually the parents agreed to let the children come into the house and we went up to the room where granny was lying. We stood beside the bed in silence for a while then one of the children said, 'How beautiful granny looks'. Death was no longer something frightening, something to be dreaded.

T.W.: You haven't said anything about your mother, but I believe she was very close to you.

Bloom: She was a marvellous woman, very simple and direct.

My own experience of death came through my mother because she had cancer. Life acquired a tremendous significance – everything we said or did could have been a last gesture, everything had to embody forty years of love.

T.W.: Being an émigré and having this feeling of not really belonging must have made a difference to you. Looking back on your life, would you say that your Christian faith was influenced by this experience?

Bloom: I think this is true. During the Revolution we lost the Christ of the great cathedrals, the Christ of the spendidly architected liturgies; and we discovered the Christ who is vulnerable just as we were vulnerable, we discovered the Christ who was rejected just as we were rejected, and we discovered the Christ who had nothing at his moment of crisis, not even friends, and this was similar to our experience.

God helps us when there is no one else to help. God is there at the point of greatest tension, at the breaking point, at the centre of the storm. In a way despair is at the centre of things – if only we are prepared to go through it. We must be prepared for a period when God is not there for us and we must be aware of not trying to substitute a false God. One day, as I describe in the book, a girl came to my surgery and condemned the Gospels without having read them. On her honeymoon she went to the cinema with her husband and she suddenly went blind. Later they discovered that she had an incurable disease. In the final stages of her illness she wrote to me, 'My heart hasn't the strength to beat Godwards' and she had the courage to accept real absence and would not substitute a false God, a comforter. The tremendous courage of this person impressed me immensely and I have never forgotten that.

The day when God is absent, when he is silent – that is the beginning of prayer. Not when we have a lot to say, but when we say to God 'I can't live without you, why are you so cruel, so silent?' This knowledge that we must find or die – that makes us break through to the place where we are in the Presence. If we listen to what our hearts know of love and longing and are never afraid of despair, we find that victory is always there the other side of it.

And there is that time when there is a longing in the heart for God himself, not for his gifts, but for God himself. There is sadness in the eyes that grow deep and look into infinity, often in the midst of fulfilment and happiness. There is longing for home, but a home that has no geography, home where there is love, depth and life.

T.W.: I remember you saying 'I am mad, but it is an odd kind of madness because other people want to catch it'. What did you mean by that?

Bloom: As Christians we are always in tension – in anguish and at the same time in bliss. This is mad, ridiculous. But it is true – accepting the dark night just as we accept the brilliance of the day. We have to make an act of surrender – if I am in Christ, there are moments when I must share the cry of the Lord on the cross and the anguish in the garden of Gethsemane. There is a way of being defeated, even in our faith – and this is a way of sharing the anguish of the Lord. I don't believe that we should ever say, 'This cannot happen to you'. If we are Christians we should go through this life, accepting the life and the world, not trying to create a falsified world.

But, on the other hand, the Christian is like someone who lives in three dimensions in a world in which the majority of people live in two. People who live freely and within a dimension of eternity will always find that something is wrong, they will always find themselves being the odd man out. The same problem was faced by the early Christians when they said that their only king was God. People turned round to them and said, 'If you say that you are disloyal to our king' and often persecuted them. But the only true way of being loyal to this two-dimensional world is to be loyal to the three-dimensional world, because in reality the world is three-dimensional. If you really live in three dimensions and do not simply live in two and imagine the third, then life will be full and meaningful. The early Christians were able to do it and Christians today are also able to do that.

T.W.: I'd like to ask you one final question – about Russia. You go there quite often. What happens?

Bloom: I go to Russia once a year to report to the Patriarch about church life in western Europe, to lecture in the theological colleges and also to keep in touch with the Russian Church. I celebrate there, I preach in the churches and I talk to ordinary people.

T.W.: Do you get politically involved?

Bloom: What we have tried to achieve is a creative tension between belonging unreservedly to the Church of Russia and asserting that we are political émigrés. In the position of tension in which we are, between churchmanship and citizenship, our churchmanship is much freer than if we had a better harmony between Church and State.

T.W.: How much active religion is there in Russia today?

Bloom: I think there is a great deal of it. Statistically we would reckon that we have about thirty million churchgoers in Russia, which is a large number after fifty years of systematic eradication of the faith in the Stalin period by extreme violence and then systematic propaganda. But in fact young people in Russia have become increasingly interested in matters of the spiritual life. and there is an increasing number of young people who come to church, either to investigate or to remain members of it. There is a vast circle of young people who belong to this realm in which God, spiritual matters, are of great importance.

T.W.: There is a sense when you speak, I don't mean when you talk of Russia, but in general, of making huge demands of people. You talked earlier about 'paying the cost' and you have this feeling about death not really being important.

Bloom: I think this is true. Perhaps I can illustrate this from a story taken from the late history of the Russian Church. I think it shows what I am trying to say about being a Christian. In the years of the Civil War when the opposing armies were contending for power, conquering and losing ground in the course of three years, a small town fell into the hands of the Red army which had been held by the remnants of the Imperial troops. A woman found herself there with her two small children, four and five years of age, in danger of death because her husband belonged to the opposite camp. She hid in an abandoned house hoping that the time would come when she would be able to escape. One evening a young woman, Natalie, of her own age, in the early twenties, knocked at the door and asked her whether she was so-and-so. When the mother said she was, the young woman warned her that she had been discovered and would be fetched that very night in order to be shot. The young woman added, 'You must escape at once.' The mother looked at the childen and said, 'How could I?' The young woman, who thus far had been nothing but a physical neighbour, became at that moment the neighbour of the Gospel. She said, 'You can, because I will stay behind and call myself by your name when they come to fetch you.' 'But you will be shot,' said the mother. 'Yes, but I have no children.' And she stayed behind.

We can imagine what happened then. We can see the night coming, wrapping in darkness, in gloom, in cold and damp, this cottage. We can see there a woman who was waiting for her death to come and we can remember the Garden of Gethsemane. We can imagine Natalie asking that this cup should pass her by and being met like Christ by divine silence. We can imagine her turning in intention towards those who might have supported her, but who were out of reach. The disciples of Christ slept; and she could turn to no one without betraying. We can imagine that more than once she prayed that at least her sacrifice should not be in vain.

Natalie probably asked herself more than once what would happen to the mother and the children when she was dead, and there was no reply except the word of Christ, 'No one has greater love than he who lays down his life for his friend.' Probably she thought more than once that in one minute she could be secure! It was enough to open the door and the moment she was in the street she no longer was that woman, she became herself again. It was enough to deny her false, her shared identity. But she died, shot. The mother and the children escaped.

METROPOLITAN ANTHONY
OF SOUROZH

Living Prayer

CONTENTS

FOREWORD*

Worship to me means a relationship. I used not to be a believer, then one day I discovered God and immediately he appeared to me to be the supreme value and the total meaning of life, but at the same time a person. I think that worship can mean nothing at all to someone for whom there is no object of worship. You cannot teach worship to someone who has not got a sense of the living God; you can teach him to act as if he believed, but it will not be the spontaneous attitude which is real worship. Therefore, as a foreword to this book on prayer, what I would like to convey is my certitude in the personal reality of a God with whom a relationship can be established. Then I would ask my reader to treat God as a neighbour, as someone, and value this knowledge in the same terms in which he values a relationship with a brother or a friend. This, I think, is essential.

One of the reasons why communal worship or private prayer seem to be so dead or so conventional is that the act of worship, which takes place in the heart communing with God, is too often missing. Every expression, either verbal or in action, may help, but they are only expressions of what is essential, namely, a deep silence of communion.

We all know in human relationships that love and friendship are deep when we can be silent with someone. As

* Adaptation of a talk given on the BBC in the 'Ten to Eight' programme first broadcast in 1965.

long as we need to talk in order to keep in touch, we can safely and sadly assume that the relationship is still superficial; and so, if we want to worship God, we must first of all learn to feel happy, being silent together with him. This is an easier thing to do than one might think at first; it needs a little time, some confidence and the courage to start.

Once the Curé d'Ars, a French saint of the eighteenth century, asked an old peasant what he was doing sitting for hours in the church, seemingly not even praying; the peasant replied: 'I look at him, he looks at me and we are happy together.' That man had learned to speak to God without breaking the silence of intimacy by words. If we can do that we can use any form of worship. If we try to make worship itself out of the words we use, we will get desperately tired of those words, because unless they have the depth of silence, they are shallow and tiresome.

But how inspiring words can be once they are backed by silence and are infused with the right spirit:

'O Lord, open Thou my lips; and my mouth shall show forth thy praise' (Ps 51:15).

I

The Essence of Prayer

THE GOSPEL OF St Matthew confronts us almost from the beginning with the very essence of prayer. The Magi saw the long-expected star; they set out without delay to find the king; they arrived at the manger, they knelt, they worshipped and they presented their gifts: they expressed prayer in its perfection, which is contemplation and adoration.

Often, in more or less popular literature about prayer, we are told that prayer is an enthralling adventure. It is a commonplace to hear: 'Come on, learn to pray; prayer is so interesting, so thrilling, it is the discovery of a new world; you will meet God, you will find the way to a spiritual life.' In a sense of course this is true; but something very much more far-reaching is being forgotten when such statements are made: it is that prayer is a dangerous adventure and that we cannot enter upon it without risk. As St Paul says, it is a fearful thing to fall into the hands of the living God (Heb 10:31). Therefore to set out deliberately to confront the living God is a dread adventure: every meeting with God is, in a certain sense, a last judgement. Whenever we come into the presence of God, whether in the sacraments or in prayer, we are doing something which is full of danger because, according to the words of scripture, God is a fire. Unless we are ready to surrender ourselves without reservation to the divine fire and to become that burning bush of the desert, which burned but was never consumed, we shall be scorched, because the experience of prayer can only be known from the inside, and is not to be dallied with.

Coming nearer to God is always a discovery both of the beauty of God and of the distance there is between him and us. 'Distance' is an inadequate word, because it is not determined by the fact that God is holy and that we are sinful. Distance is determined by the attitude of the sinner to God. We can approach God only if we do so with a sense of coming to judgement. If we come having condemned ourselves; if we come because we love him in spite of the fact that we are unfaithful, if we come to him, loving him more than a godless security, then we are open to him and he is open to us, and there is no distance; the Lord comes close to us in an act of compassionate love. But if we stand before God wrapped in our pride, in our assertiveness, if we stand before him as though we had a right to stand there, if we stand and question him, the distance that separates the creature and the creator becomes infinite. There is a passage in the *Screwtape Letters* in which C. S. Lewis suggests that distance, in this sense, is a relative thing: when the great archangel came before God to question him, the moment he asked his question, not in order to understand in humility but in order to compel God to give account, he found himself at an infinite distance from God. God had not moved, nor had Satan, and yet without any motion, they were infinitely far apart (Letter XIX).

Whenever we approach God the contrast that exists between what he is and what we are becomes dreadfully clear. We may not be aware of this as long as we live at a distance from God, so to speak, as long as his presence or his image is dimmed in our thoughts and in our perceptions; but the nearer we come to God, the sharper the contrast appears. It is not the constant thought of their sins, but the vision of the holiness of God that makes the saints aware of their own sinfulness. When we consider ourselves without the fragrant background of God's presence, sins and virtues become small and somewhat irrelevant matters; it is against the background of the divine presence that they stand out in full relief and acquire their depth and tragedy.

Every time we come near God, it is either life or death we are confronted with. It is life if we come to him in the right spirit, and are renewed by him. It is death if we come to him without the spirit of worship and a contrite heart; it is death if we bring pride or arrogance. Therefore, before we set out on the so-called thrilling adventure of prayer, it cannot be too strongly stated that nothing more significant, more awe-inspiring, can occur than meeting the God we set out to meet. It is essential to realise that we will lose our life in the process: the old Adam we are must die. We are intensely attached to the old man, afraid for him, and it is very difficult, not only at the outset but years after we have begun, to feel that we are completely on the side of Christ, against the old Adam.

Prayer is an adventure which brings not a thrill but new responsibilities: as long as we are ignorant, nothing is asked of us, but as soon as we know anything, we are answerable for the use we make of that knowledge. It may be a gift, but we are responsible for any particle of truth we have acquired; as it becomes our own, we cannot leave it dormant but have to take it into account in our behaviour, and in this sense we are to answer for any truth we have understood.

It is only with a feeling of fear, of adoration, with the utmost veneration that we can approach this adventure of prayer, and we must live up to it outwardly as completely and precisely as possible. It is not enough to lounge in an armchair, saying: now, I place myself in an act of veneration in the presence of God. We have to realise that if Christ were standing in front of us, we would comport ourselves differently, and we must learn to behave in the presence of the invisible Lord as we would in the presence of the Lord made visible to us.

This implies primarily an attitude of mind and then its reflection upon the body. If Christ was there, before us, and we stood completely transparent to his gaze, in mind as well as in body, we would feel reverence, the fear of God, adoration, or else perhaps terror, but we should not be so easy in our behaviour as we are. The modern world has to a great extent lost the sense of prayer and physical attitudes have become secondary in people's minds, although they are anything but secondary. We forget that we are not a soul dwelling in a body, but a human being, made up of body and soul, and that we are called, according to St Paul, to glorify God in our spirit and in our body; our bodies as well as our souls are to be called to the glory of the kingdom of God (I Cor 6:20).

Too often prayer has no such importance in our lives that everything else fades away to give it room. Prayer is additional to a great many things; we wish God to be present, not because there is no life without him, not because he is the supreme value, but because it would be so nice, in addition to all the great benefits of God, to have also his presence. He is additional to our needs, and when we seek him in that spirit we do not meet him. Yet notwithstanding all that has just been said, prayer, dangerous as it appears, is the best way to go ahead towards the fulfilment of our calling, to become fully human, which means in full communion with God and, ultimately, what St Peter calls partakers of the divine nature.

Love and friendship do not grow if we are not prepared to sacrifice a great deal for their sake, and in the same way we must be ready to put aside many things in order to give God the first place.

'Thou shalt love the Lord thy God with all thy heart, and with all thy soul, and with all thy strength, and with all thy mind' (Lk 10:27). This seems to be a very simple command, and yet those words contain much more than one sees at a first glance. We all know what it is to love someone with all one's heart; we know the pleasure, not only of meeting but even of thinking of the beloved, the warm comfort it gives. It is in that way that we should try to love God, and whenever his name is mentioned, it should fill our heart and soul with infinite warmth. God should be at all times in our mind, whereas in fact we think of him only occasionally.

As for loving God with all our strength, we can only do it if we cast off deliberately everything that is not God's in us; by an effort of will we must turn ourselves constantly towards God, whether in prayer, which is easier, because in prayer we are already centred on God, or in action, which requires training, because in our actions we are concentrated on some material achievement and have to dedicate it to God by a special effort.

The Wise Men travelled a long way and nobody knows the difficulties they had to overcome. Each of us also travels as they did. They were loaded with gifts, gold for the king, frankincense for the God, myrrh for the man who was to suffer death. Where can we get gold, frankincense and myrrh, we who are indebted for everything to God? We know that everything we possess has been given us by God and is not even ours for ever or with certainty. Everything can be taken away from us except love, and this is what makes love unique and something we can give. Everything else, our limbs, our intelligence, our possessions can be taken by force from us, but with regard to love, there is no means of getting it, unless we give it. In that sense we are free with regard to loving, in a way in which we are not free in other activities of soul or body. Although fundamentally even love is a gift of God, because we cannot produce it out of ourselves, yet, once we possess it, it is the only thing that we can withold or offer.

Bernanos says in the *Diary of a Country Priest* that we can also offer our pride to God, 'Give your pride with all the rest, give everything.' Pride offered in that context becomes a gift of love, and everything which is a gift of love is well pleasing to God.

'Love your enemies, bless them that hate you' (Mt 5:44), is a command that may be more or less easy to follow; but to forgive those who inflict suffering on one's beloved is altogether different, and it makes people feel as if taken in disloyalty. Yet, the greater our love for the one who suffers, the greater our ability to share and to forgive, and in that sense the greatest love is achieved when one can say with Rabbi Yehel Mikhael 'I am my beloved'. As long as we say 'I' and 'he' we do not share the suffering and we cannot accept it. The mother of God at the foot of the cross was not in tears, as shown so often in western paintings; she was so completely in communion with her son that she had nothing to protest against. She was going through the crucifixion, together with Christ; she was going through her own death. The mother was fulfilling now what she had begun on the day of the presentation of Christ to the temple, when she had given her son. Alone of all the children of Israel he had been accepted as a sacrifice of blood. And she, who had brought him then, was now accepting the consequence of her ritual gesture which was finding fulfilment in reality. As he was then in communion with her, she was completely in communion with him now and she had nothing to protest against.

It is love that makes us one with the object of our love and makes it possible for us to share unreservedly, not only the suffering but also the attitude towards suffering and the executioner. We cannot imagine the mother of God or John the disciple protesting against what was the explicit will of the son of God crucified. 'No one is taking my life from me, I lay it down of myself' (Jn 10:18). He was dying willingly, of his own accord for the salvation of the world; his death was this salvation and therefore those who believed in him and wanted to be at one with him could share the suffering of his death, could undergo the passion together with him; but they could not reject it, they could not turn against the crowd that had crucified Christ, because this crucifixion was the will of Christ himself.

We can protest against someone's suffering, we can protest against someone's death, either when he himself, rightly or wrongly, takes a stand against it, or else when we do not share his intention and his attitude towards death and suffering; but then our love for that person is an incomplete love and creates separation. It is the kind of love shown by Peter when Christ, on the way to Jerusalem, told his disciples that he was going to his death; Peter 'took him and began to rebuke him', but Christ answered: 'Get thee behind me, Satan, for thou savourest not the things that be of God, but the things that be of men' (Mk 8:33). We can imagine that the wife of the thief on the left of Christ was full of the same protest against her husband's death as he himself was; in this respect there was complete communion between them, but they were sharing a wrong attitude.

But to share with Christ his passion, his crucifixion, his death, means to accept unreservedly all these events, in the same spirit as he did, that is, to accept them in an act of free will, to suffer together with the man of sorrows, to be there in silence, the very silence of Christ, interrupted only by a few decisive words, the silence of real communion; not just the silence of pity, but of compassion, which allows us to grow into complete oneness with the other so that there is no longer one and the other, but only one life and one death.

On many occasions throughout history people witnessed

persecution and were not afraid, but shared in the suffering
and did not protest; for instance, Sophia, the mother who
stood by each of her daughters, Faith, Hope and Charity,
encouraging them to die, or many other martyrs who
helped one another but never turned against the tormentors.
The spirit of martyrdom can be brought out by several
examples. The first expresses the spirit of martyrdom in
itself, its basic attitude: a spirit of love which cannot be
defeated by suffering or injustice. A very young priest, who
was imprisoned at the beginning of the Russian revolution,
and came out a broken man, was asked what was left of
him, and he answered: 'Nothing is left of me, they have
burnt out every single thing, love only survives.' A man
who can say that has the right attitude and anyone who
shares his tragedy must also share in his unshakeable love.

There is the example of a man who came back from
Buchenwald and, when asked about himself, said that his
sufferings were nothing compared to his broken-hearted-
ness about those poor German youths who could be so
cruel, and that thinking about the state of their souls, he
could find no peace. His concern was not for himself, and
he had spent four years there, nor for the innumerable
people who had suffered and died around him; but for the
condition of the tormentors. Those who suffered were on
the side of Christ, those who were cruel were not.

Thirdly, there is this prayer written in a concentration
camp by a Jewish prisoner:

> Peace to all men of evil will! Let there be an end to all
> vengeance, to all demands for punishment and retribution . . .
> Crimes have surpassed all measure, they can no longer be
> grasped by human understanding. There are too many martyrs

... And so, weigh not their sufferings on the scales of thy justice, Lord, and lay not these sufferings to the torturors' charge to exact a terrible reckoning from them. Pay them back in a different way! Put down in favour of the executioners, the informers, the traitors and all men of evil will, the courage, the spiritual strength of the others, their humility, their lofty dignity, their constant inner striving and invincible hope, the smile that staunched the tears, their love, their ravaged, broken hearts that remained steadfast and confident in the face of death itself, yes, even at moments of the utmost weakness . . . Let all this, O Lord, be laid before thee for the forgiveness of sins, as a ransom for the triumph of righteousness, let the good and not the evil be taken into account! And may we remain in our enemies' memory not as their victims, not as a nightmare, not as haunting spectres, but as helpers in their striving to destroy the fury of their criminal passions. There is nothing more that we want of them. And when it is all over, grant us to live among men as men, and may peace come again to our poor earth – peace for men of goodwill and for all the others . . .*

There was also a Russian bishop who said that it is a privilege for a christian to die a martyr, because none but a martyr can, at the last judgement, take his stand in front of God's judgement seat and say, 'According to thy word and thy example, I have forgiven. Thou hast no claim against them any more.' Which means that the one who suffers martyrdom in Christ, whose love is not defeated by suffering, acquires unconditional power of forgiving over the one who has inflicted the suffering. And this can be applied on a much lower level, on the level of everyday life; anyone who suffers a minor injustice from someone else can forgive or refuse to forgive. But this is a two-edged

* Found in the archives of a German concentration camp and published in the Suddeutsche Zeitung.

sword; if you do not forgive, you will not be forgiven either.

French Roman Catholics, with their acute sense of justice and the honour of God, are very conscious of the victory which Christ can gain through the suffering of people: since 1797 there has existed an Order of Reparation, which by perpetual adoration of the Blessed Sacrament asks forgiveness for the crimes of the world and the forgiveness of individual sinners by their victim's prayers. This Order is also educational and aims to give children and adults the spirit of love.

Typical also is the story of the French general Maurice d'Elbée during the revolutionary wars; his men captured some *Bleus* and wanted to shoot them; the general, unwillingly, had to consent, but he insisted that they should first read the Lord's Prayer aloud, which they did, and when they came to the words 'Forgive us our trespasses as we forgive them that trespass against us', they understood, they wept and let the prisoners go. Later on, in 1794, General d'Elbée was himself shot by the *Bleus*.

Jean Daniélou, the French Jesuit writer, says in *Holy Pagans* that suffering is the link between the righteous and sinners, the righteous man who endures suffering and the sinner who inflicts it. If there were not that link, they would drift apart and sinners and righteous would remain on parallel lines that never meet. In that case, the righteous would have no power over the sinner because one cannot deal with what one does not meet.

II

The Lord's Prayer

ALTHOUGH IT IS very simple, and is used so constantly, The Lord's Prayer is a great problem and a difficult prayer; it is the only one which the Lord gave, yet, reading the Acts, one never finds it used by anyone at all, which is not what one would expect from the words that introduce the prayer in Luke 11:1, 'Lord, teach us to pray, as John also taught his disciples.' But not being quoted does not mean not being used, and in a way the Lord's Prayer is not only a prayer but a whole way of life expressed in the form of a prayer: it is the image of the gradual ascent of the soul from bondage to freedom. The prayer is built with striking precision. Just as when a pebble falls into a pond we can observe the ripples spreading from the place where the pebble fell, farther and farther towards the banks, or on the contrary, we may begin with the banks and work back to the source of the movement, in the same way the Lord's Prayer can be analysed either beginning with the first words, or else with the last. It is infinitely easier to begin the progression from the outside towards the centre of the prayer, although for Christ and for the Church it is the other way which is right.

This is a prayer of sonship – 'Our Father' – and in a certain sense, although it may be used by anyone who approaches the Lord, it expresses adequately only the relationship of those who are in the Church of God, who, in Christ, have found their way to their father, because it is only through Christ and in him that we become the sons of God.

This teaching of a spiritual life can best be understood when set in parallel with the story of Exodus and within the experience of the beatitudes. Starting with the last words of the prayer and moving towards the first, we see it as a way of ascent; our starting-point at the end defines a captivity, the last word at the beginning defines our state of sonship.

The people of God, who had come free to the land of Egypt, had gradually become enslaved. The conditions of their life brought home to them their state of slavery: work was heavier and heavier, the conditions of living more and more miserable; but this was not enough to make them move towards real freedom. If misery increases beyond a certain point, it may lead to rebellion, to violence, to attempted escape from the painful, unbearable situation; but essentially neither rebellion nor flight make us free, because freedom is first of all an inner situation with regard to God, to self and to the surrounding world.

Every time they attempted to leave the country, new and heavier tasks were given to the Jews. When they had to make bricks, they were refused the necessary straw, and Pharaoh said: 'Let them go and gather straw for themselves' (Ex 5:7), and 'Let more work be laid upon them, that they may labour therein.' He wanted them so completely exhausted, so completely concerned with the toil that they should have no thought for rebellion or deliverance any more. In the same way there is no hope for us as long as we are enthralled by the prince of this world, the devil, with all the powers at his disposal to enslave human souls and bodies and keep them away from the living God. Unless God comes himself to deliver us, there will be no deliverance, but eternal slavery; and the first words we find in the Lord's Prayer are for this very thing: 'Deliver us from Evil.' Deliverance from evil is exactly what was done in the land of Egypt through Moses, and what is achieved at baptism by the power of God, given to his Church. The word of God resounds in this world, calling everyone to freedom, giving the hope that comes from heaven to those who have lost their hope on earth. This word of God is preached and resounds in the human soul, making a man a learner of the Church, making him one who stands as an outsider in the porch, one who has heard the call and has come to listen (Rom 10:17).

When the learner is determined to become a free man in the kingdom of the Lord, the Church undertakes certain actions. What would be the good of asking a slave, who is still in the power of his master, whether he wants to be free? If he dares ask for the freedom which is offered, he knows that he will be cruelly punished the moment he is left alone again with his master. Through fear and from a habit of slavery a man cannot ask for freedom until he is delivered from the authority of the devil. Therefore, before any question is asked of the one who stands there, with a new hope in divine salvation, he is made free from the power of Satan. This is the meaning of the exorcisms which are read at the outset of the baptismal service both in the Orthodox and Roman Catholic Churches. It is only when a man is free from the bonds of slavery that he is asked if he renounces the devil and if he wants to join Christ. And only after a free answer does the Church integrate him into herself, into the Body of Christ. The devil wants slaves, but God wants free men in harmony of will with him. The evil one in terms of Exodus was Egypt and Pharaoh, and all the values attached to them, namely, to be fed and kept alive, on condition that they were submissive slaves. And for us the act of prayer, which is a more essential, final act of rebellion against slavery than taking up arms, is at the same time a sort of return into our sense of responsibility and relatedness to God.

So the first situation with which Exodus begins, and we begin, is the discovery of slavery and that it cannot be resolved by an act of rebellion or flight, because whether we flee or whether we rebel we remain slaves, unless we re-establish ourselves, with regard to God and to all the situations of life, in the way taught by the first beatitude: 'Blessed are the poor in spirit, for theirs is the Kingdom of Heaven.' In itself, poverty, the state of a slave, is no passport to the kingdom of heaven; the slave can be deprived not only of earthly goods but also of heavenly goods; such poverty can be more overwhelming than simple deprivation of what we need for earthly life. St John Chrysostom says that the poor man is not so much he who does not possess, but he who wants what he does not possess.

Poverty is not rooted in what we have or have not, but in the degree to which we long for what is out of reach. When we think of our human condition we can discover quite easily that we are utterly poor and destitute because whatever we possess is never ours, however rich and wealthy we seem to be. When we try to grasp anything we discover quite soon that it has gone. Our being is rooted in nothing except the sovereign creative word of God who called us out of total, radical absence into his presence. The life and health that we possess we cannot keep, and not only health but so many of our psychosomatic qualities: a man of great intelligence, because a minute vessel has burst in his head, becomes senile and is finished intellectually. In the realm of our feelings, for some accountable or unaccountable reason, say 'flu or tiredness, we cannot at the right moment, and at will, feel the sympathy for someone which we wish so much to feel, or we go to church and we are of stone. This is the basic poverty, but does it make us the children of the kingdom? It does not, because if at every moment of our life we feel in a state of misery, that all things escape us, if we are aware only of the fact that we do not possess them, it does not make us the joyful children of a kingdom of divine love, but the miserable victims of a situation over which we have no power and which we hate.

This brings us back to the words 'poor *in spirit*'; the poverty that opens the kingdom of heaven lies in the knowledge that if nothing that is mine is really mine, then everything that is mine is a gift of love, divine or human love, and that makes things quite different. If we realise that we have no being in ourselves, and yet we exist, we can say that there is a sustained unceasing act of divine love. If we see that whatever we have, we can in no wise compel to be ours, then everything is divine love, concretely expressed

at every single moment; and then poverty is the root of
perfect joy because all we have proves love. We should
never attempt to appropriate things to ourselves because
to call something 'ours', and not a constant gift of God,
means less and not more. If it is mine, it is alien to the
relationship of mutual love; if it is his and I possess it from
day to day, from split second to split second, it is a continuously renewed act of divine love. Then we come to the
joyful thought: 'Thanks be to God, it is not mine; if it
were mine, it would mean possession, but alas without
love.' The relationship to which this thought brings us is
what the gospel calls the kingdom of God. Only those
belong to the kingdom who receive all things from the
king in the relationship of mutual love and who do not
want to be rich, because to be rich means to be dispossessed
of love while possessed of things. The moment when we
discover God within the situation and that all things are
God's and everything is of God, then we begin to enter
this divine kingdom and acquire freedom.

It was only when the Jews, guided and enlightened by
Moses, realised that their state of enslavement had something to do with God, and was not simply a man-made
situation, it was only when they turned to God, when they
re-established a relationship which is that of the kingdom,
that something could happen; and that is true for all of us,
because it is only when we realise that we are slaves, when
we realise that we are destitute, but when we also realise
that this happens within the divine wisdom and that all
things are within the divine power, that we can turn to
Him and say, 'Deliver us from the evil one.'

As the Jews were called by Moses to escape from the

country of Egypt, to follow him in the dark night, to cross
the Red Sea, so also is each individual brought into the
wilderness, where a new period begins. He is free, but not
yet enjoying the glory of the promised land, because he
has taken with him, out of the land of Egypt, the soul of a
slave, the habits of a slave, the temptations of a slave; and
the education of a free man takes infinitely more time than
the discovery of his enslavement. The spirit of slavery
remains very close, and its standards are still there and very
potent: a slave has somewhere to rest his head, a slave is
assured of food, a slave has a social standing, however low,
he is secure because his master is responsible for him. So
to be a slave, however painful, humiliating and distressing
the situation, is also a form of security, while to become a
free person is a state of utter insecurity; we take our destiny
into our own hands and it is only when our freedom is
rooted in God that we become secure in a new way, and a
very different one.

This sense of insecurity is brought out in Samuel, when
the Jews asked the prophet to give them a king. For
centuries they had been led by God, that is by men who,
being saints, knew God's ways; as Amos says (3:7), a
prophet is one with whom God shares his thoughts. And
then in the time of Samuel, the Jews discover that to be
under God alone is, in a worldly sense, total insecurity
because it depends on saintliness, on dedication, on moral
values which are hard to get, and they turn to Samuel and
ask him to give them a king, because 'We want to be like
every other nation with the security which every nation
has.'

Samuel does not want to agree to what he sees is an

apostasy but God tells him 'Hearken to the voice of thy
people . . . for they have not rejected thee, but they have
rejected me, that I should not reign over them' (I Sam 8:9).
And a whole picture follows of what their life will be:
'This will be the manner of the king that shall reign over
you: he will take your sons, and appoint them for himself,
for his chariots, and to be his horsemen; and some shall run
before his chariots . . . And he will take your daughters
to be confectionaries, and to be cooks and to be bakers.'
'Nevertheless the people refused to obey the voice of
Samuel and they said, Nay; but we will have a king over
us' (I Sam 8:19). They want to buy security at the cost of
freedom. It is not what God wills for us, and what happens
is exactly the reverse of the events of Exodus: God's will is
that the security of slaves is to be forsaken and replaced by
the insecurity of free men in the making. This is a difficult
situation because while we are in the making we do not
yet know how to be free and we do not want to be slaves
any more. Remember what happened to the Jews in the
wilderness, how often they regretted the time when they
were enslaved in Egypt, but fed. How often they complained that now they were without a roof, without food,
dependent on the will of God, which they had not yet
learned to rely upon completely; for God gives us grace,
but leaves it to us to become new creatures.

Like the Jews in Egypt we have spent all our lives as
slaves; we are not yet in our souls, in our wills, in our whole
selves, real free men: left to our own powers we may fall
into temptation. And these words 'Lead us not into temptation' – submit us not to the severe test – must remind us
of the forty years the Jews spent crossing the short expanse

of territory between the land of Egypt and the promised land. They took so long because whenever they turned away from God, their path turned away from the promised land. The only way in which we can reach the promised land is to follow in the steps of the Lord. Whenever our heart turns back to the land of Egypt, we retrace our steps, we go astray. We have all been set free by the mercy of God, we are all on our way, but who will say that he does not retrace his steps constantly, or turn from the right path? 'Lead us not into temptation', let us not fall back into our state of slavery.

Once we have become aware of our enslavement, and have passed from mere lamentation and a sense of misery into a sense of brokenheartedness and poverty of spirit, our imprisonment in the land of Egypt is answered by the words of the next beatitudes: 'Blessed are they that mourn, for they shall be comforted', 'Blessed are the meek, for they shall inherit the earth'. This mourning that is the result of the discovery of the kingdom, of one's own responsibility, of the tragedy of being a slave, is a more bitter mourning than that which is the lot of the simple slave. The slave complains about an outer situation; this mourner, who is blessed by God, does not complain, he is brokenhearted, and he is aware that his outer enslavement is the expression of something far more tragic: his inner enslavement, his severance from the closeness of God. And nothing can be done to escape this situation unless meekness is attained.

Meekness is a difficult word which has acquired various connotations and since it is extremely rare in practice, we cannot turn to our experience of meek people, which would

give us a clue to the meaning of the word. We find in
J. B. Phillips' translation: 'Happy are those who claim
nothing', meaning 'Blessed are those who do not try to
possess'. The moment you do not want to possess, you
become free because, whatever you do possess, by that
you are possessed. Another interpretation of the word
meek is found in the translation of the Greek word into a
slavonic word meaning 'made tame'. A person or an animal
that has been tamed is not simply terrified of punishment
and subject to the authority of the master; it is someone in
whom the process has gone farther, someone who has
acquired a new quality and who by this tameness escapes
the violence of coercion.

At the threshold of our salvation from the slavery of
Egypt stands the condition that we should be tamed; in
other words, that we should recognise in the situation in
which we are, depth, significance, the presence of the
divine will, and it should be neither flight nor rebellion,
but a movement guided by God, which begins with the
kingdom of heaven that is within us and develops into the
kingdom on earth. It is a period of wavering and of inner
struggle: 'Lead us not into temptation O Lord, Protect us
in the trial, help us in the fight which has begun for us.'
And now we are at the point when a move can be made.
Look back at Exodus, at the Jews' awareness that they are
not simply slaves but the people of God that had become
enslaved because of their moral weaknesses. They had to
take risks, because no one is ever freed by a slave owner,
and they had to cross the Red Sea; but beyond the Red Sea
it was not yet the promised land, it was the burning desert
and they were aware of it and knew that they would have

to cross it in the face of great difficulties. And so are we when we decide to make a move that will liberate us from our enslavement: we must be aware that we shall be attacked by violence, by beguilement, by the inner enemies that are our old habits, our old craving for security, and that nothing is promised us, except the desert beyond. Beyond that is the promised land, but far beyond, and we must accept the risks of the journey.

There is one thing that stands as a line of demarcation between Egypt and the desert, between slavery and freedom; it is a moment when we act decisively and become new people, establishing ourselves in an absolutely new moral situation. In terms of geography it was the Red Sea, in terms of the Lord's Prayer it is 'Forgive us our trespasses as we forgive'. This 'as we forgive' is the moment when we take our salvation into our own hands, because whatever God does depends on what we do; and this is tremendously important in terms of ordinary life. If these people who are moving out of Egypt into the promised land take with them, out of the Land of Egypt, their fears, their resentments, their hatreds, their grievances, they will be slaves in the promised land. They will not be freemen, even in the making. And this is why at the demarcation line between the trials of fire and the beguilement of old habits, stands this absolute condition which God never relaxes: as you forgive, the measure which you use will be used for you; and as you forgive, you will be forgiven; what you do not forgive will be held against you. It is not that God does not want to forgive, but if we come unforgiving, we check the mystery of love, we refuse it and there is no place for us in the kingdom. We cannot go farther if we are not forgiven, and we cannot be forgiven as long as we have not forgiven everyone of those who have wronged us. This is quite sharp and real and precise and no one has any right to imagine that he is in the kingdom of God, that he belongs to it, if there is still unforgiveness in his heart. To forgive one's enemies is the first, the most elementary characteristic of a christian; failing this, we are not yet christian at all, but are still wandering in the scorching wilderness of Sinai.

But forgiveness is something extremely difficult to achieve. To grant forgiveness at a moment of softening of the heart, in an emotional crisis is comparatively easy; not to take it back is something that hardly anyone knows how to do. What we call forgiveness is often putting the other one on probation, nothing more; and lucky are the forgiven people if it is only probation and not remand. We wait impatiently for evidence of repentance, we want to be sure that the penitent is not the same any more, but this situation can last a lifetime and our attitude is exactly the contrary of everything which the gospel teaches, and indeed commands us, to do. So the law of forgiveness is not a little brook on the boundary between slavery and freedom: it has breadth and depth, it is the Red Sea. The Jews did not get over it by their own effort in man-made boats, the Red Sea was cut open by the power of God; God had to lead them across. But to be led by God one must commune with this quality of God which is the ability to forgive. God remembers, in the sense that, once we have done wrong, he will for ever, until we change, take into account that we are weak and frail; but he will never remember in terms of accusation or condemnation; it will never be brought up against us. The Lord will yoke himself together with us, into our lives, and he will have more weight to carry, he will have a heavier cross, a new ascent to Calvary which we are unwilling or incapable of undertaking.

To be able to say the first sentence that we have discussed – 'Deliver us from the evil one' – requires such a reassessment of values and such a new attitude that we can hardly begin to say it otherwise than in a cry, which is as yet unsubstantiated by an inner change in us. We feel a longing which is not yet capable of achievement; to ask God to protect us in the trial is to ask for a radical change in our situation. But to be able to say 'Forgive as I forgive' is even more difficult; it is one of the greatest problems of life. Thus, if you are not prepared to leave behind you every resentment that you have against those who were your overlords or slavedrivers, you cannot cross. If you are capable of forgiving, that is of leaving behind in the land of slavery, all your slavish mentality, all your greed and grasping and bitterness, you can cross. After that you are in the scorching wilderness, because it will take time for a free man to be made out of a slave.

All that we possessed as slaves in the land of Egypt we are deprived of – no roof, no shelter, no food, nothing but the wilderness and God. Earth is no longer capable of feeding us; we can no longer rely on natural food, so we pray 'give us day by day our daily bread'. God gives it even when we go astray, because if he did not we should die before we could reach the border of the promised land. Keep us alive, O God, give us time to err, to repent, to take the right course.

'Our daily bread' is one of the possible ways of trans-

lating the Greek text. This bread, which in Greek is called
epiousion, may be daily, but it may also be the bread that
is beyond substance. The Fathers of the Church, beginning
with Origen and Tertullian, have always interpreted this
passage as referring not only to our human needs but also
to the mysterious bread of the eucharist. Unless we are
fed in this new way, mysteriously, by divine bread (because
we depend now for our existence on God alone) we will
not survive (Jn 6:53). God sent to his people the manna
and gave them water from the rock, struck by the
rod of Moses. The two gifts are images of Christ: 'Man
shall not live by bread alone but by every word that pro-
ceedeth from the mouth of God.' This is what Christ
recalled from the Old Testament (Dt 8:3) to confound
Satan. This 'word' is not simply words but first of all the
Word that resounds for ever, upholding all things created,
and then also the Word incarnate, Jesus of Nazareth;
furthermore, it is the bread of which manna was the image,
the bread which we receive in communion. The waters
that ran and filled the brooks and the rivers at the command
of Moses, are the image of that water which was promised
to the Samaritan woman and of the blood of Christ which
is our life.

Exodus is a complex image in terms of the Lord's Prayer;
in the beatitudes we find the same progression: 'Blessed are
they which do hunger and thirst after righteousness, for
they shall be filled', 'Blessed are the merciful, for they shall
obtain mercy'. First a simple bodily hunger and thirst, a
deprivation of all possessions, which were a gift of corruption, a gift of the earth from the overlord, a stamp of
slavery, and then exactly in the way in which the mourning

of the second beatitude is increased, the moment we are turned Godwards, so this thirst and hunger are turned towards righteousness. A new dimension has been disclosed to men, one of longing, of craving, a dimension which is defined in one of the secret prayers in the liturgy as 'The Kingdom for to come', when we thank God that he has given us his kingdom for which we are longing. In the liturgy the kingdom is there, but in the journey through the desert it is ahead, in a germinal state, still beyond reach. It is within us, as an attitude, as a relationship, but certainly not as something which is already life, on which we can feed and by which we can be kept alive. There is the bodily hunger, born of our past and of our present, and the spiritual hunger, born of our future and of our vocation.

'Blessed are the merciful.' This journey is not a lonely one; in terms of Exodus it was the whole people of God who were launched out, side by side, as a unit; in terms of the Lord's Prayer and our vocation, it is the Church, it is mankind, it is everyone who is on this journey; and there is one thing of immense importance that we must learn, namely, mercy for our brothers who are journeying together with us. Unless we are willing to bear one another's burdens, to carry one another's weight, to receive one another as Christ receives us, in mercy, there is no way across the wilderness. This journey in the scorching heat, in the thirst and hunger, in the exertion of becoming a new man, is a time of mercy, of mutual charity; otherwise none will come to the place where God's law is proclaimed, where the tables of the law are offered. Thirst for righteousness and fulfilment goes hand in hand with mercy for the companions who walk side by side through the heat and the sufferings; and this thirst and hunger imply more, now, than just absence of food. When the Jews arrive one day at the foot of Sinai, they are capable of understanding and of being; they have been tamed and have become one people with one consciousness, with one direction, one intention. They are God's people, in motion towards the promised land. Their hearts that were darkened have become more transluscent, more pure. At the foot of the mountain it will be given them, to each according to his strength and capabilities, to see something of God (because 'Blessed are the pure in heart, for they shall see God'), to each of them in a different way, exactly as the disciples saw Christ transfigured on Mount Tabor, according to what they could comprehend.

At this point a new tragedy occurs: Moses discovers that the Jews have betrayed their vocation and he breaks the tables of the law; those which are afterwards given are the same, yet not the same: the difference is perhaps shown in the fact that when Moses brought the law the second time, he had a shining on his face which no one could bear (Ex 34:30); neither could they bear the Lord revealed in all his glory and fragrance. What they are given is what they can bear, but it is a law written by Moses (Ex 34:27) and not simply a divine revelation of love, 'written by the finger of God' (Ex 31:18). The law stands half way between lawlessness and grace; one can trace three steps in striking progression: in Genesis we see the violent Lamech, who says that if he is offended he will avenge himself seventy and seven fold (Gn 4:24); when we come to Sinai, we are told, an eye for an eye and a tooth for a tooth; and when we hear Christ, we are told 'seventy times seven shalt thou forgive thy brother'. These are the measures of human revolt against equity and against grace.

Khomiakov, a Russian theologian of the nineteenth century, says that the will of God is a curse for the demons, law for the servants of God and freedom for the children of God. This seems so true when we examine the gradual progression of the Jews from Egypt to the promised land. They departed slaves, who had just become aware of their potentialities as prospective children of God; they had to outgrow the mentality of slaves and attain the spirit and stature of sons; this took place gradually in the course of a long and extremely painful process. We see them slowly being built into a community of servants of God, of people who recognised that their Lord was no longer Pharaoh but the Lord of Hosts, to whom they acknowledged that they owed allegiance and unconditional obedience; they could expect from him both punishment and reward, knowing that he was leading them beyond what they then knew, into something which was their final vocation.

It is a very common thought in the writings of the early christian ascetics that man must go through these three stages – slave, hireling and son. The slave is one who obeys for fear, the hireling is one who obeys for reward and the son is one who acts for love. We can see in Exodus how gradually the people of God had become more than slaves and hirelings and the law stands at the threshold, geographically speaking, of the promised land.

At this threshold they discover, each with the ability that is his, with the depth of spirit that is his, God's own will, God's own mind, for this law can be seen in several ways: if we take it formally, sentence by sentence, it is a series of commandments: 'Thou shalt, thou shalt not,' in that sense it is law in the mentality of the Old Testament. But on the other hand, if we look at it with the eyes of the New Testament, with the eyes of our human vocation, as an increasing number were able to look at this law in the course of time after Exodus, we see that these various commandments, these imperatives, coalesce into two commandments: the love of God and the love of man. The first four of the ten are the love of God expressed concretely; and in the six other commandments we have the love of man, also made concrete, tangible, workable. The law is discipline and rule for those who are still in the making, who are still in the process of becoming sons, but at the same time it is already the law of the New Testament. The problem between man and man and between man and God is that of establishing divine peace, peace in the name of God, peace which is not built on mutual attraction or sympathy, but which is built on more basic facts; our common sonship, our common Lord, our human solidarity and our narrower church solidarity. Divine and human love must be summed up first of all in the establishment of the right relationships, the right relationship with God, with men and also with one's self.

We have seen that to exist in the desert, the absolute prerequisite is mutual forgiveness, now another step must be taken; whereas we find in Exodus the imperative law which expresses the mind and will of God, we find in the Lord's Prayer 'Thy will be done'. 'Thy will be done' is not a submissive readiness to bear God's will, as we often take it to be. It is the positive attitude of those who have gone

through the wilderness, who have entered the promised
land and who set out to make the will of God present and
real on earth as it is in heaven. St Paul says that we are a
colony of heaven (Phil 3:20; Moffat's translation). He
means a group of people whose mother city is heaven, who
are on earth to conquer it for God and to bring the kingdom
of God if only to a small spot. It is a peculiar type of conquest, which consists in winning over people to the realm
of peace, making them subject to the prince of peace and
making them enter into the harmony which we call the
kingdom of God. It is indeed a conquest, a peacemaking
that will make us sheep among wolves, seeds scattered by
the sower, which must die in order to bear fruit and to feed
others.

'Thy will be done' seen in this way from within our
situation as sons is something quite different from the
kind of obedience, submissive or resistant, which we have
seen in the beginning of Exodus, when Moses tried to put
his countrymen in motion towards freedom. Now they
have, we have, the mind of Christ, now we know the will
of God, we are no longer servants but friends (Jn 15:15).
He does not mean a vague relationship of goodwill, but
something extremely deep that binds us together. This is
the situation in which we walk into the promised land,
when we say in a new way 'Thy will be done', not as an
alien will, not as a will strong and able to break us, but as
a will with which we have become completely harmonious.
And we must, the moment we do this, accept all that is
implied in being sons of God, in being members of the one
body. As he came into the world to die for the salvation
of the world, so are we elect for this purpose; and it may

be at the cost of our own lives that we are to bring peace around us and establish the kingdom.

There is a difference between God the king, perceived in the land of Egypt, or in the scorching wilderness, and in the new situation of the promised land. First, his will would prevail anyhow, whatever resistance one opposed to it would be broken: obedience means subjection. Secondly, a gradual training shows that this king is not an overlord, a slavedriver, but a king of goodwill, and that obedience to him transforms all; that we can be not just subjects but his own people, his army in motion. Lastly, we discover the king in the full sense of this word as summed up by St Basil: 'Every ruler can rule, only a king can die for his subjects.' There is here such identification of the king with his subjects, that is with his kingdom, that whatever happens to the kingdom happens to the king; and not only identification, but an act of substitutive love which makes the king take the place of his subjects. The king becomes man, God is incarnate. He enters into the historical destiny of mankind, he puts on the flesh that makes him part and parcel of the total cosmos, with its tragedy caused by the human fall. He goes to the very depth of human condition, up to judgement, iniquitous condemnation and death, the experience of having lost God and so being able to die. The kingdom of which we speak in this petition is the kingdom of this king. If we are not at one with him and with all the spirit of the kingdom, now understood in a new way, we are not capable of being called the children of God, or of saying 'Thy Kingdom come'. But what we must realise is that the kingdom we ask for is a kingdom which is defined by the last beatitudes: 'Blessed are they which are persecuted.' 'Blessed are ye, when men shall revile you, and persecute you and shall say all manner of evil against you, for my sake.' If the kingdom is to come, we are to pay the cost which is defined in these beatitudes. The kingdom of which we are speaking is a kingdom of love and it would be superficially, seemingly, so nice to enter it; yet it is not nice, because love has got a tragic side, it means death to each of us, the complete dying out of our selfish, self-centred self, and not dying out as a flower fades away but dying a cruel death, the death of the crucifixion.

Only within the situation of the kingdom can the Name of God be hallowed and receive glory from us; because it is not our words and our gestures, even liturgical, that give glory to the name of God, it is our being the kingdom, which is the radiance and the glory of our maker and our saviour. And this name is love, one God in the Trinity.

As we see it now, the Lord's Prayer has a complete universal value and significance, expressing, though in reverse order, the ascent of every soul, from the captivity of sin to the plenitude of life in God; it is not just a prayer, it is *the* prayer of christians. The first words 'Our Father' are characteristically christian. In St Matthew 11:27 the Lord says: 'No man knoweth the Son but the Father, neither knoweth any man the Father, save the Son and he to whomsoever the Son will reveal him.' To know God as our father in an approximate way is given not only to christians but to many people, yet to know him as our father in the way in which Christ revealed it to us, is given only to christians in Christ. Outside the biblical revelation God appears to us as the creator of all things. A life attentive and worshipful may teach us that this creator is merciful, loving, full of wisdom, and by analogy may lead us to speak of the creator of all things in terms of fatherhood; he deals with us in the way in which a father deals with his children.

Even before the revelation of Christ we find in scripture one striking example of a man who was strictly speaking a pagan, but was on the verge of this knowledge of God in terms of sonship and fatherhood; it is Job. He is termed a pagan because he does not belong to the race of Abraham, he is not one of the inheritors of the promises to Abraham. He is one of the most striking figures of the Old Testament because of his contest with God. The three men who argue with him know God as their overlord: God is entitled to do what he has done to Job, God is right in whatever he does because he is the Lord of all things. And that is just the point which Job cannot accept, because he knows God differently. In his spiritual experience he knows already that God is not simply the overlord that is above all. He cannot accept him as one wielding arbitrary power, as an almighty being who can and has a right to do anything he chooses. Since, however, God has not yet said anything about himself, all this is a hope, a prophetic vision and not yet the very revelation of God in his fatherhood.

When the Lord appears to Job and answers his questions, he speaks in terms of the pagan revelation, which is typified by the words of the Psalm: 'The heavens declare the glory of God and the firmament sheweth his handywork' (Ps 19:1). Job understands, because, as Paul says, repeating Jeremiah (31:33), 'The Law of God is written in our hearts' (Rom 2:15). God confronts Job with a vision of all the created world and reasons with him; then, in spite of the fact that Job is apparently found wrong, God declares that he is more right than his gainsayers, than those who regard God as an earthly overlord. Although he fell short of a real knowledge of the divine fatherhood he had gone beyond what his friends knew about God. One may say that in the Old Testament we find in Job the first prophetic vision of the fatherhood of God and of that salvation of mankind that can be achieved only by someone who is the equal of both God and man. When Job turns accusingly towards God, and says, 'Neither is there any daysman (mediator) betwixt us, that might lay his hand upon us both' (Job 9:33), we see in him one who has outgrown the understanding of his contemporaries, but who has as yet no ground to affirm his faith and his knowledge, because God has not yet spoken through Christ.

The mystery of sonship and the mystery of fatherhood are correlative: you cannot know the father, unless you know the son, neither can you know the son, unless you are the father; there is no knowledge from without. Our relationship with God is based on an act of faith, supplemented by God's response, that brings this act of faith to fruition. The way in which we become members of Christ is an act of faith, fulfilled by God in baptism. In a way which is known only to God and to those who have been called and renewed, we become, by participation, what Christ is by birth. It is only by becoming members of Christ that we become sons of God. What we must not forget is that the fatherhood of God is more than an attitude of warmth and affection, it is more real and more sharply true: God becomes in Christ, the father of those who become members of the body of Christ, but one does not get linked with Christ by any kind of loose sentimentality: it is an ascetical effort which may take a lifetime and cost far more than one guessed at the start.

The fact that Christ and we become one, means that what applies to Christ applies to us, and that we can, in a way unknown to the rest of the world, call God our father, no longer by analogy, no longer in terms of anticipation or prophecy, but in terms of Christ. This has a direct bearing upon the Lord's Prayer: on the one hand, the prayer can be used by anyone, because it is universal, it is the ladder of our ascent towards God, on the other hand, it is absolutely particular and exclusive: it is the prayer of those who are, in Christ, the sons of the eternal father, who can speak to him as sons.

When the prayer is envisaged in its universal meaning, it is safer to study and analyse it in terms of an ascent, but it is not the way in which Christ has given it to those who, in him and together with him, are the children of God, because for them it is no longer an ascent that is spoken of, it is a state, a situation; we are, in the Church, the children of God, and these first words 'Our Father' establish the fact and make us take our stand where we belong. It is no good saying we are unworthy of this calling. We have accepted it, and it is ours. We may be the prodigal son and we will have to answer for it, but what is certain is that nothing can transform us back into that which we no longer are. When the prodigal son returned to his father, and was about to say: 'I am no more worthy to be called thy son, make me as one of thy hired servants' (Lk 15:19), the father allowed him to pronounce the first words: 'I have sinned against heaven and in thy sight and am no more worthy to be called thy son', but there he stopped him. Yes, he is not worthy, but he is a son in spite of his unworthiness. You cannot cease to be a member of your family, whatever you do, whether worthy or not. Whatever we are, whatever our life is, however unworthy we we are to be called the sons of God, or to call God our father, we have no escape. That is where we stand. He is our father, and we are answerable for the relationship of sonship. We are created by him as his children and it is only by rejecting our birthright that we become prodigal sons. Imagine that the prodigal son did not come back, but settled and married in the strange land, the child born of this marriage would be organically related to the prodigal's father. If he went back to his father's native land he would be received as one of the family; if he did not go back he would be answerable for not returning and choosing to remain a stranger to his father's family.

It is baptism which is the return of the children of many generations to the household of the father. And we baptise a child in the same spirit in which we cure a baby born with a disease. If later on he wrongly comes to think that it would have been more convenient to have kept his infirmity, to be of no use to society and to be free from the burden of social obligations, that is another matter. The Church, in baptising a child, heals it in order to make it a responsible member of the only real society.

Rejection of one's baptism amounts to the rejection of an act of healing. In baptism we not only become healthy but we become organically members of the body of Christ.

At that point, calling God 'Our Father' we have come

to Zion, to the top of the mount, and at the top of the mount we find the Father, divine love, the revelation of the Trinity; and just without the walls the small hill which we call Calvary, with history and eternity blending there in this vision. From there we can turn round and look back. This is where the christian should begin his christian life, having fulfilled this ascent, and should begin to say the Lord's Prayer in the order in which the Lord gives it to us as the prayer of the only begotten Son, the prayer of the Church, the prayer of each of us in our togetherness with all, as a person who is a son within the Son. And it is only then that we can go down from the top of the mountain, step by step, to meet those who are still on their way or those who have not yet begun their way.

III

The Prayer of Bartimaeus

―――――――――――――●―――――――――――――

THE CASE OF Bartimaeus, as recorded in Mark 10:46, gives us some insight into a certain number of points relating to prayer.

> And they came to Jericho; and as he went out of Jericho with his disciples and a great number of people, blind Bartimaeus, the son of Timaeus, sat by the highway side, begging. And when he heard that it was Jesus of Nazareth, he began to cry out, and say, 'Jesus, thou son of David, have mercy upon me.' And many charged him that he should hold his peace; but he cried the more a great deal, 'Thou, son of David, have mercy on me.' And Jesus stood still, and commanded him to be called, and they called the blind man, saying to him, be of good comfort, rise; he calleth thee. And he, casting away his garment, rose, and came to Jesus. And Jesus answered and said unto him, 'What wilt thou that I should do unto thee?' The blind man said unto Him, 'Lord, that I might receive my sight.' And Jesus said unto him: 'Go thy way; thy faith hath made thee whole.' And immediately he received his sight, and followed Jesus in the way.

This man, Bartimaeus, was not a young man apparently; he had sat for a number of years at the gate of Jericho, receiving his sustenance from the mercy or the indifferent wealth of those who passed by. It is likely that in the course of his life he had tried all existing means and all possible ways of being healed. As a child, he had probably been brought to the temple, prayers and sacrifices had been offered. He had visited all those who could heal, either because they had a gift, or because they had knowledge. He had surely fought for his sight and he had been constantly disappointed. Every human device had been tried, yet blind he remained. He had probably also heard in the previous months that a young preacher had appeared in Galilee, a man who loved people, who was merciful and who was a holy man of God, a man who could heal and work miracles. He had probably often thought that if he could he would have gone to meet him; but Christ was going from one place to another and there was little chance that a blind man should find his way to him. And so, with that spark of hope that made despair even deeper and more acute, he sat by the gate of Jericho.

One day a crowd passed him, a crowd greater than usual, a noisy oriental crowd; the blind man heard it and asked who was there, and when he was told that it was Jesus of Nazareth, he began to call out. Every spark of hope that had survived in his soul suddenly became a fire, a burning fire of hope. Jesus, whom he had never been able to meet, was passing his way. He was passing by, and every step was bringing him nearer and nearer, and then every step would take him farther and farther away, hopelessly so; and he began to cry, 'Jesus, thou son of David, have mercy upon me.' This was the most perfect profession of faith that he could make at that moment. He recognised in him the son of David, the Messiah; he could not yet call him the son of God, because even the disciples did not yet know; but he recognised in him the one who was expected. Then something happened which happens constantly in our lives: they told him to be quiet.

How often does it not happen that after seeking and struggling for years on our own, when on a sudden we begin to cry to God, many voices try to silence our prayers, outward voices as well as inward voices. Is it worth praying? How many years did you struggle and God did not care? Is he to care now? What is the use of praying? Go back into your hopelessness, you are blind, and blind for ever. But the greater the opposition, the greater also is the evidence that help is at hand. The devil never attacks us so violently as when we are quite close to the term of our struggle, and we might yet be saved, but often are not, because we give way at the last moment. Give in, says the devil, make haste, it is too much, it is more than you can stand, you can put an end to it at once, do not wait, you cannot endure it any more. And then we commit suicide, physically, morally, spiritually; we renounce the struggle and accept death, just a minute before help was at hand and we might have been saved.

We must never listen to these voices; the louder they shout, the stronger should be our purpose; we must be ready to cry out as long as necessary, as loud as Bartimaeus did. Jesus Christ was passing by, his last hope was passing by, but the people who were surrounding Christ were either indifferent or trying to silence him. His grief and suffering were out of place. They, who perhaps needed

Christ less, but surrounded him, wanted him to be busy with them. Why should that blind man in distress interrupt them? But Bartimaeus knew that there was no hope for him if this last one vanished. This depth of hopelessness was the well from which sprang a faith, a prayer full of such conviction and such insistence that it broke through all barriers – one of those prayers which beat at the gates of heaven as St John Climacus says. Because his despair was so profound he did not listen to the voices commanding him to be quiet, to hold his peace; and the more they tried to prevent him from reaching out to Christ, the louder he said: 'Thou, son of David, have mercy on me!' Christ stood still, asked for him to be brought forward and worked a miracle.

We can learn from Bartimaeus in our practical approach to prayer that when we turn to God wholeheartedly, God always hears us. Usually when we realise that we can no longer depend upon all that we are accustomed to find reliable around us, we are not yet ready to renounce these things. We can see that there is no hope as far as human, earthly ways are concerned. We are aiming at something, we search for our sight and we are constantly frustrated; it is torment and hopelessness and if we stop there, we are defeated. But if at that moment we turn to God, knowing that only God is left, and say: 'I trust thee and commit into thy hands my soul and body, my whole life,' then despair has led us to faith.

Despair is conducive to a new spiritual life when we have got the courage to go deeper and farther, realising that what we are despairing about is not the final victory but the means we have employed to reach it. Then we start at rock bottom in quite a new way. God may bring us back to one of the means we have already tried, but which, under him, we may be able to use successfully. There should always be real cooperation between God and man and then God will give intelligence, wisdom, power to do the right thing and achieve the right goal.

IV

Meditation and Worship

———————————————

MEDITATION AND PRAYER are often confused, but there is no danger in this confusion if meditation develops into prayer; only when prayer degenerates into meditation. Meditation primarily means thinking, even when God is the object of our thoughts. If as a result we gradually go deeper into a sense of worship and adoration, if the presence of God grows so powerful that we become aware of being with God, and if gradually, out of meditation we move into prayer, it is right; but the contrary should never be allowed, and in this respect there is a sharp difference between meditation and prayer.

The main distinction between meditation and our usual haphazard thinking is coherence; it should be an ascetical exercise of intellectual sobriety. Theophane the Recluse, speaking of the way in which people usually think, says that thoughts buzz around in our heads like a swarm of mosquitoes, in all directions, monotonously, without order and without particular result.

The first thing to learn, whatever the chosen subject of thought, is to pursue a line. Whenever we begin to think of God, of things divine, of anything that is the life of the soul, subsidiary thoughts appear; on every side we see so many possibilities, so many things that are full of interest and richness; but we must, having chosen the subject of our thinking, renounce all, except the chosen one. This is the only way in which our thoughts can be kept straight and can go deep.

The purpose of meditation is not to achieve an academic exercise in thinking; it is not meant to be a purely intellectual performance, nor a beautiful piece of thinking without further consequences; it is meant to be a piece of straight thinking under God's guidance and Godwards, and should lead us to draw conclusions about how to live. It is important to realise from the outset that a meditation has been useful when, as a result, it enables us to live more precisely and more concretely in accordance with the gospel.

Every one of us is impervious to certain problems and open to others; when we are not yet accustomed to thinking, it is better to begin with something which is alive for us, either with those sayings which we find attractive, which 'make our heart burn within us', or else, on the contrary, with those against which we rebel, which we cannot accept; we find both in the gospel.

Whatever we take, a verse, a commandment, an event in the life of Christ, we must first of all assess its real objective content. This is extremely important because the purpose of meditation is not to build up a fantastic structure but to understand a truth. The truth is there, given, it is God's truth, and meditation is meant to be a bridge between our lack of understanding and the truth revealed.

It is a way in which we can educate our intelligence, and gradually learn to have 'the mind of Christ' as St Paul says (1 Cor 2:16).

To make sure of the meaning of the text is not always as simple as it sounds; there are passages that are quite easy, there are other passages where words are used which can be understood only against the background of our experience, or of the traditional understanding of these words. For instance, the phrase 'The Bride of the Lamb' can be understood only if we know what scripture means by the word 'Lamb'; otherwise it becomes completely nonsensical and will be misunderstood. There are words which we can understand adequately only if we ignore the particular or technical meaning they may have acquired.

One such word is 'spirit'. For a christian, 'spirit' is a technical work; it is either the Holy Spirit, the third person of the Trinity or one of the components of the human body – body and soul. It does not always convey with the same simplicity and breadth what the writers of the gospel meant to convey; it has become so specialised that it has lost contact with its root. To make sure of the text and what it means, there is also the definition given in the dictionary. The word spirit, or any other word, can be looked up and immediately seems simple and concrete, although it may have developed into a deeper meaning as a result of the efforts of theologians. But we should never start with the deeper meaning before we have got the simple concrete one, which everyone could understand at the time Christ spoke with the people around him.

There are things which we cannot understand except within the teaching of the Church; scripture must be understood with the mind of the Church, the mind of Christ, because the Church has not changed; in its inner experience it continues to live the same life as it lived in the first century; and words spoken by Paul, Peter, Basil or others within the Church, have kept their meaning. So, after a preliminary understanding in our own contemporary language, we must turn to what the Church means by the words; only then can we ascertain the meaning of the given text and have a right to start thinking and to draw conclusions. Once we have got the meaning of the text, we must see whether in its utter simplicity it does not already offer us suggestions, or even better, a straight command. As the aim of meditation, of understanding scripture, is to fulfil the will of God, we must draw practical conclusions and act upon them. When we have discovered the meaning, when in this sentence God has spoken to us, we must look into the matter and see what we can do, as in fact we do whenever we stumble on a good idea; when we come to realise that this or that is right, we immediately think how to integrate it into our life, in what way, on what occasion, by what method. It is not enough to understand what can be done and enthusiastically to start telling our friends all about it; we should start doing it. Paul the Simple, an Egyptian saint, once heard Anthony the Great read the first verse of the first Psalm: 'Blessed is the man that walketh not in the counsel of the ungodly,' and immediately, Paul departed into the wilderness. Only after some thirty years, when Anthony met him again, St Paul said to him with great humility: 'I have spent all this time trying to become the man that does not walk in the counsel of the ungodly.' We do not need understanding on many points to reach perfection; what we need is thirty years of work to try to understand and to become that new man.

Often we consider one or two points and jump to the next, which is wrong since we have just seen that it takes a long time to become recollected, what the Fathers call an attentive person, someone capable of paying attention to an idea so long and so well that nothing of it is lost. The spiritual writers of the past and of the present day will all tell us: take a text, ponder on it hour after hour, day after day, until you have exhausted all your possibilities, intellectual and emotional, and thanks to attentive reading and re-reading of this text, you have come to a new attitude. Quite often meditation consists in nothing but examining the text, turning over these words of God addressed to us, so as to become completely familiar with them, so imbued with them that gradually we and these words become completely one. In this process, even if we think that we have not found any particular intellectual richness, we have changed.

On many occasions we can do a lot of thinking; there are plenty of situations in our daily life in which we have nothing to do except wait, and if we are disciplined – and this is part of our spiritual training – we will be able to concentrate quickly and fix our attention at once on the subject of our thoughts, of our meditation. We must learn to do it by compelling our thoughts to attach themselves to one focus and to drop everything else. In the beginning, extraneous thoughts will intrude, but if we push them away constantly, time after time, in the end they will leave us in peace. It is only when by training, by exercise, by habit, we have become able to concentrate profoundly and quickly, that we can continue through life in a state of collectedness, in spite of what we are doing. However, to become aware of having extraneous thoughts, we must already have achieved some sort of collectedness. We can be in a crowd, surrounded by people and yet completely alone and untouched by what is going on; it depends on us whether to allow what is happening outside to become an event in our inner life or not; if we allow it to, our attention will break down, but if we do not, we can be completely isolated and collected in God's presence whatever happens around us. There is a story by Al Absihi about this sort of concentration. A Moslem's family used to keep a respectful silence whenever he had a visitor, but they knew that they could make as much noise as they wanted while he was praying, because at such times he heard nothing; in fact, one day he was not even disturbed by a fire that broke out in his house.

We may sometimes find ourselves in a group of people arguing hotly with no hope of a solution. We cannot leave without causing further disorder, but what we can do is mentally to withdraw, turn to Christ and say, 'I know that you are here, help!' And just be with Christ. If it did not sound so absurd one would say, make Christ present in the situation. Objectively he is always present, but there is some difference between being there objectively and being introduced by an act of faith into a given situation. One can do nothing but sit back and just remain with Christ and let the others talk. His presence will do more than anything one could say. And from time to time, in an unexpected way, if one keeps quiet and silent together with Christ, one will discover that one can say something quite sensible that would have been impossible in the heat of argument.

Parallel with mental discipline, we must learn to acquire a peaceful body. Whatever our psychological activity, our body reacts to it; and our bodily state determines to a certain degree the type or quality of our psychological activity. Theophane the Recluse, in his advice to anyone wishing to attempt the spiritual life, says that one of the conditions indispensable to success is never to permit bodily slackness: 'Be like a violin string, tuned to a precise note, without slackness or supertension, the body erect, shoulders back, carriage of the head easy, the tension of all muscles oriented towards the heart.' A great deal has been written and said about the ways in which one can make use of the body to increase one's ability to be attentive, but on a level accessible to many, Theophane's advice seems to be simple, precise and practical. We must learn to relax and be alert at the same time. We must master our body so that it should not intrude but make collectedness easier for us.

Meditation is an activity of thought, while prayer is the rejection of every thought. According to the teaching of the eastern Fathers, even pious thoughts and the deepest and loftiest theological considerations, if they occur during prayer, must be considered as a temptation and suppressed; because, as the Fathers say, it is foolish to think about God and forget that you are in his presence. All the spiritual guides of Orthodoxy warn us against replacing this meeting with God by thinking about him. Prayer is essentially standing face to face with God, consciously striving to remain collected and absolutely still and attentive in his presence, which means standing with an undivided mind, an undivided heart and an undivided will in the presence of the Lord; and that is not easy. Whatever our training may give us, there is always a short cut open at any time: undividedness can be attained by the person for whom the love of God is everything, who has broken all ties, who is completely given to God; then there is no longer personal striving, but the working of the radiant grace of God.

God must always be the focus of our attention for there are many ways in which this collectedness may be falsified; when we pray from a deep concern, we have a sense that our whole being has become one prayer and we imagine that we have been in a state of deep, real prayerful collectedness, but this is not true, because the focus of attention was not God; it was the object of our prayer. When we are emotionally involved, no alien thought intrudes, because we are completely concerned with what we are praying about; it is only when we turn to pray for some other person or need that our attention is suddenly dispersed, which means that it was not the thought of God, not the sense of his presence that was the cause of this concentration, but our human concern. It does not mean that human concern is of no importance, but it means that the thought of a friend can do more than the thought of God, which is a serious point.

One of the reasons why we find it so difficult to be attentive is that the act of faith which we make in affirming: 'God is here,' carries too little weight for us. We are intellectually aware that God is here, but not aware of it physically in a way that would collect and focus all our energies, thoughts, emotions and will, making us nothing but attention. If we prepare for prayer by a process of imagination: 'The Lord Christ is here, that is what he looks like, this is what I know about him, this is what he means to me . . .', the richer the image, the less real the presence, because it is an idol that is built which obscures the real presence. We can derive some help from it for a sort of emotional concentration, but it is not God's presence, the real, objective presence of God.

The early Fathers and the whole Orthodox tradition teach us that we must concentrate, by an effort of will, on the words of the prayer we pronounce. We must pronounce the words attentively, matter-of-factly, without trying to create any sort of emotional state, and we must leave it to God to arouse whatever response we are capable of.

St John Climacus gives us a simple way of learning to concentrate. He says: choose a prayer, be it the Lord's Prayer or any other, take your stand before God, become aware of where you are and what you are doing, and pronounce the words of the prayer attentively. After a certain time you will discover that your thoughts have wandered; then restart the prayer on the words or the sentence which was the last you pronounced attentively. You may have to do that ten times, twenty times or fifty times; you may, in the time appointed for your prayer, be able to pronounce only three sentences, three petitions and go no farther; but in this struggle you will have been able to concentrate on the words, so that you bring to God, seriously, soberly, respectfully, words of prayer which you are conscious of, and not an offering that is not yours, because you were not aware of it.

John Climacus also advises us to read the prayer of our choice without haste, in a monotonous way, slowly enough to have time to pay attention to the words, but not so slowly as to make the exercise dull; and to do it without trying to experience anything emotionally, because what we aim at is a relationship with God. We should never try to squeeze out of the heart any sort of feeling when we come to God; a prayer is a statement, the rest depends on God.

In this way of training a given amount of time is set apart for prayer, and if prayer is attentive, it does not matter what this length of time is. If you were meant to read three pages in your rule of prayer and saw that after half an hour you were still reading the first twelve words, of course it would raise a feeling of discouragement; therefore, the best way is to have a definite time and keep to it. You know the time fixed and you have the prayer material to make use of; if you struggle earnestly, quite soon you will discover that your attention becomes docile, because the attention is much more subject to the will than we imagine, and when one is absolutely sure that however one tries to escape, it must be twenty minutes and not a quarter of an hour, one just perseveres. St John Climacus trained dozens of monks by this simple device – a time limit, then merciless attention, and that is all.

The outward beauty of the liturgy must not seduce us into forgetting that sobriety in prayer is a very important feature in Orthodoxy. In the *Way of a Pilgrim* a village priest gives some very authoritative advice on prayer: 'If you want it to be pure, right and enjoyable, you must choose some short prayer, consisting of few but forcible words, and repeat it frequently, over a long period. Then you will find delight in prayer.' The same idea is to be found in the *Letters of Brother Lawrence*: 'I do not advise you to use multiplicity of words in prayer; many words and long discourses being often the occasions of wandering.'

John of Kronstadt was asked once how it was that priests, in spite of their training, experience wandering, intrusive thoughts, even in the course of the liturgy. The answer was: 'Because of our lack of faith.' We have not faith enough, faith being understood in the terms of St Paul as 'the evidence of things not seen' (Heb 11:1). But it would be a mistake to think that those distracting thoughts all come from outside; we must face the fact that they come from our own depths: they are our continual inner preoccupations coming to the fore, they are just the thoughts that usually fill our life, and the only way to get radically rid of unworthy thoughts is to change our outlook on life fundamentally. Again, as Brother Lawrence puts it in his eighth letter: 'One way to recollect the mind easily in the time of prayer, and preserve it more in tranquillity, is not to let it wander too far at other times; you should keep it strictly in the presence of God; and being accustomed to think of him often, you will find it easy to keep your mind calm at the time of prayer, or at least to recall it from its wanderings.'

As long as we care deeply for all the trivialities of life, we cannot hope to pray wholeheartedly; they will always colour the train of our thoughts. The same is true about our daily relations with other people, which should not consist merely of gossip but be based on what is essential in every one of us, otherwise we may find ourselves unable to reach another level when we turn to God. We must eradicate everything meaningless and trivial in ourselves and in our relations with others, and concentrate on those things we shall be able to take with us into eternity.

It is not possible to become another person the moment we start to pray, but by keeping watch on one's thoughts one learns gradually to differentiate their value. It is in our daily life that we cultivate the thoughts which irrepressibly spring up at the time of prayer. Prayer in its turn will change and enrich our daily life, becoming the foundation of a new and real relationship with God and those around us.

In our struggle for prayer the emotions are almost irrelevant; what we must bring to God is a complete, firm determination to be faithful to him and strive that God should live in us. We must remember that the fruits of prayer are not this or that emotional state, but a deep change in the whole of our personality. What we aim at is to be made able to stand before God and to concentrate on his presence, all our needs being directed Godwards, and to be given power, strength, anything we need that the will of God may be fulfilled in us. That the will of God should be fulfilled in us is the only aim of prayer, and it is also the criterion of right prayer. It is not the mystical feeling we may have, or our emotions that make good praying. Theophane the Recluse says: 'You ask yourself, "Have I prayed well today?" Do not try to find out how deep your emotions were, or how much deeper you understand things divine; ask yourself: "Am I doing God's will better than I did before?" If you are, prayer has brought its fruits, if you are not, it has not, whatever amount of understanding or feeling you may have derived from the time spent in the presence of God.'

Concentration, whether in meditation or in prayer, can only be achieved by an effort of will. Our spiritual life is based on our faith and determination, and any incidental joys are a gift of God. St Seraphim of Sarov, when asked what it was that made some people remain sinners and never make any progress while others were becoming saints and living in God, answered: 'Only determination.' Our activities must be determined by an act of will, which usually happens to be contrary to what we long for; this will, based on our faith, always clashes with another will, our instinctive one. There are two wills in us, one is the conscious will, possessed to a greater or lesser degree, which consists in the ability to compel ourselves to act in accordance with our convictions. The second one is something else in us, it is the longings, the claims, the desires of all our nature, quite often contrary to the first will. St Paul speaks of two laws that fight against each other (Rom 7:23). He speaks of the old and the new Adam in us, who are at war. We know that one must die in order that the other should live, and we must realise that our spiritual life, our life as a human being taken as a whole, will never be complete as long as these two wills do not coincide. It is not enough to aim at the victory of the good will against the evil one; the evil one, that is the longings of our fallen nature, must absolutely, though gradually, be transformed into a longing, a craving for God. The struggle is hard and far-reaching.

The spiritual life, the christian life does not consist in developing a strong will capable of compelling us to do

what we do not want. In a sense, of course, it is an achievement to do the right things when we really wish to do the
wrong ones, but it remains a small achievement. A mature
spiritual life implies that our conscious will is in accordance
with the words of God and has remoulded, transformed our
nature so deeply, with the help of God's grace, that the
totality of our human person is only one will. To begin
with, we must submit and curb our will into obedience to
the commandments of Christ, taken objectively, applied
strictly, even when they clash with what we know about
life. We must, in an act of faith, admit against the evidence
that Christ is right. Experience teaches us that certain
things do not seem to work as the gospels say they should;
but God says they do, so they must. We must also remember that when we fulfil God's will in this objective
sense, we must not do it tentatively, thinking of putting it
to the test, to see what comes of it, because then it does not
work. Experience teaches us that when we are slapped on
one cheek, we want to retaliate; Christ says 'turn the other
cheek'. What we really expect when we finally determine
to turn the other cheek is to convert the enemy and win
his admiration. But when instead we are slapped again, we
are usually surprised or indignant, as though God has
cheated us into doing something quite unworkable.

We must outgrow this attitude, be prepared to do
God's will and pay the cost. Unless we are prepared to pay
the cost, we are wasting our time. Then, as a next step,
we must learn that doing is not enough, because we must
not be drilled into christianity, but we must *become*
christians; we must learn, in the process of doing the will
of God, to understand God's purpose. Christ has made his

intentions clear to us and it is not in vain that in St John's gospel he no longer calls us servants but friends, because the servant does not know the mind of the master, and he has told us all things (Jn 15:15). We must, by doing the will of God, learn what this doing implies, so that in thought, in will, in attitude, we may become co-workers with Christ (1 Cor 3:9). Being of one mind we shall gradually become inwardly what we try to be outwardly.

We see that we cannot partake deeply of the life of God unless we change profoundly. It is therefore essential that we should go to God in order that he should transform and change us, and that is why, to begin with we should ask for conversion. Conversion in Latin means a turn, a change in the direction of things. The Greek word *metanoia* means a change of mind. Conversion means that instead of spending our lives looking in all directions, we should follow one direction only. It is a turning away from a great many things which we valued solely because they were pleasant or expedient for us. The first impact of conversion is to modify our sense of values: God being at the centre of all, everything acquires a new position and a new depth. All that is God's, all that belongs to him, is positive and real. Everything that is outside him has no value or meaning. But it is not a change of mind alone that we can call conversion. We can change our minds and go no farther; what must follow is an act of will and unless our will comes into motion and is redirected Godwards, there is no conversion; at most there is only an incipient, still dormant and inactive change in us. Obviously it is not enough to look in the right direction and never move. Repentance must not be mistaken for remorse, it does not consist in feeling terribly sorry that things went wrong in the past; it is an active, positive attitude which consists in moving in the right direction. It is made very clear in the parable of the two sons (Mt 21:28) who were commanded by their father to go to work at his vineyard. The one said, 'I am going', but did not go. The other said, 'I am not going', and then felt ashamed and went to work. This was real repentance, and we should never lure ourselves into imagining that to lament one's past is an act of repentance. It is part of it of course, but repentance remains unreal and barren as long as it has not led us to doing the will of the father. We have a tendency to think that it should result in fine emotions and we are quite often satisfied with emotions instead of real, deep changes.

When we have hurt someone and realise that we were wrong, quite often we go and express our sorrow to the person, and when the conversation has been emotionally tense, when there were a lot of tears and forgiveness and moving words, we go away with a sense of having done everything possible. We have wept together, we are at peace and now everything is all right. It is not all right at all. We have simply delighted in our virtues and the other person, who may be goodhearted and easily moved, has reacted to our emotional scene. But this is just what conversion is not. No one asks us to shed tears, nor to have a touching encounter with the victim, even when the victim is God. What is expected is that having understood the wrong, we should put it right.

Nor does conversion end there; it must lead us farther in the process of making us different. Conversion begins but it never ends. It is an increasing process in which we gradually become more and more what we should be, until, after the day of judgement, these categories of fall, conversion and righteousness disappear and are replaced by new categories of a new life. As Christ says: 'I make all things new' (Rev 21:5).

One can pray everywhere and anywhere, yet there are places where prayer finds its natural climate; those places are churches, fulfilling the promise; 'I will make them joyful in my house of prayer' (Is 56:7).

A church, once consecrated, once set part, becomes the dwelling-place of God. He is present there in another way than in the rest of the world. In the world he is present as a stranger, as a pilgrim, as one who goes from door to door, who has nowhere to rest his head; he goes as the lord of the world who has been rejected by the world and expelled from his kingdom and who has returned to it to save his people. In church he is at home, it is his place; he is not only the creator and the lord by right but he is recognised as such. Outside it he acts when he can and how he can; inside a church he has all power and all might and it is for us to come to him.

When we build a church or set apart a place of worship we do something which reaches far beyond the obvious significance of the fact. The whole world which God created has become a place where men have sinned; the devil has been at work, a fight is going on constantly; there is no place on this earth which has not been soiled by blood, suffering or sin. When we choose a minute part of it, calling upon the power of God himself, in rites which convey his grace, to bless it, when we cleanse it from the presence of the evil spirit and set it apart to be God's foothold on earth, we reconquer for God a small part of this desecrated world. We may say that this is a place where the kingdom of God reveals itself and manifests itself with power. When we come to church we should be aware that we are entering upon sacred ground, a place which belongs to God, and we should behave accordingly.

The icons seen on church walls are not merely images or paintings: an icon is a focus of real presence. St John Chrysostom advises us, before we start praying, to take our stand in front of an icon and to shut our eyes. He says 'shut your eyes', because it is not by examining the icon, by using it as a visual aid, that we are helped by it to pray. It is not a substantial presence in the sense in which the bread and wine are the body and blood of Christ. An icon is not, in this sense, Christ, but there is a mysterious link between the two. By the power of grace an icon participates in something which can best be defined in the words of Gregory Palamas as the energies of Christ, as the active power of Christ working for our salvation.

An icon is painted as an act of worship. The wood is chosen and blessed, the paint is blessed, the man who wishes to paint prepares himself by fasting, by confession, by communion. He keeps ascetical rules while working and when his work is completed, it is blessed with holy water and chrismated (this last part of the blessing is now often omitted, unfortunately). Thus, by the power of the Holy Spirit, the icon becomes more than a painting. It is loaded with presence, imbued with the grace of the Spirit and linked with the particular saint it represents in and through the mystery of the communion of saints and the cosmic unity of all things. One cannot say of the icon that the indwelling of the saint is identical with or even similar to that which we find in the holy gifts, and yet it is a focus of real presence as it is experienced and taught by the Church. An icon is not a likeness, it is a sign. Certain icons have been singled out by the power and wisdom of God to be miraculous icons. When you stand in their presence you feel challenged by them.

A priest who visited Russia recently took services in a church where there was a well-known wonder-working icon of Our Lady and was deeply conscious of her active participation in the service. The icon had become very dark in the course of centuries, and from the place where he stood he could not distinguish the features, so he continued to celebrate with his eyes shut. Suddenly he felt that the Mother of God in the icon was as it were compelling him to pray, directing his prayers, shaping his mind. He became aware of a power originating from the icon that filled the church with prayer and guided the diffuse thoughts. It was almost a physical presence, there was a person standing there, compelling a response.

V

Unanswered Prayer and Petition

IN THE EPISODE of the Canaanite woman (Mt 15: 22) we see Christ, at least at first, refusing to answer a prayer; it is the case of a prayer tested in an extremely hard way. The woman asks for something which is absolutely right, she comes with complete faith and does not even say 'if you can', she just comes, sure that Christ can and that he will be willing, and that her child will be cured. To all this faith the answer is 'No'. It is not that the prayer is not worthy, or the faith not sufficient, simply that she is the wrong sort of person. Christ has come for the Jews, she is a pagan; he has not come for her. But she insists, saying, 'Yes, I am the wrong kind, but even the dogs eat the crumbs which fall from their master's table.' And she stands, trusting in the love of God, in spite of what God says, trusting so humbly despite the reason he gives. She does not even invoke the love of God, she just appeals to its expression in daily life: I have no right to a loaf, just give me some crumbs. Christ's clear and sharp refusal tests her faith and her prayer is fulfilled.

So often we implore God, saying, 'O God, if . . . if

Thou wilt . . . if Thou canst . . .', just like the father, who says to Christ: 'Your disciples have not been able to cure my little boy, if you can do anything, do it' (Mk 9:22). Christ answers with another 'if': if you believe, however little, everything is possible with faith. Then the man says: 'I believe, help thou mine unbelief.' The two 'ifs' are correlative, because if there is no faith there is also no possibility for God to enter into the situation.

The fact that one turns to God should be the proof of belief, but it is so only to a certain extent; we believe and we do not believe at the same time, and faith shows its measure by overcoming its own doubts. When we say: 'Yes, I doubt, but I do believe in God's love more than I trust my own doubts,' it becomes possible for God to act. But if one believes in law and not in grace, if one believes that the world as we know it with its mechanical laws is mechanical because God willed it to be nothing but a machine, then there is no place for God. Yet the heart's experience, as well as modern science, teaches us that there is no such thing as the absolute law in which men believed in the nineteenth century. Whenever by faith the kingdom of God is re-created, there is a place for the laws of the kingdom to act, that is for God to come into the situation with his wisdom, his ability to do good within an evil situation, without, however, upsetting the whole world. Our 'if' refers less to the power of God than to his love and concern; and God's reply 'if you can believe in my love, everything is possible' means that no miracle can happen unless, even in an incipient way, the kingdom of God is present.

A miracle is not the breaking of the laws of the fallen

world, it is the re-establishment of the laws of the kingdom of God; a miracle happens only if we believe that the law depends not on the power but on the love of God Although we know that God is almighty, as long as we think that he does not care, no miracle is possible; to work it God would have to enforce his will, and that he does not do, because at the very core of his relationship to the world, even fallen, there is his absolute respect for human freedom and rights. The moment you say: 'I believe, and that is why I turned to you,' implies: 'I believe that you will be willing, that there is love in you, that you are actually concerned about every single situation.' The moment this grain of faith is there the right relationship is established and a miracle becomes possible.

Apart from this type of 'if', which refers to our doubt in the love of God, and which is wrong, there is a legitimate category of 'if'. We can say: 'I am asking this, if it is according to thy will, or if it is for the best, or if there is no secret evil intention in me when I ask,' and so on. All these 'ifs' are more than legitimate, because they imply a diffident attitude to our own selves; and every prayer of petition should be an 'if-prayer'.

As the Church is an extension of Christ's presence in time and space, any christian prayer should be Christ praying although it implies a purity of heart that we do not possess. The prayers of the Church are Christ's prayers, particularly in the canon of the liturgy, where it is entirely Christ praying; but any other prayer in which we ask for something involving a concrete situation is always under 'if'. In the majority of cases we do not know what Christ would have prayed for in this situation and so we introduce the 'if', which means that as far as we can see, as far as we know God's will, this is what we wish to happen to meet his will. But the 'if' also means: I am putting into these words my desire that the best should happen, and therefore you can alter this concrete petition to anything you choose, taking my intention, the desire that your will be done, even if I am unwise in stating how I should like it to be done (Rom 8:26). When, for example, we pray for someone to recover, or to be back from a journey at a certain time, for some purpose we think essential, our real intention is the good of the person, but we are not clear-sighted about it, and our timing and planning may be wrong. 'If' implies that so far as I can see what is right, be it done that way, but if I am mistaken, do not take me at my word but at my intention. The Staretz Ambrose of Optina had the kind of vision which allowed him to see a person's real good. The monastery's icon painter had just received a large sum of money and was about to start his journey home. He must have prayed that he might be on his way immediately; but the Staretz deliberately delayed the artist for three days, and in so doing saved him from being murdered and robbed by one of his workmen. When he eventually departed the villain had left his ambush, and it was only years later that the painter discovered from what danger the Staretz had protected him.

We sometimes pray for someone we love, who is in need and whom we are not able to help. Very often we do not know what the right thing is, we do not find the words to help even the most beloved. Sometimes we know that nothing can be done except to be silent, though we are ready to give our life to help. In that spirit we can turn to

God, put the whole situation into his care and say: 'O God, who knowest everything and whose love is perfect, take this life into thine hand, do what I long to do, but cannot.' Prayer being a commitment, we cannot pray in all truth for those whom we are not ourselves prepared to help. With Isaiah we must be ready to hear the Lord say 'Whom shall I send, and who will go for us?' and to answer: 'Here am I, send me' (Is 6:8).

Many are dismayed at the thought of praying for the dead, and they wonder what one is aiming at, what one can hope in doing so. Can the destiny of the dead be changed if one prays for them, will the praying convince God to do an injustice and grant them what they have not deserved?

If you believe that prayers for the living are a help to them, why should you not pray for the dead? Life is one, for as St Luke says: 'He is not the God of the dead but of the living' (20:38). Death is not an end but a stage in the destiny of man, and this destiny is not petrified at the moment of death. The love which our prayer expresses cannot be in vain; if love had power on earth and had no power after death it would tragically contradict the word of scripture that love is as strong as death (Song 8:6), and the experience of the Church that love is more powerful than death, because Christ has defeated death in his love for mankind. It is an error to think that man's connection with life on earth ends with his death. In the course of one's life one sows seeds. These seeds develop in the souls of other men and affect their destiny, and the fruit that is born of these seeds truly belongs not only to those who bear it but also to those who sow. The words written or spoken that change a human life or the destiny of mankind, as the words of preachers, philosophers, poets or politicians, remain their authors' responsibility, not only for evil but also for good; the authors' destiny is bound to be affected by the way they have influenced those living after them.

The life of every person continues to have repercussions until the last judgement, and man's eternal and final destiny is determined not only by the short space of time he has lived on this earth but also by the results of his life, by its good or evil consequences. Those who have received seed sown as in fertile ground, can influence the destiny of the departed by prayerfully beseeching God to bless the man who has transformed their lives, given a meaning to their existence. In turning to God in an act of enduring love, faithfulness and gratitude they enter this eternal kingdom which transcends the limits of time, and they can influence the destiny and the situation of the departed. It is not injustice that is asked of God; we do not ask him merely to forgive a man in spite of what he has done but to bless him because of the good he has done, to which other lives bear witness.

Our prayer is an act of gratitude and love, in so far as our life is the continuation of something that he stood for. We do not ask God to be unjust, and we do not imagine that we are more compassionate and more loving than he is, nor do we ask him to be more merciful than he would otherwise be; we are bringing new evidence for God's judgement, and we pray that this evidence should be taken into account and that the blessing of God should come abundantly for the one who has meant so much in our life. It is important to realise that we pray not in order to convince God of something but to bear witness that this person has not lived in vain, neither loving nor inspiring love.

Any person who has been the origin of love in any way has something to put forward in his defence, but it is for those who remain to bear witness to what he has done for them. Here again it is not simply a matter of goodwill or emotion. St Isaac of Syria says: do not reduce your prayer to words, make the totality of your life a prayer to God. Therefore, if we wish to pray for our departed, our life must back up the prayer. It is not enough to wake up to a certain feeling for them from time to time and then ask God to do something for them. It is essential that every seed of good, truth and holiness that has been sown by them should bear fruit, because then we can stand before God and say: he has sown good, there was some quality in him which inspired me to do well, and this particle of good is not mine but his and is in a way his glory and his redemption.

The Orthodox Church has very firm views about death and burial. The burial service starts by 'Blessed is our God'; we should realise what weight this carries, because these words are said in spite of the death, in spite of the bereavement, in spite of the suffering. The service is based on Matins, which is a service of praise and light, the mourners stand holding lighted candles in their hands as a symbol of the resurrection. The basic idea of the service is that we are indeed faced with death, but death does not frighten us any more when we see it through the resurrection of Christ.

At the same time the service gives a sense of the ambiguity of death, the two sides to it. Death cannot be accepted, it is a monstrosity: we have been created in order to live, and yet in the world which human sin has made monstrous, death is the only way out. If our world of sin were fixed unchangeable and eternal, it would be hell; death is the only thing that allows the earth, together with suffering and sin, to escape from this hell.

The Church perceives the two sides to this; St John of Damascus has written about it with extreme realism, crudely, because a Christian cannot be romantic about death. Dying is dying in the same way in which, when we speak of the cross, we must remember that it is an instrument of death. Death is death with all its tragic ugliness and monstrosity, and yet death ultimately is the only thing that gives us hope. On the one hand, we long to live; on the other hand, if we long sufficiently to live, we long to die, because in this limited world it is impossible to live fully. There is decay indeed, but a decay which, in conjunction with the grace of God, leads to a measure of life which otherwise we would never have. 'Death is a gain,' says St Paul (Phil 1:21), because living in the body we get separated from Christ. When we have reached a certain measure of life – independent of time – we must shed this limited life to enter into unlimited life.

The Orthodox burial service is strikingly centred round the open coffin, because the person is still considered in his entirety as body and soul, both being the concern of the Church. The body has been prepared for the burial; the body is not a piece of outworn clothing, as some seemingly devout people like to say, which has been cast off for the soul to be free. A body is much more than this for a Christian; there is nothing that befalls the soul in which the body does not take part. We receive impressions of this world, but also of the divine world partly through the body. Every sacrament is a gift of God, conferred on the soul by means of physical actions; the waters of baptism, the oil of chrismation, the bread and wine of communion are all taken from the material world. We can never do either good or evil otherwise than in conjunction with our body. The body is not there only, as it were, for the soul to be born, mature and then to go, abandoning it; the body, from the very first day to the last, has been the co-worker of the soul in all things and is, together with the soul, the total man. It remains marked for ever as it were by the imprint of the soul and the common life they had together. Linked with the soul, the body is also linked through the sacraments to Jesus Christ himself. We commune to his blood and body, and the body is thus united in its own right with the divine world with which it comes into contact.

A body without a soul is a corpse and not our concern, and a soul without a body, even the soul of a saint that goes 'straight to heaven', does not yet enjoy the bliss which the whole human being is called to enjoy at the end of time when the glory of God shines through soul and body.

As St Isaac the Syrian says, even eternal bliss cannot be enforced on the human being without the consent of the body. It is extremely striking to find this comment upon the importance of the body in the sayings of St Isaac, who is one of the great ascetics, one of those about whom people might easily say that he spent all his life killing his body. But in the words of St Paul, the ascetics were killing the body of sin, to reap out of corruption, eternity (Rom 6:6) and not killing the body for the soul to escape an imprisonment.

Thus the dead body is an object of care on the part of the Church, even when it is the body of a sinner; and all the attention we pay to it when alive is nothing to the veneration shown it at the burial service.

In the same way the body is linked with the soul in the life of prayer. Every perversity, every excess, every vulgarity to which we ourselves subject our bodies degrades one member of this partnership in a way which damages the other; to put the matter another way, indignity imposed from without can be overcome by prayer; self-inflicted indignity destroys prayer.

The characteristic of christian prayer is that it is the prayer of Christ, brought to his father, from generation to generation in constantly renewed situations, by those who, by grace and participation, are Christ's presence in this world; it is a continuous, unceasing prayer to God, that God's will should be done, that all should happen according to his wise and loving plan. This means that our life of prayer is at the same time a struggle against all that is not Christ's. We prepare the ground for our prayer each time we shed something which is not Christ's, which is unworthy of him, and only the prayer of one who can, like St Paul, say: 'I live, yet not I, but Christ liveth in me' (Gal 2:20) is real christian prayer.

Yet, instead of praying for the will of God to be done, we often try to convince him to do things as we want. How can such prayers not be defeated?

However well we pray, we must be aware at every
moment that our best idea may be wrong. However
sincere, however truthful our intentions, however perfect
it is according to our lights, every prayer may go wrong
at a certain moment, and this is why, when we have said
everything we had to say to God, we must add, as Christ
did in the garden of Gethsemane: 'Not as I will, but as
Thou wilt' (Mt 26:39). In the same spirit we may make
use of the intercession of the saints: we bring them our
intentions which are good, but let them frame them in
accordance with the will of God, which they know.

'Ask and it shall be given' (Mt 7:7). These words are
a thorn in the christian consciousness, they can neither be
accepted nor rejected. To reject them would mean a refusal
of God's infinite kindness, but we are not yet christian
enough to accept them. We know that the father would
not give a stone instead of bread (Mt 7:9), but we do not
think of ourselves as children who are unconscious of
their real needs and what is good or bad for them. Yet
there lies the explanation of so many unanswered prayers.
It can also be found in the words of St John Chrysostom:
'Do not be distressed if you do not receive at once what
you ask for: God wants to do you more good through
your perseverance in prayer.'

'Could not the silence of God be the tragic aspect of our
own deafness?' *

'Again I say unto you that if two of you shall agree on
earth as touching anything that they shall ask, it shall be
done for them of my Father which is in heaven' (Mt

* A. de Chateaubriant, *La Réponse du Seigneur*, p. 170.

18:19). This quotation is sometimes used as a stick with which to beat christians, because often enough things are asked earnestly by several persons together and yet not granted. But objections crumble the moment it appears that the being together is a wordly one, the agreement is coalition and not unity, and the belief that God can do anything he likes is interpreted in the same way that it was by Job's comforters.

As for the seeming untruth that 'All things, whatsoever Ye shall ask in prayer, believing, ye shall receive' (Mt 21:22), it is answered by Christ's prayer in the garden of Gethsemane and partly also by St Paul (Heb 11:36–40):

> And others had trial of cruel mockings and scourgings, yea moreover of bonds of imprisonment: They were stoned, they were sawn asunder, were tempted, were slain with the sword; they wandered about in sheepskins and goatskins; being destitute, afflicted, tormented; (of whom the world was not worthy) they wandered in deserts, and in mountains, and in dens and caves of the earth. And all these, having obtained a good report through faith, received not the promise. God having provided some better things for us, that they, without us, should not be made perfect.

Surely in all those situations there was a great deal of prayer, not perhaps for deliverance on the part of those who were ready to lay down their lives for God, but for help; and yet they were not given all they could expect.

When God sees that you have faith enough to stand his silence or to accept being delivered to torment, moral or physical, for a greater fulfilment of his kingdom, he may keep silent, and in the end the prayer will be answered, but in quite a different way from what you expected.

St Paul says, speaking of the prayer of Christ in the garden of Gethsemane, that his prayer was heard (Heb 5:7), and God raised him from the dead. St Paul does not speak here of an immediate answer from God, who could have taken away the cup, which was what Christ was asking; but in fact God gave Christ strength to accept, to suffer, to fulfil his work, and it is the absoluteness of his faith which made it possible for God to say No. But it is also this very absoluteness of Christ's faith which made it possible for the world to be saved.

Many of our prayers are prayers of petition, and people seem to think that petition is the lowest level of prayer; then comes gratitude, then praise. But in fact it is gratitude and praise that are expressions of a lower relationship. On our level of half-belief it is easier to sing hymns of praise or to thank God than to trust him enough to ask something with faith. Even people who believe half-heartedly can turn to thank God when something nice comes their way; and there are moments of elation when everyone can sing to God. But it is much more difficult to have such undivided faith as to ask with one's whole heart and whole mind with complete confidence. No one should look askance at petition, because the ability to say prayers of petition is a test of the reality of our faith.

When the Mother of Zebedee's children came to ask Christ for the two best places in paradise for her two sons, she came with complete confidence that the Lord could do what she was asking, but she was thinking of the power of Christ to grant her request as the Lord's right to act simply according to his will, which was not in accordance with the teaching: 'My judgement is just because I seek not mine own will, but the will of the Father which hath sent me' (Jn 5:30).

What the Mother of Zebedee's children expected was that the Lord would arbitrarily fulfil her desire as a favour, because she was the first to put forward the claim. The refusal of Christ pointed out that what the mother was asking was for a situation of pride in the kingdom of God, when the whole kingdom is based on humility. The mother's prayer was conditioned by the Old Testament attitude to the coming of the Messiah.

VI

The Jesus Prayer

THOSE WHO HAVE read *The Way of a Pilgrim* are familiar
with the expression 'The Jesus Prayer'. It refers to a short
prayer the words of which are: 'Lord Jesus Christ, Son of
God, have mercy on me, a sinner,' constantly repeated. *The
Way of a Pilgrim* is the story of a man who wanted to learn
to pray constantly (I Thes 5:17). As the man whose experience is being related is a pilgrim, a great many of his
psychological characteristics, and the way in which he
learned and applied the prayer, were conditioned by the
fact that he lived in a certain way, which makes the book
less universally applicable than it could be; and yet it is the
best possible introduction to this prayer, which is one of
the greatest treasures of the Orthodox Church.

The prayer is profoundly rooted in the spirit of the
gospel, and it is not in vain that the great teachers of Orthodoxy have always insisted on the fact that the Jesus Prayer
sums up the whole of the gospel. This is why the Jesus
Prayer can only be used in its fullest sense if the person who
uses it belongs to the gospel, is a member of the Church of
Christ.

All the messages of the gospel, and more than the messages, the reality of the gospel, is contained in the name, in the person of Jesus. If you take the first half of the prayer you will see how it expresses our faith in the Lord: 'Lord Jesus Christ, Son of God.' At the heart we find the name of Jesus; it is the name before whom every knee shall bow (Is 45:23), and when we pronounce it we affirm the historical event of the incarnation. We affirm that God, the Word of God, co-eternal with the father, became man, and that the fullness of the godhead dwelt in our midst (Col 2:9) bodily in his person.

To see in the man of Galilee, in the prophet of Israel, the incarnate Word of God, God become man, we must be guided by the spirit, because it is the spirit of God who reveals to us both the incarnation and the lordship of Christ. We call him Christ, and we affirm thereby that in him were fulfilled the prophecies of the Old Testament. To affirm that Jesus is the Christ implies that the whole history of the Old Testament is ours, that we accept it as the truth of God. We call him son of God, because we know that the Messiah expected by the Jews, the man who was called 'son of David' by Bartimaeus, is the incarnate son of God. These words sum up all we know, all we believe about Jesus Christ, from the Old Testament to the New, and from the experience of the Church through the ages. In these few words we make a complete and perfect profession of faith.

But it is not enough to make this profession of faith; it is not enough to believe. The devils also believe and tremble (Jas 2:19). Faith is not sufficient to work salvation, it must lead to the right relationship with God; and so, having professed, in its integrity, sharply and clearly, our faith in the lordship and in the person, in the historicity and in the divinity of Christ, we put ourselves face to face with him, in the right state of mind: 'Have mercy on me, a sinner.'

These words 'have mercy' are used in all the Christian Churches and, in Orthodoxy, they are the response of the people to all the petitions suggested by the priest. Our modern translation 'have mercy' is a limited and insufficient one. The Greek word which we find in the gospel and in the early liturgies is *eleison*. *Eleison* is of the same root as *elaion*, which means olive tree and the oil from it. If we look up the Old and New Testament in search of the passages connected with this basic idea, we will find it described in a variety of parables and events which allow us to form a complete idea of the meaning of the word. We find the image of the olive tree in Genesis. After the flood Noah sends birds, one after the other, to find out whether there is any dry land or not, and one of them, a dove – and it is significant that it is a dove – brings back a small twig of olive. This twig conveys to Noah and to all with him in the ark the news that the wrath of God has ceased, that God is now offering man a fresh opportunity. All those who are in the ark will be able to settle again on firm ground and make an attempt to live, and never more perhaps, if they can help it, undergo the wrath of God.

In the New Testament, in the parable of the good Samaritan, olive oil is poured to soothe and to heal. In the anointing of kings and priests in the Old Testament, it is again oil that is poured on the head as an image of the grace of God that comes down and flows on them (Ps 133:2) giving them new power to fulfil what is beyond human capabilities. The king is to stand on the threshold, between

the will of men and the will of God, and he is called to
lead his people to the fulfilment of God's will; the priest
also stands on that threshold, to proclaim the will of God
and to do even more: to act for God, to pronounce God's
decrees and to apply God's decision.

The oil speaks first of all of the end of the wrath of God,
of the peace which God offers to the people who have
offended against him; further it speaks of God healing us
in order that we should be able to live and become what
we are called to be; and as he knows that we are not capable
with our own strength of fulfilling either his will or the
laws of our own created nature, he pours his grace abundantly on us (Rom 5:20). He gives us power to do what
we could not otherwise do.

The words *milost* and *pomiluy* in slavonic have the same
root as those which express tenderness, endearing, and
when we use the words *eleison*, 'have mercy on us', *pomiluy*,
we are not just asking God to save us from His wrath – we
are asking for love.

If we turn back to the words of the Jesus Prayer, 'Lord
Jesus Christ, Son of God, have mercy on me, a sinner', we
see that the first words express with exactness and integrity
the gospel faith in Christ, the historical incarnation of the
Word of God; and the end of the prayer expresses all the
complex rich relationships of love that exist between God
and his creatures.

The Jesus Prayer is known to innumerable Orthodox,
either as a rule of prayer or in addition to it, as a form of
devotion, a short focal point that can be used at any
moment, whatever the situation.

Numerous writers have mentioned the physical aspects

of the prayer, the breathing exercises, the attention which is paid to the beating of the heart and a number of other minor features. The Philocalia is full of detailed instructions about the prayer of the heart, even with references to the Sufi technique. Ancient and modern Fathers have dealt with the subject, always coming to the same conclusion: never to attempt the physical exercises without strict guidance by a spiritual father.

What is of general use, and God given, is the actual praying, the repetition of the words, without any physical endeavour – not even movements of the tongue – and which can be used systematically to achieve an inner transformation. More than any other prayer, the Jesus Prayer aims at bringing us to stand in God's presence with no other thought but the miracle of our standing there and God with us, because in the use of the Jesus Prayer there is nothing and no one except God and us.

The use of the prayer is dual, it is an act of worship as is every prayer, and on the ascetical level, it is a focus that allows us to keep our attention still in the presence of God.

It is a very companionable prayer, a friendly one, always at hand and very individual in spite of its monotonous repetitions. Whether in joy or in sorrow, it is, when it has become habitual, a quickening of the soul, a response to any call of God. The words of St Simeon, the new theologian, apply to all its possible effects on us: 'Do not worry about what will come next, you will discover it when it comes' (Quoted in the *Guild of Pastoral Psychology*, No. 95, p. 91).

VII

Ascetic Prayer

WHEN WE ARE in the right frame of mind, when the heart is full of worship, of concern for others, when as St Luke says, our lips speak from the fullness of the heart (6:45), there is no problem about praying; we speak freely to God in the words that are most familiar to us. But if we were to leave our life of prayer at the mercy of our moods, we should probably pray from time to time fervently and sincerely, but lose for long periods any prayerful contact with God. It is a great temptation to put off praying till the moment when we feel alive to God, and to consider that any prayer or any move Godwards at other periods lacks sincerity. We all know from experience that we have a variety of feelings which do not come to the fore at every moment of our lives; illness or distress can blot them from our consciousness. Even when we love deeply, there are times when we are not aware of it and yet we know that love is alive in us. The same is true with regard to God; there are inner and outward causes that make it difficult at times to be aware of the fact that we believe, that we have hope, that we do love God. At such moments we must act not on the strength of what we feel but of what we know. We must have faith in what is in us, although we do not perceive it at that particular moment. We must remember that love is still there, although it does not fill our hearts with joy or inspiration. And we must stand before God, remembering that he is always loving, always present, in spite of the fact that we do not feel it.

When we are cold and dry, when it seems that our prayer is a false pretence, carried out by routine, what should we do? Would it be better to stop praying until prayer comes alive again? But how shall we know that the time has come? There is a grave danger of being seduced by the desire for perfection in prayer when we are still so far from it. When prayer is dry, instead of giving way we should make a wider act of faith and carry on. We should say to God: 'I am worn out, I cannot pray really, accept, O Lord, this monotonous voice and the words of prayer, and help me.' Make prayer a matter of quantity when unable to make it a matter of quality. Of course, it is better to utter only 'Our Father', with all the depth of understanding of the words, than to repeat the Lord's Prayer twelve times; but it is just what we are sometimes incapable of. Prayer being quantitative does not mean the utterance of more words than usual; it means keeping to the usual rule of prayer fixed for oneself and accepting the fact that it is nothing but a certain quantity of repeated words. As the Fathers say, the Holy Spirit is always there when there is prayer and according to St Paul: 'No man can say that Jesus is the Lord, but by the Holy Ghost' (I Cor 12:3). It is the Holy Spirit who will in due time fill prayer, faithful and patient as it has been, with the meaning and depth of new life. When we stand before God in these moments of dejection we must use our will, we must pray from conviction if not from feeling, out of the faith we are aware of possessing, intellectually if not with a burning heart.

At such moments the prayers sound quite different to us, but not to God; as Julian of Norwich says, 'Pray inwardly though thou thinkest it savour thee not, for it is profitable, though thou feel not, though thou see nought, yea though thou think thou canst not. For in dryness and in barrenness, in sickness and in feebleness, then is thy prayer well pleasant to me, though thou thinkest it savour thee nought but little and so is all thy believing prayer in my sight' (*The Cloud of Unknowing*).

In those periods of dryness, when prayer becomes an effort, our main support is faithfulness and determination; it is by an act of will, including them both, that we compel ourselves, without considering our feelings, to take our stand before God and speak to him, simply because God is God and we are his creatures. Whatever we feel at a given moment our position remains the same; God remains our creator, our saviour, our lord and the one towards whom we move, who is the object of our longing and the only one who can give us fulfilment.

Sometimes we think that we are unworthy of praying and that we even have no right to pray; again, this is a temptation. Every drop of water, from wherever it comes, pool or ocean, is purified in the process of evaporation; and so is every prayer ascending to God. The more dejected we feel, the greater the necessity for prayer, and that is surely what John of Kronstadt felt one day when he was praying, watched by a devil who was muttering, 'You hypocrite, how dare you pray with your filthy mind, full of the thoughts I read in it.' He answered, 'It is just because my mind is full of thoughts I dislike and fight that I am praying to God.'

Whether it is the Jesus Prayer that is being used or any other readymade prayer, people often say: what right have I to use it? How can I say those words as my own? When we make use of prayers which have been written by saints, by men of prayer, and are the result of their experience, we can be sure that if we are attentive enough, the words will become our own, we shall grow into their underlying feeling and they will remould us by the grace of God, who responds to our effort. With the Jesus Prayer the situation, in a way, is simpler, because the worse our position is, the easier it is to realise that, having taken our stand before God, all we can say is *Kyrie Eleison*, 'Have mercy'.

More often than we may admit to ourselves, we pray hoping for a mysterious illumination, hoping that something will happen to us, that a thrilling experience will come our way. It is a mistake, the same kind of mistake we make sometimes in our relationships with people which may in fact destroy the relationship completely. We approach a person and we expect a definite sort of response, and when there is no response whatever or else when it is not the one we expected, we are disappointed, or we dismiss the reality of the given answer. When we pray, we must remember that the Lord God, who lets us come freely into his presence, is also free with regard to us; which does not mean that the freedom he takes is an arbitrary one, as ours, to be gracious or rude according to our mood, but that he is not bound to reveal himself to us simply because we have come and are gazing in his direction. It is very important to remember that both God and we are free either to come or to go; and this freedom is of immense importance because it is characteristic of a real relationship.

Once, a young woman, after a period of prayerful life in which God seemed to be immensely familiar and close, suddenly lost touch with him completely. But more than the sorrow of losing him she was afraid of the temptation of trying to escape that absence of God by building up a false presence of him; because the real absence of God and his real presence are equally good proofs of his reality and of the concreteness of the relationship which prayer implies.

So we must be prepared to offer our prayer and be ready for whatever God may give. This is the basic principle of the ascetic life. In the struggle to keep ourselves directed Godwards and to fight against anything in us that is opaque, that prevents us from looking in the direction of God, we can be neither altogether active nor passive. We cannot be active in the sense that, by agitating ourselves, by making efforts, we cannot climb into heaven or bring God down from heaven. But we cannot just be passive either and sit doing nothing, because God does not treat us as objects; there would be no true relationship if we were merely acted upon by him. The ascetic attitude is one of vigilance, the vigilance of a soldier who stands in the night as still as he can and as completely alert and aware as possible of anything that is happening around him, ready to respond in the right way and with speed to anything that may happen. In a way he is inactive because he stands and does nothing; on the other hand, it is intense activity, because he is alert and completely recollected. He listens, he watches with heightened perception, ready for anything.

In the inner life it is exactly the same. We must stand in God's presence in complete silence and collectedness, alert and unstirring. We may wait for hours, or for longer periods of time, but a moment will come when our alertness will be rewarded, because something will be happening. But again, if we are alert and vigilant, we are on the lookout for anything that may come our way, and not for one particular thing. We must be ready to receive from God whatever experience is sent. When we have prayed for some time and have felt a certain warmth, we fall quite easily into the temptation of coming to God the next day expecting the same thing to happen. If we have in the past prayed with warmth or with tears, with contrition or joy, we come to God looking forward to an experience we have already had, and quite often, because we are looking for the old one, we miss the new contact with God.

God's coming close to us may find expression in a variety of ways; it may be joy, it may be dread, it may be contrition or anything else. We must remember that what we are going to perceive today is something unknown to us, because God as we knew him yesterday is not God as he might reveal himself tomorrow.

VIII

The Prayer of Silence

PRAYER IS PRIMARILY an encounter with God; on certain occasions we may be aware of God's presence, more often dimly so, but there are times when we can place ourselves before him only by an act of faith, without being aware of his presence at all. It is not the degree of our awareness that is relevant, that makes this encounter possible and fruitful; other conditions must be fulfilled, the basic one being that the person praying should be real. In social life we have a variety of facets to our personalities. The same person appears as one in one setting and quite different in another, authoritative in any situation in which he commands, quite submissive at home, and again quite different among friends. Every self is complex, but none of these false personalities or of those which are partly false and partly true, are our real selves to such an extent as to be able to stand in our name in the presence of God. This weakens our prayer, it creates dividedness of mind, heart and will. As Polonius says in *Hamlet*: 'To thine own self be true, and it must follow as the night the day, Thou canst not then be false to any man.'

To find the real self, among and beyond those various false persons, cannot be done at an easy cost. We are so unaccustomed to be ourselves in any deep and true sense that we find it almost impossible to know where to begin the search. We all know that there are moments when we are nearer to being our true selves; those moments should be singled out and carefully analysed in order to make an approximate discovery of what we really are. It is our vanity that usually makes it so difficult to discover the truth about ourselves; our vanity in itself and in the way it determines our behaviour. Vanity consists of glorying in things that are devoid of value and of depending for our judgement about ourselves, and consequently for our whole attitude to life, on the opinion of people who should not have this weight for us; it is a state of dependence on other people's reactions to our personality.

Thus vanity is the first enemy to be attacked, although, as the Fathers say, it remains the last to be defeated. We find an instance of the defeat of vanity in the story of Zacchaeus (Lk 19:1), which can teach us a great deal. Zacchaeus was a rich man with social standing, he was an official of the Roman Empire, a publican who had a position to maintain. He was an important citizen of his little city; the attitude which is summed up in 'what will people say?' might have stopped him from meeting Christ. When Zacchaeus heard that Christ was passing through Jericho, his desire to see him was so strong that he forgot that he might become ridiculous – which is for us much worse than a great many evils – and he ran, this respectable citizen, and he climbed up a tree! He could be seen by the whole crowd and it is difficult to doubt that a great many laughed.

But such was his desire to meet Jesus that he forgot to worry about the opinions of other people; he became for a short time independent of anyone's judgement and at that moment he was completely himself; he was Zacchaeus the man, not Zacchaeus the publican, or the rich man, or the citizen.

Humiliation is one of the ways in which we may unlearn vanity, but unless it is accepted willingly, humiliation may only increase our hurt feelings and make us even more dependent on the opinions of others. Statements concerning vanity in St John Climacus and in St Isaac of Syria seem to conflict: one says that the only way to escape vanity is through pride; the other, that the way lies through humility. They both express their opinions in a given context and not as an absolute truth, but it allows us to see what the two extremes have in common, which is that whether you grow proud or humble, you take no notice of human opinions, in both cases the judgement of men is set aside. In the life of St Macarius we have an illustration of the first.

St Macarius, approaching a monastery over which he had oversight, saw several of the brethren laughing and mocking at a very young monk, who was taking no notice of them at all, and he was amazed at the serenity of the young man. Macarius had great experience of the difficulties of the spiritual struggle and thought it slightly suspicious. He asked the monk how it was that, young as he was, he had attained such a measure of impassibility. The answer was: 'Why should I take any notice of barking dogs? I pay no attention to them, God is the only one whom I accept as a judge.' This is an example of how pride can free us from dependence upon the opinions of other people. Pride is an attitude in which we set ourselves at the centre of things, we become the criterion of truth, of reality, of good and evil, and then we are free from any other judgement and also free from vanity. But it is only perfect pride that can dispel vanity completely, and perfect pride is fortunately beyond our human capabilities.

The other remedy is humility. Basically humility is the attitude of one who stands constantly under the judgement of God. It is the attitude of one who is like the soil. Humility comes from the latin word *humus*, fertile ground. The fertile ground is there, unnoticed, taken for granted, always there to be trodden upon. It is silent, inconspicuous, dark and yet it is always ready to receive any seed, ready to give it substance and life. The more lowly, the more fruitful, because it becomes really fertile when it accepts all the refuse of the earth. It is so low that nothing can soil it, abase it, humiliate it; it has accepted the last place and cannot go any lower. In that position nothing can shatter the soul's serenity, its peace and joy.

There are moments when we are shaken out of our dependence on people's reactions; these are moments of profound sorrow and also of real overwhelming joy. When King David danced before the ark (II Sam 6:14), many, like Michal, the daughter of Saul, thought that the king was behaving in a very unseemly way. They probably smiled or turned away, embarrassed. But he was too full of joy to notice. It is the same with sorrow; when it is genuine and deep a person becomes real; poses and attitudes are forgotten and that is so precious in sorrow, in our own as much as in someone else's.

The difficulty is that when we are real because we are in sorrow, or because we are in joy, we are neither in a mood nor in a position to watch ourselves, to observe the features of our personality that come through; and yet there is a moment when we are still feeling deeply enough to be real, but sufficiently recovered from the ecstasy of joy or of grief as to be struck by the contrast between what we are at this particular moment and what we are usually; then our depth and our shallowness appear to us clearly. If we are attentive, if we do not move thoughtlessly from one state of mind and heart into the other, forgetting things as they pass by, we can gradually learn to preserve those characteristic features of reality which appear for a moment.

Several spiritual writers say that we must try to discover Christ in us. Christ is the perfect, completely true man and we can begin to discover what is true in us by discovering what is akin to him. There are passages in the gospel against which we rebel and other passages which make our heart burn within us (Lk 24:32). If we single out the passages which either provoke a revolt, or which we feel with all our heart to be true, we will already have discovered the two extremes in us; in short, the anti-Christ and the Christ in us. We must be aware of both kinds of passages and concentrate on those which are close to our heart, because we may safely assume that they mark one point at least in which Christ and we are akin, a point at which a man is already – certainly not fully, but at least in an incipient way – a real man, an image of Christ. But it is not enough to be emotionally moved, to give complete intellectual agreement to this or that passage of the gospel;

we must embody the words of Christ. We may have been
touched and yet abandon all we have thought and felt on
the first occasion that offers itself for applying the discovery.

There are times when we are in a mood to make peace
with our enemies, but if the other person resists, the peacemaking mood is soon changed into a bellicose one. That
happened to Miusov, in Dostoyevsky's *The Brothers Karamazov*. He had just been rude and intolerant to others and
then regained his own self-esteem by making a new start,
but Karamazov's unexpected insolence at once changed
his feelings again and 'Miusov passed immediately from
the most benevolent frame of mind to the most savage. All
the feelings that had subsided and died down in his heart
revived instantly.'

It is not enough to be struck by the passages which appear
to be so true, the struggle to become at every moment of
our life what we are at the best moments must follow, and
then we will gradually shed the superficial and become
more real and more true; just as Christ is truth and reality
itself, so shall we become more and more what Christ is.
This does not consist in imitating Christ in his outer
expression only, but of being inwardly what he is. The
imitation of Christ is not an aping of his conduct or of his
life; it is a hard and complex struggle.

This marks a difference between the Old and the New
Testament: the commandments of the Old Testament were
rules of life and he who faithfully kept to these rules
became a righteous man, and yet he could not derive
eternal life from them. On the contrary, the commandments of the New Testament never make a man righteous.
Christ once said to his disciples: 'When ye shall have done

all those things which are commanded you, say, We are unprofitable servants; we have done that which was our duty to do' (Lk 17:10). But when we fulfil the commandments of Christ, not merely as rules of behaviour, but because the will of God has impregnated our heart, or even when we simply curb our ill-will into fulfilling them outwardly and stand in repentance, knowing that there is nothing in us beyond this outer compliance, we gradually grow into the knowledge of God, which is inward, not intellectual, rational or academic.

A person who has become real and true can stand before God and offer prayer with absolute attention, unity of intellect, heart and will, in a body that responds completely to the promptings of the soul. But until we have attained such perfection we can still stand in the presence of God, aware that we are partly real and partly unreal, and bring to him all that we can, but in repentance, confessing that we are still so unreal and so incapable of unity. At no moment of our life, whether we are still completely divided or in process of unification, are we deprived of the possibility of standing before God. But instead of standing in the complete unity that gives drive and power to our prayer, we can stand in our weakness, recognising it and ready to bear its consequences.

Ambrose of Optina, one of the last Russian Staretz, said once that two categories of men will attain salvation: those who sin and are strong enough to repent, and those who are too weak even to repent truly, but are prepared, patiently, humbly and gratefully, to bear all the weight of the consequences of their sins; in their humility they are acceptable to God.

God is always real, always himself, and if we could stand face to face with him as he is and perceive his objective reality, things might be simpler; but we manage, in a subjective way, to blur this truth, this reality in front of which we stand, and to replace the real God by a pale picture of him, even worse, by a God who is unreal because of our one-sided and poor conception of him.

When we have to meet someone, the reality of the meeting does not depend only on what we are and on what the other is, but very much on the preconceived idea we have formed about the other person. It is not to the real person we are then speaking, but to the image we have formed and it usually takes a great deal of effort on the part of the victim of this prejudice to break through and establish a real relationship.

We have all formed ideas about God; however lofty, beautiful, even true in its component parts the idea may be, it will, if we are not careful, stand between us and the real God and may become simply an idol before which we pray while the real God is hidden by it. This happens particularly when we turn to God with requests or for intercession; then we do not come to God as to a person with whom we want to share a difficulty, in whose love we believe and from whom we expect a decision; but we come trying to consider God under a certain aspect, and we direct our prayers not towards God but towards a concept of God, which at that particular moment is useful to us.

We must not come to God in order to go through a range of emotions, nor to have any mystical experience. We must just come to God in order to be in his presence, and, if he chooses to make us aware of it, blessed be God, but if he chooses to make us experience his real absence, blessed be God again, because as we have seen he is free to come near or not. He is as free as we are, although, when we do not come into God's presence, it is because we are busy with something else that attracts us more than he does. As for him, if he does not manifest his presence, it is because we must learn something about him and about ourselves. But the absence of God which we may perceive in our prayer, the sense that he is not there, is also part of the relationship and very valuable.

Our sense of God's absence may be the result of his will; he may want us to long for him and to learn how precious his presence is by making us know by experience what utter loneliness means. But often our experience of God's absence is determined by the fact that we do not give ourselves a chance of becoming aware of his presence. A woman who had been using the Jesus Prayer for fourteen years complained that she had never had any sense that God was there. But when she had it pointed out to her that she was talking all the time, she agreed to take her stand silently for a few days. As she was doing it she became aware that God was there, that the silence that surrounded her was not emptiness, absence of noise and agitation, but that there was a solidity in this silence, that it was not something negative, but positive, a presence, the presence of of God who made himself known to her by creating the same silence in her. And then she discovered that the prayer came up quite naturally again, but it was no longer the sort of discursive noise that had prevented God from making himself known.

If we were humble or even reasonable we should not expect, just because we had decided to pray, that we should at once have the experience of St John of the Cross, or St Theresa or St Seraphim of Sarov. However, it is not always the experience of the saints which we long to have, but simply to repeat a former one of our own; although to concentrate on a previous experience may blind us to the one which should come our way quite normally. Whatever we have felt belongs to the past and is linked with what we were yesterday, not with what we are today. We do not pray in order to provoke any particular experience in which we may delight, but in order to meet God with whatever may happen as a consequence, or to bring him what we have to bring and leave it to him to use it the way he chooses.

We must also remember that we should always approach God knowing that we do not know him. We must approach the unsearchable, mysterious God who reveals himself as he chooses; whenever we come to him, we are before a God we do not yet know. We must be open to any manifestation of his person and of his presence.

We may have understood a great deal about God from our own experience, from the experience of others, from the writings of the saints, from the teaching of the Church, from the witness of the scriptures; we may know that he is good, that he is humble, that he is a burning fire, that he is our judge, that he is our saviour and a great many other things, but we must remember that he may at any time reveal himself in a way in which we have never perceived him, even within these general categories. We must take our stand before him with reverence and be ready to meet whoever we shall meet, either the God who is already familiar or a God we cannot recognise. He may give us a sense of what he is and it may be quite different from what we expect. We hope to meet Jesus, mild, compassionate, loving, and we meet God who judges and condemns and will not let us come near in our present state. Or we come in repentance, expecting to be rejected, and we meet compassion. God, at every stage, is for us partly known and partly unknown. He reveals himself, and thus far we know him, but we shall never know him completely, there will always be the divine mystery, a core of mystery which we shall never be able to penetrate.

The knowledge of God can only be received and given in communion with God, only by sharing with God what he is, to the extent to which he is communicable. The Buddhist world of thought has illustrated it in a story about a doll of salt.

A doll of salt, after a long pilgrimage on dry land, came to the sea and discovered something she had never seen and could not possibly understand. She stood on the firm ground, a solid little doll of salt, and saw there was another ground that was mobile, insecure, noisy, strange and unknown. She asked the sea, 'But what are you?' and it said, 'I am the sea.' And the doll said, 'What is the sea?' to which the answer was, 'It is me.' Then the doll said, 'I cannot understand, but I want to; how can I?' The sea answered, 'Touch me.' So the doll shyly put forward a foot and touched the water and she got a strange impression that it was something that began to be knowable. She withdrew her leg, looked and saw that her toes had gone, and she was afraid and said, 'Oh, but where is my toe, what have you done to me?' And the sea said, 'You have given something in order to understand.' Gradually the water took away small bits of the doll's salt and the doll went farther and farther into the sea and at every moment she had a sense of understanding more and more, and yet of not being able to say what the sea was. As she went deeper, she melted more and more, repeating: 'But what is the sea?' At last a wave dissolved the rest of her and the doll said: 'It is I!' She had discovered what the sea was, but not yet what the water was.

Without drawing an absolute parallel between the buddhist doll and christian knowledge of God, one can see much truth in this little story. St Maxim uses the example of a sword that becomes red hot: the sword does not know where the fire ends and the fire does not know where the sword begins, so that one can, as he says, cut with fire and burn with iron. The doll knew what the sea was when she had become, minute as she was, the vastness of the sea. So also when we enter into the knowledge of God, we do not contain God, but are contained in him, and we become ourselves in this encounter with God, secure in his vastness.

Saint Athanasius said that man's ascent to deification begins from the moment he is created. From the first, God gives us uncreated grace to achieve union with him. From the Orthodox point of view there is no 'natural man' to whom grace is super-added. The first word of God that called us out of nothingness was our first step towards the fulfilment of our calling, that God should be in all and that we should be in him as he is in us.

We must be prepared to find that the last step of our

relationship with God is an act of pure adoration, face to face with a mystery into which we cannot enter. We grow into the knowledge of God gradually from year to year until the end of our life and we will continue to do so through all eternity, without coming to a point when we shall be able to say that now we know all that is knowable of God. This process of the gradual discovery of God leads us at every moment to stand with our past experience behind us and the mystery of God knowable and still unknown before us. The little we know of God makes it difficult for us to learn more, because the more cannot simply be added to the little, since every meeting brings such a change of perspective that what was known before becomes almost untrue in the light of what is known later.

This is true of any knowledge which we acquire; every day teaches us something in science or the humanities, but the learning we have acquired makes sense only because it brings us to the borderline beyond which there is something we can still discover. If we stop just to rehearse what we know, we shall waste our time. So the first thing, if we want to meet the real God in prayer, is to realise that all the knowledge previously acquired has brought us to stand before him. All this is precious and meaningful, but if we go no farther it becomes ghostly, phantom-like, it will cease to be real life; it will be a memory and one cannot live on memories.

In our relations with people we turn inevitably just one facet of our personality to one facet of the other person's; it may be good when it is a way of establishing contact, it may be evil when we do so to exploit the other person's weaknesses. To God also we turn the facet which is closest to him, the trusting or loving side. But we must be aware of the fact that it is never a facet of God we meet: we meet God in his entirety.

When we come to pray we hope to experience God as someone who is present and that our prayer will be, if not a dialogue, at least a discourse to someone who listens. We are afraid that we may sense no presence at all and have the impression of speaking in the void, with no one there to listen, to answer, to be interested. But this would be a purely subjective impression; if we compare our experience of prayer with our normal daily human contacts, we know that someone may be listening very intently to what we say and yet we may feel that our words are being poured out in vain. Our prayer always reaches God but it is not always answered by a sense of joy or peace.

When we speak in terms of taking a stand, we always think that here we are and there is God, outside us. If we search for God, above, or in front, or around us, we will not find him. St John Chrysostom said: 'Find the door of the inner chamber of your soul and you will discover that this is the door into the kingdom of Heaven.' St Ephraim of Syria says that God, when he created man, put in the deepest part of him all the kingdom, and that the problem of human life is to dig deep enough to come upon the hidden treasure. Therefore, to find God we must dig in search of this inner chamber, of this place where the whole kingdom of God is present at the very core of us, where God and we can meet. The best tool, the one which will go through all obstacles, is prayer. The problem is one of praying attentively, simply and truthfully without replacing the real God by any false God, by an idol, by a product of our imagination and without trying to have a preview of any mystical experience. Concentrating on what we say, believing that every word we pronounce reaches God, we can use our own words or the words of greater men to express, better than we could, what we feel or what we sense dimly within us. It is not in a multitude of words that we shall be heard by God but in their veracity. When we use our own words we must speak to God with precision, neither trying to be short nor trying to be long, but trying to be true.

There are moments when prayers are spontaneous and easy, others when it feels as if the spring has dried up. This is the time to use the prayers of other men which express basically what we believe, all those things which are not at present made vivid by any deep response of the heart. Then we must pray in a double act of faith, not only faith in God but also in ourselves, trusting in the faith which is dimmed, in spite of its being part of us.

There are times when we do not need any words of prayer, neither our own nor anyone else's and then we pray in perfect silence. This perfect silence is the ideal prayer, provided, however, that the silence is real and not daydreaming. We have very little experience of what deep silence of body and soul means, when complete serenity fills the soul, when complete peace fills the body, when there is no turmoil or stirring of any sort and when we stand before God, completely open in an act of adoration. There may be times when we feel physically well and mentally relaxed, tired of words because we have used so many of them already; we do not want to stir and we feel happy in this fragile balance; this is on the borderline of slipping into daydreaming. Inner silence is absence of any sort of inward stirring of thought or emotion, but it is complete alertness, openness to God. We must keep complete silence when we can, but never allow it to degenerate into simple contentment. To prevent this the great writers of Orthodoxy warn us never to abandon completely the normal forms of prayer, because even those who reached this contemplative silence found it necessary, whenever they were in danger of spiritual slackness, to reintroduce words of prayer until prayer had renewed silence.

The Greek Fathers set this silence, which they called *hesychia*, both as the starting-point and the final achievement of a life of prayer. Silence is the state in which all the powers of the soul and all the faculties of the body are completely at peace, quiet and recollected, perfectly alert yet free from any turmoil or agitation. A simile which we find in many writings of the Fathers is that of the waters of a pond. As long as there are ripples on the surface, nothing can be reflected properly, neither the trees nor the sky; when the surface is quite still, the sky is perfectly reflected, the trees on the bank and everything is there as distinct as in reality.

Another simile of the same sort used by the Fathers is that as long as the mud which is at the bottom of a pond has not settled, the water is not clear and one can see nothing through it. These two analogies apply to the state of the human heart. 'Blessed are the pure in heart for they shall see God' (Mt 5:8). As long as the mud is in motion in the water there is no clear vision through it, and again as long as the surface is covered with ripples there can be no adequate reflection of what surrounds the pond.

As long as the soul is not still there can be no vision, but when stillness has brought us into the presence of God, then another sort of silence, much more absolute, intervenes: the silence of a soul that is not only still and recollected but which is overawed in an act of worship by God's presence; a silence in which, as Julian of Norwich puts it, 'Prayer oneth the soul to God.'

EPILOGUE*

Prayer for Beginners

WE ARE ALL beginners and I do not intend to give you a course of lectures, but I wish to share with you some of the things I have learned, partly by experience, and probably more through the experiences of others.

Prayer is essentially an encounter, a meeting between a soul and God, but to be real an encounter takes two persons each being really himself. To a very great extent we are unreal and God so often in our relationship is unreal to us because we believe that we turn to God, when we are in fact turning to something we imagine to be God; and we think that we are standing before him in all truth, whereas we are putting forward someone who is not our real self, who is an actor, a sham, a stage personality. Every one of us is a variety of persons at the same time; it may be a very rich blending, but also it may be an unfortunate meeting of discordant personalities. We are different according to circumstances and surroundings: the various people that meet us know us as different persons.

* From the BBC television series 'The Epilogue', first shown in 1958.

There is a Russian proverb that says, 'He is a lion when meeting sheep, but he is a sheep when he meets lions.' Which is quite true in more ways than one: we all know the lady who is all smiles with outsiders and who is a holy terror at home, or the big boss who is so tame in private life.

When it comes to praying, our first difficulty is to find which one of our personalities should be put forward to meet God. It is not simple because we are so unaccustomed to be our real self that in all truth we do not know which one that is; and we do not know how to find it. But if we were to give a few minutes a day to think over our various activities and contacts, we would probably come much closer to the discovery. We could find out the sort of person we were when we met so and so, and the other person we were when we were doing this or that. And we could ask ourselves: but when was I really myself? Perhaps never, perhaps only for a split second or perhaps to a certain extent under special circumstances, while meeting particular people. Now, in these five or ten minutes which you can spare, and I am sure everyone can spare them in the course of the day, you will discover that there is nothing more boring for us than to be left alone with ourselves! We usually live some sort of reflected life. Not only are we a variety of people successively under various circumstances but also the very life that is in us belongs so often to other people. If you look into yourself, and if you dare to question how often you act from the very core of your personality, how often you are expressing your own self, you will see that it happens rarely enough. Too often we are immersed in what is happening around us, all the unnecessaries we gather from the wireless, television, newspapers, but during this period, these few minutes of concentration, we must shed everything that is not essential to life.

Then of course you run the risk of remaining bored with yourself; all right, be bored. But this does not mean that there is nothing left in us, because at rock bottom we are made in the image of God, and this stripping is very much like the cleaning of an ancient, beautiful wall painting, or of a painting by a great master that was painted over in the course of the centuries by tasteless people who had intruded upon the real beauty that had been created by the master. To begin with, the more we clean, the more things disappear, and it seems to us that we have created a mess where there was at least a certain amount of beauty; perhaps not much, but some beauty. And then we begin to discover the real beauty which the great master has put into his painting; we see the misery, then the mess in between, but at the same time we have a preview of the authentic beauty. And we discover that what we are is a poor person who needs God; but not God to fill the gap – God to be met.

So let us set out to do this and let us also every evening of this week, pray a very simple prayer:

'Help me, O God, to put off all pretences and to find my true self.'

Grief and joy, both great gifts of God, are often the meeting point with our real self, when monkey tricks are put aside and when we become invulnerable, out of reach of the falsities of life.

Next we have to investigate the problem of the real God,

because obviously if we are to address God, this God must be real. We all know what a headmaster is for schoolboys; when they have to go and see him they go to the headmaster and it never occurs to them until they have grown up and no longer in his power that the headmaster is a man. They think of him in terms of a function; but this empties his human personality of every human characteristic and there can be no kind of human contact with him.

Another example: when a boy is in love with a girl, he adorns her with all sorts of perfections; but she may not have any of them and this person constructed out of nothing is very often 'nothing', clad in qualities that are artificial. Here again there can be no contact because the boy is addressing someone who does not exist. This is true also of God. We have a lot of mental or visual pictures of God, collected from books, from church, from what we hear from adults when we are children and eventually from clergymen when we are older. Quite often these pictures prevent us from meeting the real God. They are not quite false because there is some truth in them, and yet they are perfectly inadequate to the reality of God. If we wish to meet God we must, on the one hand, make use of the knowledge acquired either personally, or by means of reading, hearing, listening, but also, go farther.

The knowledge of God which we possess today is a result of yesterday's experience and if we set ourselves in front of God as we know him, we will always turn our backs to the present and to the future, looking only at our own past. It is not God that we are going to meet, it is what we have already learned about him. This illustrates the function of theology, since theology is our whole knowledge of God and not the small amount we have personally already known and learned about him. You must, if you wish to meet God as he really is, come to him with a certain experience, allow it to bring you close to God, and leave it at that, standing before not the God you know but the God both known and unknown.

What will happen next? Something quite simple: God who is free to come to you, to respond, to answer your prayers, may come to you and make you feel, perceive, his presence; he may also choose not to do so. He may just give you a sense of his real absence, and this experience is as important as the other, because in both cases you come upon the reality of God's right to answer or to stand back.

Try, then, to discover your own real self and to stand it face to face with God as he is, having shed all false images or idols of God; and to help you in this search, to give you support in this effort, I suggest that you should, this week, pray the following prayer:

'Help me, O God, to discard all false pictures of thee, whatever the cost to my comfort.'

In the search for our true self we may come not only to boredom, which I have mentioned, but to fear, or even to despair. It is this nakedness that brings us to our senses; then we can begin to pray. The first thing to avoid is lying to God; it seems quite obvious, and yet we do not always observe it. Let us speak frankly to God, say to him what sort of person we are; not that he does not know it, but there is a great difference between assuming that someone we love knows all about us, and having the courage and

real love for the person to speak truthfully and tell everything about ourselves. Let us say to God openly that we
stand before him with a feeling of uneasiness, that we do
not really want to meet him, that we are tired and would
rather go to bed, but we must beware of being frivolous or
just presumptuous: he remains our God. After that the
ideal would be to remain happily in his presence, as when
we are with people we love dearly, when there is real
intimacy. But more often than not we are not on those
terms with God. We do not feel so happy and intimate with
him as to be able just to sit and look at him and feel glad.
As we must talk, let it be genuine talk. Let us put all our
worries to God, squarely, and then, having told him everything, so that he should know them from us, we should
drop them, leave them to him. Now that he is in the know,
it is no longer any of our concern: we can freely think of
him.

The exercise of this week, obviously, must be added to
the exercises of the previous weeks, and it will consist in
learning to put everyone of our concerns to God, after
having settled ourselves in front of him, and then drop
these concerns; and to help us in this, let us from day to
day repeat a very simple and precise prayer, that will define
our way of dealing with God:

'Help me O God to let go all my problems, and fix my
mind on thee.'

If we did not put our worries to God, they would stand
between him and us in the course of our meeting, but we
have also just seen that the next move, which is essential,
is to drop them. We should make that in an act of confi-

dence, trusting God enough to give him the troubles we wish to get off our shoulders. But then, what next? We seem to have emptied ourselves, there is nothing much left, what are we going to do? We cannot remain empty, because if we do we shall be filled by the wrong things, by feelings, thoughts, emotions and reminiscences and so on. We must, I believe, remember that an encounter is not meant to be a one-sided discourse on our part. Conversation means not only talking but hearing what the other has to say. And to achieve this we must learn to be silent; although it seems trifling it is a very important point.

I remember that one of the first people who came to me for advice when I was ordained was an old lady who said: 'Father, I have been praying almost unceasingly for fourteen years, and I have never had any sense of God's presence.' So I said: 'Did you give him a chance to put in a word?' 'Oh well,' she said. 'No, I have been talking to him all the time, because is not that prayer?' I said: 'No, I do not think it is, and what I suggest is that you should set apart fifteen minutes a day, sit and just knit before the face of God.' And so she did. What was the result? Quite soon she came again and said: 'It is extraordinary, when I pray to God, in other words when I talk to him, I feel nothing, but when I sit quietly, face to face with him, then I feel wrapped in his presence.' You will never be able to pray to God really and from all your heart unless you learn to keep silent and rejoice in the miracle of his presence, or if you prefer, of your being face to face with him although you do not see him.

Quite often, having said what we have to say and having sat for a certain time, we are at a loss: what shall we do?

What we should do I believe is to start on some set prayers. Some find set prayers too easy, and at the same time see a danger of taking for actual praying the repetition of what someone else has said in the past. Indeed, if it is just mechanical it is not worth doing, but what is overlooked is that it depends on us whether it is mechanical or not, by paying attention to the words we say. Others complain that set prayers would be unreal because it is not quite what they would express, it is not theirs. In a sense it is unreal, but only in the same way in which the painting of a great master is unreal for a schoolboy, or the music of a great composer is unreal for a beginner, and yet that is just the point: we go to concerts, we visit art galleries to learn what real music or real painting is, to form our taste; and that is partly why we should use set prayers, to learn which feelings, which thoughts, which ways of expressions we should employ, if we belong to the Church. It also helps in time of dryness, when we have very little to say.

Apart from the stripped, naked, reduced-to-bone person which we are when we remain just alone, we are also in the image of God and the child of God that is in each of us is capable of praying with the loftiest and holiest prayers of the Church. We must remember that and make use of them. I suggest we add to the exercises we have been doing, a period of silence, a few minutes – three or four minutes – which we shall end with a prayer:

'Help me, O God, to see my own sins, never to judge my neighbour, and may the glory all be thine!'

Before I enter into the subject of 'Unanswered Prayer', I would like to pray to God that he might enlighten both me and you, because it is a difficult subject, yet such a vital one. It is one of the great temptations which everyone may meet on his way, which makes it very hard for beginners, and even for proficient people, to pray to God. Many times people pray and it seems to them that they are addressing an empty heaven; quite often it is because their prayer is meaningless, childish.

I remember the case of an old man telling me that when he was a child he prayed for several months that he would be given by God the amazing gift which his uncle possessed – that of every evening taking his teeth out of his mouth, and putting them into a glass of water – and he was terribly happy later on that God did not grant his wish. Often our prayers are as puerile as this, and of course they are not granted. Quite frequently when we pray we believe that we are praying rightly, but we pray for something which involves other people, of whom we do not think at all. If we pray for wind in our sails, we do not realise that it may mean a storm at sea for others, and God will not grant a request that affects others badly.

Besides these two obvious points, there is another side to unanswered prayer which is more basic and deep: there are cases when we pray to God from all our heart for something which, from every angle, seems to be worthy of being heard, and yet there is nothing but silence, and silence is much harder to bear than refusal. If God said 'No', it would be a positive reaction of God's, but silence is, as it were, the absence of God and that leads us to two temptations: when our prayer is not answered, we either doubt God, or else we doubt ourselves. What we doubt in God is not his might, his power to do what we wish, but we doubt his love, his concern. We beg for something essential and he does not even seem to be concerned; where is his love and his compassion? This is the first temptation.

There is another: we know that if we had as much faith as a mustard seed, we could move mountains and when we see that nothing budges, we think, 'Does that mean that the faith I have got is adulterated, false?' This again is untrue, and there is another answer: if you read the gospel attentively, you will see that there is only one prayer in it that was not answered. It is the prayer of Christ in the garden of Gethsemane, and yet we know that if once in history God was concerned for the one who prayed, it was then for his son, before his death, and also we know that if ever perfect faith was exemplified, it was in his case, but God found that the faith of the divine sufferer was great enough to bear silence.

God withholds an answer to our prayers not only when they are unworthy but when he finds in us such greatness, such depth – depth and power of faith – that he can rely upon us to remain faithful even in the face of his silence.

I remember a young woman with an incurable disease and after years of the awareness of God's presence, she suddenly sensed God's absence – some sort of real absence – and she wrote to me saying, 'Pray to God, please, that I should never yield to the temptation of building up an illusion of his presence, rather than accept his absence.' Her faith was great. She was able to stand this temptation and God gave her this experience of his silent absence.

Remember these examples, think them over because one day you will surely have to face the same situation.

I cannot give you any exercise, but I only want you to

remember that we should always keep our faith intact, both in the love of God and in our honest, truthful faith, and when this temptation comes upon us, let us say this prayer, which is made of two sentences pronounced by Jesus Christ himself:

'Into Thy hands I commend my spirit,
Thy Will, not mine, be done.'

Whatever I have tried to give as an outline of the main ways in which we should approach prayer, does it mean that if you do all I have suggested you will be able to pray? Indeed not, because prayer is not simply an effort which we can make the moment we intend to pray; prayer must be rooted in our life and if our life contradicts our prayers, or if our prayers have nothing to do with our life, they will never be alive nor real. Of course we can deal with that difficulty and make an easy escape by excluding from our prayers everything that, in our life, does not fit into the framework of prayer – all those things we are ashamed or uneasy about. But it does not solve anything satisfactorily.

Another difficulty which we meet constantly is to fall into daydreaming, when our prayer expresses a sentimental trend and is not the expression of what our life is basically. There is one common solution for these two difficulties; that of joining together life and prayer, making them one, by living our prayer. To help us along this line, set prayers, of which I have already spoken, are most precious because they are an objective, hard outline of a way of praying. You may say that they are unnatural, and it is true in the sense that they express the life of people who are im- measurably greater than we are, of real christians, but that is just why you can make use of them, trying to become the sort of people for whom those prayers are natural.

You remember Christ's words: 'Into Thy hands I commend my Spirit.' Of course it is not within our own experience, but if we learn from day to day to become the sort of person who is capable of pronouncing these words sincerely, in all honesty, we will not only make our prayers real, but we will make ourselves real, with a new reality, the true reality of becoming the sons of God.

If you take, for instance, the five prayers which I have suggested and if you take one after the other, each of the petitions of these prayers, and if you try to make each of them in turn the motto, the slogan that will direct the day, you will see that prayer becomes the criterion of your life; it will give you a framework for it, but also your life will stand in judgement, against you or for you, giving you the lie when you pronounce these words, or, on the contrary, affirming that you are true to them. Take each sentence of each prayer and make it the rule of one day after the other, so for weeks and weeks, until you become the sort of person for whom these words are life.

We have to part now; I have immensely enjoyed being with you, although I do not see you, but we are united in prayer and in our common interest for the life of the spirit. May the Lord God be with each of you and in our midst for ever.

And before we part, I would like us to say together one short prayer that will unite us before the throne of God:

O Lord, I know not what to ask of thee; thou alone knowest what are my true needs. Thou lovest me more than I know how to love myself. Help me to see my real needs which are concealed from me. I dare not ask either a cross or consolation. I can only wait on thee. My heart is open to thee. Visit and help me for thy great mercy's sake, strike me and heal me, cast me down and raise me up. I worship in silence thy holy will and thine inscrutable ways. I offer myself as a sacrifice to thee. I put all my trust in thee. I have no other desire than to fulfil thy will. Teach me how to pray, pray thou thyself in me.

AMEN

METROPOLITAN ANTHONY
OF SOUROZH

School for Prayer

CONTENTS

I

The Absence of God

AS WE START learning to pray, I would like to make it clear that what I mean by 'learning to pray' is not an attempt to justify or explain this in a speculative way. Rather, I would like to point out what one should be aware of, and what one can do if one wishes to pray. As I am a beginner myself, I will assume that you are also beginners, and we will try to begin together. I am not speaking to anyone who aims at mystical prayer or higher states of perfection, because these things will teach themselves. When God breaks through to us or when we break through to God, in certain exceptional circumstances, either because things suddenly disclose themselves with a depth we have never before perceived or when we suddenly discover in ourselves a depth where prayer abides and out of which it can gush forth, there is no problem of prayer. When we are aware of God, we stand before Him, worship Him, speak to Him.

At the outset there is, then, one very important problem: the situation of one for whom God seems to be absent. This is what I would like to speak about now. Obviously I am not speaking of a real absence – God is never really absent – but of the *sense* of absence which we have. We stand before God and we shout into an empty sky, out of which there is no reply. We turn in all directions and He is not to be found. What ought we to think of this situation?

First of all, it is very important to remember that prayer is an encounter and a relationship, a relationship which is deep, and this relationship cannot be forced either on us or on God. The fact that God can make Himself present or can leave us with the sense of His absence is part of this live and real relationship. If we could mechanically draw Him into an encounter, force Him to meet us, simply because we have chosen this moment to meet Him, there would be no relationship and no encounter. We can do that with an image, with the imagination, or with the various idols we can put in front of us instead of God; we can do nothing of the sort with the living God, any more than we can do it with a living person. A relationship must begin and develop in mutual freedom. If you look at the relationship in terms of *mutual* relationship, you will see that God could complain about us a great deal more than we about Him. We complain that He does not make Himself present to us for the few minutes we reserve for Him, but what about the twenty-three and a half hours during which God may be knocking at our door and we answer 'I am busy, I am sorry' or when we do not answer at all because we do not even hear the knock at the door of our heart, of our minds, of our conscience, of our life. So there is a situation in which we have no right to complain of the absence of God, because we are a great deal more absent than He ever is.

The second very important thing is that a meeting face to face with God is always a moment of judgment for us. We cannot meet God in prayer or in meditation or in contemplation and not be either saved or condemned. I do not mean this in major terms of eternal damnation or eternal salvation already given and received, but it is always a critical moment, a crisis. 'Crisis' comes from the Greek and means 'judgment'. To meet God face to face in prayer is a critical moment in our lives, and thanks be to Him that He does not always present Himself to us when we wish to meet Him, because we might not be able to endure such a meeting. Remember the many passages in Scripture in which we are told how bad it is to find oneself face to face with God, because God is power, God is truth, God is purity. Therefore, the first thought we ought to have when we do not tangibly perceive the divine presence, is a thought of gratitude. God is merciful; He does not come in an untimely way. He gives us a chance to judge ourselves, to understand, and not to come into His presence at a moment when it would mean condemnation.

I would like to give you an example of this. Many years ago a man came to see me. He asked me to show him God. I told him I could not but I added that even if I could, he would not be able to see Him, because I thought – and I do think – that to meet God one must have something in common with Him, something that gives you eyes to see, perceptiveness to perceive. He asked me then why I thought as I did, and I suggested that he should think a few moments and tell me whether there was any passage in the Gospel that moved him particularly, to see what was the connection between him and God. He said 'Yes, in the eighth chapter of the Gospel according to St John, the passage concerning the woman taken in adultery.' I said 'Good, this is one of the most beautiful and moving passages. Now sit back and ask yourself, who are you in the scene which is described? Are you the Lord, or at least on His side, full of mercy, of understanding and full of faith in this woman who can repent and become a new creature? Are you the woman taken in adultery? Are you one of the older men who walk out at once because they are aware of their own sins, or one of the young ones who wait?' He thought for a few minutes then said 'No, I feel I am the only Jew who would not have walked out but who would have stoned the woman.' I said 'Thank God that He does not allow you to meet Him face to face.'

This may be an extreme example, but how often could we recognise similar situations in ourselves? Not that we flatly refuse God's word or God's example, but that in a less violent way we do what the soldiers did during the Passion. We would love to cover Christ's eyes, to be able to deal him blows freely without being seen. Do we not do this, to a certain extent, when we ignore the divine presence and act according to our own desires, our moods, contrary to everything which is God's will? We try to blind him, but in fact we blind ourselves. At such moments, how can we come into His presence? We can indeed, in repentance, broken-hearted; but we cannot come in the way in which we immediately wish to be received – with love, with friendship.

Look at the various passages in the Gospel. People much greater than ourselves hesitated to receive Christ. Remember the centurion who asked Christ to heal his servant. Christ said 'I will come', but the centurion said 'No, don't. Say a word and he will be healed.' Do we do that? Do we turn to God and say 'Don't make your-self tangibly, perceptively present before me. It is enough for You to say a word and I will be healed. It is enough for You to say a word and things *will* happen. I do not need more for the moment.' Or take Peter in his boat after the great catch of fish, when he fell on his knees and said 'Leave me, O Lord, I am a sinner.' He asked the Lord to leave his boat because he felt humble – and he felt humble because he had suddenly perceived the greatness of Jesus. Do we ever do that? When we read the Gospel and the image of Christ becomes compelling, glorious, when we pray and we become aware of the greatness, the holiness of God, do we ever say 'I am unworthy that He should come near me?' Not to speak of all the occasions when we should be aware that He cannot come to us because we are not there to receive Him. We want something *from* Him, not *Him* at all. Is that a relationship? Do we behave in that way with our friends? Do we aim at what friendship can *give* us or is it the friend whom we love? Is this true with regard to the Lord?

Let us think of our prayers, yours and mine; think of the warmth, the depth and intensity of your prayer when it concerns someone you love or something which matters to your life. Then your heart is open, all your inner self is recollected in the prayer. Does it mean that God matters to you? No, it does not. It simply means that the subject matter of your prayer matters to you. For when you have made your passionate, deep, intense prayer concerning the person you love or the situation that worries you, and you turn to the next item, which does not matter so much – if you suddenly grow cold, what has changed? Has God grown cold? Has He gone? No, it means that all the elation, all the intensity in your prayer was not born of God's presence, of your faith in Him, of your longing for Him, of your awareness of Him; it was born of nothing but your concern for him or her or it, not for God. How can we feel surprised, then, that this absence of God affects us? It is we who make ourselves absent, it is we who grow cold the moment we are no longer concerned with God. Why? Because He does not matter so much.

There are other ways too in which God is 'absent'. As long as we ourselves are real, as long as we are truly ourselves, God can be present and can do something with us. But the moment we try to be what we are not, there is nothing left to say or have; we become a fictitious personality, an unreal presence, and this unreal presence cannot be approached by God.

In order to be able to pray, we must be within the situation which is defined as the kingdom of God. We must recognise that He is God, that He is King, we must surrender to Him. We must at least be concerned with His will, even if we are not yet capable of fulfilling it. But if we are not, if we treat God like the rich young man who could not follow Christ because he was too rich, then how can we meet Him? So often what we would like to have through prayer, through the deep relationship with God which we long for, is simply another period of happiness; we are not prepared to sell all that we have in order to buy the pearl of great price. Then how should we get this pearl of great price? Is that what we expect to get? Is it not the same as in human relationships: when a man or a woman experiences love for another, other people no longer matter in the same way. To put it in a short formula from the ancient world, 'When a man has a bride, he is no longer surrounded by men and women, but by people.'

Isn't that what could, what should happen with regard to all our riches when we turn to God? Surely they should become pale and grey, just a general background against which the only figure that matters would appear in intense relief? We would like just one touch of heavenly blue in the general picture of our life, in which there are so many dark sides. God is prepared to be outside it, He is prepared to take it up completely as a cross, but He is not prepared to be simply part of our life.

So when we think of the absence of God, is it not worth while to ask ourselves whom we blame for it? We always blame God, we always accuse Him, either straight to His face or in front of people, of being absent, of never being there when He is needed, never answering when He is addressed. At times we are more 'pious' (very much in inverted commas), and we say piously 'God is testing my patience, my faith, my humility.' We find all sorts of ways of turning God's judgement on us into a new way of praising ourselves. We are so patient that we can put up even with God!

Is this not true? When I was a young priest I preached a sermon, one of the many I preached in a parish, and a young girl came up to me and said 'Father Anthony, you must be appallingly evil.' I said 'I am certainly evil, but how do you know that?' She said 'Because you have described our sins so well that you must have committed them all yourself!' Of course, the shocking description of evil thoughts and evil attitudes which I am giving you now are probably mine and not yours, but perhaps they are yours too, however little.

What we must start with, if we wish to pray, is the certainty that we are sinners in need of salvation, that we are cut off from God and that we cannot live without Him and that all we can offer God is our desperate longing to be made such that God will receive us, receive us in repentance, receive us with mercy and with love. And so from the outset prayer is really our humble ascent towards God, a moment when we turn Godwards, shy of coming near, knowing that if we meet Him too soon, before His grace has had time to help us to be capable of meeting Him, it will be judgment. And all we can do is to turn to Him with all the reverence, all the veneration, the worshipful adoration, the fear of God of which we are capable, with all the attention and earnestness which we may possess, and ask Him to do something with us that will make us capable of meeting Him face to face, not for judgment, nor for condemnation, but for eternal life.

I would like to remind you of the parable of the Pharisee and the Publican. The Publican comes and stands at the rear of the church. He knows that he stands condemned; he knows that in terms of justice there is no hope for him because he is an outsider to the kingdom of God, the kingdom of righteousness or the kingdom of love, because he belongs neither to the realm of righteousness nor to the realm of love. But in the cruel, the violent, the ugly life he leads, he has learnt something of which the righteous Pharisee has no idea. He has learnt that in a world of competition, in a world of predatory animals, in a world of cruelty and heartlessness, the only hope one can have is an act of mercy, an act of compassion, a completely unexpected act which is rooted neither in duty nor in natural relationships, which will suspend the action of the cruel, violent, heartless world in which we live. All he knows, for instance, from being himself an extortioner, a moneylender, a thief, and so forth, is that there are moments when for no reason, because it is not part of the world's outlook, he will forgive a debt, because suddenly his heart has become mild and vulnerable; that on another occasion he may not get someone put into prison because a face will have reminded him of something or a voice has gone straight to his heart. There is no logic in this. It is not part of the world's outlook nor is it a way in which he normally behaves. It is something that breaks through, which is completely nonsensical, which he cannot resist; and he knows also, probably, how often he himself was saved from final catastrophe by this intrusion of the unexpected and the impossible, mercy, compassion, forgiveness. So he stands at the rear of the church, knowing that all the realm inside the church is a realm of righteousness and divine love to which he does not belong and into which he cannot enter. But he knows from experience also that the impossible does occur and that is why he says 'Have mercy, break the laws of righteousness, break the laws of religion, come down in mercy to us who have no right to be either forgiven or allowed in'. And I think this is where we should start continuously all over again.

You probably remember the two passages from St Paul where he says 'My power is manifest in weakness'. Weakness is not the kind of weakness which we show by sinning and forgetting God, but the kind of weakness which means being completely supple, completely transparent, completely abandoned in the hands of God. We usually try to be strong and we prevent God from manifesting His power.

You remember how you were taught to write when you were small. Your mother put a pencil in your hand, took your hand in hers and began to move it. Since you did not know at all what she meant to do, you left your hand completely free in hers. This is what I mean by the power of God being manifest in weakness. You could think of that also in the terms of a sail. A sail can catch the wind and be used to manoeuvre a boat only because it is so frail. If instead of a sail you put a solid board, it would not work; it is the weakness of the sail that makes it sensitive to the wind. The same is true of the gauntlet and the surgical glove. How strong is the gauntlet, how frail is the glove, yet in intelligent hands it can work miracles because it is so frail. So one of the things which God continues to try to teach us is to replace the imaginary and minute amount of disturbing strength we have by this frailty of surrender, of abandonment in the hands of God. I will give you an example of this.

Twenty-five years ago a friend of mine who had two children was killed during the liberation of Paris. His children had always hated me because they were jealous that their father had a friend, but when the father died they turned to me because I had been their father's friend. One of his children was a girl of fifteen who came to see me one day in my surgery (I was a doctor before I became a priest), and she saw that, apart from my medical paraphernalia, I had a book of the Gospels on my desk. So with all the certainty of youth she said 'I can't understand how a man who is supposed to be educated can believe in such stupid things.' I said 'Have you read it?' She said 'No'. Then I said 'Remember it is only the most stupid people who pass judgments on things they do not know.' After that she read the Gospels and she was so interested that her whole life changed. because she started to pray and God gave her an experience of His presence and she lived by it for a while. Then she fell ill with an incurable disease and she wrote me a letter when I had already become a priest and was in England, and said 'Since my body has begun to grow weak and to die out, my spirit has become livelier than ever and I perceive the divine presence so easily and so joyfully.' I wrote to her again: 'Don't expect it will last. When you have lost a little bit more of your strength, you will no longer be able to turn and cast yourself Godwards and then you will feel that you have no access to God.' After a while she wrote again and said 'Yes, I have become so weak now that I can't make the effort of moving Godwards or even longing actively and God has gone', but I said 'Now do something else. Try to learn humility in the real, deep sense of this word.'

The word 'humility' comes from the Latin word 'humus' which means fertile ground. To me, humility is not what we often make of it: the sheepish way of trying to imagine that we are the worst of all and trying to convince others that our artificial ways of behaving show that we are aware of that. Humility is the situation of the earth. The earth is always there, always taken for granted, never remembered, always trodden on by everyone, somewhere we cast and pour out all the refuse, all we don't need. It's there, silent and accepting everything and in a miraculous way making out of all the refuse new richness in spite of corruption, transforming corruption itself into a power of life and a new possibility of creativeness, open to the sunshine, open to the rain, ready to receive any seed we sow and capable of bringing thirtyfold, sixtyfold, a hundredfold out of every seed. I said to this woman 'Learn to be like this before God; abandoned, surrendered, ready to receive anything from people and anything from God.' Indeed she got a great deal from people; within six months her husband got tired of having a dying wife and abandoned her, so refuse was poured generously, but God also shone His light and gave His rain, because after a little while she wrote to me and said 'I am completely finished. I can't move Godwards, but it is God who steps down to me.'

This is not only a story to illustrate what I said, but something to the point; this is the weakness in which God can manifest His power and this is the situation in which the absence of God can become the presence of God. We cannot capture God. But whenever we stand, either like the Publican or like this girl, outside the realm of 'right', only in the realm of mercy, we can meet God.

Try and think about the absence of God, and do

realise that before you can knock at the door – and remember that it is not only at the door of the Kingdom understood in the general way, but that Christ really says 'I am the door' – before you knock at the door, you must realise that you are outside. If you spend your time imagining that in a mad way you are already in the kingdom of God, there is certainly no point in knocking at any door for it to be opened. Obviously, you must look round trying to see where are the angels and the saints, and where the mansion is which belongs to you, and when you see nothing but darkness or walls, you can quite legitimately find it surprising that Paradise is so unattractive. We must all realise that we are not yet in it, that we are still outsiders to the kingdom of God, and then ask ourselves 'Where is the door and how does one knock at it?'

In the next chapter we will try to go deeper into this subject of knocking at the door and the attempt to go inside, to become an inmate of Paradise, of the place where prayer is possible.

II

Knocking at the Door

AS I SAID in speaking of the way in which we
perceive the absence of God – which is obviously not
objective but subjective – unless we are aware that we
are outside the kingdom of God, that we need to knock
at a door to be allowed in, we may spend a great deal
of our lives in imagining that we are inside, behaving
as though we were, and never reaching that depth where
the kingdom of God unfolds itself in all its beauty, its
truth and its glory.

When I say that we are outsiders, I do not mean
simply that there is a situation in which we are radically
outside or radically inside. We should think rather in
terms of an increasing progression from depth to depth,
from height to height, whichever formula you prefer, so
that at every step we already possess something which
is rich, which is deep, and yet always go on longing for
and moving towards something richer and deeper. This
is very important to remember, because we are extraordinarily rich, even while we are outside. God gives us
so much, we are so rich intellectually and emotionally,
our lives are so full, that we may imagine that there
can be nothing more than this, that we have found
fulfilment and wholeness, that we have reached the end
of our search. But we must learn that there is always
more. We must rejoice that, poor as we are, we are so

rich; yet we must long for the true riches of the Kingdom, being careful not to be beguiled by what we
already possess so that we turn away from what is ahead
of us.

We must remember that all we possess is a gift. The
first Beatitude is one of poverty, and only if we live
according to this Beatitude can we enter into the kingdom of God. This Beatitude has two aspects. First, there
is the very clear fact that we possess nothing which we
can keep, whether we want to or not; it is the discovery
that I am nothing and that I have nothing – total,
irremediable, hopeless poverty. We exist because we
have been willed into existence and brought into
existence. We have done nothing for it, it was not an
act of our free will. We do not possess life in such a
way that it is impossible for anyone to take it away from
us, and all that we are and all that we possess is
ephemeral in this way. We have a body – it will die. We
have a mind – yet it is enough for one minute vessel to
burst in a brain for the greatest mind to be suddenly
extinguished. We have a heart, sensitive and alive – and
yet a moment comes when we would like to pour out all
our sympathy, all our understanding for someone who is
in need, and at that moment there is nothing but a stone
in our breast.

So, in a way, we can say that we possess nothing
because we are masters of nothing which is in our possession. And this could lead us, not to the sense of belonging to the kingdom of God and rejoicing in it, but to
despair – if we did not remember that although none of
these things are ours in such a way that they cannot be
taken away from us, yet we *are* in possession of them.
This is the second aspect of the Beatitude. We are rich,
and everything which we possess is a gift and a sign of
the love of God and the love of men, it is a continuous

gift of divine love; and as long as we possess nothing,
love divine is manifested continuously and fully. But
everything we take into our own hands to possess is taken
out of the realm of love. Certainly it becomes ours, but
love is lost. And it is only those who give everything away
who become aware of true, total, final, irremediable,
spiritual poverty, and who possess the love of God expressed in all His gifts. One of our theologians has said
'All the food of this world is divine love made edible.'
I think this is true and the moment we try to be rich by
keeping something safely in our hands, we are the losers,
because as long as we have nothing in our hands, we can
take, leave, do whatever we want.

This is the Kingdom, the sense that we are free from
possession, and this freedom establishes us in a relationship where everything is love – human love and love
divine.

Now if we reason in these terms, we can transfer the
same idea to what was said earlier. Yes, we are rich. Yet
we should never be beguiled by what we possess into
imagining that now we can demolish the old barns and
build new ones in order to store more of our riches.
Nothing can be stored – nothing except the kingdom of
God itself. And so we can discard one thing after
another in order to go ahead free – free of being rich.
Have you never noticed that to be rich always means
an impoverishment on another level? It is enough for
you to say 'I have this watch, it is mine', and close your
hand on it, to be in possession of a watch and to have
lost a hand. And if you close your mind on your riches,
if you close your heart so that you can keep what is in
it safe, never to lose it, then it becomes as small as the
thing on which you have closed yourself in.

Now if that is true, the moment you reach rock
bottom, the moment you are aware of your utter

dispossession of all things, then you are on the fringe of the kingdom of God, you are nearly aware that God is love and that He is upholding you by his love. And at that point you can say two things simultaneously. You can pray out of your utter misery, dereliction and poverty, and you can rejoice that you are so rich with the love of God. But this is only if you have come to the point of discovering it, because as long as you imagine you are rich there is nothing to thank God for, and you cannot be aware of being loved. Too often the kind of thanksgiving we offer is too much a general thanksgiving, and the kind of repentance we bring to God is too much a general repentance.

I have experienced this once, in a most unromantic and unspiritual way. When I was a teenager I remember going to a place, and I calculated my journey very well because I hoped I would arrive at the moment when people have lunch, and I thought that if I arrived in time they couldn't possibly make me wait in the next room without giving me something to eat. But, of course, my train was later and I arrived after lunch, ravenously hungry. I was with a friend, and since we were really too hungry to go on we asked whether there was anything they could give us. They said 'We have half a cucumber.' We looked at this cucumber and at each other and thought 'Is that all God can give us?' Then my friend said 'And now, let us say grace.' I thought 'Goodness for a cucumber!' My friend was a better believer than I and more pious, so we read None together, and then we read a few more prayers, then we read the blessing of the food, and all the time I had difficulty in detaching myself from the half cucumber, of which a quarter would be mine, and then we broke the cucumber and ate it. In all my life I haven't been so grateful to God for any amount or quantity of food. I

ate it as one would eat sacred food. I ate it carefully, not
to miss any moment of this rich delight of the fresh
cucumber, and after we had finished I had no hesitation
in saying, 'And now, let us give thanks to the Lord', and
we started again in gratitude.

We cannot live a life of prayer, we cannot go ahead
Godwards, unless we are free from possession in order to
have two hands to offer and a heart absolutely open –
not like a purse which we are afraid of keeping open
because our money will drop out of it, but like an open
and empty purse – and an intelligence completely open
to the unknown and the unexpected. This is the way in
which we are rich and yet totally free from richness.
And this is the point at which we can speak of being
outside the Kingdom and yet be so rich, inside and yet
also so free.

This is true, for instance, when we fast. I don't mean
the fasting and abstinence that affects only the stomach
but that attitude of sobriety which allows you, or
compels you, never to get enslaved by anything. This is
a question of our whole conduct of life. First of all it
affects our imagination because that is a point at which
sin begins. One of our Orthodox writers, in the ninth
century, said that the sins of the flesh are the sins which
the spirit commits against the flesh. It is not the flesh
that is responsible, and I think in that sense we must
learn to control our imagination. As long as our
imagination has not taken hold of us, things are outside
us; once our imagination has got entangled and
imprisoned in things, then we are glued to things. You
know there are such things as meat and vegetables and
puddings and so on. As an objective fact you know it. If
you settle down and ask yourself 'I'm not really hungry
but there are so many nice things one can eat, what
would I fancy?' in five minutes' time you will have

projected tentacles over a variety of things. You will be like Gulliver, knit to the ground by one hair and another hair and another hair; each of the hairs are really nothing, but the sum total will keep you solidly tied down. Once you have allowed your imagination full sway, things are much more difficult. In that respect we must be sober and we must fight for freedom. There is a great deal of difference between attachment and love, between hunger and greed, between a live interest and curiosity, and so forth. Every one of our natural propensities has got a counterpart which is marked by evil and which is one of the ways in which we get enslaved. This is what I meant by withdrawing tentacles. To begin with, say 'no'. If you haven't said 'no' in time, you are in for a fight. But then be ruthless about it, because reason and detachment is more precious than what you get as a slave in terms of enjoyment.

Now if what I have said so far is true, we must knock at a door. At this point certain problems become very acute. If the door was that of some church, it would be very simple, we would come and knock. But the trouble is that we usually do not know where to knock. How often people want to pray and they ask themselves 'Now where is the focus of this prayer? Where should I turn my gaze and my heart?' If you are a Moslem, it is simple. You turn towards Mecca. But even so, once we have turned eastwards, what then? You cannot focus on things which are less than God. The moment you try to focus on an imaginary god, or a god you can imagine, you are in great danger of placing an idol between yourself and the real God. This is a thought which was expressed as early as the fourth century by St Gregory of Nazianzus. He said that the moment we put a visible sign in front of ourselves, whether it be a crucifix, a tabernacle, an icon or an invisible image – God as we imagine Him, or Christ as we have seen Him in paintings – and we focus our attention on that, then we have placed a barrier between ourselves and God, because we take the image which we have formed for the person to whom we address our prayer. What we must do is to collect all the knowledge of God which we possess in order to come into His presence, but then remember that all we know about God is our past, as it were, behind our back, and we are standing face to face with God in all His complexity, all His simplicity, so close and yet unknown. Only if we stand completely open before the unknown, can the unknown reveal itself, Himself, as He chooses to reveal Himself to us as we are today. So, with this open-heartedness and open-mindedness, we must stand before God without trying to give Him a shape or to imprison Him in concepts and images, and we must knock at a door.

Where? The Gospel tells us that the kingdom of God is within us first of all. If we cannot find the kingdom of God within us, if we cannot meet God within, in the very depth of ourselves, our chances of meeting Him outside ourselves are very remote. When Gagarin came back from space and made his remarkable statement that he never saw God in Heaven, one of our priests in Moscow remarked 'If you have not seen Him on earth, you will never see Him in Heaven.' This is also true of what I am speaking about. If we cannot find a contact with God under our own skin, as it were, in this very small world which I am, then the chances are very slight that even if I meet Him face to face, I will recognise Him. St John Chrysostom said 'Find the door of your heart, you will discover it is the door of the kingdom of God.' So it is inward that we must turn, and not outward – but inward in a very special way. I am not saying that we must become introspective. I don't mean that we must go inward in the way one does in psychoanalysis or psychology. It is not a journey into my *own* inwardness, it is a journey *through* my own self, in order to emerge from the deepest level of self into the place where He is, the point at which God and I meet.

So this question of incipient prayer has, therefore, two aspects: first, this going inwards, and secondly, the use of words in prayer and the direction in which to turn them.

I will speak now of the second point. Towards what, towards whom shall I turn the sharp edge of my prayer? Very often people try to shout into the sky and they are surprised to discover that the sky is empty and does not echo back. It is not there that one can find an echo. A spiritual writer of the seventh century, St John Climacus, has written that a prayer, words of prayer, are like an arrow. But to possess an arrow is not enough. If you want to hit a target, you must have a bow with a good string, and a good arm to pull. If you have a good bow and cannot pull, your arrow will just fly a few yards and fall short. If you do not shoot your shaft with a powerful arm, it will not hit the target. What we need is the bow, the string and the arm, and the strength. Now, given that the words of prayer are the shaft, we are aiming at the deepest point where God is to be found within us; we must turn our bow inwards to hit ourselves at that deepest point. Secondly, we must provide the arrow with all the conditions that will allow it to fly forcefully. Very often we are inattentive in prayer, our heart is not in it, and our prayer is not upheld by our life. Here, if you wish, are analogies with the bow, the string and the strength.

There are moments when one can make attempts at breaking through into the depths by calling to Him who is at the root and depth of all things, but you will see perfectly well where you are going and where to aim the prayer: not back, not upwards, but deeper, deeper – at every resistance there is in the way, at every covering fallacy, at everything that prevents you from piercing through into that very depth. And so prayer will become something perfectly feasible, although a hard, arduous daring exercise.

First of all, then, we must choose a prayer. That is very important. Just as it is important to use the right words if you are in a relationship with someone, so it is with a prayer. Whichever one we choose, it must be a prayer that makes sense to us and a prayer which does not make us uneasy. I must admit that the perusal of manuals of prayer very often leaves me very uneasy. I feel that if God was really present, concretely there in front of me, I would certainly not dare to make all these flat discourses to Him and tell Him things about Himself that He has known long before I ever came into the world. So there is a need for choice, because if you are ashamed of your prayer, God may be uneasy about you and the prayer too, and you will never be able to bring it to God wholeheartedly. The first thing, then, is really to find words of prayer that are worthy of you and worthy of God. I say 'worthy of you and worthy of God' because if they are good enough for you, then God can accept them, but if they are not good enough for you, leave God alone, He has heard better things than that. Yet we must not try to find extraordinary words; one of the dangers in prayer is to try to find words that will be somehow on the level of God. Unfortunately, as none of us are on a level with God, we fall short and waste a great deal of time in trying to find the right words.

Without attempting to cover all the ground, I would just like to give you an image of the worthiness of an act of worship or words of worship. In the life of Moses, in Hebrew folklore, there is a remarkable passage. Moses finds a shepherd in the desert. He spends the day with the shepherd and helps him milk his ewes, and at the end of the day he sees that the shepherd puts the best milk he has in a wooden bowl, which he places on a flat stone some distance away. So Moses asks him what it is for, and the shepherd replies 'This is God's milk.' Moses is puzzled and asks him what he means. The shepherd says 'I always take the best milk I possess, and I bring it as an offering to God.' Moses, who is far more sophisticated than the shepherd with his naïve faith, asks 'And does God drink it?' 'Yes' replies the shepherd, 'He does.' Then Moses feels compelled to enlighten the poor shepherd and he explains that God, being pure spirit, does not drink milk. Yet the shepherd is sure that He does, and so they have a short argument, which ends with Moses telling the shepherd to hide behind the bushes to find out whether in fact God does come to drink the milk. Moses then goes out to pray in the desert. The shepherd hides, the night comes, and in the moonlight the shepherd sees a little fox that comes trotting from the desert, looks right, looks left and heads straight towards the milk, which he laps up, and disappears into the desert again. The next morning Moses finds the shepherd quite depressed and downcast. 'What's the matter?' he asks. The shepherd says 'You were right, God is pure spirit and He doesn't want my milk.' Moses is surprised. He says 'You should be happy. You know more about God than you did before.' 'Yes, I do' says the shepherd, 'but the only thing I could do to express my love for Him has been taken away from me.' Moses sees the point. He retires into the desert and prays hard. In the night in a vision, God speaks to him and says 'Moses, you were wrong. It is true that I am pure spirit. Nevertheless I always accepted with gratitude the milk which the shepherd offered me, as the expression of his love, but since, being pure spirit, I do not need the milk, I shared it with this little fox, who is very fond of milk.'

I have tried to point out, first of all, that your prayer must be turned inwards, not towards a God of Heaven nor towards a God far off, but towards God who is closer to you than you are aware; and secondly, that the first act of prayer is to choose such words of prayer as are completely true to what you are, words which you are not ashamed of, which express you adequately and are worthy of you – and then offer them to God with all the intelligence of which you are capable. You must also put all the heart you can into an act of worship, an act of recognition of God, an act of cherishing, which is the true meaning of charity, an action which involves you in the mind, in the heart, and an action which is completely adequate to what you are.

The first thing which I suggest, therefore, is that you should ask yourself what words of prayer make sense for you to offer to God, whether they be your own or those of other people. Ask yourself also how much they touch your heart, to what extent you are capable of concentrating your mind on them – for if you cannot be attentive to the words you say, why should God? How can He receive them as an expression of love if you do not put your heart into them, if you have only put in a certain amount of courtesy together with a certain amount of absent-mindedness?

And then if you learn to use a prayer you have chosen at moments when you can give all your attention to the divine presence and offer God this prayer, gradually what happens is that the awareness of God grows within you to such an extent that whether you are with people, listening, speaking or whether you are alone working, this awareness is so strong that even if you are with people you will still be able to pray. The analogy which some of our spiritual writers give works on two different levels: one is simpler and cruder and, I think, expresses very well what they are trying to say, the other is loftier.

The simpler and cruder one is something which one of our great spiritual guides, Theophan the Recluse, says: 'The awareness of God shall be with you as clearly as a toothache.' When you have a toothache, you don't forget it at all. You may be talking, you may be reading, you may be scrubbing, you may be singing, you may be doing anything; the toothache is there continuously present and you cannot escape the ache of its presence. He says in the same way we should develop an ache in our hearts. I don't mean the physical heart, but at the core of us, an ache that will be a desperate longing for God, a feeling that 'I am alone, where is He?' at the moment when you have lost touch in prayer.

The loftier way of putting it, of course, is to say that when a great joy has come upon us or a great pain or a great sorrow, we do not forget it in the course of the day. We listen to people, we do our work, we read, we do what we are supposed to, and the pain of bereavement, the awareness of joy, of the exhilarating news is with us incessantly. This should also be the sense of the presence of God. And if the sense of the presence of God is as clear as that, then one can pray while one does other things. One can pray while one works physically, but one can also pray when one is with people, listening or being engaged in some sort of conversation or relationship. But, as I said, this is not the first thing that happens to us, and I think we must school ourselves to

an attitude of worshipful attention and of brokenheartedness first, in those conditions which allow it,
because it is so easy to get inattentive, to slip from
alertness to dreaming in prayer. Let us start to learn this
sort of prayerful attention, of complete stability, of
worshipful adoration, and of surrender to God at
moments when we can do it with an undivided mind
and heart, and then one can make attempts in other
situations.

We will go on with this subject in the next chapter
by showing the way one can take one or two prayers
and use them to break through into our own depth,
towards the place where God is. In addition to that, I
will try to explain how one can go inward, for this is
another exercise. Do not forget the little fox, he can be
most useful for your life of prayer. And while we are on
the subject of foxes, if you want to learn how one makes
friends with God, learn from another fox in the book of
St Exupery called *The Little Prince* about how one
makes friends with one who is extremely sensitive,
vulnerable and shy.

III

Going Inwards

I HAVE SAID that one of the problems which we
must all face and solve is: where should I direct my
prayer? The answer I have suggested is that we should
direct it at ourselves. Unless the prayer which you intend
to offer to God is important and meaningful to you first,
you will not be able to present it to the Lord. If you are
inattentive to the words you pronounce, if your heart
does not respond to them, or if your life is not turned
in the same direction as your prayer, it will not reach
out Godwards. So the first thing is, as I said, to choose a
prayer which you can say with all your mind, with all
your heart and with all your will – a prayer which does
not necessarily have to be a great example of liturgical
art, but which must be true, something which should
not fall short of what you want to express. You must
understand this prayer, with all the richness and
precision it possesses.

In the use of words there are three things we can do.
We can use spontaneous prayer, the kind of prayer that
gushes out of our own souls; we can use short vocal
prayers which are very short, extremely intense in their
content and wide so that they can contain as many
meanings as possible; and we can use what one calls, at
times in a rather unpleasant way, ready-made prayers,
which range from the flattest productions of people who

are trying to invent prayers for all occasions, to the
expressions of the saints' deepest experience, expressed
in the prayers that they did not invent but which the
Holy Spirit coined within their lives and within their
hearts. I would like to say something about each of these
categories.

Spontaneous prayer is possible in two situations:
either at moments when we have become vividly aware
of God, when this awareness calls out of us a response of
worship, of joy, all the forms of response which we are
capable of giving, being ourselves and facing the living
God, or when we become aware suddenly of the deathly
danger in which we are when we come to God, moments
when we suddenly shout out from the depths of despair
and dereliction, and also from the sense that there is no
hope of salvation for us unless God saves us.

These two situations are the two extreme poles – the
vision of ourselves in the desperate situation in which we
are, Godless, lonely, longing, and yet incapable of breaking through; or the marvel of suddenly finding ourselves
face to face with God when we can pray spontaneously
and it doesn't matter much what words we use. We can
go on repeating 'my joy, my joy'. We can say words
because the words do not matter, the words are merely
a way of sustaining a mood, of speaking foolishly,
madly, of our love or of our despair. You remember the
passage in the Gospel concerning the Transfiguration in
which Peter says to Christ 'Shall we make three tents
for you, for Moses and for Elijah?' The Gospel says
he was speaking nonsense because he was out of himself.
He was faced with something so overwhelming that he
said whatever came into his mind, he blundered out
something that expressed his feelings.

Now, if we imagine that we can sustain spontaneous
prayer throughout our life, we are in a childish delusion.

Spontaneous prayer must gush out of our souls, we cannot simply turn on a tap and get it out. It is not there for us to draw from to use at any moment. It comes from the depths of our soul, from either wonder or distress, but it does not come from the middle situation in which we are neither overwhelmed by the divine presence nor overwhelmed by a sense of who we are and the position in which we are. So that, at those moments, to try to use a spontaneous prayer is a completely illusory exercise. There are whole periods when you are neither at the bottom of the sea nor at the top of the peak, when you have got to do something about praying, and that is the period when you cannot pray from spontaneity but you can pray from conviction. This is very important, because many people who begin a life of prayer think that unless they feel very strongly about the words and phrases they use, they are not being sincere. This is not true. One can at times be perfectly sincere in the lucidity of one's mind, in the straightness of one's will, although at a given moment these words, or it can be gestures, do not express what I feel now.

The example that comes to me is this. When you live in your family, and you work out of doors and are doing a heavy kind of work, you may come back physically worn out. If at that moment your mother, your sister, your father or whoever else, said 'Do you love me?' you would say 'I do.' If the other person goes on investigating, 'Do you really love me at this moment?' what you could honestly have said is 'No, I feel nothing but my aching back and worn out body.' But you are perfectly right in saying 'I love you' because you know that underneath all the exhaustion, there is a live current of love. And when Christ says 'those who love me will keep my commandments' He does not say that 'if you love me you will go from one emotion into another, one state of rapture into another, one theological vision to another', He just says 'If you believe my words then live up to what you have received', and 'live up' means always live a little bit above one's means, as it were. To do more than you could have done spontaneously.

So there is a need for some sort of prayer which is not spontaneous but which is truly rooted in conviction. To find this you can draw from a great many of the existing prayers. We already have a rich panoply of prayers which were wrought in the throes of faith, by the Holy Spirit. For example, we have the psalms, we have so many short and long prayers in the liturgical wealth of all the Churches from which we can draw. What matters is that you should learn and know enough of such prayers so that at the right moment you are able to find the right prayers. It is a question of learning by heart enough meaningful passages, from the psalms or from the prayers of the saints. Each of us is sensitive to certain particular passages. Mark these passages that go deep into your heart, that move you deeply, that make sense, that express something which is already within your experience, either of sin, or of bliss in God, or of struggle. Learn those passages, because one day when you are so completely low, so profoundly desperate that you cannot call out of your soul any spontaneous expression, any spontaneous wording, you will discover that these words come up and offer themselves to you as a gift of God, as a gift of the Church, as a gift of holiness, helping our simple lack of strength. And then you really need the prayers you have learnt and made a part of yourself.

In the Orthodox Church, we have morning and evening prayers, which are, on the whole, longer than the ones commonly used in the West. It should take about half an hour in the morning, half an hour in the even-

ing, to read these prayers. A person will try to learn
them by heart so that at other moments he or she can
draw from them. But it is not enough just to learn
prayers by heart. A prayer makes sense only if it is
lived. Unless they are 'lived', unless life and prayer
become completely interwoven, prayers become a sort of
polite madrigal which you offer to God at moments
when you are giving time to Him.

If in your morning prayers you have said a phrase, you
must live up to this phrase in the course of the day. And
I think that, apart from learning as many meaningful
passages as you can, you must make a rule that when
you have discovered one phrase which makes sense to
you – in the reading of the Gospel, in the reading of the
New or Old Testament in general, in praying with words
from the liturgy – you must try to apply it in the course
of the day ruthlessly, for as long as you can. You may
imagine that you are capable of taking up a phrase
like this and living it throughout the course of a whole
day. But it is extremely difficult. If you can keep to one
sentence of one prayer for an hour without breaking the
rule you will be lucky, but do it! Say 'I have read this
prayer, my heart is ready O Lord, my heart is ready,
for half an hour I will make sure that my heart is open
to God and ready to obey His will.' Half an hour, not
more, then give yourself a respite and turn to something else because, if you try to keep to one sentence
which is absolute and difficult, in the end you will simply
say to yourself 'Can't do it any more' and you will end
up doing nothing. But if you say 'I have three or four or
five sentences as slogans for the day and I will try to
apply this from the moment I have read it until 10
o'clock in the morning, then I'll move to the next one,
then to the next one', you will see that gradually all the
words of prayer, all the thoughts and feelings the saints

express in their prayers come alive in you, they begin to go deep into your will and to mould your will and your body, because it is with your body that you have to apply commandments.

However, you may say 'I don't feel very strongly about these words.' If these words express a basic conviction but you feel nothing at the moment, turn to God in repentance and say to God 'This is my basic Christian faith, and look, I don't feel anything about it', and then from that point you may discover that you suddenly burst into spontaneous prayer. You can express to God your sorrow, your misery, your disgust with yourself, and you come back with the determined will to tell God what is true and that your will is united with His will.

A last way in which we can pray is the use, more or less continuous, of a vocal prayer that serves as a background, a walking stick, throughout the day and throughout life. What I have in mind now is something which is specifically used by the Orthodox. It is what we call the 'Jesus prayer', a prayer which is centred on the name of Jesus. 'Lord Jesus Christ, son of God, have mercy on me a sinner.' This prayer is used by monks and nuns but also it is used by our lay people. It is the prayer of stability, because it is the prayer that is not discursive – we do not move from one thought to the other – it is a prayer that places us face to face with God through a profession of faith concerning Him, and it defines a situation concerning us. It is the profession of faith which, according to the mind of most Orthodox ascetics and mystics, is a summing up of the whole Gospels. We profess the Lordship of Christ, His sovereign right upon us, the fact that He is our Lord and Our God, and this implies that all our life is within His will and that we commit ourselves to His will and to no other way. That is the name of 'Jesus' in which we confess the reality of the Incarnation and all that the Incarnation stands for. Christ in whom we see the Incarnate Word of God in the line of the Old and the New Testament, the anointed of Yahweh. Then the perfect profession of faith, of what He is – the Son of God. This is not only a profession of faith in Jesus Christ, but it also opens up the Trinitarian way because He is the Son of the Father and no one can recognise in the prophet of Galilee the Incarnate Son of God unless the Holy Spirit teaches him to see, to understand and to commit himself. So here we have the fourth profession of faith that allows us to stand face to face with God in truth, and profess in spirit. And then, 'have mercy on us.' 'Have mercy' is the English rendering of the word 'eleison'. When you say the Kyrie Eleison you are using Greek words which mean, 'Lord have mercy.'

Why I want to insist on these words which we use in prayer is that in all modern languages words have specialised and narrowed meanings as contrasted with ancient languages. Very often we use words of prayer which are extremely rich but we do not notice the depth of what we say, because we take the words for what they mean in our ordinary speech, while they could have deep echoes in our hearts if we only connected them with other things we know.

I would like to give you an example of this which may shock classical scholars because the philology implied is doubtful, but since it is based on a pun made centuries ago by the Greek Spiritual Fathers, who knew their language and were not shy of making a pun, I will take advantage of it too. Most of us use the words 'Kyrie eleison', or 'Lord have mercy', at some moments of our lives. We are at least aware that they exist, and know approximately what we mean by them. On the whole, it is an appeal to God for mercy, for compassion, for warmth of heart. Now the point at which the classical student may find fault with me and with the Greek Fathers is that some of them derive 'eleison' from the same root as the Greek words 'olive tree', 'olive', 'olive oil'. However, let us leave the argument to scholars and have a look at what could be conveyed to us from the point of view of the Scriptures. When we say 'Kyrie eleison', we may be content with the sense that it is a general appeal to God's mercy. In this case it will not satisfy us, because we cannot put the whole of our life into this 'Lord have mercy', and besides, the words themselves do not mean much in our ordinary speech. But if you think of the olive tree, of the olive in the Old and New Testaments, you will see the following: the first time the olive and the twig of the olive tree appear is at the end of the Flood, when the twig is brought to Noah by a dove. (Is it the same dove that hovered over Christ on the day of His baptism?) This olive twig means that the wrath of God has come to an end, that forgiveness is freely given, that time and new possibilities open up ahead of us. This is the first situation. However, we cannot always follow this way, because it is not enough just to have time and new possibilities opening up if we are sick at heart, if we are broken in will or if we are incapable in mind or body either of discerning or of following the path. We need healing, so remember the oil which the Good Samaritan poured on the wounds of the man who had fallen victim to the robbers. The healing power of God will make it possible for us to take advantage of the cessation of His wrath, of the gift of forgiveness that is offered and, indeed, of the gift of time and space and eternity.

Another image is that of the anointing of priests and

kings, who among the people of Israel were called upon
to stand on a threshold between the world divine and
the human world, between the unity and harmony of
the will of God and the diversity and complexities – not
to speak of the tensions and oppositions – of the human
world. To be able to stand there, a man needs more
than human capability; he needs a divine gift. This was
signified at the anointing given to both priests and
kings. But in the New Testament all of us are priests
and kings, and our vocation as human beings and as
Christians is beyond what a human being could achieve.
We are called upon to become and to be living members
of the Body of Christ, temples on a soil pure and worthy
of the Holy Spirit, and partakers of the divine nature.
All this is beyond our own human capabilities, and yet
we need to be human to the full, in the profound way
in which a Christian thinks of humanity in the image
of the Incarnate Son of God. To do this we need the
grace and the help of God. All this is shown us in the
same image.

Now, if we reflected with the same simplicity – it takes
only a dictionary and a Bible and some thinking – and
if we thought as simply and as directly about the other
words we use in prayer, then they would grow remark-
ably rich intellectually. Then we could pay more attention to what we say, and our prayer would not just be
one of empty words or words which are merely the
symbol of something from which the true meaning is
lost. Then before we said 'Kyrie eleison' – 'Lord have
mercy on me, Lord show me compassion, Lord pour
out Thy love and tenderness on me' – we should have
thought about the situation we are in. Have we fallen
to our lowest depth? Are we faced with infinite possibilities, and at the same time unable to realise any of
them because we are so deeply wounded? Are we healed,

and yet confronted with a vocation so great that it humbles us to think of it because it is beyond us? Yet it can be fulfilled only if God grants us the power to do so. This implies an attentive perusal of words. It also implies such a treatment of words as to make them part of our emotions and that we bring and collect around them all the intensity and depth of our personal life. But if the words we use are not made real by the way we live, they will still be meaningless and lead nowhere, because they will be like a bow that we cannot shoot for lack of a string. It is absolutely pointless to ask God for something which we ourselves are not prepared to do. If we say 'O God make me free from this or that temptation' while at the same time seeking every possible way of falling to just such a temptation, hoping now that God is in control, that He will get us out of it, then we do not stand much chance. God gives us strength but we must use it. When, in our prayers, we ask God to give us strength to do something in His Name, we are *not* asking Him to do it *instead* of us because we are too feeble to be willing to do it for ourselves.

The lives of the saints are enlightening in this respect, and in the life of St Philip Neri just such an occasion is described. He was an irascible man who quarrelled easily and had violent outbursts of anger and of course endured violent outburst from his brothers. One day he felt that it could not go on. Whether it was virtue or whether he could no longer endure his brothers his *Vita* does not tell us. The fact is that he ran to the chapel, fell down before a statue of Christ and begged Him to free him of his anger. He then walked out full of hope. The first person he met was one of the brothers who had never aroused the slightest anger in him, but for the first time in his life this brother was offensive and unpleasant to him. So Philip burst out with anger and went on, full of rage, to meet another of his brothers, who had always been a source of consolation and happiness to him. Yet even this man answered him gruffly. So Philip ran back to the chapel, cast himself before the statue of Christ and said 'O Lord, have I not asked you to free me from this anger?' And the Lord answered 'Yes, Philip, and for this reason I am multiplying the occasions for you to learn.'

I think it is very important for us to realise that God will act in this way. He is not going to be crucified for you every day. There is a moment when you must take up your own cross. We must each take up our own cross, and when we ask something in our prayers, we undertake by implication to do it with all our strength, all our intelligence and all the enthusiasm we can put into our actions, and with all the courage and energy we have. In addition, we do it with all the power which God will give us. If we do not do this, we are wasting our time praying. This implies that 'Kyrie eleison', or any similar words which we may utter, must be turned against ourselves. Our mind must be formed, moulded to the words, filled and harmonised with them. Our heart must accept them with complete conviction and express them with all the strength of which we are capable, and our will must take hold of them and transform them into action. Therefore, prayer and action should become two expressions of the same situation vis-a-vis God and ourselves and everything around us. Short of that, we are wasting our time. What is the point of telling God about things, and when He gives us strength to combat them, sitting back to wait until He does it for us? What point is there in repeating words which have grown so thin, so meaningless, that they just allow us to keep a cobweb, as it were, between ourselves and God?

Therefore, choose the right words, choose them and fasten all your attention to them, because they are words of truth and the words that God will hear because they are true. Put all your heart into them. Make these words so live with intellectual consciousness because they are true, and make them pierce through to the very depths of your own heart.

Words of prayer have the quality of always being words of commitment. You cannot simply say words of prayer without implying 'If I say that, then that is what I am going to do when the occasion lends itself.' When you say to God 'At all costs, at all costs, O Lord, save me', you must remember that you must put all your will into that, because one day God will say 'Here is the price to pay.' The ancient writers said 'Give your blood and God will give you the Spirit.' That is the price. Abandon all, you will receive heaven; abandon enslavement, you will acquire freedom. As your will is already engaged not only in the act of praying but in all the consequences of this prayer, so also must your body be, because a human being is not simply a soul engaged for a while in a body. It is a being which is body and soul, one unique being which is Man.

There is a physical effort to be made in prayer, the physical attention, the physical way in which you pray. Fasting, if food has made you too heavy for prayer, is involved in it too. If you do this, you will be knocking at a door.

Now if we want to go inwards with all these words, to bore down deeper and deeper, the way one bores to get something from the depths of the earth, then we must take a risk, and this risk is that it is very difficult to go inwards. It sounds simple. We all assume that we are deep and that the deeper we go, the more delightful it

will be. It is not quite as simple as that. True, when we
have come to a certain depth it is all right, but on the
way it looks very much like the stories of the quest of
the Grail. There are all sorts of monsters to be met with
on the way, and the monsters are not devils, they are
not our neighbour, they are just ourselves. This makes
it more distasteful and much more difficult to do.

Generally, it is greed, fear and curiosity which make
us live outwardly. A French scientist who worked in
America, Alexis Carrell, said in a book called *Man the
Unknown* that if you ask yourself where your
personality ends you will see that the tongue of a greedy
person is projected like tentacles towards all the edibles
of the world; the eyes of the curious person are like
tentacles projected and attached to everything around;
the ears of the eavesdropper become long and wide and
go far far afield. If you could draw a picture of what you
look like in those terms, you would see that precious
little is left of you inside, because everything is extrover-
ted. So that the first thing one must do is to detach
the tentacles and bring them in. You cannot go inwards
if you are completely outward.

Try an experiment and you will see, you will discover
a number of other useful things on the way. Try to find
time to stay alone with yourself: shut the door and
settle down in your room at a moment when you have
nothing else to do. Say 'I am now with myself', and just
sit with yourself. After an amazingly short time you
will most likely feel bored. This teaches us one very
useful thing. It gives us insight into the fact that if after
ten minutes of being alone with ourselves we feel like
that, it is no wonder that others should feel equally
bored! Why is this so? It is so because we have so little
to offer to our own selves as food for thought, for
emotion and for life. If you watch your life carefully

you will discover quite soon that we hardly ever live from within outwards; instead we respond to incitement, to excitement. In other words, we live by reflection, by reaction. Something happens and we respond, someone speaks and we answer. But when we are left without anything that stimulates us to think, speak or act, we realise that there is very little in us that will prompt us to action in any direction at all. This is really a very dramatic discovery. We are completely empty, we do not act from within ourselves but accept as our life a life which is actually fed in from outside; we are used to things happening which compel us to do other things. How seldom can we live simply by means of the depth and the richness we assume that there is within ourselves.

There is a passage in Dickens' *Pickwick Papers* which is a very good description of my life and probably also of your lives. Pickwick goes to the club. He hires a cab and on the way he asks innumerable questions. Among the questions, he says 'Tell me, how is it possible that such a mean and miserable horse can drive such a big and heavy cab?' The cabbie replies 'It's not a question of the horse, Sir, it's a question of the wheels', and Mr Pickwick says 'What do you mean?' The cabbie answers 'You see, we have a magnificent pair of wheels which are so well oiled that it is enough for the horse to stir a little for the wheels to begin to turn and then the poor horse must run for its life.' Take the way in which we live most of time. We are not the horse that pulls, we are the horse that runs away from the cab in fear of its life.

Because we don't know yet how to act without an outer reason, we discover that we don't know what to do with ourselves, and then we begin to be increasingly bored. So first of all, you must learn to sit with yourself and to face boredom, drawing all the possible conclusions.

After a while this becomes worse than boredom, because we are not simply bored in a way that allows us to say 'I am an active person and am of use to my neighbour. I always do good, and for me to be in the state of suspense where I am not doing anything for anyone else is a severe trial.' We begin to discover something else. We are bored when we try to get out of this boredom by turning inward to see if there is anything in ourselves that will put an end to it. Quite soon we discover that there is nothing, since all we have to think about we have already thought about dozens of times. All the range of emotions which we have in store are there like a piano which we have closed because we are not used to the piano playing itself. We must have someone else playing on the keys. We are not in the habit of doing nothing, and so it becomes worrying and can lead us to the point of anguish. If you read the Desert Fathers, who had good experience of this, or the monks who spent their lives in monasteries, you will see that there are moments when they simply ran out of their cells shouting for help, trying to meet something or someone, whatever they could find. The devil himself would have been better than this emptiness of self-contemplation. One of the spiritual writers, Theophan the Recluse, says 'Most people are like a shaving of wood which is curled round its central emptiness.' If we are really honest, we must admit that this is a very apt description of the state of practically all of us.

Then we must be able to fight this anguish and to say 'No, I will stick it through, and I will come to the point where the anguish itself will prompt me to do what good will is incapable of doing.' Indeed, a moment comes, a moment of despair and anguish and terror, which makes us turn even deeper inward and cry 'Lord have mercy! I am perishing, Lord save me!' We discover that there is nothing in us that can give life, or rather is life; that all we called life, imagine life to be, was outside and inside there was nothing.

Then we look into the abyss of nonentity and we feel that the deeper we go into it the less there will be left of us. This is a dangerous moment, this is the moment when we must hesitate.

At this point we have reached the first layer of depth where we begin to be able to knock at a door. For on the layer where we were just resting from our neighbour before we felt bored, on the layer where we are simply bored and feel offended that we should be, on the layer on which we begin to fidget and worry, then feel slightly anguished, we have as yet no reason to cry and shout with a despair that fills all our mind, all our heart, all our will and all our body with a sense that unless God comes I am lost, there is no hope, because I know that if I emerge out of this depth I will simply be back in the realm of delusion, of reflected life, but not real life.

This is the point at which we can begin to knock at a door which is still closed, but beyond which there is hope, that hope which Bartimaeus, the blind man at the gates of Jericho, felt, out of his utmost despair, when Christ was passing.

We know from the Gospels that Bartimaeus found himself landed by the side of the road, hopelessly blind, having lost all faith and all hope in human help, and reduced to beg for his living, to hope not really on charity (the word meaning 'cherishing'), but on the kind of charity which consists in throwing coins to someone without ever having seen him. And one day this man, who had now given up hope, who was installed in the dust in his present blindness, heard about the man, a new prophet, who was now working miracles throughout the Holy Land. Had he had eyes he would probably have got up and run throughout the country to find him, but he couldn't possibly keep pace with this itinerant wondermaker. And so he stayed where he was, and the presence of one who might possibly have cured him must have made his despair even greater, even more poignant. And one day he heard a crowd that passed by, a crowd which did not sound like any other crowd. Probably, as the blind do, he had developed the sense of hearing and a sensitiveness greater than ours, because he asked 'Who is it that passes by?' and he was told 'Jesus of Nazareth'. And then he stood at the point of utmost despair and of utmost hope. Utmost hope because Christ was passing within reach, but at the background the looming despair because a few paces would have brought Him level with Bartimaeus, a few more paces and He had gone and would probably never pass by him again. And out of this desperate hope he began to cry and shout 'Jesus, son of David, have mercy on me.' It was a perfect profession of faith. And at that moment it was because his despair was so deep that he could summon such daring hope in order to be healed, saved, made whole. And Christ heard him.

There is a degree of despair that is linked with total, perfect hope. This is the point at which, having gone inward, we will be able to pray; and then 'Lord have mercy' is quite enough. We do not need to make any of the elaborate discourses we find in manuals of prayer. It is enough simply to shout out of despair 'Help!' and you will be heard.

Very often we do not find sufficient intensity in our prayer, sufficient conviction, sufficient faith, because our despair is not deep enough. We want God in addition to so many other things we have, we want His help, but simultaneously we are trying to get help wherever we can, and we keep God in store for our last push. We address ourselves to the princes and the sons of men, and we say 'O God, give them strength to do it for me.' Very seldom do we turn away from the princes and sons of men and say 'I will not ask anyone for help, I would rather have Your help'. If our despair comes from sufficient depth, if what we ask for, cry for, is so essential that it sums up all the needs of our life, then we find words of prayer and we will be able to reach the core of the prayer, the meeting with God.

And now, more about turmoil. The link here is also Bartimaeus. He cried, but what does the Gospel say of everyone around? They tried to silence him, and we can see all the pious people with good sight, with solid legs, with good health, surrounding Christ, speaking of high matters, the kingdom to come, and the mysteries of the Scriptures, turning on Bartimaeus and saying, 'What, can't you keep quiet? Your eyes, your eyes, what do they matter whilst speaking of God?' Bartimaeus was like someone jumping out of context to ask God for something he needed desperately while some ceremonial is going on, and destroying the good harmony. He would be thrown out immediately. He would be silenced. But the Gospel says also that, in spite of all these people who wanted to shout him down, he insisted because it mattered so much to him. The more they tried to silence him, the more he shouted.

Here is my message. There is a saint of Greece called Maxim, a young man, who went to church one day and heard the reading of the Epistle in which it says that we should pray unceasingly. It struck him in such a way that he thought he could do nothing else than fulfil this commandment. He walked out of the church, went into the neighbouring mountains and set out to pray unceasingly. Being a Greek peasant of the fourth century, he knew the Lord's Prayer and some other prayers. So he proceeded, as he tells us, to recite them, again and again and again. Then he felt very well. He was praying, he was with God, he was elated, everything seemed to be so perfect, except that gradually the sun began to go down and it became colder and darker, and as it became darker he began to hear all sorts of worrying sounds – cracking branches under the paws of wild beasts, flashing eyes, sounds of smaller beasts being killed by larger beasts, and so forth. Then he felt that he was really alone, a small, unprotected thing in a world of danger, of death, of murder, and that he had no help if God didn't give it. He no longer continued saying the Lord's Prayer and the Creed; he did exactly what Bartimaeus did, he began to shout 'Lord Jesus Christ, Son of God, have mercy on me'. And he shouted like that all the night because the creatures and the flashing eyes didn't give him a chance to go to sleep. Then the morning came and he thought, because all the beasts had gone to sleep, 'Now I can pray', but by then he felt hungry. He thought he would collect some berries and he started towards a bush, but then he realised that all those flashing eyes and savage paws must be hidden somewhere in the bushes. So he began to make his way very softly and at every step said 'Lord Jesus Christ save me, help me, help me, save me. O God help me, protect me', and for every berry he collected he had certainly prayed several times.

Time passed and after many years he met a very old and experienced ascetic who asked him how he had learnt to pray unceasingly. Maxim said 'I think it's the devil who taught me to pray unceasingly.' The other man said 'I think I understand what you mean, but I would like to be sure that I understand you rightly'.

Nicholas explained how he had gradually become accustomed to all these noises and dangers of the day and night. But then temptations came upon him, temptations of the flesh, temptations of the mind, of the emotions, and later more violent attacks from the devil. After that there was no moment day or night when he did not shout Godwards, saying 'Have mercy, have mercy, help, help, help'. Then one day after fourteen years of that, the Lord appeared to him; and the moment the Lord appeared, stillness, peace, serenity came on him. There was no fear left – of darkness or of bushes, no fear of the devil – the Lord had taken over. 'By then' Maxim said 'I had learned that unless the Lord Himself comes, I am hopelessly and completely helpless. So even when I was serene and peaceful and happy I went on praying 'Lord Jesus Christ, Son of God have mercy on me', because he knew that only in the divine mercy was there any peace of heart and peace of mind and stillness of body and rightness of will.

So Nicholas learnt to pray not in spite of the turmoil, but because of the turmoil, and because the turmoil was a real danger. If we could be aware that we are in much greater turmoil, that the devil is lurking, trying to catch and destroy us, that every human meeting is judgment, is crisis, is a situation in which we are called either to receive Christ or to be Christ's messenger to the person whom we are meeting, if we realised that the whole of life has this intensity of meaning, then we would be able to cry and to pray continuously, and turmoil would be not a hindrance but the very condition which teaches us to pray while we are still too inexperienced to pray from the depth without any prompting, without any incitement into prayer.

When we know nothing about prayer, when we have not prayed at all in our lives or not enough, how can we learn to pray in the conditions of life in which we live? I have experimented on that in a variety of situations: in the years when I was in medical work, five years in the war, in the priesthood and so forth, and it does work. It does work if you are simple enough to do it. It works in this way.

Awake in the morning and the first thing you do, thank God for it, even if you don't feel particularly happy about the day which is to come. 'This day which the Lord has made, let us rejoice and be grateful in it'. Once you have done this, give yourself time to realise the truth of what you are saying and really mean it – perhaps on the level of deep conviction and not of what one might call exhilaration. And then get up, wash, clean, do whatever else you have got to do, and then come to God again. Come to God again with two convictions. The one is that you are God's own and the other is that this day is also God's own, it is absolutely new, absolutely fresh. It has never existed before. To speak in Russian terms, it is like a vast expanse of unsoiled snow. No one has trodden on it yet. It is all virgin and pure in front of you. And now, what comes next? What comes next is that you ask God to bless this day, that everything in it should be blessed and ruled by Him. After that you must take it seriously, because very often one says 'O God bless me', and having got the blessing we act like the prodigal son – we collect all our goods and go to a strange country to lead a riotous life.

This day is blessed by God, it is God's own and now let us go into it. You walk in this day as God's own messenger; whoever you meet, you meet in God's own way. You are there to be the presence of the Lord God, the presence of Christ, the presence of the Spirit, the presence of the Gospel – this is your function on this particular day. God has never said that when you walk into a situation in His own Name, He will be crucified and you will be the risen one. You must be prepared to walk into situations, one after the other, in God's name, to walk as the Son of God has done: in humiliation and humility, in truth and ready to be persecuted and so forth. Usually what we expect when we fulfil God's commandments is to see a marvellous result at once – we read of that at times in the lives of the saints. When, for instance, someone hits us on one cheek, we turn the other one, although we don't expect to be hit at all, but we expect to hear the other person say 'What, such humility' – you get your reward and he gets the salvation of his soul. It does not work that way. You must pay the cost and very often you get hit hard. What matters is that you are prepared for that. As to the day, if you accept that this day was blessed of God, chosen by God with His own hand, then every person you meet is a gift of God, every circumstance you will meet is a gift of God, whether it is bitter or sweet, whether you like or dislike it. It is God's own gift to you and if you take it that way, then you can face any situation. But then you must face it with the readiness that anything may happen, whether you enjoy it or not, and if you walk in the name of the Lord through a day which has come fresh and new out of His own Hands and has been blessed for you to live with it, then you can make prayer and life really like the two sides of one coin. You act and pray in one breath, as it were, because all the situations that follow one another require God's blessing.

A number of years ago I spoke about this at Taizé, and I have remained in correspondence with about thirty of the boys and girls there. One of them wrote to me and said 'I have tried your advice. I have tried it with all my energy. I have not yet had a minute in which I was not praying and acting, praying and acting, and now I can't hear the word of God, I can't bear this sort of prayer.' I said to her 'You've got indigestion. You should have used common sense in prayer, as one uses common sense in life. You cannot, having never prayed before, start with eighteen hours of dialogue and prayer with God continuously like this while you do other things. But you can easily single out one or two moments and put all your energy into them. Simply turn your eyes Godwards, smile at Him and go into it. There are moments when you can tell God "I simply must have a rest, I have no strength to be with You all the time", which is perfectly true. You are still not capable of bearing God's company all the time. Well, say so. God knows that perfectly well, whatever you do about it. Go apart, say for a moment "I'll just have a rest. For a moment I accept to be less saintly".'

In this way we can just rest and look at things which are also God's things – trees and buildings – and then after a while we go back to Him. If we try to pray continuously, we will be defeated quite soon; but if we choose moments intelligently we can do it.

If you do that you will be able to pray. You can experiment, but don't forget to be sober because there is a sin which the Spiritual Fathers call 'spiritual greed', which consists of wanting to have more and more of God at a moment when you should be put on a diet and have just a little and enough for you.

IV

Managing Time

IN THE tense modern life which we live, the problem
of managing time is an all important one. I am not going
to try and convince you that you have plenty of time
and can pray if you want to; I want to speak of managing time within the tensions, the rush of life. I will spare
you any description of the way in which one can make
time: I will only say that if we try and waste a little less
of it, there will be more of it. If we use crumbs of
wasted time to try to build short moments for recollection and prayer, we may discover that there is quite a
lot of it. If you think of the number of empty minutes
in a day when we will be doing something because we
are afraid of emptiness and of being alone with ourselves, you will realise that there are plenty of short
periods which could belong both to us and to God at the
same time. But what I want to speak about is something
which I believe is more important. It is the way in which
we can control and stop time. We can pray to God only
if we are established in a state of stability and inner
peace face to face with God, and these things release us
from the sense of time – not objective time, the kind
we watch – but the subjective sense that time is running
fast and that we have no time left.

First of all I would like to draw your attention to
something which we all know and we all discuss. There

is absolutely no need to run after time to catch it. It does not run away from us, it runs towards us. Whether you are intent on the next minute coming your way, or whether you are completely unaware of it, it will come your way. The future, whatever you do about it, will become the present, and so there is no need to try to jump out of the present into the future. We can simply wait for it to be there, and in that respect we can perfectly well be completely stable and yet move in time, because it is time that moves. You know the situation when you are in a car or on a train and you sit back, if you are not driving, and you look out of the window; you can read, you can think, you can relax, and yet the train moves, and at a certain moment, what was the future, whether it is the next station or the last station to which you are going, will be present. I think this is very important. The mistake we often make with our inner life is to imagine that if we hurry we will be in our future sooner – a little like the man who ran from the last carriage of the train to the first, hoping that the distance between London and Edinburgh would be shortened as a result. When it is that kind of example we see how absurd it is, but when we continually try to live an inch ahead of ourselves, we do not feel the absurdity of it. Yet that is what prevents us from being completely in the present moment, which I dare say is the only moment in which we can be, because even if we imagine that we are ahead of time or ahead of ourselves, we are not. The only thing is that we are in a hurry, but we are not moving more quickly for this. You must have seen that more than once. Someone with two heavy suitcases, trying to catch a bus, rushes: he is as quick as he can be, he runs as fast as the suitcases allow, and he is all intent on being where he is not.

But you know what happens when we take a walk

on holiday. We can walk briskly, gaily and quickly, or if we are of the right age and condition, we can even run, but we don't feel in a hurry at all, because what matters at that moment is the running, not the arriving. This is the kind of thing we must learn about prayer, to establish ourselves in the present. Usually we think or we behave as though the present was an imaginary line, very very thin indeed, between the past and the future, and we roll from the past into the future, continually passing this line in the same way as you can roll an egg on a cloth. If you do this, it runs continuously, it is nowhere at any moment, there is no present, because it is always in the future.

Not everyone is lucky enough to have decisive experiences, 'disclosure situations', which teach him things, but I would like to tell you in a few words about a very useful experience which I had.

During the German occupation of France I was in the resistance movement and, coming down into the Underground, I was caught by the police. This is one of the most interesting experiences I have had. Leaving aside all the romantic trimmings as to what happened and how it happened, I will put it in more philosophical terms concerning time. What took place at that moment was this: I had a past, I had a future, and I was moving out of one into the other by walking briskly down the steps. At a certain moment someone put a hand on my shoulder said 'Stop, give me your papers.' At that moment several things happened. For one thing, I began to think very quickly, feel very intensely, and to be aware of the whole situation with a relief and a colourfulness which I had never before perceived on the last steps of Metro Etoile. The second thing was that I realised that I had no past, because the real past I had was the thing for which I should be shot. So, that past was not there any more. The false past which I was prepared to talk about had never existed, and so I found myself standing there like the lizard who had been caught by the tail and had run away leaving the tail somewhere behind, so that the lizard ended where the tail had been. Then I discovered another thing which was very interesting (though I did not elaborate so much on the philosophy of time at that moment) but what I perceived at once, and what I understood gradually, is that you have a future only to the extent to which you can foresee a minute before it happens, or an inch before you reach it, what will come next – i.e. nothing is coming next because you have no idea of what could come – you are like someone standing in an unknown room in the dark. You stand there and all that's there is darkness pressing on your eyes. There may be nothing ahead of you or infinity ahead of you, it is all the same thing. You end exactly where darkness begins. So I discovered that I had no future either. It was then I discovered that living in the past on the one hand and in the future on the other hand was simply not possible. The lizard had no tail, and darkness was on my face. I discovered that I was pressed into the present moment, and all my past, that is, all the things that could be, were condensed in the present moment with an intensity, a colourfulness that was extremely exhilarating and which allowed me eventually to get away!

Now as far as time is concerned, there are moments, without going into so much detail, when one can perceive that the present moment is there, the past is irremediably gone – it is irrelevant except to the extent to which it is still in the present – and the future is irrelevant because it may happen or it may not. That happens for instance, when you are in an accident, when you are at a moment of danger which requires

extremely quick action. You have no time to roll comfortably from the past into the future. What you have
got to do is to be so completely in the present that all
your energies and all your being is summed up in the
word 'now'. You discover with great interest that *you*
are in the 'now'. You know the very, very thin plane
which geometry teaches us has no thickness. This
geometric plane which has absolutely no thickness,
which is 'now', moves along the lines of time, or rather
time runs under it, and brings to you 'now' everything
you will need in the future. This is the situation we
must learn, and we must learn it in a more peaceful way.
I think we must do exercises in stopping time and in
standing in the present, in this 'now' which is my
present and which is also the intersection of eternity
with time.

What can we do? This is the first exercise. It can be
done at moments when you have absolutely nothing to
do, when nothing pulls you either backward or forward
and when you can use five minutes, three minutes or
half an hour for leisure and for doing nothing. You sit
down and say 'I am seated, I am doing nothing, I will do
nothing for five minutes', and then relax, and continually throughout this time (one or two minutes is the
most you will be able to endure to begin with) realise, 'I
am here in the presence of God, in my own presence and
in the presence of all the furniture that is around me,
just still, moving nowhere.' There is, of course, one more
thing you must do: you must decide that within these
two minutes, five minutes, which you have assigned to
learning that the present exists, you will not be pulled
out of it by the telephone, by a knock on the door, or
by a sudden upsurge of energy that prompts you to
do at once what you have left undone for the past ten
years. So you settle down and say 'Here I am', and you

are. If you learn to do this at lost moments of your life when you have learned not to fidget inwardly, but to be completely calm and happy, stable and serene, then extend the few minutes to a longer time and then to a little while longer still. A moment will come, of course, when you will require some defences, because you can sit quietly for two minutes even if the telephone does ring or someone knocks at the door, whereas fifteen minutes may be too long for either the telephone to ring or for the person to stand at the door. But then make up your mind that if you were not at home you would not open the door, nor would you answer the telephone. Or, if you have more courage, or are more convinced of what you are doing, you can do what my father did. He had a little note on the door saying 'Don't go to the trouble of knocking. I am at home but I will not open the door.' This is a way which is much more decisive, because people understand it at once, whereas if you say 'Kindly wait five minutes', the kindness usually dies out within two minutes!

Then when you have learned this stability, this serenity, you will have to learn to stop time not only at moments when it drags or has stopped anyway, but at moments when it rushes, when it puts forward claims. The way to do it is this. You are doing something which you feel is useful; you feel that unless this is done the world will falter on its course; and then if at a certain moment you say 'I stop', you will discover many things. First, you will discover that the world does not falter and that the whole world – if you can imagine it – can wait for five minutes while you are not busy with it. This is important, because we usually deceive ourselves, saying 'Well, I must do it: it is charity, it is duty, I cannot leave it undone.' You can, because at moments of sheer laziness you will leave it undone for much longer than

the five minutes you have chosen. So the first thing you
say is: 'Whatever happens, I stop here.' The simplest
way to do it is to have an alarm clock. Wind it and say
'Now I am working without looking at the clock until
it rings.' That is very important; one of the things which
we must unlearn, is looking at the clock. If you are
walking somewhere and are aware that you are late, you
look at your watch. But you cannot walk as quickly
while you look at your wrist as if you simply look
straight ahead. And whether you are aware that it is
seven minutes or five or three minutes, you are none
the less late. So add a starting time and you will be there
on time, or else if you are late, walk as fast and as briskly
as you can. When you are at the door, have a look to see
how contrite you must look when the door is opened!
Then, when the alarm clock goes off, you know that for
the next five minutes the world has come to an end and
you will not move from the spot. It is God's own time and
you settle back in His own time quietly, silently and
peacefully. In the beginning you will see how difficult
it is, and you will feel that it is of great importance
that you should finish, say, writing a letter or reading
a paragraph. In reality, you will discover quite soon that
you can very well postpone it for three, five or even ten
minutes and nothing happens. And if you are doing
something that requires attention, you will discover how
much better and more quickly you can do it.

I will give you another example. In the beginning,
when I was a physician, I felt it was most unfair to the
people who were in the waiting room if I was slow in
seeing the person who was with me in the consulting
room. So the first day I tried to be as quick as I could
with those in the consulting room. I discovered by the
end of my surgery hours that I had not the slightest
recollection of the people I had seen, because all the

time a patient was with me, I was looking beyond him with clairvoyant eyes into the next room and counting the heads of those who were not with me. The result was that all the questions I asked I had to ask twice, all the examinations I made I had to make twice or even three times. When I had finished, I could not remember whether I had done these things or not. Of course everyone is not like me, you may be able to recollect much better than I, but this is just an example of what may happen even to one of you.

Then I felt this was simply dishonest, and I decided that I would behave as if the person who was with me was the only one who existed. The moment I began to feel 'I must be quick', I would sit back and engage in small talk for a few minutes just to prevent myself from hurrying. I discovered within two days that you no longer need to do anything like that. You can simply be completely concerned with the person or task that is in front of you, and when you have finished, you will discover that you have spent half the time doing it, instead of all the time you took before; yet you have seen everything and heard everything.

Since then I have often given this kind of advice to many people in a variety of walks of life, and it works. So if you do these exercises, beginning with stopping time that is not moving, and ending with time that is trying to move fast, and you stop and say 'no', you will discover that the moment you have overcome the inner tension, the inner agitation, the fidgeting and the anguish, time passes perfectly well. Can you imagine that only one minute goes by every minute? That is exactly what happens. It is strange, but it is true, though from the way we behave one might think that five minutes could rush past in thirty seconds. No, every minute counts as much as the next minute, every hour as much as the next hour. Nothing disastrous happens at all. You may say 'Shall I have time to do it all?' I will answer you in a very Russian way: 'If you do not die first, you will have time to do it. If you die before it is done, you don't need to do it.' There is another saying of the same kind which you can keep for future reference: 'Do not worry about death. When death is there, you are no longer there, but as long as you are there, death is not.' It is the same principle. Why should I worry about a situation which will resolve itself?

Once you have learned not to fidget, then you can do anything, at any speed, with any amount of attention and briskness, without having the sense of time escaping you or catching up with you. It is like the feeling I spoke of, when you are on holiday, with all your holiday ahead of you. You can be quick or slow, without any sense of time, because you are only doing what you are doing, and there is no purpose. And then you will see that you can pray in every single situation in the world, that there is no situation which can prevent you from praying. What *can* prevent you from praying is that you allow yourself to be in the storm, or you allow the storm to come inside you instead of raging around you.

You may remember the story in the Gospel of the storm on the Sea of Galilee: Christ asleep in the boat and the storm raging around. At first the apostles work hard and hopefully in order to survive. Then at a certain moment they lose heart, and the storm that was outside comes inside – the storm is within them too. Anguish, death no longer simply circle round, they come inside. And then they turn to Christ and do what we very often do with God: we look at God in time of stress and tragedy, and we are indignant that He is so peaceful. The story in the Gospel underlines it by saying that Christ was sleeping with His head on a pillow – the final insult. They are dying and He is comfortable. This is exactly what we feel about God so often. How dare He be blissful, how dare He be so comfortable when *I* am in trouble? And the disciples do exactly what we do so very often. Instead of coming to God and saying 'You are peace, you are the Lord, say a word and my servant will be healed, say a word and things will come right', they shake Him out of His sleep and say 'Don't you care that we are perishing?' In other words, 'If you can do nothing, at least don't sleep. If you can do nothing better, then at least die in anguish with us.' Christ reacts, he gets up and says 'Men of little faith!' and brushing them aside, He turns towards the storm and, projecting His inner stillness, His harmony and peace on the storm He says 'Be still, be quiet' and everything is quiet again.

This we can do, and we must be able to do it. But it requires systematic intelligent training, in exactly the same way as we train to do other things. Learn to master time, and you will be able, whatever you do, whatever the stress, in the storm, in tragedy, or simply in the confusion in which we continuously live – to be still, immobile in the present, face to face with the Lord, in silence or in words. If you use words, then you can bring to God all that is around you, all the storm. If you are silent, you can rest in the 'eye' of the cyclone or the hurricane, in the calm there, but leaving the storm around you to rage, while you are where God is, at the only point of total stability. But this point of total stability is not a point where nothing happens. It is the point where all the conflicting tensions meet and are counterbalanced by one another and are held in the powerful hand of God.

Real silence is something extremely intense, it has density and it is really alive. I remember a passage from the lives of the desert saints in which one of them was asked by his brothers to deliver a spiritual discourse for the benefit of a bishop who was to visit them, and he said 'No, I won't because if my silence doesn't speak to him, my words will be useless.' This is the kind of silence we should try to learn about, or to learn to achieve. How can we do it? What I can try to direct you to is a parable or an image, that of birdwatching.

If we want to watch birds in their stirring in the woods or the fields, we must be awake before them We must be prepared to be alert, alive, completely out of sleep before the first bird wakes. Indeed, before the birds are aware that morning has come. We must go into the fields or into the woods and settle there absolutely still, absolutely silent, absolutely relaxed, so that we should never stir and frighten the light sleepers which are around us, because otherwise they will make their way into the distance and fly off where we can neither hear nor see them. Birdwatching implies on the one hand this stillness, this quiet, this repose, and at the same time an intense alertness, because if you sit in the fields dreaming the undreamt dreams of your short night, all the birds will have gone long before you realise that the sun is warming your back. It is essential to be alert and alive, and at the same time still and relaxed, and this is contemplative preparation for contemplative silence; this very difficult balance between the kind of alertness that will allow you with a completely open mind, completely free from prejudice, from expectation, to receive the impact of anything that will come your way, and at the same time this stillness that will allow you to receive the impact without dreaming into it the picture of your own presence that will be destructive of it.

About twenty years ago, soon after my ordination, I

was sent before Christmas to an old people's home.
There lived an old lady, who died some time later at
the age of 102. She came to see me after my first celebra-
tion and said 'Father, I would like to have advice about
prayer.' So I said 'Oh yes, ask So-and-so.' She said 'All
these years I have been asking people who are reputed to
know about prayer, and they have never given me a
sensible reply, so I thought that as you probably know
nothing, you may by chance blunder out the right
thing.' That was a very encouraging situation! And so
I said 'What is your problem?' The old lady said 'These
fourteen years I have been praying the Jesus Prayer
almost continually, and never have I perceived God's
presence at all.' So I blundered out what I thought. I
said 'If you speak all the time, you don't give God a
chance to place a word in.' She said 'What shall I do?' I
said 'Go to your room after breakfast, put it right, place
your armchair in a strategic position that will leave
behind your back all the dark corners which are always
in an old lady's room into which things are pushed so
as not to be seen. Light your little lamp before the ikon
that you have and first of all take stock of your room.
Just sit, look round, and try to see where you live,
because I am sure that if you have prayed all these fourteen years it is a long time since you have seen your
room. And then take your knitting and for fifteen
minutes knit before the face of God, but I forbid you
to say one word of prayer. You just knit and try to
enjoy the peace of your room.'

She didn't think it was very pious advice but she took
it. After a while she came to see me and said 'You know,
it works.' I said 'What works, what happens?' because
I was very curious to know how my advice worked. And
she said 'I did just what you advised me to do. I got up,
washed, put my room right, had breakfast, came back,

made sure that nothing was there that would worry me, and then I settled in my armchair and thought "Oh how nice, I have fifteen minutes during which I can do nothing without being guilty!" and I looked round and for the first time after years I thought "Goodness what a nice room I live in – a window opening onto the garden, a nice shaped room, enough space for me, the things I have collected for years".' Then she said 'I felt so quiet because the room was so peaceful. There was a clock ticking but it didn't disturb the silence, its ticking just underlined the fact that everything was so still and after a while I remembered that I must knit before the face of God, and so I began to knit. And I became more and more aware of the silence. The needles hit the armrest of my chair, the clock was ticking peacefully, there was nothing to bother about, I had no need of straining myself, and then I perceived that this silence was not simply an absence of noise, but that the silence had substance. It was not absence of something but presence of something. The silence had a density, a richness, and it began to pervade me. The silence around began to come and meet the silence in me.' And then in the end she said something very beautiful which I have found later in the French writer, Georges Bernanos. She said 'All of a sudden I perceived that the silence was a presence. At the heart of the silence there was Him who is all stillness, all peace, all poise.'

After that she lived for about ten more years and she said that she could always find the silence when she was quiet and silent herself. This does not mean that she stopped praying, it means that she could sustain this contemplative silence for a while, then her mind began to quiver and she turned to vocal prayer until the mind was still and settled again, then she dropped out of words into silence as before. Very often this could happen to us – if instead of being so intent on doing things, we could simply say 'I am in God's presence, what a joy, let us be still.'

In the life of a Catholic priest of France, the Curé d'Ars, Jean Marie Vianney, there is a story of an old peasant who used to spend hours and hours sitting in the chapel motionless, doing nothing. The priest said to him 'What are you doing all these hours?' The old peasant said 'I look at Him, He looks at me and we are happy.'

This can be reached only if we learn a certain amount of silence. Begin with the silence of the lips, with the silence of the emotions, the silence of the mind, the silence of the body. But it would be a mistake to imagine that we can start at the highest end, with the silence of the heart and the mind. We must start by silencing our lips, by silencing our body in the sense of learning to keep still, to let tenseness go, not to fall into day-dreaming and slackness, but to use the formula of one of our Russian saints, to be like a violin string, wound in such a way that it can give the right notes, neither wound too much to breaking point, nor too little so that it only buzzes. And from then onwards we must learn to listen to silence, to be absolutely quiet, and we may, more often than we imagine, discover that the words of the Book of Revelation come true: 'I stand at the door and knock.'

In the next chapter we will consider the basic conditions for establishing prayer in connection with address-ing God and being able to speak to Him.

V

Addressing God

IN THIS chapter I would like to say something about
the moment when we are so disposed that prayer
becomes really possible and live. In view of what I have
said before and the assumptions that have been constantly present in the background, prayer is obviously
a relationship, an encounter a way in which we have
a relationship with the living God. There is a moment
when this relationship becomes something live. And
since it is a question of relationship, I want to start with
something that refers equally to prayer and to human
relationships.

A relationship becomes personal and real the moment
you begin to single out a person from the crowd. That
is when this person becomes unique in his own right,
when he ceases to be anonymous. Someone has spoken
of 'the anonymous society' in which instead of having
names and surnames and qualities and personality, we
are defined in general terms like 'the ratepayers', and
so forth. In our relationships with people there is very
often this element of anonymity: 'they'. We speak in
the third person when we feel that someone can easily
be replaced by someone else, because the relationship
is functional, not personal, and this *function* can be
fulfilled by someone else, while this *person* would not be
replaceable by anyone else. In other languages I would

have said that a relationship becomes real the moment when one begins to think of a person in terms of 'thou' instead of 'you'. It does not require a change of language, it is an inner change. You know very well, I am sure, that one can have this 'I' and 'thou' relationship or an 'I' and 'it' relationship with someone.

Prayer begins at the moment when, instead of thinking of a remote God, 'He', 'The Almighty', and so forth, one can think in terms of 'Thou', when it is no longer a relationship in the third person but in the first and second persons. Take, for instance, the Book of Job, where there is a conflict. Take so many other instances in Scripture and in life, in the lives of saints and sinners, when there was tension and a violent confrontation. This is always a personal thing. There is no prayer as long as there is a cautious, distant and chilly relationship, as long as there is ceremonial between us and God, as long as we cannot speak to Him but must go through a long and complex series of words and actions. But there is a moment when, instead of all this, we pierce through and speak in the first and second person. We say 'I' and we expect Him to be 'Thou', or 'You' in the singular. Let it not be the polite, the royal 'You' but the singular and unique 'You.'

And then there is another moment in a warm human relationship: the moment when we look for a name for a person. I am not speaking now of a general surname empty of meaning, but of when we begin to see how this person relates to a name. You know, for instance, how personal in a positive and also a negative way a nickname can be. A nickname may be a way of crushing you down, of ruling you out, of destroying everything there is between two people; but it may also be a name which only two people use, or a very small group of persons, who are so deeply and so intimately linked to each other

that the name is filled with meaning for them, because
it is supremely personal. The more absurd it is, in a way,
the more personal it is, because no one else would invent
it except you.

Then there is the surname. The surname often seems
to us to be alien, a general term like 'humanity'; so many
people have the same surname. And yet if we look at
it more attentively in human relationships, we can
realise that the surname is the mark of a community.
From generation to generation back in history, people
who are of our blood, whose life is within our bones,
within our heredity, within our minds, have had this
name, and this name links us back very far to generations of people and will probably link us forward to
others, and by the various links of marriage and family
will constitute a vast network of people deeply connected
with each other. If, instead of thinking of surnames, you
think of heredity, of genealogy, is it not what we find in
two of the Gospels concerning the Lord? Is this not the
very thing which this genealogy points to: a link from
generation to generation with concrete, real human
beings? So a surname is something that we can treat
with immense interest, because it holds all our past in
one word, and if we thought of other people in these
terms, surnames could themselves come to life. Instead
of being an expression of someone's uniqueness and of
his uniqueness in his relationship with us, as is a nickname, it would link us all of a sudden to this unique
person, to a whole world of beings . . .

Then there is the Christian name, the name which
we receive in baptism: it is the name by which God
takes possession of the person. The Christian name
links the person with God, because as he receives it he
dies with Christ and rises again, but also it links him
with a variety of people who have been granted this

same name, and first of all with the one who made a pagan name into a Christian name, the first saint who brought it to the Church.

We also have another name, one which we do not know. You remember the passage in the Book of the Revelation which says that in the Kingdom each will receive a white stone with a name written on it, a name which is known only to God and to him who receives it. This is no nickname, no family name, no Christian name. It is a name, a word, that is exactly identical with us, which coincides with us, which *is* us. We may almost say it is a word which God pronounced when he willed us into existence and which is us, as we are it. This name defines our absolute and un-repeatable uniqueness as far as God is concerned. No one can know the name, as no one can, in the last analysis, know anyone as God knows him; and yet it is out of this name that everything else comes that can be known about us.

You may be wondering why I am concentrating on names. It is because part of our prayer is related directly to God and is our personal link with Him, but another part of our prayer is our link with the whole outside world, and when we pray for each other, when we pray for the world, we are bringing to God names and nothing else. But these names are full of meaning or empty of meaning according to circumstances, accord-ing to whether or not we are able to sense the depth of what we say. If we name people before God without any sense of name, simply using names as labels, empty of depth, our relationship is of poor quality; if we pronounce a name with any of the significance I have tried very briefly to express, then our prayer becomes not only a bringing forth of a person on our open hands, as it were, but it links us to this person with a depth not of compassion, not of love, but of identification, sharing, solidarity, which has quite a different quality.

This is also true in the other direction. Unless we can find the right name for God, we have no free, real, joyful, open access to Him. As long as we have to call God by general terms like 'The Almighty,' 'The Lord God', as long as we have got to put 'the' before the word to make it anonymous, to make it a generic term, we cannot use it as a personal name. But there are moments when the sacred writers, for instance, burst out with something which has the quality of a nick-name, something which no one else could possibly say, which is at the limit of the possible and the impossible, which is made possible only because there is a relation-ship. Remember the psalm in which, after more restrained forms of expression, suddenly David bursts out, 'You, my Joy!' That is the moment when the whole psalm comes to life. Saying 'O Thou our Lord', 'O You are the Almighty', and the like, was stating to God facts about Him, but bursting out and saying 'O You my Joy!' was quite a different thing. And when we can say to God 'O You my Joy!' or when you can say 'O You the pain of my life, O You who are standing in the midst of it as torment, as a problem, as a stumbling block!', when we can address Him with violence, then we have established a relationship of prayer.

And so it is very important for us to have a look and find out whether there are names in our experience that apply to God. For one thing, the use of names may change from time to time. There are moments when we perceive one aspect of our relationship with God, and at other times we see other aspects, exactly in the same way in which, in friendly or affectionate relationships with each other, we do not choose one single expression for speaking to one another, but a variety of shades and nuances. We have 'The Almighty', we have 'The Lord', we have 'The Creator', we have 'The Provider', we have 'Wisdom', but we also have a very simple name like Jesus, which is, shall I say, a Christian name.

It may sound rather strange to say that Christ has a Christian name, and I hope you will understand what I mean. It reminds me of a discussion which one of my parishioners, who is a Christian, had with her husband, who is not. He spent forty years of his life trying to give her evidence that Christianity is worthless, and one day, in desperation, she said 'How *can* you say that, when God was first of all a Jew and then became a Christian?' The way in which I say that Jesus is a Christian name may remind you very much of this very primitive approach, yet it is a human name, the first Christian written in the roll of the Church. And if we remember this, if we become aware of the closeness it establishes between Him and us, then we will understand why generations of Christians have fastened on this name; probably not because St. Paul says 'At the Name of Jesus every knee shall bow', for though it is certainly true, it is not this which makes a name warm, lovable. That would be tantamount to speaking of 'The Almighty' or 'The Lord', but the name of Jesus is a live, real, personal name.

And you may find many other names. I am quite certain that if some day 'O Thou my Joy!' or any other cry of this kind bursts out of you, it will be the moment when you will have discovered a relationship between Him and you which is your own, which is not a relationship that you share with many other people. I do not mean to say that you should not share it. We have words for God which belong to all of us, but there are words that belong only to me or to you in the same way in which, in human relationships, there are surnames.

there are Christian names, there are nicknames. It is good if you can have a nickname by which you can call the Almighty God, a nickname that has all the depth of your heart, all the warmth you are capable of; it becomes your way of saying 'In my uniqueness this is the way I perceive your uniqueness.'

If in the process of discovering where you stand in relation to God – how far you are an outsider – you come to the point of knocking, of going deeper and deeper into yourself, turning your prayer *on yourself,* bringing yourself to the point where there *is* a door to knock on, the point where it *can* be opened – there *will* come a moment when the door *will* open, but then you must have a name for God. You must be able to say a word that shows that it is *you* who have been in search of Him, and not just an interchangeable human being in quest of an anonymous God.

In the process of searching you will have endured pain, anguish, hope, expectation – all the range of human emotions. God will have been the desired One and He will have been the frustrating One. He will have been the One you long for and the One you hate because He escapes you, the One you love beyond everything, without whom you cannot live, and whom you cannot forgive, because He does not respond, and many other things. And out of this search there will gradually emerge words which you can speak to God out of your own experience of the quest of the Grail, words which are your own. You may discover that they coincide with many words which others have used. Then they will cease to be anonymous words, they will be words which you have in common with other people but which have become truly yours. But do not use words which are in the common dictionary, words which do not belong to you. When you begin to hear a chain rattling on the door, when you have a feeling that it will open, then come out with the words which are your own and call God by the name which He has won in your own life. At that moment you will have met. In the ever deepening and enriching relationship that follows, you will have a great deal of time to discover other words, to discard the words of hatred and anguish. Like the martyrs spoken of in the Book of Revelation, you will say 'Thou hast been just and true in all Thy ways' (Rev. 15:3). And these words then will wipe out all the words of bitterness, all the names that sound cruel; but you will keep names which are personal, which are your own, and which will be a real relationship and a real way of being related to the living God.

What I have said about 'learning to pray' is, I think, practical enough so that you can experiment. Quite obviously there is a great deal more that should have been said about the same things and a great deal more that one should say about other things, but do try to experiment along the lines I have suggested and you will see that it is not a waste of time. Search for a name, and if you have no name, do not be surprised that no one hears you: you are not calling.

VI

Two Meditations

THE MOTHER OF GOD

THERE ARE two types of ikons of the Mother of God. The usual type is that which you find in East and West – the Virgin holding the child. This is an image of several things and not only the Mother of God as a person. It is an image of the Incarnation, an assertion of the Incarnation and its reality. It's an assertion of the true and real motherhood of the Virgin. And, if you look attentively at the ikon, you will see that the Mother of God holding the Child never looks at the Child. She always looks neither at you nor into the distance but her open eyes look deep inside her. She is in contemplation. She is not looking at things. And her tenderness is expressed by the shyness of her hands. She holds the Child without hugging him. She holds the Child as one would hold something sacred that one is bringing as an offering, and all the tenderness, all the human love, is expressed by the Child, not by the mother. She remains the Mother of God and she treats the child, not as baby Jesus, but as the Incarnate Son of God who has become the son of the Virgin and He, being true man and true God, expresses to her all the love and tenderness of man and God both to His mother and to His creature. This is one image.

Another image, which you find very seldom, is the image of the Mother of God alone, without the obvious presence of Christ. I will describe just one of them. It is a Russian ikon of the 17th century. You see a Russian peasant girl who has lost her veil, whose hair, parted in the middle just falls down on a rather square face. Her eyes are big and she is looking into infinity or into the depths. Certainly not a view of anything which is in front of her. If you look more you see two hands. Two hands that couldn't be where they are simply because anatomy wouldn't allow it. They are not there to be part of a realistic picture, they are there to express what neither the face nor the hands nor the eyes could express without ceasing to express something more important. They are hands of anguish. And then, in the corner of the ikon, almost invisible, pale yellow on pale yellow background, a little mount and an empty cross. This is the mother contemplating the crucifixion and death of her only begotten son.

When we turn to the Mother of God in prayer, we should realise more often than we do that any prayer we offer to the Mother of God means this: 'Mother, I have killed thy son. If you forgive me, I can be forgiven. It you withhold forgiveness *nothing* can save me from damnation.' And it is amazing that the Mother of God, in all which is revealed in the Gospel, has made us understand, and made us bold to come to her with this very prayer, because there is nothing else we can say. To us she is the Mother of God. She is the one who brought God Himself into our earthly situation. In that sense we insist on this term 'Mother of God'. Through her God became Man. He was born into the human situation through her. And she is not to us simply an instrument of the Incarnation. She is the one whose personal surrender to God, her love of God, her readi-

ness to be whatever God wills, her humility in the sense
in which I have spoken about it to you already, is such
that God could be born of her. There is, in one of our
great saints and theologians of the 14th century, a
passage on the Mother of God in which he says 'The
Incarnation would have been as impossible without the
"Here am I, the handmaid of God" of the Virgin, just
as it would have been impossible without the will of the
Father.' Here there is a total co-operation between
her and God. Speaking of the Incarnation and the
attitude of the Blessed Virgin, I think an English writer
has put it in a remarkable way – Charles Williams in
his novel *All Hallows Eve*. He says of the Incarnation
that what makes its uniqueness is that 'one day a virgin
of Israel was capable of pronouncing the sacred name
with all her heart, all her mind, all her being, all her
body, in such a way that in her word became flesh'. I
think this is a very good theological statement that
signifies the place which she has in the Incarnation.

We love her, we feel perhaps in her in a peculiar
way we see the Word of God spoken by Paul who says
'My power is made manifest in weakness.' We can see
this frail virgin of Israel, this frail girl, defeating sin in
her, defeating hell, defeating everything by the power of
God which is in her. And this is why at moments like
persecutions, when indeed the power of God is made
manifest in nothing but weakness, the Blessed Virgin
stands out so miraculously, so powerfully in our eyes. If
she could defeat earth and hell then we have in her a
tower of strength and one who can intercede and save,
and we mark the fact that in her there is no discrepancy
with the will of God, that she is in perfect harmony with
Him, by using a formula of prayer which we use only
for God and for her, 'Save us'. We don't say 'Pray for
us'.

STARETZ SILOUAN

In 1938 a man died on Mount Athos*. He was a very simple man, a peasant from Russia who came to Mount Athos when he was in his twenties and stayed for about fifty years. He was a man of utmost simplicity. He had gone to Athos because he had read in a pamphlet about the Holy Mountain that the Mother of God had given a promise that anyone who would serve the Lord in these monasteries, she would stand for him and pray for him. So he just abandoned his village and said 'If the Mother of God is prepared to stand for me, there I go, and her business is to save me.' He was a most remarkable man and for a long time he was in charge of the workshops of the monastery. The workshops of the monastery were manned by young Russian peasants who used to come for one year, for two years, in order to make some money, really farthing added to farthing, in order to go back to their villages with a few pounds, perhaps, at the utmost to be able to start a family by marrying, by building a hut and by buying enough to start their crops. One day other monks, who were in charge of other workshops, said 'Father Silouan, how is it that the people who work in your workshops work so well while you never supervise them, while we spend our time looking after them and they try continuously to cheat us in their work?' Father Silouan said 'I don't know. I can only tell you what I do about it. When I come in the morning, I never come without having prayed for these people and I come with my heart filled with compassion and with love for them, and when I walk into the workshop I have tears in my soul for love of them.

* A book has been written about his life: Archimandrite Sofrony, *The Undistorted Image*, trans. by Rosemary Edmunds, The Faith Press 1958.

And then I give them the task they have to perform in the day and as long as they will work I will pray for them, so I go into my cell and I begin to pray about each of them individually. I take my stand before God and I say "O Lord, remember Nicholas. He is young, he is just twenty, he has left in his village his wife, who is even younger than he, and their first child. Can you imagine the misery there is there that he has had to leave them because they could not survive on his work at home. Protect them in his absence. Shield them against every evil. Give him courage to struggle through this year and go back to the joy of a meeting, with enough money, but also enough courage, to face the difficulties".' And he said 'In the beginning I prayed with tears of compassion for Nicholas, for his young wife, for the little child, but as I was praying the sense of the divine presence began to grow on me and at a certain moment it grew so powerful that I lost sight of Nicholas, his wife, his child, his needs, their village, and I could be aware only of God, and I was drawn by the sense of the divine presence deeper and deeper, until of a sudden, at the heart of this presence, I met the divine love holding Nicholas, his wife, and his child, and now it was with the love of God that I began to pray for them again, but again I was drawn into the deep and in the depths of this I again found the divine love. And so', he said, 'I spend my days, praying for each of them in turn, one after the other and when the day is over I go, I say a few words to them, we pray together and they go to their rest. And I go back to fulfil my monastic office.'

Here you can see how contemplative prayer, compassion, active prayer was an effort and a struggle, because it was not just saying 'Remember O Lord, him, him and him.' It was hours and hours spent just praying with compassion, praying with love, both blending together.

METROPOLITAN ANTHONY
OF SOUROZH

God and Man

CONTENTS

CHAPTER ONE

THE ATHEIST AND THE ARCHBISHOP[1]

Marghanita Laski and Archbishop Anthony Bloom

I

Laski: You believe in God, and you think this is good and right. I don't believe in God, and I think it's good and right. Now we're neither of us frivolous people, we're serious, we've reached our decision as carefully as we can. There's a lot of people like me, there's a lot of people, probably a lot more people, like you. How do you explain this basic, one could say this *fundamental* difference?

Bloom: I really don't know how to explain it but it seems to me that the word 'belief' is misleading. It gives an impression of something optional, which is within our powers to choose or not. What I feel very strongly about it, is that I believe because I know that God exists, and I'm puzzled how you manage not to know.

Laski: This brings me to the next thing I wanted to ask you, which is about faith. I know that faith is a major Christian virtue but to me it's nearer a vice and I cannot see why you need it. When you say 'I know that God exists' and many people do say this for one reason or another because they've experienced God or because they see God in the shape of the universe. But if you know, you don't need faith. And if you don't know, to me as an unbeliever, it's almost throwing away the most important

[1] Transcript of televised interviews, transmitted 5th and 12th July, 1970; with grateful acknowledgement to the BBC.

thing about a human being, to substitute faith for not knowing. To me, the right thing when you don't know is to wait on knowledge or to say 'I don't know'. If you know that God exists, why should faith be considered a virtue?

Bloom: I think it's a question of the definition of faith. I remember having read in a rather facetious theological book a definition of faith as the ability which grown-ups possess to assert that things are true when they know that they are not true.

Laski: That's rather nice . . . .

Bloom: If that is faith, I'm afraid I don't possess it. I think faith is best defined in the words of the Epistle to the Hebrews, when the writer says 'Faith is certainty about things invisible.' It is certainty, that is the operative word, and things which are invisible are not simply things imagined. Speaking for instance of myself and a number of other people, I'm sure we began with an experience that was totally convincing. Now at a certain moment this experience faded away, as does every experience of beauty, of love, of joy, of pain. There is a moment when it is no longer actual, but the certainty of it has remained. And this is the moment when faith comes into it. But faith doesn't mean credulity; it means that the certainty remains about something which is not our actual present experience of things.

Laski: If you use the word faith, surely it must imply that you have faith in the face of possible doubt? But if you have certainty, then there's no room for doubt, and so I'm sorry, I can't see any need for faith—isn't certainty enough?

Bloom: You are in the same position as I in a way. You have a certainty, concerning the non-existence of God, which in a way is an act of faith, because you have as little evidence you can produce outwardly as I have to produce outwardly.

Laski: Wouldn't you say there was a fundamental difference in way of thinking about, or way of approaching problems of the invisible, that there could be a temperamental preference for having certainty about the invisible, and for reserving judgment about the invisible?

Bloom: I'm not sure, I think my attitude to things is very much determined by the kind of education I have had. I was trained to be a scientist and I treat things as experimental science—perhaps wrongly, perhaps rightly. But as far as faith is concerned, for instance, I started with something which was an experience which seemed to be convincing, that God does exist. Doubt comes into it not as questioning this fundamental experience but as questioning my intellectual workings out of it. And in that respect the doubt of the believer should be as creative, as daring, as joyful, almost as systematic as the doubt of a scientist who, having discovered facts that have convinced him up to a point of something, will begin to find the flaw in his reasoning, the error in his system, or new facts that will invalidate his model of the universe.

Laski: But his moment of discovering, as it seems to him, a new pattern in the universe, is equally convincing whether his examination of the pattern shows it to be true or false. The scientist will no doubt value the feeling that comes with the new discovery, but he wouldn't regard that feeling as validating, as you say; he would afterwards make tests and so on. But you don't, do you, admit an experience of feeling as if God exists which doesn't necessarily say whether God exists or not?

Bloom: I don't think it's wholly a question of feeling. I don't think for instance that feeling can be simply unreasonable or completely absurd, and yet kept against every other evidence. But I would say for instance if you transfer, for a moment, from faith in God to other fields—music, say—from the point of view of a scientist, music can be put in drawing, in line, in mathematical formula. When you've got them all it does not give you a clue as to whether this is a beautiful piece of music or whether it is just discordant noise. There is a moment when you listen and you say this is music and not simply noise.

Laski: Certainly, although one of the things I most want to know about is why good music, good poetry, good art, has the effect on us it does, and I always assume that experiences of God include such a patterning. I as an atheist would never want to doubt the profound knowledge that the Churches, synagogues, mosques, have acquired over the centuries, into human nature, into human thought, into human physical responses. Now you've written greatly about interior prayer and even before I read your book I was very much interested in this because it seemed to me clearly that it worked. That is to say, people who attempted contemplative prayer received benefit from it. And this I have tried, I have tried it a great deal recently, because I've just had a very bad slipped disc, and I don't like painkillers. And it seemed to me that to try contemplative prayer, as St Gregory describes it, meditating on the Lord's Prayer for instance, might help my pain. And indeed it did. So I assume that here the Church has discovered a mental technique which is therapeutic, which is beneficial. But it seems to me that in the case of this experience of prayer, as in other experiences called religious, the Church has, so to speak, pre-empted them, said 'These are our experiences, these lead to God.' I'm not pretending my attempts compare with anything that a trained religious could do, but are you not holding to yourselves and giving explanations which are unacceptable to atheists of various techniques and modes of living that could help all humanity, perhaps even in this time of recourse to drugs —could help humanity with greater need than ever before?

Bloom: As far as techniques and methods are concerned, I quite agree that you are right, and I could give you an example in your favour as it were, about a group of drug addicts who by chance read 'The Cloud of Unknowing' and addressed themselves to a priest, not to me, to say: 'We have discovered that this is exactly what we are looking for and it would be a much cheaper thing for us to get it that way than through the drugs we are using—'

Laski: —And much healthier.

Bloom: Much healthier. And we have experience now of a number of drug addicts for instance who discover through meditation what they were looking for through drugs, and move away from drugs into another world. As far as technique is concerned I think it is completely true, because techniques are founded on our common humanity. Whatever the object you pursue, your thinking is your human thinking, your emotions and feelings are your human emotions and so forth. What the believer would say is that for some reason, the same kind of reason that makes you recognise beauty in music, in nature, in art and so on, he would say: 'This experience which I had is neither my emotions nor my wishful thinking, nor my physical condition at that moment; it was a meeting with something different, profoundly other than myself, and which I cannot trace back even with decent knowledge of sociology, or psychology, or biology, to anything which is me, and within me.'

Laski: This is the fundamental difference between us, isn't it? Whether this feeling that we have encountered is something other than oneself, is a self-induced feeling or is an other-induced feeling, an other-derived feeling. Is this not what separates us most?

Bloom: Yes. A believer would say: 'I objectively know that he exists, which means I have knowledge acquired and not manufactured.' But doesn't it apply in the same way to things like irrational experiences in common life? Like love, like the sense of beauty, in art, music and so on?

Laski: I would guess that the sense of beauty is irrational only for the present until explained. I always think of the philosopher Hume, who two hundred years ago said we know that bread does us good but we shall never know why and of course now we do know why. And I think we shall, perhaps in the not very distant future, come to learn what kind of patterning it is that affects us and that we call beautiful.

Bloom: That may well be, but why don't you think that we may by the same process come to a point when by the study, say, of brainwaves and that kind of thing, we will be able to discover that at such a moment something has intruded or come into our experience which is not intrinsic to our physical body. Logically, it's as credible as the other one.

Laski: This is what I would most like to know and of course if the experiment worked your way, there would be no alternative to being a believer. I simply suspect it would work my way. But Archbishop, supposing I had, as any of us unbelievers might have, a sudden experience of the kind you describe as certainty that God existed. Supposing that it didn't take place in any religious context. Let's say like St Ignatius Loyola, I was sitting by a river. Now I know I was brought up a Jew, but I've lived in England, which is as they say the country of a hundred religions and one sauce, why should anything follow from this? I can understand that it would be sensible to join a religion for fear of the kind of arrogant madness that falls upon people who think that they have a direct personal line to God, but from this experience of God, what should lead me to suppose I've encountered a Christian, a Jewish, a Moslem God? That he would want me to be a Methodist or a Russian Orthodox or a Church of England? What should make one take a step further than having this experience and saying: 'Fine, I now have the certainty that God exists?'

Bloom: It would proceed in different steps—if you had, and I'm certain one can have an experience of God outside any context, of previous religiosity or religious background, then you will probably discover that if God does exist it has immediate implications as to your situation with regard to men in general. . . .

Laski: Please explain because this is what I want to understand.

Bloom: Readily. My experience in childhood was that life was violent, brutal, heartless, that men were to one another adversaries and causes of suffering, that there were on the whole just a few, the closest around you, who belonged together, and who were no danger to you. And my situation when I was a young teenager, was that all these people were dangers. One had to fight, to overcome in order to survive, and eventually to hit back as hard as one could in order to win the day.

Laski: This was truly your situation, I believe, wasn't it?

Bloom: That was the experience I had, in a slum school, and in the early years of revolution and so on—not in Russia but abroad. Now, when I discovered God and I discovered Him in connection with the Gospel, the first thing that struck me is that here was a God for whom everyone was meaningful, who was not segregating people, who was not the God of the good versus the bad, the God of the believer versus the unbeliever, the God of one type versus another. That everyone existed for him as a completely meaningful and valuable person. And if I had discovered that God, then that was the attitude I had to discover with regard to all my surroundings. And you know, I felt with amazement that the fact that I had discovered that God was such, and that that was his relatedness to everyone else, upturned me completely. I looked around and I no longer saw the detestable hateful creatures, but people who were in relationship with Him, and with whom I could come into a new relationship, if I believed about them what God believes about them.

Laski: But it is a fact that non-believers can have this experience of respectful love, charitable love, to all creatures, without the need for God. I'm not a good Socialist, but I think that people who are really good Socialists, in the basic sense, not the political sense of the word, have this feeling. It's not necessary to have God to have the sense of the worth of each human being.

Bloom: No, I don't mean to say that it is necessary. I would say it is not necessary to know that God exists to be a human being, and not below the mark as I was quite definitely. Neither is it necessary I would say, to know that God exists for Him to exist in fact. To me the problem of God is this. He is not something I need to have a world outlook. I don't need God to fill gaps in my world outlook. I have discovered that he exists and I can't help it, exactly in the same way as I have discovered facts in science. He is a fact for me, and that's why He has significance and plays a role in a way exactly in the same sense in which having discovered that a person exists, life becomes different from the moment before you had become aware of the person.

Laski: Could I ask you to be a bit concrete about this? For instance this is rather a debating point I'm going to make, but I thing it's a valid one. For the past five hundred years, since science escaped from the bounds of the Church, it's leapt ahead, so that it's a commonplace now to say that our technological, our scientific knowledge is beyond our moral capacity. The Church, on the other hand, has had two thousand years to develop our moral capacity, if this is one of its functions. But you have said that one can come to this awareness of the real individual—what's the Christian word I want?—for the existence, the respectful existence of every human being. And this entails, I think, a kind of behaviour to human beings which makes a link between belief in God and morals. Is there a necessary link between belief in God and morals? What is it? And since the Church doesn't seem in two thousand years to have made us good—in fact I would claim that it's secular thought that has done most to improve us over the past two hundred years—can the Church be said to have fulfilled this function? In other words, how do morals follow from belief in God? Why has the Church failed to make us moral beings?

Bloom: I think quite certainly morals should follow our belief in God because if we see the world structured around a certain number of great principles, it should make a difference to our behaviour...

Laski: What are the great principles?

Bloom: Love, let us say... love, justice.

Laski: Because you feel love when you encounter God? Because God seems to be a creature of love and justice?—I mean where do these virtues come into the encounter with God?

Bloom: Let me limit myself to the Gospel which will be easier than to try to embrace a wider field. The whole teaching of the Gospel is really a teaching about loving. Now the fact that we fall short of it condemns us, but doesn't make its declaration less true. I'm quite prepared to say that individually and collectively we have fallen very short of that ideal. Now what I'm more doubtful about, is what you said about secular thought because my impression is that west European secular thought at least, or the secular thought developed from west European culture is impregnated with the Gospel, for instance the notion of the value of the person is something which the Gospel has introduced into ancient society which simply didn't possess it. And there are so many things which now have become common ground, universally accepted, which were novelties in their time and which now work in society as leaven works in dough.

Laski: I would agree with you completely about this. I'm only saying that over the past two hundred years, at least since the middle of the eighteenth century, these principles which do seem to me to be the glory of western civilisation, have passed effectively into the hands of the seculars and from the hands of the religious, that insofar as there has been a moral leap forward over this period, and I think there has been one, it's not I think, the Churches, the synagogues, that we have to thank for it.

Bloom: There are two things that strike me—the one is that the believers have had and still have a most unfortunate tendency to escape the difficulties and the problems of life into 'worship' in inverted commas.

Laski: Yes, I'm glad you brought that up.

Bloom: That quite certainly. It's much easier to retire to one's room and say: 'Oh God, give bread to the hungry,' than to do something about it. I have just been in America and someone was making discourse about his readiness to give his life for the hungry and the needy, and I asked him why he was a chain smoker and didn't give simply a packet of cigarettes for it.

Laski: And I can throw another example at you. All of us who have children and meet a lot of young people . . . . meet the people who ask for more love in the world but find it impossible to give it to the older generation.

Bloom: Yes, that's true too. So that is quite definite. We have been escaping into a world of irresponsible prayer, instead of realising that if I say to God, 'Here is a need. Help,' I must be prepared to hear God answer within me, without waiting for a revelation. 'You have seen that—well go and do it.' So that is a way in which we have failed, and which is one of the reasons why we have gone wrong.

Laski: Could I suggest that another reason why I think you and

the secular do-gooders also have failed is because of a rejection
of the world not just as you say, going into one's room
and failing to do the good that lies to hand, but a feeling that
the world and particularly the urban world of today, is a hell—
a Satanic mill, a place to be avoided. There's no gaiety in
religion, for instance, there's no enjoyment of a jolly life. The
pleasures that we normally take in society, even if you like the
pleasures of amassing possessions, of sitting in our little castles
with our refrigerators round us and our children playing at our
feet—these to me are healthful pleasures. But I think that serious
people, serious religious people, serious non-religious people, have
always regarded these things that we genuinely enjoy as human
animals, as clogs in the way of the good life.

Bloom: I think they are right up to a point. I think it takes a
great deal of mastery of self not to forget what is deepest
in oneself to the profit of what is more superficial. It's easier to
be superficial than deep, it's easier to be on that level rather than
face things that may be tragic. You see the difficulty is that we
have made it into a false moral attitude, into an attitude that
if you are a Christian you must be stern, almost sinister, never
laugh—

Laski: —Or very, very simple, so simple and innocent that the
realities of life seem irrelevant to you.

Bloom: Yes. But if you are really aware of things, of how tragic
life is, then there is restraint in your enjoyment. Joy is another
thing. One can possess a great sense of inner joy and elation,
but enjoying the outer aspects of life with the awareness of so
many people suffering and so on, is something which I find
difficult. When I was a professional man, we made a decision with
my mother never to live beyond the minimum which we need for
shelter and food because we thought and I still think, that whatever you spend above that, it is stolen from someone else who
needs it while you don't need it. That doesn't make you sinister,
it gives you a sense of joy in sharing, and in giving and receiving.
But I do feel that as long as there is one person who is hungry,
excess of happiness—excess of amenities—is a theft. . .

Laski: And yet each one person is so vulnerable, so prone to tragedy, so likely to fall into danger that when I see people, for instance on a beach, with excessive possessions and enjoying themselves excessively, here I think, is gaiety, a little happiness stored, a moment of gaiety that is not wrong.

Bloom: I wouldn't say it is wrong. I think it could be deeper and it could be more permanent. One of the problems of the modern person is that we have so much that we no longer enjoy little things. Say, in the years when life was extremely hard, in my experience, the slightest joy was a miracle. Now, my level of miracle has come up; it takes more for me to find that things are so miraculous.

Laski: Yes, and yet sometimes people rediscover simplicity through excess. I'm not morally disagreeing with what you are saying but I am wondering whether this—to put forward such a moral point as you do—isn't to impose guilt on most of us who are not so austere. This would be a general charge, not against you only.

Bloom: Guilt is always wrong and guilt is a sickly attitude to life. It's useless. It's destructive and it does away with the very sense that all things are possible, that one can put things right. No, I believe that guilt is wrong but I think that it is a challenge of greater joy. If I say, for instance, I won't do this because I can have the joy of sharing, instead of parasitically, in a predatory way, devouring it for myself, I'm not diminishing my joy and I'm not developing a sense of guilt.

Laski: The only thing I'd say is that if you are wrong—guilty—have done wrong, it's better to bear it yourself than to put it on to other people. It may be necessary to bear your own guilt and work through it.

Bloom: I think it's better to leave the word guilt alone and *do* something. . .

Laski: Certainly, do something, but don't push it on to somebody else.

Bloom: I don't see any advantage in pushing it on somebody else except if somebody is prepared, in terms of affection, friendship, love or whatever you call it, I mean relatedness to you, to share with you your problem, your predicament, not your sense of guilt, not your drowning, but your getting out of it.

Laski: I've been pushing my questions at you and you've been very generous, but have I left out—I'm sure I have—some important area that you would like to put forward? Have I given you insufficient scope to say what's really important to you?

Bloom: No, I think it was very exciting as it was. We never can cover all the ground, anyhow. What I feel, to put it in two very short statements about God and religion, is that to me God is not someone I need to fill gaps. It's someone I have got to accept because from the experience of life I have He does exist; I can't avoid the fact. And the second thing is that all the morals that develop from His existence are part not of a duty to Him or a duty to people—I don't like the word duty—but an act of happiness and gratitude for God and for people, and that links with worship—a worshipful attitude to God, a worshipful attitude to people, a worshipful attitude to life; I think the sense of worship and joy and of a challenge which will make me grow into a full stature is really what matters in practical life.

II

Bloom: What strikes me in the discussion we had before is that we are both on a level of conviction and belief. That is, I said that I had some sort of evidence that God exists. What is your evidence that he does not exist? On what do you base your belief?

Laski: I think I've got to put it in a more negative way. I see no evidence that God exists. No reason to believe that God exists. What you take as evidence seems to me not to count as evidence, not to be sufficient evidence.

Bloom: You call that over-belief—?

Laski: Over-belief? I would say that undoubtedly you and people like you know a feeling that seems as if something that might be called God could exist, but this seems to me to be a feeling that something it might be useful to call God exists, not evidence that God exists. It seems to me more probably to be a feeling of it than true evidence.

Bloom: Where do you draw the line between evidence that is something that does exist and the superstructure which we'll call over-belief? How do you distinguish the one and the other?

Laski: That is a difficult question, but I suppose that evidence would be something that if accepted as valid made a difference to one's entire mental patterning, something that had to be taken into account and which, if not taken into account, falsified every previous picture you'd held of how the world was, how it was constructed. I would rather find, I think, that to believe that God exists in supererogatory. Isn't it William of Occam who said you shouldn't multiply entities unnecessarily? I don't see a need to believe that God exists, or that if I did my picture of the world would be improved. In fact, I think my picture of the world would be falsified in that I would tend to make overtidy patterns about how things are if I believe that God exists, instead of confronting the much greater difficulties that seem to me to be there when I can't accept this.

Bloom: Yes, I see. But is an experience valid when it says to you God does exist? Can you invalidate that kind of statement?

Laski: It doesn't seem to me to be a valid statement at all because there are all kinds of statements I can make from my experience. I can say at a moment of loving infatuation: 'This person is the person I shall be happy with all my life. He is the most beautiful, wonderful creature in the world.' But my eyes are blinded. Or I may have a fever and be hallucinated. Or the sun may shine and I may have an improper optimism about a situation. Or the sun may not shine and I may have an improper pessimism. Surely experience must be tempered by authority, just as authority must be tempered by experience, but on experience alone, I may be mad.

Bloom: That's the kind of thing which the atheists and the believers say about one another quite freely, so we can both accept that kind of qualification. But what is the basic difference between saying 'I know that God exists' and saying 'I know that love exists'?

Laski: I don't think I would say 'I know that love exists' because I wouldn't use abstract words like this. I would say I know several different kinds of feelings that are called love, and it would be better, I think, if we restricted the word a bit more and used it for rather fewer feelings than rather many, but I can certainly say I know various feelings that people call love and I probably don't know all the feelings that people call love. For instance, I don't know your feeling of love of God in any adult sense.

Bloom: What if I simply denied the fact that love does exist, that there is such feeling—whatever the nuance you give it—I suppose you would say there is something lacking in me?

Laski: But haven't you changed the words a bit? I say I know a feeling that it's reasonable to call love, just like I know a feeling of being right and a feeling of being wrong, but I wouldn't myself—I may be only quibbling with words—find it useful to say love exists, right exists, wrong exists. I know what it is to feel loving, let me put it that way, I know what it is when people are feeling loving towards me.

Bloom: Yes I see. But it's an irrational feeling, something which is pure feeling which you accept as an experience without assuming that at the back of it there is such a thing as love, as it were.

Laski: No. You seem to be using irrational there as a rude word.

Bloom: On the contrary.

Laski: But it's a feeling that has all kinds of validations hasn't it? I mean, for instance, you can observe my behaviour when I say I feel loving and say: 'Is my behaviour consonant with what counts as feeling loving?' And if I say I am feeling loving when in fact my eyes are glazed, my hands are cold, I have no energy, you would then be justified in saying: 'Well she may call this love but I think she's mad.' There are references for feeling loving, aren't there?

Bloom: Yes. You moved from some sort of child's belief into unbelief . . . . . or is it too personal a question, how did you make the move into discarding God? Simply by the fact that there was no evidence that satisfied your more adult mind?

Laski: Would you agree that a child's belief in God need have very little to do with an adult's belief in God, except when the adult comes to God he'll make a recognition? This is what was presented to me as God when I was a child and now I can see more clearly. I see that it was right to present this to me. The God I knew and loved as a child was a God presented to me by my parents and He was an imaginary friend, as many children have, and I think I had the same kind of belief in Him that I had, say, in the fairies or that I had, say, in that somewhere there was a country called China. These were all things that came by authority and had to stand the test of time.

Bloom: So it wasn't a God whom you would have said you had met in a sort of intimate relationship. It was a God whom someone else had met and about whom you had been told?

Laski: A little more than that because I think every child's imaginary friend is somebody you meet in a personal relationship and I was certainly very convinced that this God whom I loved was on my side, so to speak. That when my parents said *this* was right and I thought, no, *that* was right, God was with me not with them.

Bloom: You find, say in the Bible, in the Gospels in particular, a sort of poetic evidence but no sort of objective evidence?

Laski: No objective evidence of the existence of God but an objective evidence of the kind of reasons that led people to believe in God and, of course, a great many statements of permanent validity without which I couldn't live nearly so well as I try to.

Bloom: But do you think one can have a convincing poetic

evidence which is founded on nothing but hallucination or nothing but fantasy or wishful thinking?

Laski: Now you are using rude words and unnecessarily because it seems to me that religion would not have existed in every community we know of unless it corresponded to people's deepest needs which couldn't in other ways be satisfied and when you say poetic, we in our post-Renaissance world, take poetry as being something fairly slight compared with religion. But I would have thought that religion was the expression of something we had so far no other means of expressing, something that is to do with our whole best development as human beings, and so when I say I accept this as a poetic myth it's not to denigrate it; in fact it's rather greedily and jealously to say what can I learn from it and in what ways human beings can without the mythical basis of the myth still continue to develop in a life that's a continuance from this and not a break from it.

Bloom: When I think of poetry as far as the human scene is concerned, I always feel that it carries weight, it makes sense because it is an expression in its own terms of something so profoundly real that poetry is the only medium which can be used to transmit the experience or to share it, but what makes it so convincing, so powerful is that there is a reality, human reality, at the root of it.

Laski: But here we agree. I mean I think we were almost reaching the point of difference before, ... if you would say that poetry is an expression of a very deep human reality I am not away from you at all. It's when you suggest, if you are going to suggest, that there is something outside, something other, that we would disagree. It seems to me in fact that the subject of poetry, to take poetry literally now, that the subject that is most often used in poetry is the subject of this very deep emotional pattern-making, in some way closely related to a religious experience, that this is the thing poetry is most about.

Bloom: So that the human experience is genuine and the way it is interpreted you would feel is beyond the evidence as it were, the loss of words, imagination or fantasy.

Laski: Beyond the evidence but not destructively beyond the evidence if one is able to accept it as mythical. We met before on television, I think a year ago, and I remember saying to you I understand you. I still believe that I understand you and I think perhaps this is what I am trying to say, that nothing that you put forward seems to me to be alien or strange but rather to be poetry in its deepest sense.

Bloom: And you would accept, for instance, that passages of the Gospel, to take the Gospel as an example, as being humanly true, without implying that it goes beyond the human truth of it.

Laski: I would not only take them, I would seek them and use them.

Bloom: Because you mentioned the Lord's Prayer, for instance . . . What does the Lord's Prayer mean, apart from the God whom you call 'Our Father' in the beginning, or about Whose kingdom, will and so on you speak? Is it an incantation? You said that you used it.

Laski: Yes, it's hard to say because its meaning changes from one pondering to another. You must find this too. And, except for using it as I think I do in a somewhat incantatory way, it wouldn't be perhaps the words that would most come to my lips, except for this purpose. I mean some of it I would accept, some I would reject. For instance: 'Lead us not into temptation' or, as it says in the New English Bible 'Do not bring us to the test'. This I would reject. This seems to me to be cowardly, but, on the other hand, the pious wish: 'Thy Kingdom Come' this seems an expression of Glory, this is splendid, this is life-giving.

Bloom: My difficulty is not so much such-and-such a sentence but the fact that the Lord's Prayer, for instance, is addressed to someone. If the someone doesn't exist at all, how does it affect you?

Laski: I don't know the answer to that. I mean there is maybe still a childish recourse to a someone. I don't think there often is. Maybe I'm using your image. Could I produce another text, perhaps which I might find easier? One I often think of: 'I Will

Lift up Mine Eyes to the Hills from Whence Cometh My Help'. Now this is more meaningful to me because the help that comes from looking at hills, to those of us who are helped by looking at hills, is a very real thing. We don't know, it may be, as people have said, something to do with the shape of the hills, whatever it may be, but I don't need then to assume a someone, a something that moves on the mountains. I just know, as a human being, that looking at hills is good for many human beings. It helps.

Bloom: I can't see that. My difficulty was that a prayer is addressed to someone or to a void and then I would feel that if there is a void towards which it is addressed then I couldn't use it.

Laski: In moments of deep distress and disaster where it would be natural to pray, in that sense I can't pray and this is one of the things we atheists must do without. I can see that it could be the greatest of strength and comfort to feel you could address a prayer and this perhaps is why I think people address prayers, but we can't do it.

Bloom: My feeling about it is not so much that there is someone to whom you can address a prayer but that the God who I believe exists, makes sense, and is a key of harmony even when the whole piece of music is totally discordant. Where is your key of harmony? Or is the world completely nonsensical?

Laski: Perhaps there isn't a harmony but certainly I think that the attempt to impose a harmony goes far beyond anything we have a right, on what evidence we have, to do. But we can seek for harmony in ourselves, harmony in our surroundings. We can seek the things that give us harmony. This I think is our duty. This is an important thing to do, but to say there is a great . . . a universal, an overall harmony, no, I think this is something we impose and God is one of the means by which we impose it.

Bloom: I won't say that there is one, but I would say that we are in a dynamic process of disharmony and tragedy that is aiming at and moving towards a final resolution, a meaning. How can you build meaning on the sort of patchwork which is life day by day?

Laski: First, I wouldn't seek for anything in the nature of a final resolution because that would seem to me to be atrophy and death. The play, as you put it, of a movement towards tragedy and disorder, a movement towards harmony, is the very ebb and flow out of which creativity comes; but meaning, in any large sense, isn't something I would look for, no. I don't understand what this means.

Bloom: What do you feel of life then? You just exist, you act according to—I wouldn't say principles—but to promptings . . .

Laski: Experience and authority—my experience, as purely as I can get it, the best authority I can find to try to be a good animal, a good human being, to the best of my capacity in my society, making as many choices as I feel it's in me to make, reconciling myself where I can't choose.

Bloom: And what about this scale of values? Is there such a thing as a scale of values between things bad and good, better or worse, ugliness and beauty? Is there any sort of base on which one can build a scale of values?

Laski: I've got to be very simple here because what I go by is as easy as comes. What makes me feel better is good. What makes me feel worse is bad. But authority must come in. You see, again, I could be mad. I could be a sadist. If I feel better at beating a child then I must defer to authority. There's something wrong with me, I should go to a doctor. But what makes me feel better, in society, as a social animal, I think, if tested by authority—and part of the authority I could certainly use would be the authority of religion—what tends towards health, the health of me in my society, is good. What tends to unhealth is bad.

Bloom: Yes, but health and unhealth are very relative notions.

Laski: Need they be? Just as you, as a doctor, as you have been, can recognize a state of greater or lesser physical health, surely we are moving towards a point where we are able to recognise a larger kind of health than that, a health. . . a social health for instance as a community, a psychosomatic health of the individual as a whole and one of the things we should be able to do in ourselves, and always with this check of authority, is to know what's good for us and the word good is quite important there, to know what's bad for us.

Bloom: What troubles me is that for instance that in the case where the physical well-being of people has improved they feel happier and yet often I feel so sorry for them because they are missing something more important and I would rather be back to more misery but be alive in the way I was than be more stable, more happy, more satisfied and less dynamically alive.

Laski: I don't think this is wiped out by what I've said. Are you saying better Socrates dissatisfied than the pig satisfied? I think the polarity between unhappiness and happiness, between ill-health and good health, between stagnation and movement, all this is what makes for movement and creativity. And so the last thing I would be saying is that I want to be in a state of perfect endless bliss because this would be similar to your final harmony. You know the atheist poet, William Cory, who said: 'Your chilly heavens I can forego, this warm, kind world is all I know', and the chilly heavens do indeed seem to me to be the area of cold movementlessness like an icy sea.

Bloom: I don't think that harmony is bound to be a stagnation or immobility. When, for instance, you spin a top, there is a moment when the movement is so perfect and intense that it coincides with complete poise.

Laski: But your harmony—I mean if we are talking about music —the harmony of music is made by playing on your nerves, by the exacerbation of discords, by the expectation that isn't fulfilled. There's no peace but the grave.

Bloom: True, there is no peace but in the grave, but I don't see harmony as a grave. What do you think of the people who are sure that there is an otherness which they call God, how do you take into account their experience or what they assert? Do you think that all of them were completely mistaken in their judgment or hallucinated?

Laski: You lead me to the besetting sin of the atheist which is

arrogance, so I think I have to say I don't know. I guess there
to be a temperamental difference. I guess there to be a difference
between people who prefer a minuscule putting together of pieces
that may never reach a whole and people like Plato, perhaps,
who saw a perfection in ideals. There do seem to me to be people
who yearn for an otherness and people who yearn for a here and
now, and this is not to make judgment between them but to say
that perhaps it's something to do with the way your brain works.

Bloom: Yes, but you spoke of authority as one of the bases for
decision and thought. If you take the total authority of mankind
in the sense that it occupies a place which seems to be discordant with another line, with the line you have taken, do you feel
you need integrate them somehow or would you say, as an atheist
once said to me: 'Your belief comes either from hopeless
ignorance, *or*, from the fact that you are a crack-pot and as you
are not hopelessly ignorant'—or rather he thought I was hopeless
but he didn't think I was sufficiently ignorant—'then you must
be a hopeless crack-pot.'

Laski: When I said authority I wasn't thinking again of authority
for a great big thing, but for little things. 'The hedgehog knows
one big thing and the fox knows many things.' I'm a fox. You're
a hedgehog. So when I refer to authority, I want to know what
authority has said about charity, what authority has said about
adultery, what authority has said about lies and anger. But not
what it's said about God. It simply seems to me that where these
human problems are concerned, what should I do? How should
I behave? How can I find consolation? The Fathers of the
Church and the Fathers of the Synagogue have been into all this
and they've found answers that suit human beings, so there is
likely to be an answer that suits me. I don't have to take their
source of their answer, but their answer is very likely to suit my
condition.

Bloom: I find it surprising because in our time particularly people
are so interested in knowing all that exists—travelling and having
seen, having read, having heard, being aware of the total reality.
My question about this reality is that I feel God is perhaps part

of this reality or is not and it's not immaterial to know whether He exists any more than it is immaterial to know whether something else of the material world exists. It's as important in a way, not for a world outlook, but for the sake of my passionate interest in what there is.

Laski: But I have said I don't think God exists. How would my life be changed if I thought otherwise? How would my very imperfect world picture be made more perfect, how would my life be different?

Bloom: What is the difference for your life to have discovered that music exists? In a way, you could very well live without ever having had any experience of music. It may not have made you any better, any worse, but it's an enrichment. It is part of a real and wider experience of life and that's how I would put the problem about God.

Laski: I see this. But surely God doesn't exist for my enrichment. You're suggesting almost that there's another art form I haven't come across. I'm tone deaf to God and I would have a richer life, just as I might if I could understand another art that I don't understand. But God must be something more than this.

Bloom: And yet, as far as my human experience is concerned, when in times past I've said: 'I've no use for music, I am not interested and I dislike it', people have said: 'Oh poor one. You miss so much and you are short of part of life.'

Laski: But at least you knew that music existed. You could watch us listening to it. You could see these people scraping away.

Bloom: With great thought and meditation. . . But what about us scraping away? What about, say, the great people like St Theresa?

Laski: I don't go greatly for St Theresa, because it seems to me that whenever she didn't find people who would agree with her exact interpretation of God, she sought for another adviser, so she is not my favourite saint. But I think she's a good example because she, more than most people, actually believed she perceived God beyond the point which Christianity allows in fact and yet she did not really submit her visions to authority. As I say, she changed her authority whenever it didn't suit her vision.

Bloom: Yet here is a woman and here are many people who possess something they say is real. And you would go a long way to discover a new writer, a new artist, in terms of painting or sculpture, a new world of discovery and yet you would say this is not worth investigating and discovering. That's what puzzles me.

Laski: I don't think I'm saying that. I would certainly probably not have investigated it so far as you would think proper. It's certain that I don't see any substitute for this world of yours because since the Renaissance for instance, it's been all too sadly apparent that in all the arts there has been no inspiration comparable with the inspiration that religion gave. There have been no words for secular music that compare with the music of a Mass. I certainly think that belief in God and the religions that arose from belief in God did give a shaping and a pattern to life for which I can see no conceivable substitute and to that extent I would certainly grant to you that my life is poorer than that of a believer. My justification for it, and I say it as humbly as I can, is that it's founded on the truth as I see it and the truth has to make me free of perfection. I'm not entitled to it.

Bloom: I feel terribly happy about what you said because I think what really matters first of all is integrity and truth and I'm certain that if God exists, which I believe He does, He's happier about truth of unbelief than falsified belief. Now I think I must give you the chance you gave me to say what you would like to say in addition to our discussion.

Laski: I probably haven't made atheism seem at all rich and I don't think it is. I think it's a very Protestant, a very puritanical faith that, as I say, does tend towards arrogance because we lack authority. But there is one thing I would say for atheism, as against religion, and that is this: if you try to practice it, it trains you in a virtue that I value highly which is endurance without whimpering and without seeking help you can't properly expect to have. But we must—I say 'we', I don't know who 'we' are, I don't know who atheists are and this is, again, where arrogance comes in—but we must depend very deeply on religions which have a great many things that we can't have—rite, ritual, festival, words beyond any words we've managed to maintain. I think sometimes that we could have more help.

CHAPTER TWO

DOUBT AND THE CHRISTIAN LIFE[1]

I DO NOT mean to give a complete exposition of Christianity. I want to take a certain number of points which I think are relevant for the Christian and which are relevant for anyone who wishes to understand himself and the situation in which we as Christians find ourselves. Perhaps when I say 'we Christians' I go beyond the limits of what I should say; perhaps I should say 'the way in which one Christian who belongs to the Russian Church understands it', because it will be a personal contribution. It is offered not as a teaching but to stimulate thought.

Periodically there are words that emerge that characterise a situation. When one uses the words 'problem' and 'problematic', one means things that had seemed to be absolutely clear to the generation before but which now have unfolded themselves in a new way and have acquired a depth of vision which requires new thinking. We are no longer content with a simple repetition of views which belonged to a previous generation. I am talking about such things as the historical meaning of tragic events like the Russian Revolution, suffering—communal or family—and national tragedies.

Nowadays it seems that the words which come easily to mind are *bewilderment*, *perplexity*, and they result in an attitude of mind because the trouble with words is that they begin by defining a situation that exists and then they try to crystallise the

[1] Chapters two, three, and five are edited versions of talks given at Birmingham University in 1970.

situation, making out of it a sort of world outlook. People confronted with a problem are perplexed; they say so, and that is right. Later, however, people have come to the perplexity before the problem and think that they are up to date if they are perplexed, but that doesn't always lead to a solution.

Therefore, before we start to consider anything more concrete in our faith or world outlook, I would like to focus attention on perplexity and on doubt, in an attempt to provoke thought about a few words like faith, doubt, reality and truth. I am not a theologian; I am a scientist by training and a physician, so you will not find in my words any depth of philosophical probing into things. I am writing as an ordinary human being who is confronted with life and its problems.

First of all, concerning faith, one preliminary remark. Faith is very often understood by people as a defeat of intelligence. In other words, faith begins when I can no longer think creatively, when I let go of any attempt at rational understanding, and when I say 'I believe' because it is so absurd that it is the only way of facing the problem. This may be an act of credulity, it may be an act of cowardice, it may be a preliminary act, full of wisdom and intelligence, that teaches us not to draw conclusions or to come to conclusions before we have understood. But this is not faith as understood by the great men of all religions, and particularly the Christian faith. In the Epistle to the Hebrews in the eleventh chapter, faith is defined as 'certainty of things unseen'. We usually lay the stress on 'things unseen' and forget the 'certainty' about them. So when we think of faith we usually think of the invisible and instead of certainty put against it an interrogation mark. Then to solve the problem, we accept in a childish way, in an unintelligent way very often, what we are told by others—usually our grandparents of three generations back, or whoever else we choose to believe for reasons that are not always reasonable. But if you try to see the way in which faith originates in those people who were the great men of faith, the heroes of faith, you can see that it always originates in an experience that makes the invisible certain, and which allows them, having discovered that the invisible is as real as the visible, to go further in searching the invisible by methods of their own.

There is a passage for instance, in the works of Macarius of Egypt, a man who lived in the fourth century. He says 'The experience of God, the vision of the world in God, is something which can happen only at a moment when all our thoughts, all emotions, are arrested to such a degree that we can no longer both be within the experience, perceive the things, and step out of the experience, watch ourselves and analyse what is going on. The moment when an experience is "lived" is a moment when we cannot observe it.' And he says that this would be quite sufficient for someone who has had an experience of God. He would not wish to go back to another stage. But he also says, 'God has concern, not only for those who have this experience, but also for the people who haven't got it; that someone should come to them as a witness of things unseen, and yet experienced, real, and he steps back away from them.' At that moment begins, as he says, the realm of faith. The certitude remains even though the experience is already of the past; the certainty is there because what has happened to him is as certain as anything around him, is tangible, visible, perceived by the senses, so that the moment of faith begins as a result of a first contact with the invisible, discovered, disclosed somehow.

That means that we must be very severe and sober when we speak of our faith, for we often say 'I believe this and that' when we have taken it from someone else that it is true—we don't care to investigate it in depth, and as long as this truth or illusory truth is not destroyed or broken down, then we take it for granted. This is a bad faith; this is what one of our Russian theologians called 'the aged sacrament of the faith that does not think'.

What we *should* do whenever we are faced with that kind of faith is to confront it with experience. We ask ourselves whether we have any experience of it. If we haven't, it must remain a field to be investigated. It remains a field that was conveyed to us by someone who knows, but which is not known to us. It is promising, but it must hold its promise in the future. We cannot yet say 'I know, I am certain, I understand with experience.'

This kind of faith—the faith of one who simply takes things on trust—sooner or later will be badly battered by life and by problems, by doubt in fact, or if you prefer, by perplexity. What happens so often with people is that when they are young, they are given a number of certainties which they accept on trust from their parents, their teachers, their surrounding, the milieu in which they live. After that, this minimum of faith is kept as a sort of treasure. We develop in all sorts of ways, but our awareness of the world invisible and of the certainties it entails does not grow with it. A moment comes round the age of 18, perhaps earlier or later, when a child in us, the little child of 8 who has collected all the faith he was capable of and formed a world outlook which is childish, is confronted with an opponent, an adversary within himself. A girl, a young man, of 18, 20 or 25, says 'Nonsense, you can't believe that', and then an argument starts which is doomed to lead to the defeat of faith simply because it is the argument between a little child with a pure heart and uninvolved thinking, against someone who poses to the childish nature the problems of another age, another level of understanding, another level of perception of the world.

At 8 the world can be taken on trust; at 18, at 25, it cannot; and in certain circumstances, there are things that can never be taken on trust. I will give you an example. The Eucharist, the central event of Christian worship, is centred on an act of thanksgiving in which we say to God 'Thank you for all things'. Now, can we honestly say, 'thank you for all things' in the face of the tragedies of the world unless we have a reason to see beyond the tragedy to their solution and a meaning within them?

Doubt is not simply contradiction. Doubt is a moment of dividedness, a dichotomy in our minds; a moment when, having followed a very simple straight road, we come to a fork, and we ask ourselves 'Do I go this way or that way?' The one may be more convincing, the other may be more alluring. Which one are we going to choose? It is the situation of someone who has been weighing up the problems of life in a very simple way and suddenly discovers there is a much more subtle balance between things and that a simple solution is no solution at all. What are we going to do at that moment?

There are two absolutely different attitudes to doubt in the mind—there is that of the scientist and that of the believer. For the scientist, doubt is a systematic weapon; it is a joy. For the believer when he takes the wrong attitude to doubt and to the problems he is facing, it is a moment of anguish. What happens usually to the believer is that having believed in all simplicity that everything is clear, simple, straightforward, he suddenly discovers that life gives the lie to what he thought to be true. Then his answer is 'I am disloyal to what I thought, I am disloyal to my faith, to my Church, to my God'. The problem is not only about subtleties but about basic things, about God Himself, about the Church, about what is at the core of the believer's life. Then he feels that what is at stake is the breaking down, the destruction, the disappearance of the object of faith, and God's existence is now questionable. The values which were essential, which were existential values for him, are questionable, and therefore his very existence becomes a problem and seems to be insuperably problematic.

But when a scientist engages in research, he gathers together all the facts he is capable of collecting. Once he has gathered his facts, he must hold them together in a way that makes it possible for him to handle the totality of the facts, and he builds a hypothesis, a theory, a model, a construction, an architectural building, that is capable of holding everything together. If the whole object of research for the scientist was to make himself a name, he will try to protect his model against any criticism, against any doubt and against any questioning, with greater or lesser honesty. But if as a scientist he is a man who is out to discover what things are in reality, his first action will be to go round and round his model in all directions, examining and trying to find where the flaw is, what the problems are which are generated by the model he has built, by the theory he has proposed, by the hypothesis he has now offered for the consideration of others. If he cannot find a flaw, then he will try through research to go farther in the field and discover such facts that do not fit with his theory or his model, because when he will find a fact that will explode his model, make his theory questionable, he will have opened up a new window on reality. So the aim of the good research scientist is to create models of theories or hypotheses as a preliminary exercise to questioning and to discovering something which will make him break them down in order to create another model which is as doubtful as the preceding one, but which allows him to keep the new facts together in a manageable way.

At the root of the scientist's activity there is the certainty that what he is doubting is the model he has invented—that is, the way in which he has projected his intellectual structures on the world around him and on the facts; the way in which his intelligence has grouped things. But what he is also absolutely certain of is that the reality which is beyond his model is in no danger if his model collapses. The reality is stable, it is there; the model is an inadequate expression of it, but the reality doesn't alter because the model shakes.

'Model' can be replaced by another word when it is not used in a scientific way—it can be replaced by the word 'truth'. Truth is something which is an expression of reality, and an expression means two things: first, that the reality which surrounds us is perceived (obviously incompletely); secondly, that it is expressed (also incompletely, because of our inability to express identically in words and in expressions). Only one occasion in human history sees the moment when truth and reality coincide. That moment is in the incarnation Christ, because he is God, the plenitude, the fullness of creation, and at the same time the perfect expression of it. Then truth no longer answers the question 'What?', it answers the question 'Who?', and when Pilate said 'What is truth?' Christ gave him no answer for the simple reason that if he had said to him what he had said to the disciples, 'I am the Truth' Pilate would have understood even less than the disciples, and the disciples understood nothing at that particular moment.

Truth and the expression of it is bound to be formulated in human terms, in the language of a given tribe, a nation, an epoch and so forth. Obviously it is limited, but it has also another quality: truth can be either static or dynamic. You can express the truth in two ways. A snapshot is true and yet it is perfectly untrue. Everyone must have seen snapshots of preachers, lecturers or politicians delivering a speech. They are usually taken at a moment when the subjects stand with their mouths open like a hippopotamus. Well, the snapshot is perfectly true, but it expresses only a split second and gives you a ridiculous image of something that perhaps at that moment was profoundly moving for the people. It is a petrification, a sort of fossil of something which is dynamic; it is true, and yet it does not express the truth because the truth at that moment was emotion. When you want to express the truth—that is, reality—dynamically, you discover that the truth becomes a problem of a quite different sort. Perhaps an example or two will explain what I mean.

There is a painting by the French painter Géricault called *The Derby at Epsom.* If you look at the painting, you will see that the horses are galloping, but if you are interested in zoology or in the mechanics of movement and examine the horses, you will discover that no horse gallops that way. Some are spread out in such a way that if they went on they would fall flat on their bellies; others stand with their four feet gathered together and couldn't even jump from the position in which they are painted. But what was Géricault aiming at? He aimed at showing the gallop and not the horses. The problem was to express the movement and not the anatomy, the physiology. And he chose deliberately (because he knew perfectly well how to draw a horse) to falsify things as the only way of convincing the viewer that the horses were moving.

This is what we are always doing in theology or philosophy: we falsify things when we want to convey a dynamic moment, but often the reader takes them to be an adequate and immobile picture of what reality it. This is true, for instance, of the Trinity.

There is another example which I should like to give about reality. It is that of false teeeth. When we say these are false teeth, we are making a judgement of value but not of reality. We start with the common assumption that real teeth grow spontaneously in peoples' mouths. This is true; from this point of view those teeth which you can remove in the evening, wash under the tap and keep in a glass are evidently false. But from the point of view of the dentist, they are perfectly real (false) teeth. It sounds like a joke, but that is the kind of mistake which we make continually. We don't notice it, but we start to speak of something from an angle, move to another and we discover that the two don't work together.

No, reality is something within us which is the total thing

which includes God and all things visible and invisible. This is what we aim at expressing in glimpses when we speak in terms of truth. These terms of truth may be adequate, they are never identical with their object. In the field of art something very interesting may be discovered in the works of primitive painters particularly of one Russian painter called Rublev who lived 6oo years ago. He was trained by a man who had mastery of three-dimensional painting, and strangely enough, for most of his painting he reverted to two-dimensional. A Soviet historian of art made a study of the problem, and he showed that Rublev expresses all historical events in three-dimensional, because particularly in time and in space they have thickness. But things which belong to the eternal, he expresses only in two dimensions because they have no thickness—they are not within time and within space. When you look out of the window during the night in a thunderstorm, you may see the scenery in a flash—but it goes so quickly that you can't see whether one tree is farther or nearer than another, or any so precise detail. This is the way that truth is both adequate and inadequate. When we say that the truth is inadequate, that our intellectual, philosophical, theological, scientific model is inadequate in comparison with reality, it simply means that we are saying 'How marvellous, I have come to a point when I can outgrow the limitations in which I have lived and I can move into a greater, deeper, more enthralling vision of things as they are.'

If we think of a scientist and a believer, then we will see that the scientist's doubt is systematic, it is surging, it is hopeful, it is joyful, it is destructive of what he has done himself because he believes in the reality that is beyond and not in the model he has constructed. This we must learn as believers for our spiritual life both in the highest forms of theology and in the small simple concrete experience of being a Christian. Whenever we are confronted with a crossroads, whenever we are in doubt, whenever our mind sees two alternatives, instead of saying 'Oh God, make me blind, Oh God help me not to see, Oh God give me loyalty to what I know now to be untrue', we should say 'God is casting a ray of light which is a ray of reality on something I have outgrown—the smallness of my original vision. I have come to a point when I can see more and deeper, thanks be to God.' That is not perplexity, it is not bewilderment, it is not the anguished doubt of the believer who hides his head and hopes that he will be able to revert to the age of 8.

This is very important because unless you are prepared to see reality and your own thoughts and the thoughts of others with keen interest, with courage, but with the certainty that the last word is not doubt, not perplexity and not bewilderment, but that it is discovery, then you are wasting your time. You will die in the way in which in ancient mythology we are told: an ass that stood between a bucket of water and some straw and could never decide whether he was more hungry than thirsty or more thirsty than hungry.

I should like to talk now of the situation of being a Christian in the world; and I should like to preface my remarks by saying that we have a tendency to exaggerate the meaning which we attach to the expression 'the contemporary world'. The world is always contemporary to someone: at every moment it will be contemporary to a generation of people, and there are general rules that are human and historical which I believe can serve as a basis for our judgement and action. Another thing which I should like to underline is the fact that God is always contemporary. This we very often forget, trying by all sorts of theological efforts to make Him contemporary with us, when He is perfectly contemporary, needs no change to be Himself and to be up to date.

This being said, I take as a first starting point two stories of the Gospel which are too well known for me to describe them in detail—the stories of two storms on the Lake of Galilee. The scheme of these two stories is practically identical. The disciples leave the shore, they are caught up in a storm and they are confronted with the unexpected in the person of their Lord and of their God, Jesus Christ. In the first story the disciples left the shore, then they were caught up in the storm alone in their boat. Christ had remained behind, dismissing the crowds after the miracle of the multiplication of the bread and fish. Their only protection against the storm was the frail shell of their boat. They fought with all their energy, with all their skill, with all their courage, yet death was enveloping them on every side, pressing hard, trying to break through their precarious security. At a certain moment they saw, right in the middle of the storm, walking on the seas, blown around by the wind, Christ himself. They looked and saw and they cried out in fear because they knew it could not be Christ, they knew it was a ghost. Why? Because they knew that God, their God, their Master, their Teacher, stood for harmony, for peace, for salvation, for life, and there he was right in the middle of the storm which spelt death, disharmony and horror; it could not be God, because God's presence could not be in harmony with what was going on.

This is the reaction we have so often, and we react as wrongly as the disciples when dramatic events occur in our lives. Whether it is history at large—wars and earthquakes—whether it is the small history in which we are involved—our own lives, our own families, our own religion, colour, group—if the presence of God is felt and is not accompanied by immediate harmony, by the coming of peace, by salvation, by the relief of pain and by the relief of anguish, we shout out that it is a ghost. He cannot be there. We forget that God is the Lord of the storm just as he is the Lord of the stillness, the serenity and the harmony of things.

I will leave this story at this point and take the next one, and come back to both. In this one we read that Christ has left the shore with his disciples. He is asleep in the prow of the boat; he is asleep comfortably, resting his head on a cushion. A storm springs up, death is abroad, fear enters and conquers the hearts of the disciples. They fight again within the precarious protection of the shell of the boat, and they feel that they are being defeated. Then they turn towards Him who is their salvation, or should be; and they see Him who should be their salvation completely indifferent, asleep, at rest, and—to add insult to injury—he is not only asleep but he has made himself comfortable with his head on a cushion.

This is what we accuse God of continuously. We never stop accusing him of that. We are fighting against death; anguish disrupts our lives; fear makes them unbearable; death is abroad, suffering is killing us, and God is not only there, indifferent, but in perfect comfort because he is beyond reach of these things. Are we fair and are we right? I will try to answer this question a little later. Let us go back to more features of the story.

In the first story, having cried out their fear, the disciples hear the Lord say 'Fear not, it is I'. They hear a voice which is strangely like the familiar and loved voice of their master. And Peter acting once more quickly than he thinks, says, 'If it is you, tell me to walk on the seas and join you'. And then, because Christ says 'Yes, it is I, come', Peter of a sudden—because he has recognised Him who is life, who is meaning, who is harmony, in himself—of a sudden abandons the frail protection of their boat, and begins to walk and indeed he walks, and as long as he looks at Christ, and as long as his only desire is to be with Him, to be at that point where God stands in the storm, he can walk. But suddenly he remembers himself. He remembers that he is a man of flesh and blood, that he has gravity, that he has never walked on the sea, never withstood the raging waves, that he will drown; and the moment he turns his gaze, his interest, his concern on himself, he indeed begins to drown because he is still in that part of the storm where death is abroad.

In the case of the second story, the disciples feel defeated—death is there, they have no strength left, no hope, no peace left. Turmoil has overcome them completely; they turn to him, they awake him, perhaps even brutally, for their words are brutal. 'For all you care, we are dead'. This is the translation which Moffatt gives of that passage. 'For all you care, we are dead'. They don't turn to him saying, 'You are the Lord, a word of yours will be sufficient for us to be saved'. No, they recognise defeat, they accept the ruthlessness and indifference of God, they have no word for Him. What they want of this God become man who proves incapable of being a help and their salvation, if he can do nothing better, is to be in anguish, in despair, together with them and to die with them—not be drowned unconsciously, all unwitting of the oncoming defeat of life by death. And Christ turns away from them, brushes them away saying 'How long shall I be with you, men of little faith?' Then, turning to the storm, he commands the seas to be still and the wind to cease, projecting as it were, his own serenity, his own peace, his own stillness, his own harmony, on all things around Him. In the case of Peter as well as in the case of the other apostles, they had allowed the storm not only to rage around them, but to enter into them; the storm had become an internal experience; it had conquered. In Christ it remains outside himself; it is conquered. In a passage of St John's Gospel, the Lord says 'the Prince of the world has nothing in him which he can use to kill'. They are not His words but the implication is that He is free, He has overcome the world; he can project on it the measurement, the categories of eternity, stability, serenity, salvation, security, not the precarious and frail security of the little boat, but another security; not the peace, the naive peace of those who say 'That will never happen to me', or console others by saying 'Don't worry it won't happen to you', but the peace of one who has said 'It may happen, it will happen, it has happened, and yet because I have lost all human hope, I stand firm and unshaken on divine hope.'

I have said that Christ was at the point of a storm, at a certain point of the storm which we should reach in order to be with God in the storm; that Peter nearly drowned because he did not reach it. Where is this point? This point of the storm is not a point where there is no storm, it is what one calls the eye of the hurricane, it is the point where all conflicting forces meet and where an equipoise is reached because there is no violence—not because there is no tension, not because there is no tragedy, but because the tragedy and the tension have come to such a pitch that they meet so violently as to balance each other; they are at the point of breaking. This is the point where God stands, and when we think of God, the God of history, the God of human life, the God whom we accuse all the time, to whom we give from time to time a chance by saying 'He must be right because he is God'—this is the God who has chosen to stand at the breaking point of things, and this is why He can be respected, why we can treat Him with consideration, why we can believe in Him and not despise Him.

Now, where is this point? Long ago a man once stood in anguish, in despair, before the face of God and before the judgement of his friends. This man was called Job. He was afflicted with all that can afflict a man—bereavement, loss of all he possessed, loss of all that was dear, but more than this, more tragically than this, with the loss of understanding. He no longer could understand his God. Meaning had gone out of his life, and in his argument with God and in his argument with his friends, he stood for meaning and refused consolation; he refused to be consoled and got out of tragedy and anguish by a consoling, appeasing and false image of God and of his ways. He believed, indeed he knew a living God, and that one he could no longer understand. And at a certain moment, he says, 'Where is the man that will stand between me and my judge, who will put his hand on my shoulder and on my judge's shoulder; where is he that will step into the situation, take a place at the heart of the conflict, at the breaking point of the tension, stand between the two in order to re-unite them, and to make them one?' He had a sense that only that could be the solution of his problem. Indeed of the problem of the meaning of tragedy, ultimately of the meaning of history. He had a foreboding that only that could be true, and that indeed happened. It happened when the Son of God became the Son of Man, when the Word of God became flesh, when Jesus came into the world, who being truly man, could put his hand on the man's shoulders without destroying the man by the fire of divine touch, and who could without blasphemy and sacrilege, put his hand on the shoulder of God without being destroyed.

This is what we truly mean by Intercession. Christians spend their time interceding, and at times I listen to these intercessions with fear because to me intercession means an involvement that may spell death; and I am frightened when I hear a congregation of people intercede for one need after the other, piling up on their shoulders all the needs of the world just for the time Evensong lasts. After that they put it down on God's shoulders, and they go out elevated with a new emotion.

About ten years ago I came back from India. I was asked in London to speak at a rather big meeting about hunger. I spoke about what I had seen and what had wounded me very deeply with all the passion and violence I am capable of. For a while the people sat and listened, then when we came out I stood at the west door shaking hands, and a lady came up to me and said 'Thank you for the entertaining evening.' That is intercession very often with us. We have spied a need, we have become aware of a tragedy, and then from the security of our living, we turn to God, and say 'O Lord, haven't you noticed that? What are you doing about it? And this? And that? Aren't you forgetful of your duties to mankind? This is not intercession. Intercession is a Latin word which means to take a step that brings you to the centre of the conflict, and in the image of Christ, in the person of Christ, we see that intercession means taking a step which is definitive—once and for all he becomes man, not for a while. And he doesn't become a pleading advocate or a go-between equally different to the one on either side, who will go and find terms of agreement between the one and the other. He takes his stand in total, final solidarity between Man and God; turning to God, he is man and stands condemned; turning to men he is God and stands rejected. He must die. And his solidarity doesn't go simply to the sweet selected few who will recognise him or believe in him. No, his solidarity goes to everyone. He is not God for the good versus the bad, the believers versus the unbelievers, or the creed or the colour of a nation, or of a social group. He has made himself solid with everyone. We discovered as exiled Russians in the early days of emigration when we had lost everything, when there was nothing left standing for us, when we were unwanted, rejected, despised, helpless, vulnerable to the utmost, we discovered we had also lost the God of the great cathedrals, the God of the beautifully engineered ceremonials. Where did we stand? When we looked at ourselves, we discovered that we had lost faith in ourselves, and very often self-respect. And then we discovered our God in a new way. We discovered that in Christ God has revealed himself as vulnerable, as helpless, as contemptible, as overcome and vanquished, as trodden under foot, as rejected, and we discovered that we had a God who was not ashamed of us, because he had made Himself solid with what we were, in our misery, in our deprivation, in our rejection, and also that we had no reason to be ashamed of a God who knew how to love to the extent that he was prepared to become one of us, and to show by doing this that his faith in us was unshaken and that his respect of human dignity was whole and untouched.

This God is the one who stands at the middle of history. He is the one who stands at the breaking point of the storm, and he calls us to stand where He stands, to be involved, to be committed, to be committed to life and death within the storm, and yet neither to accept this fallacy of a ghost in the storm instead of God, or to turn to God and say 'If you can do nothing more, at least be together with us, in anguish and in despair'. He wants us to take a step, to be in the world at the point which I called 'the eye of the hurricane', but not *of* the world, because we are free from the uncertainty, from the fear, from the self-centredness of Peter, remembering himself at a moment when the whole sea was death and danger for the other disciples, for all the other boats around, and when God stood there as the key of harmony, but it was not the harmony that he expected.

I should like to give you one example of what it means both to make an act of intercession and to stand where our place is. It is the story of a woman of whom we know nothing except the name. She was called Natalie. The story was told me by the other people involved in it. In 1919 at a moment when the Civil War was raging like a storm over Russia, when our cities were falling prey to one army after the other, a woman with two young children was trapped in a city which had fallen into the hands of the Red Army, while her husband was an officer of the White Army. To save her life and theirs, she hid in a small cabin at the outskirts of the city. She wanted to wait until the first surges were over and try to escape afterwards. On the second day someone knocked at her door towards the evening. She opened it in fear and she was confronted with a young woman of her age. The woman said 'You must flee at once because you have been discovered and betrayed; you will be shot tonight'. The other woman, showing her children that stood there, said, 'How could we do that? We would be recognised at once, and they can't walk far.' The young woman who so far had been nothing but a neighbour, someone living next door, became that great thing which one calls a neighbour in the Gospel. She grew to the full stature of the Gospel of God, of the good news of the dignity and graciousness of man, and she said 'They won't look for you, I shall stay behind.' And the mother said 'But they will kill you.' 'Yes', said the woman, 'but I have no children, you must go.' And the mother went.

It is not easy, I would say it is almost sacrilegious, to try to imagine what happened in the heart and mind of this woman in the course of the hours that preceded her death. But we can look back to the Gospel and see what happened in the Gospel to those who were the prototype, the archetype of this great and holy woman.

Almost two thousand years before, a young man of her age was waiting for his death. His name was Jesus. He was in a garden wrapped in the darkness of the coming night. There was no reason within him why he should die. He was young, healthy; he had done nothing wrong. He was waiting to die in a vicarious way other peoples' death. He was waiting in the darkness of the night, and death was coming to kill life eternal itself. Three times he went towards his disciples, hoping for a word that would strengthen his heart, for companionship: not to be released, not to be saved from the oncoming death, but to feel that there was a human presence, compassion, love and awe. The disciples were asleep. He got no help.

Natalie in the coming night, in the gathering darkness, in the cold that was falling from the walls and the roof, had nowhere to turn; there was no-one to whom she could turn. She was alone, facing the coming of another woman's death that would be enacted in her body, in her destiny. She could have walked out. The moment she had passed the threshold, she was again Natalie, not the mother. Two thousand years before on that same cold night when Christ was betrayed into the hands of his murderers, the strongest, the most daring of his disciples was challenged three times, twice by a little maid in the courtyard, once by a group of standers-by; he was not asked 'Are you Jesus?' he was told 'You were with him!' and three times he said 'No', and walked out of the courtyard. Into what? Into security. He turned round and the eyes of Christ met his eyes, and he remembered and he wept. But he walked out. Natalie did not walk out, she stayed inside.

How often must she have thought 'Is there any hope that at least my sacrifice will be useful?' Again, two thousand years ago

a man was waiting for death, John the Baptist, and before he
died, when he knew that death was inevitable, he sent two of his
disciples to Christ to ask Him 'Are you He for whom we waited,
or shall we expect another one?' That means 'If you are Him,
then my life of asceticism, my aloneness, my preaching, my
imprisonment and death, all the tragedy and hardship of my
life, make sense. But if you are not, then I have been betrayed
by God and by man, by my own inspiration and by the weakness
of the living God. Are you He?' Christ did not give him a direct
answer. He gave him the answer of the prophet 'Go and tell him
what you see—the blind see, the lame walk and the poor
proclaim the good news—news about God—news about man.'
The humility of the one and the greatness of the other.

Natalie probably asked herself the same question—was it in
vain that she was dying? There was no answer, only the hours
passed, the cold of the early morning came and with it, death.
The door was brutally opened and they did not even take the
trouble of dragging her out. She was shot where she was.

This is the answer which the Christian can give to the tragedy
of history. The place where we must stand. Natalie stood where
Christ had stood, and where indeed Christ stands now, risen in
Heaven with his hands and sides seared with nails and the spear.
He stands at the very heart of human history, human suffering,
human death, human anguish and tragedy. But He stands there
like a rock. He stands there firm, having endured everything,
every human suffering in thought and body, and he says to us
Christians, 'That is where you must stand, not in the dreamland
of a faith that gives you the illusion that you are already in
heaven while you have never been on earth. No, at the heart of
human suffering and tragedy but with a faith unshaken, with the
certainty that He who was expected by Job, has come'. And if
we stand there, we may undergo all that was promised by him.
You remember the passage: 'Are you prepared and capable of
drinking of the cup which I shall drink, of undergoing what I
shall go?' 'Yes', said his two disciples. This must be our answer,
and when tragedy comes, we must answer again as Isaiah spoke:
' "Whom shall I send?" said the Lord. "Here I am, send me." '
Like a sheep among the wolves; like the Son of God among men.

CHAPTER THREE

MAN AND GOD

In the 18th and 19th centuries, the centre of interest was mainly ideas and ideals, and man was the material support of these ideals or this concept. He was subservient to them, he was supposed to serve them, to live for them and eventually to die for them. There was greatness in this approach and if we forget its significance, we would certainly lose a very important dimension of humanity. Man's greatness is I believe, to be measured, not only by his potentialities but also by his ability to live for and to die for things which in his view are greater than him. But we know also that when ideals and ideas acquire such independence as to become overlords of the minds and lives of people, when men are no longer free to approach them critically, but are forced into one-sidedness that involves them in life and death without any choice of their own, then something has gone wrong. And it is not surprising that nowadays, as a revulsion against what has been happening since the beginning of the First World War, we have a sense of the value and the significance of man in his frailty, in his becoming, in his search, as well as in his achievements and in the service he can render to things great.

Nowadays man is a meeting point of all those who are in search of things true and things right. If St Paul came back into our world and was faced with an altar dedicated to the Unknown God, he might very well say 'I know his name, his name is Man', and at that point he would probably meet not only those who believe but also those whom we call unbelievers. I would like to build part of this chapter on two quotations: the one belongs to Karl Marx and the other one to St John Chrysostom. These are two poles.

Karl Marx says approximately that the society of the worker is in no need of a God because Man has become its God, and St John Chrysostom in one of his innumerable sermons says that if you wish to know how great man is, don't turn your eyes towards the thrones of the kings or the palaces of the great men, look up towards the throne of God and you will see the Son of Man seated at the right hand of Glory. In both cases it is man who is the final, the greatest vision, and greatest value.

I would like now to take up not these two quotations, but the vision of man which they imply and see whether the unbeliever, the humanist, the atheist and the Christian have got anything to say to one another about it. If you think of man conceived in atheistic terms—I am not now using the word 'atheistic' to refer to aggression against God, but to an attitude of mind and outlook in which God has no place, in which he doesn't exist—you will see that man appears in various ways. The empirical and concrete man is not the object of the exercise. The concrete man is raw material; this raw material is in the process of *becoming;* from the point of view of natural science it would be called evolution, from the point of view of social science one would speak of an evolving society, but the empirical man is not *the* reality which concerns the atheist uniquely. As raw material he exists, but he is to be set up against a certain number of visions, the first of all of which may be of the man of the future—man as he should become when he will have become what he should be. I remember a discussion I had on a plane between Moscow and the south of Russia with an atheist who said to me that we should not judge the success or failure of the Russian Revolution by what was actually achieved or not achieved as yet, because the result of the revolution will be shown when men will have been transformed in such a way that they become real men. In other words, man is always viewed as something ahead of us, something in the future towards which we move; and the empirical raw material which we all are is to be worked upon, transformed, changed and moulded, and in this recasting, as experience shows through the centuries, many bones crack and many things have to be changed with force and sometimes with violence.

The second aspect of man is society, the present-day society representing a collective vision of man and the empirical man being forced into, led into, or convinced into becoming an integral and harmonious part of the society. The level of the change may of course be valued in different ways. We may think that the society to which this man belongs is far below the mark, and at times, often perhaps, far below the mark of its individual members; but it is society which is the collective man, and the individual man must be fitted in like a little stone in a vast and complex mosaic. In that case also man has to be re-adjusted, re-formed.

Another aspect of the attitude of the unbeliever to man is that the empirical man has a right to be what he is and to become whatever he will become. That, when you think of it in an absolute sense, leads to a vision which is near the vision of the anarchist—everyone has a right to be himself whatever he is—and to the sort of idealistic idea that if everyone was allowed to be nothing but himself, unhampered, the final result would be perfect harmony.

It may also lead in the process to accepting man as he is, not only with his frailty and his becoming, but also with his right to be a problem to his neighbour, to be subservient to his passions, to his weaknesses, to refuse any idealism, any desire for change, and be content with being what he is, however low this level of being may be. I am not speaking of course of a high or low level of living which is not what the empirical man seeks, but the acceptance of himself in his laziness, in his lack of ideals, in his refusal to be part of a whole which is greater than him, and so on.

In the case of society defining man or in the case of an ideal abstract man being set up as the pattern for the future becoming, we always meet—whatever the case, whatever the kind of dictatorship or pressure group—with something which a Russian writer, Solzhenitsyn, in his book *Cancer Ward*, defined in the following way. One of the central characters has this said about him, 'He had the greatest possible love and consideration for mankind, and this is why he hated so fiercely every human being that disfigured this ideal so horribly'. This is exactly what happens when we have no other standard and no other point of reference than either an ideal which we build out of our imagination according to what we desire, or else when it is society, the concrete pack which is around us, which defines what each of the howling wolves should be. Man confronted with an abstract ideal of man or with a concrete, real society which clings to totalitarian rights, must be remoulded, must be broken, must be changed and must be brought—a blood offering very often— to this abstract ideal or perish, confronted with his inability to fit with the pack, the concrete society, the jungle in which he lives.

Christianity also sets men as the final value, but not idealistically or abstractly. We have put on the altar a concrete real man —Jesus of Nazareth—and we must have a look at what is implied. We see in the Creed that Christ was true man and true God. When we say that he was true man we imply two things: the fact that he was God has not made him into a man alien to us, a man so different from us that he has only the same shape and the same name while in reality he has nothing in common with us; on the other hand, we proclaim that being the true man means to be a revelation of man in his fulfilment, man as he is called to be, and that in Christ we have a vision—concrete, real, historical—of what we are called to become in our reality, in our historicity and in our becoming. So when we say that Christ is true man, we affirm that to be united with the Godhead does not annihilate or change the nature of mankind, and it is only in Him because man is united in Him with the Godhead; that man is revealed in his full possibility because man as a specimen of natural history is not man in the sense in which we believe man is truly human. Man becomes truly human only when he is united with God infinitely, deeply, inseparably, so that the fullness of Godhead abides in the flesh. I am using terms which are applied to Christ in the Scriptures, but which I believe are applicable to man if we take, for instance, the words of St Peter in his Epistle that our vocation is to become partakers of the divine nature—God's participation and not just human beings related to a God who remains an outsider to us.

But that implies a quite different vision of man, and it also implies something which I believe to be important, a quite different vision of the Church.

Very often we think of the Church in sociological terms; it is a society of men gathered around a teaching, round a person, round certain functions, of which some are lyrical—worship—or some are acts of God—sacraments—but which always belong to a human society directed Godward. This is a poor and insufficient vision of the Church. Looked at from this angle, the Church is nothing more than an object of historical study; it is not an object of faith, there is no invisible depth in that kind of vision of the Church. This presence of the invisible belongs to the Church because the first member of the Church is the Lord Jesus Christ who from two angles transcends the empirical, historical Church which we are, defined in the words, if you want, of St Ephraim of Syria, as not the assembly of the just, but the crowd of the sinners who repent and are seeking for eternal life. Christ transcends this empirical, historical, sociological group by the fact that as man in his very humanity, he is completely what we are, yet we doubt our brokenness, we doubt our separation from God, we doubt our separation from one another. Sin means basically separatedness, brokenness—inside, a sort of schizophrenia, outside, the fragmentation which we define when we see one another, not as parts, members, limbs of one body, but as individuals contrasted with us.

But also Christ transcends the sociological reality of the Church in another way. Even while He was within history in the days of His flesh, He belonged at the same time to the fullness of eternity because He is God, not only in his Godhead but because His humanity itself transforms life—finite, precarious, transitory as we know it—into life eternal, stable and victorious.

The Church is also the place where the Holy Spirit has taken abode, dwelling in each of us and making each of us a temple of the divine presence, and through the Holy Spirit we are united in one life, one reality, both physical and spiritual, with the Son of God, and we become, by participation, by adoption, the sons of the Father. The Church is an organism, both and equally human and divine, containing the fullness of God and the fullness of man, but also the frailty and brokenness and insufficiences of man, and in that sense the Church is simultaneously already at home and still in becoming—already at home in terms of relatedness to God by the way in which we are already grafted on God, and still in becoming because we have not reached the fullness to which we are going. In that sense, the Church also participates in this curious historicity and transcendence of Christ himself. Historical, yes, but bringing into history a dimension which is not to be imprisoned in time and space; the dimension of infinity, of eternity, of profundity, which *things* have not got apart from their participation in these qualities which are God Himself.

Now I want to turn to Christ, and to speak a little about his humanity. We read that He is truly man, and when we try to see what He has got in common with us, we see that He was born, He lived, He died. When we think of the way in which He participates in our life, we see he is not only a partaker of the glories of mankind—rather of anything but its glories. He makes himself solid, he identifies himself, not merely with those who are in glory, not merely with those who are just, righteous and saintly, not merely with those who are in no need of salvation or help—he identifies himself with everyone. We must not forget that the rich and the wealthy and the powerful also have an eternal soul, an eternal destiny; we must remember that to preach the Gospel to the poor and the derelict is only half of our mission. I am afraid the Church has forgotten that and for centuries has preached patience to one, hardly ever preaching justice to the other.

But it still remains that Christ, in his acceptance of the human situation, has identified himself with us, not only in our stability but also in our frailty and in our misery—yes, He hungered with us. He was born, rejected, there was no place for him except in a manger outside the society of man. He was surrounded with murder on the first day of His birth. He was tired, He was abandoned, lonely, hated, despised, and so forth; that is also true. He accepted the company of people whose company others didn't want—the sinners, those who were despised; that is also true. But there is something more to the way in which He accepts solidarity with us, and something much more important. He accepts solidarity with us *in death*. One says, quite naturally: he chose to become a man, so he had to die of it. No he hadn't, and this is just the point. A number of writers have pointed out the fact that death can be conceivable only through severance from the source of life. One cannot be, as it were, plugged into life eternal and die. St Maxim the Confessor underlines the fact that at the moment of his conception, at the moment of his birth, in his humanity Christ had no participation in death, because his humanity was pervaded with the eternal life of His divinity. He could not die. It is not an allegory or a metaphor when in the Orthodox Church on Thursday in Holy Week, we sing 'O Life Eternal, how can you die; O Light, how can you be quenched?'

This is a point which I think we should consider.

He died on the cross, and the operative words are the most tragic words of history: He, who is the Son of God, because he has accepted total, final, unreserved and unlimited solidarity with men in all their conditions, without participation in evil but accepting all its consequences; He, nailed on the cross, cries out the cry of forlorn humanity, 'My God, my God, why has thou forsaken me?'

People who are keen on exegesis explain to us that at that point He was rehearsing a verse of a prophetic song. If you have seen anyone die a violent death you can't well imagine him at the last moment rehearsing a prayer he had been taught when he was a little boy! Besides, it is an error of vision—for it is prophecy that is turned towards its fulfilment, not fulfilment that is supposed to recite words of prophecy. No, it was something real. When Christ said 'My God, my God why hast thou forsaken me', he was crying out, shouting out the words of a humanity that had lost God, and he was participating in that very thing which is the only real tragedy of humanity—all the rest is a consequence. The loss of God is death, is forlornness, is hunger, is separation. All the tragedy of man is in one word, 'Godlessness'. And He participates in our godlessness, not in the sense in which we reject God or do not know God, but in a more tragic way, in a way in which one can lose what is the dearest, the holiest, the most precious, the very heart of one's life and soul. And when in the Apostles' Creed, we repeat 'And he descended into Hell', we very often think 'That's one of those expressions', and we think of Dante and of the place where all those poor people are being tortured with such inventiveness by God.

But the Hell of the Old Testament has nothing to do with this spectacular hell of Christian literature. The Hell of the Old Testament is something infinitely more horrid; it is the place where God is not. It's the place of final dereliction, it's the place where you continue to exist and there is no life left. And when we say that He descended into Hell, we mean that having accepted the loss of God, to be one of us in the only major tragedy of that kind, He accepted also the consequences and goes to the place where God is not, to the place of final dereliction; and there, as ancient hymns put it, the Gates of Hell open to receive Him who was unconquered on earth and who now is conquered, a prisoner, and they receive this man who has accepted death in an immortal humanity, and Godlessness without sin, and they are confronted with the divine presence because he is both man and God, and Hell is destroyed—there is no place left where God is not. The old prophetic song is fulfilled, 'Where shall I flee from thy face—in Heaven is thy throne, in Hell (understand in Hebrew—the place where you are not), you are also'. This is the measure of Christ's solidarity with us, of his readiness to identify himself, not only with our misery but with our godlessness. If you think of that, you will realise that there is not one atheist on earth who has ever plunged into the depths of godlessness that the Son of God, become the Son of Man, has done. He is the only one who knows what it means to be without God and to die of it.

This has consequences in our attitude to people around us. If what I have been saying is true, and I believe it with all my commitment, then there is nothing which is human, including the loss of God, including death through loss of God, including all the anguish of the Garden of Gethsemane, which is the expectation of the coming of this horror of horrors, which is alien to Christ and which is outside the mystery of Christ.

And then what is our attitude as Christians to those who are the enemies of Christ, who hate him, who reject him and those who are Godless, not only because they have not yet met God, but because they have met a caricature of God, whom we have presented them with in the name of God Himself? We must realise that we stand before the judgement of those who reject

God because of us, and that Christ is not alien to them, and they are not outside Him, they are not alien to Him. There is a mystery of salvation far beyond the Church, far beyond our experience, far beyond our understanding.

What I have said about Christ is said not about the God of Heaven who becomes man, but about the Man, Jesus, who had such faith in us, in all of us, that he accepted becoming everything we are, including our Godlessness and our death. He believed in us and was prepared to vindicate the greatness of man by showing us in his person that man is so great that when God unites Himself with him, man remains in the full sense of the word—only instead of remaining small, he becomes what God has willed him to be.

ONE EXPRESSION dominated the Oxford University Mission in 1969 which is particularly clear to Ian Ramsey, the Bishop of Durham. Many could not immediately understand what it meant, but then discovered that it had a depth of meaning and it served a very useful purpose. The expression of 'cosmic disclosure'. Cosmic disclosure means to him and came to mean generally that there are moments when things which surround us—people, situations—suddenly acquire depth, become transparent, as it were, and allow us to see them with a new significance, and as I said, with depth. The nearest approximation to cosmic disclosure I could give you is something which we probably all know about. When I was small I was given a little drawing made up of a maze of lines. What you could distinguish at once in this maze of lines was a hunter in a wood, and the caption said 'Where is the rabbit?' Then you took the thing and began to look at it this way and that way in all directions, until suddenly you saw the rabbit and you couldn't understand how it was that you hadn't seen it before.

That is true as an image for everything in life. We live in a situation, live with people, see the situation at its face value, we see people apparently as they are, and one day we suddenly spot the goodness. How great, how profoundly significant that is. That happens, for instance, when we look at very familiar scenery one day when we are perceptive, when we have eyes to see, and are capable of response. We look at something which is the most ordinary thing which we have seen day after day, and suddenly we stand arrested by beauty, by meaning, by something it lends us, as though things had become translucent and we could see in depth, deeper and deeper towards a core that is full of meaning.

The same happens with people. We live among people and we see them as people. People are interchangeable with the crowd, faces move and there is always a face to be seen. But all of a sudden a face that we have seen often, which has become so familiar that we don't even look at it any more because from the first glimpse we know that's him or that's her—suddenly we have stopped to look, or because something in the eyes, something in the expression has made us stop, the face appears to us completely new, lending us a depth of meaning, a depth of significance. And someone who was an interchangeable part of the crowd is singled out in such a way that it becomes a person, and a person who is totally unique, who can't be replaced by any other person, can't be confused, is simply himself or herself.

There is a saying of Methodius Olympius, a Greek divine, who said 'As long as we don't love a person, one person, we are surrounded with men and women. The moment our heart has discovered the person it loves there is the beloved one and nothing but people around.' This is the way in which something can be singled out, seen in depth and in truth—seen, I was about to say, in glory, because in those moments things which are lifeless, colourless or dull, suddenly acquire relief, colour, beauty and meaning. In such moments occurs what Ian Ramsey, the Bishop of Durham, calls 'cosmic disclosure'. That kind of cosmic disclosure we all know, and if we are attentive to ourselves we will remember such moments—moments when suddenly, among people whom we know very well, we discover someone, with a warmth of heart, with a vision, with an emotion we never had before. A thought that has been repeatedly thrust at us in the form of quotation from the Gospel or from literature, which somehow clicks in a situation and acquires deep meaning, is no longer a quotation from Shakespeare or from the Scriptures; it is truth that has been put into words which are so significant and so powerful.

This kind of experience adjoins the experience which we have of God because God is also someone whom we can discover in this experience of cosmic disclosure. I insist on the word 'cosmic' this time because God is within the reality in which we live, and furthermore, as long as we have not discovered Him and the invisible world that is His world, we are still blind to a whole wealth of reality. This is why it is important, from my point of view, to have discovered God. In a way I would say it is rather a danger, very often a nuisance. One could very well live with less trouble without a God than with a God because— particularly with a God who has accepted solidarity to the point of death, love to the point of forgetting himself and in addition to this, is vulnerable, helpless, despised, beaten—God tells us coldbloodedly; this is the example which I give you—follow it. Or he says, here are the beatitudes: you will be hungry, you will be thirsty, you will be beaten, you will be cast out, you will be persecuted—and that is the best you can have. That kind of God is not always a discovery that brings ease in our lives. The point is not whether God will be useful, the point is whether it is true that He exists.

Now, can one attach any truth, any validity, to this kind of cosmic disclosure which includes beauty, love, human relationships, the existence of God, and a new vision of the world? What is the validity of experience? There is a point of view which I believe to be a falsification of a scientific approach that says: experience is something that can be proved according to methods of natural science or the precise sciences like physics, chemistry, biology. This, I think, is a falsification because experience is not limited to that kind of science. There is a whole world which is irrational, yet not unreasonable. When I was a student and studied physics, I had to pass the exam on acoustics. I was totally uninterested in music and totally incapable of appreciating it at all. To me, music was a system of sounds. I knew all about music as far as sound is concerned and as far as physics is involved; as to enjoying it—no, it never occurred to me that it was enjoyable. I had also met a man who took the same line about literature— a very remarkable man I met in Ireland, an old canon who was the shyest and the most reserved creature I have ever met and who found the English extraordinary, and so unbearably exuberant that he could not stand a holiday in Britain because he came back exhausted. He asked me once whether I knew Dostoevsky. I was rather surprised that he was interested in Dostoevsky and I said, 'Have you read him? How do you like his novels?' He looked at me and said, 'Novels? I never thought he wrote novels'. I said, 'What did you read then?' He mentioned all Dostoevsky's well-known books. I asked 'What were you looking for?' It turned out that he was collecting a card index on Russian religion and he had read the whole of Dostoevsky but had never noticed that he was a writer.

There is such a thing as the irrational that cannot be simply reduced to rational formulae. We know now that there is a whole world of the irrational in us which is not in the realm of intellect and reason, yet which exists and has immense power in us. Emotional troubles are not rational and yet they are more decisive in our total balance than our points of view, when in an Olympian way, that is, with total indifference, we view things. But there is another thing about the kind of experience which people would advocate, saying 'That is reliable, I have probed into it with my five senses?' But our five senses are no more reliable than any kind of inner reaction. When you look at something, you say: I am sure it is there; my eyes give me evidence. When I listen to something, I say: I am sure it is there; my ears have given me evidence. But what is the evidence? I remember very well, I went to see a patient once, who sat next to me and as I was talking to her she suddenly began to pat thin air. I said 'Oh, what's that?' And the good lady said, 'It's an ethereal lion. I live in an astral body and not only in a physical body, and I have a nice little lion that comes and sits with me'. This good lady felt the lion's fur under her hand; she could see the lion; she could probably perceive the lion in a variety of other ways. I couldn't I'm afraid. Now, from my point of view her physical perception of the lion was hallucinatory; from her point of view the reason for my lack of perception was my denseness and my blindness. With everything we see, we assume first of all that previous experience is proof that it is true, and secondly we pass a judgement of value, that this is not a hallucination and that it is reality. From the point of view of natural life, of course we may be right or wrong, but from the point of view of psychological thinking, I have a right to challenge and to doubt any visual, audible, sensory experience because your eyes are not the part of you that assert that this is a lion or that this is a watch. It is your judgement and your head, your brains that say that. And between the lion that sits here and your eyes that catch sight of him in his absence and the nervous system that brings it to your brain and your brain that takes cognisance of it and your judgement that says it is a real lion and not a fantasy is a nice long chain which I can doubt at more than one point.

One can show experimentally that many of the things which we assume so easily are more doubtful than we imagine. So that unless we are prepared, as philosophers or scientists have been to doubt systematically any experience we have, there is no logical, solid reason to question one type of experience and admit of the other, especially when a type of experience is not the experience of one unique person, but when it is corroborated by the experience, the practical knowledge of other people.

So the fact that an experience will not be transmitted directly or cannot be given evidence of by what we call objective methods is proof of nothing, because the words objective and subjective must be treated with a great deal more care. An objective judgement usually means a judgement which I can pass with total indifference, without any kind of prejudice, and in practice that's what we mean by this. But if we want to have an objective vision of something, what we should really mean by this is that we must perceive the thing as the thing perceives itself without interfering. That is obviously totally impossible; I cannot perceive a chair by identifying myself with the chair. But I do perceive something when something happens to me. So long as it remains only the object and unrelated to me, there is no perception at all, not to speak of any kind of experience. I think we must take that into account, because neither in music, nor in physics, nor in any kind of rational and precise science, is there objectivity that does not involve a subject. And if that is true, then all the complex experiences of beauty, of love, of appreciation, of evaluation of judgement, of inner certainty which we can have, have an objective significance for another person.

Now, this is an important introduction because unless we understand this, we have got to deny systematically any experience which is not tangible and we can doubt any experience which is tangible unless we accept a total interplay of immutable laws of identity in the outside world and in the laws of nature.

There is another problem. In this intercourse between subjective and objective, there are two things. First of all, an experience which has become mine, I must be able to retain, to examine and to express; and on the other hand, the people around me must be able to receive the experience, that is, to receive the message of it. There is more than one way of conveying an experience, but the most usual is by forms of speech that are meaningful simultaneously on two levels—on the level of the objective experience which you have had, but also on the level of something already known to the listener than can work as an analogy and enable him to understand what you are speaking about. So, when we speak of love, there is the love of the mother to the child, the love of the child to the mother; they are not identical. The love of friends, the mutual love of lovers; the love of husband and wife, and a variety of lofty types of love are very different from one another because you cannot understand it before you have undergone it. A little girl of seven will never be able to understand what it means that her sister of eighteen is madly in love, because there is an analogy but not yet identity between the two. So there are ways of conveying things.—

Take a man like Jeremiah. Jeremiah was shown by God, one day, a twig of almond tree, and God spoke to him at the same time and said, 'What do you see?' The answer was 'God is the keeper of Israel.' This is built on a grammatical pun in the Hebrew language which is irrelevant for what we need now. But can you imagine the state in which Jeremiah was; he saw the twig of almond tree and all of a sudden he was overwhelmed with the sense of the divine presence. Don't you think that whenever he held in his hand a twig of almond tree, he was brought back to that much more than by a sort of theological reminiscence? Don't you know what happens to you when you have been in a place where you have been miserable or happy and come back after ten years, and suddenly see the same sunlight, the same house, the same situation, how, of a sudden, all the emotions of ten years ago well up in you which you could not conjure up by any trick of intellectual imagination?

This is the first way in which any experience which was reality has become now my own past, has placed myself in the position which I defined in the first chapter as the point where certainty about something which has become visible to me at a certain moment can be retained. And then perhaps I will want to convey something about it. Then I will use words that are either words of poetry or methods of music, something that will make sense to my listener because he may have an analogical experience and be able to catch a glimpse of mine through the glimpse of his. That is what happens, for instance, to us when we have endured real suffering or enjoyed exhilerating happiness. We can understand the joy and the suffering of others, not by suffering their suffering or rejoicing with their joy, but by compassion, suffering together, or rejoicing together, with them, with understanding.

The seers, the visionaries, the people who have the experience of things invisible that they have undergone as certainties, try to express things. They usually use words that are ordinary words to convey an experience that would make sense.

Take, for instance, the old man Nicodemus, who came to see the Lord one night at Jerusalem. You can imagine the scene. They stood probably on the platform of the house to talk in the evening breeze instead of staying in the heated rooms. They were speaking of God, intangible, invisible, that cannot be caught in any kind of net. Nicodemus didn't understand, and Christ said 'Look, what do you perceive now? You perceive the wind that is blowing around us; your skin is refreshed, your clothes are freely moving in this wind. It is an actuality, a certainty that you are within this refreshing, life-giving, renewing blowing of the evening breeze. Yet, you don't know where it comes from, you don't know where it goes to. You know nothing about it except this complete personal experience that makes you say an objective thing: "The wind is blowing, I am refreshed".'

The Church in the Scriptures has been spoken of as being the Bride of the Lamb. I remember talking in those terms once in a youth group led by a very pious and dignified lady. When question time came, she said 'I can't understand, why do you and your Church use all these fairy tale expressions? What do they convey?' I thought that they did convey something, but the group wanted to know why. So I said 'Does "Bride of the Lamb" convey anything to you about the Church?' She replied 'It's ridiculous, I know what a lamb is; we have all seen Easter postcards, the little white beast with a blue or red ribbon jumping on the green meadow; and we also know what a bride is, it's a girl who has realised that it's time to get married and looks round for a boy to catch who has got a good job, a car and a future.' Now, this respectable Christian lady obviously could not see the point that the bride is a girl who proves capable and ready to love with such commitment, to love so wholeheartedly, as to choose one man, to unite her destiny with him, to be prepared to abandon all the rest, to follow him wherever he will go. And if you remember what Scripture called the lamb in the 52nd/ 53rd chapter of Isaiah, you will understand what the man of sorrows and the lamb means. Then yes, the Church is expressed by these terms. But at that point, it is human experience plus a depth of communal experience that is needed. Outside the communal experience and the vocabulary of a legal community, these words mean nothing any more.

Among the ways in which we express our knowledge of things invisible and of God in particular, there are words which try to qualify God—either in his relatedness to us, as the Creator, or in his actions within our life of freedom—or else point to something which is at the very core of the problem. And there are three such words: the one is *God*—God is a very fortunate word because it means nothing semantically. I don't mean to say that a philologist doesn't know where its roots begin; what I mean is that when you say 'God', the word itself hasn't got any content— it signifies someone or a notion, but it doesn't describe him. So that we can speak this word without prejudging anything. And there are two more words: *Jesus* and *Love*; the two ways in which we know God. In the word *Jesus*, we say 'Who is God?'

God is this man who claims to be the Eternal One, Jesus, who is God and is man at the same time; to whom I can speak personally and who reveals to me therefore that God is a person because only a person can become one with a person, and reveal a person. And on the other hand Love. Love which is not simply in Biblical terminology a feeling multiplied by infinity, but is the fullness of life that is beyond insecurity, has conquered death, and can give itself as an offering of life and death without fear.

I have already said all I wanted to say about the way in which Jesus of Nazareth, who belonged totally to history and at the same time transcends history completely in his Godhead, is involved and totally involved in our human destiny. But what I want to talk about is the fact that we do not only say that the Son of God became the Son of Man; we say, we proclaim, we believe, we see that God became flesh, the Word became flesh, and by flesh I indicate the fact that God became not only part of history or destiny, but of the material, visible, tangible reality of this world. Matter has found itself in the fact of the incarnation, united with divinity. What I have said earlier about man holds here. The incarnation reveals to us that man is so great that he can unite himself with God without ceasing to be man in the full sense of this word; that he is so vast that he contains the divine presence, that there is at the core of each of us what the Archbishop of Canterbury once called a God-shaped emptiness which nothing can fill which is of the earth or of heaven or of the created, but God alone. But here we see the greatness, not only of humanity, but of the material world revealed to us in the historical fact of the incarnation. If God has taken flesh, it means that in an exemplary manner in the human flesh of the man called Jesus, all the matter of this world has been shown to be capable of such vastness, such depth, such greatness as to be united with the Godhead without ceasing to be itself, but becoming to a degree and in a way which surpasses imagination itself in the full sense of this word. So we discover that matter—which we treat usually in almost a sacrilegious way as inert, dead, alien to the great calling of the creation—can become not only spirit-bearing, but God-bearing, pervaded with divinity. And this we can see in the way in which matter is revealed in the miracle of the transfiguration. We do not see light divine shine around Christ, we see his flesh aflame with divine light; we see his clothes become whiter than they can be made on earth; we can see that matter itself is pervaded, filled with the divine presence, and revealed in glory for however short a moment.

That is the background for the root of our belief and for our faith in a realistic theology of the sacraments and for a realistic vision of miracles. Miracles are usually thought of in a most primitive way by the least primitive people. People imagine that they are so sophisticated that they have outgrown the very notion of matter, forgetting that they eat every day, they multiply, they take baths; that they are the victims, fearful and careful of every change of temperature. What I mean by a miracle is not something which strikes the imagination because it couldn't happen and yet it does happen. The difference between a miracle and an act of magic is that an act of magic consists of an act of over-powering, of enslaving, of depriving someone of something—of freedom, of independence, of the capability to determine itself and to stand in its own right.

A miracle is, on the contrary, an act of God which is mediated by the faith of man and the divine mercy that re-establishes a harmony, destroyed and broken. And at the root of it there is this very clear vision of the Old and the New Testaments, that all things created by God are created for eternity, for destiny, created capable of hearing God, of understanding God, of obeying God in a fulfilment which is both freedom and obedience. That applies also to the sacraments in a peculiar way. In the sacraments what we believe happens is that the matter of this world is detached from the evil, sinful, Godless context in which it was betrayed by the faithlessness of men, brought back to God as an offering, received by God, made free, restored to its primeval freshness, and furthermore by an act divine, fulfilled and revealed as it should be and shall be. To take the central act of the Church, the blessing of the bread and the wine into the body and the blood of Christ—it ultimately means that we see here the matter of this world in the example of a small particle of it, of a drop of it, attain to that fulfilment which is the vocation of all things, that God should be all in all and that all things should be fulfilled by the divine presence, indeed the integration of God in them.

That is the meaning of *Jesus*, which implies incarnation, history and the taking up of flesh by the living God; it implies a personal relationship which opens up our vision of men, of all things created; and it implies that the scientist, the physician, anyone who deals with the matter of this world, is a high priest or else has betrayed his human vocation and in particular his Christian vocation.

The other word I have mentioned is Love. We read in the Scriptures that God is Love. We read also in the Scriptures, in a synthetic way by bringing together things which are not expressed as a theological statement, that God is one in the Holy Trinity. The two things are identical. I want in a few words to say something about love, then to try to show the relation of this notion of love to the Holy Trinity—One God.

We usually think of love in terms of taking of love, of giving and of receiving; and this is right. But, first of all, giving and receiving is not what we understand by it. It must be something much deeper and purer, more refined than what we imagine we do when we give and when we receive. Very often to give is a way we have of asserting ourselves. We are rich and therefore we are secure, and the proof of our security is that we can give. We are proud and generous as a result and we revel in the sense of our generosity and greatness because it gives us the right to be proud. When we are at the receiving end at times, we can receive because we are greedy. But these two actions of giving and receiving must, to become Christian actions, be free from the evils I have indicated. You cannot receive with an open heart, with a sense of worshipful gratitude, with a sense of joy or fulfilment, of exhilarating openness unless you love the person who gives, and unless you know the gift is a sign of love and has nothing to do with pride and self-assertiveness. You cannot give in the right way if giving is not committing yourself to the last and is not an expression of service, of worship, and of tenderness. And this is one aspect of love.

But love is not only this. St Gregory of Nazianzus in the 4th century, speaking of God, trying to find the link between love

and the Trinity makes an analysis of human love to try to find
the clue, because if we are using human words, human images,
it is legitimate also to see connections on the human level. He
says love that would be simply an arithmetical one, a monad
cannot be called love. It is self-love, self-adoration, narcissism.
He turns to the love of two and says, 'People imagine that the
love of two, of a couple, that know nothing any more except the
two who love one another, is fullness of love. Don't we see the
passion, the total commitment, the adoration, indeed, which
results from it?' And he says 'No, this is a fallacy, because this
love is frail. However rich and however pure the giving and
receiving between these persons, this relationship is not stable.'
The whole of literature, and unfortunately so much in our lives,
proves that the moment a third person appears, we are either in
comedy or in tragedy. It is either Othello or any other example
of the betrayed husband or wife. It is either tragic and ends in
death and murder, or else it ends in the laughter of the
onlookers. What happens is that this double link, this two-way
traffic of giving and receiving, breaks down if it is not an open
relationship, if it is a closed circuit that goes round and round.
When the third person appears, a triangular relationship is established in which giving and receiving can be pictured now in the
form of two arrows which meet each other or are directed against
each other. And a new system of relationship is established—the
newcomer establishes a golden link of adulterous love with the
one, and a bloody link of hatred with the other; it is a triangle
of complex relationships, it is not an image of love.

What Gregory of Nazianzus insists on is that love implies
a third quality—not only giving and receiving, but the ability
of sacrifice. Now, the word sacrifice in our language means always
losing something, being deprived of something. But in Latin, in
Greek, in Hebrew, in Slavonic, in all the ancient languages,
sacrifice comes from sacred—it means to make something sacred,
make something holy and not to lose it. Indeed, when you bring
life to God or a gift to God, it becomes His, it is no longer yours
in the greedy and possessive sense of the word. But it becomes
holy with the holiness of God, and we must remember that when
we speak of sacrifice, it is that which is the centre of gravity—

not what you lose, but what happens when we bring the bread and the wine, the holy and perfect sacrifice. What happens is sanctification and not simply loss, because there is no loss when we bring something to God—what we have we receive from God, more than we could provide ourselves with. 'Seek the Kingdom of God', says Christ, 'and all things will be given to you in addition', not: 'taken away from you'. This is the principle of sacrifice, of santification, of the offering that gives and receives only as an act of love and not to gain a return.

The word which I would use is self-annihilation, the ability to accept not to be, no longer to exist in a situation because something else matters more. By this I mean the following: John the Baptist said about himself, 'I am the friend of the Bridegroom'. The bride is not his bride, neither is the bridegroom his bridegroom, but such is his love for both of them that he brings them together—he is their witness and their companion in the marriage feast; he brings them to the chamber where they will meet face to face alone in a fulfilled relationship of soul and body, and he remains outside lying across the door so that no one should disturb the mystery of this love.

This act of self-annihilation is essential to love, and if there is no such thing in our love with regard not only to one person but to all persons, all situations, all things, our love is still deficient. This is very important for us to understand because in God we find the three things. We find the exulting joy of three persons who love in giving perfectly and receiving perfectly, but who being a trinitarian relationship, if I may put it in this form of speech, are not in the way of each other, in which each of them accepts every single moment not to exist for the two others to be face to face—the miracle of total communion, fusion and oneness.

Speaking of God we must consider things in the simultaneity of events and not in temporal succession. The three simultaneously give, the three simultaneously receive, the three simultaneously place themselves in such a situation that the others are alone with each other. But that means death because self-annihilation, self-nothing, sacrifice, mean death and the cross is inscribed in the mystery of the Holy Trinity.

We speak of the impassibility of God. So often the impassibility of God is understood as the inability of God to feel anything. The word doesn't mean that at all; it means simply that God is never acted upon, is never passive, is always supremely active. The incarnation and the death upon the cross, unless the cross was inscribed in the very mystery of the trinitarian life, would be an event introduced into God from the outside. In fact, on the contrary, it is the projection of one of the rich aspects of a complex mystery of love into human history through the incarnation and the death, because it is always there as the death of the one who accepts not being in order that the others may be fulfilled. But then you will say, 'Is there only death within this mystery? Is it only death which we can expect from each other if we love in a more perfect way?'

Indeed not, because there is something else to it. There is a saying of Gabriel Marcel which I feel is one of the great statements of Christian thought in our days. He says 'To tell someone "I love you" is tantamount to telling him or her, "you shall never die"'. We usually try to assert our existence, to be sure that we are, to conquer our insecurity, our doubt. We assert ourselves against. We distinguish one another by putting together common qualities of size, colour, language and so on, that allow us to say, 'He is not me'. But this is the state of the individual, and the individual is a state of fragmentation.

This is not what is the object and subject of love. It is the person that is the identity in us which makes us the same person from the baby to the old man, and from earth into heaven. This person cannot contrast himself or herself by opposition because it is uniqueness that is characteristic. But then, if you accept dying as an individual, dying as someone who tries to assert his being by not being the other, how can you survive? Only in the love of the other. And this is Trinitarian theology—the vision of three persons whose love is such that they lay down their lives and they are caught up into eternal life, into life that can no longer be taken away from them because they have given their lives and others have granted them eternity.

This is an anthropomorphic way of speaking of the Trinity, you will say. Yes it is, but the revelation of God is always in human terms because it is addressed to human beings; whatever can be revealed by God about Himself can be revealed only if there is a conformity between the object who is revealed to and the subject who reveals it. All that can be revealed must be capable of being put in human terms. What we forget and where we make our God extraordinarily small, and indeed not acceptable for many Christians and non-Christians is that we imagine God is nothing but what can be revealed about him.

Between husband and wife there is a transcendence of two persons into something greater. A German writer has put it in the following way: 'In marriage two become one in such a way that it is one personality in two persons,' and beyond that there is all the mystery of God which is beyond communicating, which is beyond being shared with us, which is Him unbelievable. In that way then we will see that God is infinitely vaster than the model and image that we have, but all these models and images belong also to the mystery of revelation. A God like Him is, on all these levels, to us a revelation of transcendence and at the same time, of humanity. He is as great as man is, and we are as great as He is. He belongs to our becoming and our tragedy, totally, and we belong to the fullness of his ability and glory, wholly by vocation, and yet, not in possession of it because we are still on the way.

If we think in that context about man and history and individual persons, about matter and science and technology, about human soul and human art, then we can have a vision of the cosmos and of the God who is within it and beyond it, that can inspire us to be creative, as creative as God, and, at the same time, to worship Him in amazement because we have been given this incredible freedom to be ourselves.

CHAPTER FOUR

HOLINESS AND PRAYER[1]

I T IS very important for the comprehension of holiness to understand that it has two poles: *God* and the *World*. Its source, its fulcrum and its content is God; but its point of impact, the place into which it is born, where it develops and also where it is expressed in terms of Christ's salvation, is the world, this ambiguous world which, on the one hand, was created by God and is the object of such love that the Father gave His only-begotten Son for its salvation, and on the other hand, has fallen into the slavery of evil. This pole of holiness which relates to the world therefore has two aspects: a vision of the world as God willed it, as He loves it, and at the same time an asceticism which requires us to disengage ourselves from the world and free the world from the grip of Satan.

This second element, this battle which is our vocation, is part and parcel of holiness. The Desert Fathers, the ascetics of early times, did not flee from the world in the sense in which modern man sometimes tries to escape its grip in order to find a haven of security, they set out to conquer the Enemy in battle. By the grace of God, in the power of the Spirit, they were engaging in combat.

One of the reasons why holiness is unsteady and why the holiness of the Fathers and heroes of the Spirit in the early days often seems so remote is that we have lost this sense of combat. The conception of the Church as the advance guard of the Kingdom, as men and women who have committed their ultimate weakness into God's hands, knowing with certainty that the very

[1] A talk given in Louvain in 1969.

power of God is able to manifest itself in their weakness, the conception of the Church as the Body of Christ, whose life is not taken from it but which gives its life, is a rare thing among Christians. More often we see that as soon as a community or an individual is confronted with danger, he turns to the Lord and says: 'Lord, help me, protect me, save me, deliver me!' Isn't this the picture which the Polish writer Sinkiewicz gave us years ago in *'Quo Vadis'* in which St Peter leaves Rome at the moment of persecution and at the gates of the city meets Christ who is on His way there. 'Where are you going, Lord?' he asks his Master. 'I am going back to Rome,' the Lord replies, 'to suffer and die there because you are leaving it.' Isn't this what we constantly expect of God? Isn't this our anguished, desperate appeal to the Lord as soon as life becomes dangerous: 'Deliver me, Lord!' When the psalmist spoke of this deliverance, his position was quite different from ours; he belonged to the Old Testament. We belong to the New Testament, we are the Body of Christ, the temple of the Holy Spirit. God has sent us into the world by His Son, just as He sent His Son into the world.

And so in this respect there is a *crisis of holiness* which does not date from our time, for it is contemporaneous with many Christian generations. But we must face it, because holiness is our absolute vocation, because contemplative holiness is not an escape, and because the activism of our time which tries to be independent of any contemplation and to become a value in itself, lacks the content of complete holiness which Christian holiness ought to have, for the content of holiness is God Himself.

If you would like to make a closer study of holiness from the point of view of the Old Testament, you can easily refer to the alphabetical index of the Jerusalem Bible. There you will find all the elements that have been considered since before Christ. I would like to single out one or two without dealing with the subject as a whole.

God alone is holy. To say that God is holy is not to define Him as having holiness as an attribute, because we do not know this attribute. In saying 'God is holy', we do not define Him, because holiness itself is unknown to us: it becomes perceptible to us in proportion to our discovering God. For Israel holiness was that which is God. Reverential fear was linked to this notion; likewise the sense of irremediable separation: God is transcendent in an absolute way, He is beyond everything. Even when God is known, He remains unknowable; even when He approaches, He remains infinitely far away; even when He speaks to us, He is still beyond all communication. To approach Him is a danger: He is the fire that consumes; one cannot see His face and remain alive. All these images show us the attitude of a people who were conscious of the holiness of God and who were face to face with this Living God.

But the scandal of the New Testament, the impossible thing, is that the Inaccessible One has become accessible, the transcendent God has become flesh and dwelt among us. The holiness which surpassed every human notion and was a separation reveals itself to be otherwise: the very holiness of God can become infinitely close without becoming any the less mysterious; it becomes accessible without our being able to possess it; it lays hold of us without destroying us. In this perspective we can understand the words of St Peter in his general epistle, that we are called to become partakers of the divine nature. In Christ we see something which could be revealed by God but which could not even be dreamed of by man: the fullness of Divinity in human flesh. Here is the crux of holiness. It is accessible to us because of the fact of the Incarnation. This does not lessen the mystery of God: a purely transcendent God is easier to understand or imagine than the God of the Incarnation. And when we see the crèche of the Nativity in our imagination or in plastic representations and can take the Child-God in our hands, we are confronted with a greater mystery than that of the imperceptible God. How can we understand that the full depth of infinity and eternity lies here, hidden and at the same time revealed by a frail human body that is fragile and transparent to the presence of God?

Here is the very crux of holiness, because our holiness can be nothing else than participation in the holiness of God. And this is possible only through Christ, although the Old Testament was aware of a created holiness within the created world. Everything which God lays hold of and which becomes His own possession, such as the Ark, a person, a holy place, participates in a certain way in God's holiness and becomes an object of reverential fear. There is a holiness of Presence: the Temple. There is a holiness disquieting for the neighbouring peoples: the People of God, who are the place of the Presence. But this place of the Presence, which was like a living Temple, does not participate in God's holiness in a personal way, in each of its members. It is only later, in the Church of the Living God, that the place of the Presence also becomes the place of a personal presence within and through each one: it is the Church, the Body of Christ, the Church which Christ is on the evening of His Resurrection, in the Holy Spirit who takes hold of the Church, brings it to birth and becomes its life; but it is also the Church each of whose members, on the day of Pentecost and through the centuries by a continuation of that mystery, become the temple of the living God. And the Church is not only linked to Christ as His Body and to the Spirit, whose temple she becomes, but it is a Church in which each member in his particular uniqueness is linked to the Father through the only-begotten Son. 'Your life', says St Paul, 'is hidden in God with Christ.' This relationship of Christ with us, this bond between the One who alone is holy and His creatures, this presence of the personal eternity and personal infinity that God is, this real and living participation in a divine holiness is the essential characteristic of the Church, or at least one of its central characteristics. I believe that the Church is holy, not simply blessed and sanctified by gifts of grace, but holy with a depth and intensity which surpass all meaure, holy with the holiness of God who resides there, in the way in which a piece of wood glows with the fire that consumes it. And this holiness is a Presence in the Church. This is why the Church, in its position in relation to God, can acquire, possess and live this holiness only in Him.

On the other hand, just as God became man, just as His holiness was present in the flesh in our midst, living, acting and saving, so too now, through the mystery of the Incarnation, the Church participates in eternity, in the holiness of God, and at the same time also in the salvation of the world. The holiness of the Church must find its place in the world in an act of crucified love, in an active and living presence. But essentially it is the holiness, the Presence of God that we should manifest in the world. This is our vocation, this is what we are. If we are not this, we are outside the mystery that we pretend to express and in which we pretend to have our part.

Nevertheless, it is necessary to locate the position of the Church and that of the individual Christian in relation to the world. It seems to me that we have only two ways of doing this: on the one hand, we can try to see what holiness has been in history, and on the other hand, we can try to understand, in the person of Christ and in divine love, what the world is for God and what the solidarity of God is with the world that He has created.

I believe that a careful study of the history of the saints will easily show us that throughout the ages holiness has been the expression of love. In the very brief and condensed history of the Russian Church—it is hardly a thousand years since we became Christians—we can see something extremely important: the forms of saintliness have changed through the centuries without disappearing once they have come into being, and these changes express through the years the way in which God, in the hearts of the faithful, have loved the world. Scanning the history of the Russian Church—the one I know best—I see that at the beginning there is an act of faith: a man or a human group who believed, and who gave God to the surrounding people. St Vladimir, Prince of Kiev, believed. And because he believed passionately, radically, Christ entered into the history of his principality, and the social and human structures began to break up and be transformed. Yet he had no social purpose, no pious work in view: he simply could not live otherwise than he had learned from God Himself. It is only because this man believed in the Gospel message that the relations and internal structures in his principality changed. It is curious to note this change during a period when there was certainly no talk of social security or of a state responsible for its citizens! We see in the first place that this man, who had been a man of war and violence, a powerful and authoritarian tribal chief, ceased to make war, opened the prisons and proclaimed the forgiveness of Christ. We see that this man, whose personal life was by no means a model of holiness, changed overnight with a sharpness and clarity which confronted his people with a choice: to follow the old vision or a new one. We see that in the structures of this poor little city of Kiev, which was no more than a market-town, the poor, the sick and the aged became the object of solicitude. All the poor who could still walk received their daily meal in the courtyards of the Prince's palace. For those who were too aged, too weak, unable to move about, the Prince sent carts loaded with bread and sustenance through the city and neighbouring hamlets. Here we have a picture of a social transformation as great, comparatively speaking, as the greatest of our time. It implies a change of mental habit more amazing than the improvements that we make from day to day within one mentality already acquired and given to us.

This is the first picture: living, active love, the diaconate of Christ.

Then, a little later, we have the witness of the martyr, a particular type of martyr. There is no doubt that the Russian Church, like all the others, has known martyrs for the faith: people who set out to preach the Gospel to tribes that were still pagans perished for their message. Among them are two men who expressed a type of holiness that we would call 'social'. They were two princes, Boris and Gleb—and even a third, Igor —who chose to give up their power and principality and their very life rather than draw the sword. They allowed themselves to be killed rather than be defended and cause bloodshed. Here again is an example of holiness contemporaneous with an era of violence, one in which violence breaks out in new forms and in a new situation. Here again we see that the Gospel creates a situation of love, and that it is love alone which defines holiness in this situation.

Then a dark age: Russia is invaded for three centuries and falls under the Mongol yoke. At this time we find only two types of holiness, that of bishops and that of princes, both of which express the same thing. Their holiness arises out of the fact that both are hard pressed, being the defenders, advocates and protectors of the people committed to their charge, and they give their life, their blood, for the people. At this moment all the other forms of holiness that have existed—monastic holiness and others—become sporadic. Then a veritable epidemic of holiness begins: that of people who give their lives for their neighbour, truly taking responsibility for him according to the image of Kings and Priests which the Old Testament gives us. They realise that sometimes, in so-called 'better' times, the heads of the Church as well as those of the state forget that they stand on the threshold of two worlds: the world of men and the world of God; the world of the unique, radiant divine will directed to the salvation and plenitude of all things, and the world of multiple, discordant, violent human will opposed to that of God,—and that their role is to unite the two and to give their life for this work. Here again we see that it is love that takes the lead.

It is not a new invention in terms of holiness, it is not the search for a contemporary holiness: it is simply the response of the holiness inherent in the Church, of the love given by God to His Church, which has found a new form of expression. It was not the moment to withdraw into the forests or to choose other valid but different forms of holiness: it was the moment for giving one's life.

The Mongol yoke withdraws: we enter a period of national anguish, a period in which the former suffering now changes to confidence. As long as this suffering was crushing the nation and destroying the very capacity to feel it, it was bearable. Now problems arise, internal ones which are not yet well expressed: God and suffering, the horror of a world which could be so frightful, and then the birth of hope and the search for a path for this hope. At this time we see giants of the spiritual life one after the other abandoning everything, the highest tasks as well as the humblest circumstances, and withdrawing into the forests of northern and central Russia to seek God there. These men leave everything because they have understood that in torment, disorder and purely earthly seeking they will not find the answer to the problems of their contemporaries. They leave everything to be with God. Their purpose is certainly not social at this time. They have to find their souls again, and with their soul, the nation, the soul of their people, the soul of their contemporaries. They are not in flight: they take up a life so arduous, so laborious that it would be ridiculous to consider it as an escape. The living conditions in a forest in northern Russia at this time, the hunger, cold, physical dangers from wild beasts, all these should make it easy for us to understand that it is not an easy and comfortable life that they are looking for. They seek only God, and they find God in the depths of their souls, which surrender to Him. They seek only Him, but at the same time their love becomes deeper and deeper, and they welcome all those who, one after the other, come in the same anguish, seeking the same haven of salvation. Monasteries grow up around them, this too by an act of love. A society of human help and work begins to appear. I will give two examples that are diametrically opposed.

In norther Russia beyond the Volga in the 15th century one of the great saints of Russia, St Nilus, settled with several companions in a desolate, swampy region. They lived in dreadful poverty, and in his *Rule* St Nilus said that a monk must be so poor that he cannot even offer physical charity beyond a piece of bread, but he should love the pilgrim or the vagabond or the brigand who has fled or the heretic who has broken away from the Church—let us say, the ꞌChurch that St Nilus belongs to— he should love him so much that he would be ready to give him all the spiritual experience, everything that his soul contained. Here is a man who chose to know only Christ, and Christ crucified, who gave up everything, physically, and who could not give anything, for he possessed nothing but God alone, by whom he was possessed. For one does not possess God: one is laid hold of by Him, filled with His breath and His presence, but one does not become the proprietor of all this.

The other man, his contemporary, lived in the region of Moscow and was an equally remarkable person. He founded a monastery in which about a thousand monks worked under a rule of incredible austerity. The monastery, in such a cold region, was never heated, the monks were not permitted to wear anything else but a hair shirt and a garment thrown over it. The offices lasted ten hours a day and the work in the fields or in the monastery was seven to eight hours. At times they groan and howl with indignation, saying, 'We are hungry, our granaries are full . . . and you do not let us eat; we are thirsty and we have water . . . and you do not let us drink.' Their holy and fierce superior answers: 'You do not work in order to be satisfied, you do not work in order to have a life of ease; you have no business to be warm, you have no business to be at rest. Look at the peasants round about, they are hungry, it is for them that we must work, they are cold, it is for them that we must cut wood; they have many orphans, it is for them that you set up this orphanage; they are ignorant, it is for them that you have this school; the old people have no place to go, it is for them that you must maintain this old people's home.' And these poor thousand monks, some of whom were doing their utmost to be holy, groaned and groaned. . . And nevertheless, under the strong hand of their Superior they lived a life which was love. There were moments when they kicked, when the flesh weakened, but they had a conscience in their midst; it was St Joseph, who did not allow them to fall as low as they would have. To use more modern terminology, he is, if you like, a collective super-ego. He is there with his absolute demands. . . And here we have another monastic type.

Other monasteries of the same kind formed round him. Hunger, cold, ignorance, neglect of the aged, neglect of the young: all this became the object of love. And if you read the works and life of St Joseph, there is no doubt that there was nothing else but love, for he had no concern for anything else. He did not care about the consequences, nor did it matter what people thought of the folly of these things. What he said was that these people were hungry and in need of help, and that we who have known Christ, who know who He is, must bring Him to them. And if it costs you your life, well, it costs you your life! If you read his writings, you will see few reassuring passages on the repose which the monks will have and a much greater number in which they are warned that if they do not toil hard, there is hell fire.

After this epoch we find ourselves in a period in which States begin to acquire a reality which we would now call secular. The principality of Moscow begins to grow in strength and size. It devours the neighbouring principalities by most unworthy means and asserts a kind of ethic, a state law. At this moment the

Christian conscience rises up in a very curious way. At this period, which was a time of renewal, when people were simply beginning to breathe again and also to attach themselves more and more to material goods—because they had begun to appear and because everyone was happy to be able to build a livable world at last—at this time a group of men and women, several dozen, appeared successively and simultaneously, who were called 'God's fools' or 'fools of Christ'. On close inspection the folly in question can be interpreted in two different ways according to the various cases. There was the folly undertaken by people of clear intelligence, burning hearts and iron will. But there was also, in certain cases, the holiness of those whose intelligence was disturbed but who, basically, had God at the heart of their interior life. They were people who denied all the social values: wealth and the impossibility of living without many of the material things so dear to man; the most primitive human relations as well as the most demanding hierarchical relations. They were men who, in this icy Russia of the North, walked the streets with bare feet in winter, dressed only in a shirt, and proclaimed the fact that if you believe, you can live by the Word of God; *if you believe*, you can give up everything, whereas if you let yourself become involved in the new tendency to accept values that are only transitory, you are lost, you belong to the world of Satan!

Was it an exaggeration or a vision of peace, a question of depth? I believe there is a question of depth here. I have no wish to say that we should all go out and do the same and that none of the human values which the Christian world has formed in the course of centuries have any meaning. But I believe that if we have a religious vocation, if we have the sense of eternity, the sense of the Presence—and if we know that God is living and active in our midst and in us—we should have a Gospel on the subject. It would consist in saying: 'Yes, all of that has a temporary, transitory, ephemeral and sometimes even necessary value taken as a whole, but we must not attach our hearts to it. We must toil with our backs and our hands, but our heart must not be put into it, for our heart should belong only to God.'

Then a more complex situation enters into Russian history: the social life, the political life and the religious life mesh into one another in a way that is increasingly rich or increasingly impoverished, according to the moments. We find here all the types of Christian life that exist in the West, or in the Christian world taken as a whole, up to the moment when the Orthodox Church became the object of persecution in communist countries. At this moment the Church and the world become linked in a new way. If you think of the martyrs of the first centuries, you find that they are distinguished by certain characteristics. They were men, women and children who had discovered that God and Christ were the ultimate value for them, that in Him resided all the meaning of life. He was all in all to them. And it was out of personal loyalty that when His name was blasphemed, when His Person was put in question, they could only die for Him. On the other hand, in this relationship between Christ and those who believed in Him, a profound change was taking place in them: they would die to be reborn. Recall the 6th chapter of the Epistle to the Romans. They died the death of Christ and lived again by His Resurrection, they were in possession of eternal life, and it was eternal life that powerfully strengthened and gave direction to their temporal life. For them to die was not to perish but to be released from a transitory, ephemeral life with a view to attaining the fullness, the plenitude of eternal life in God. To live was Christ, but to die was a gain, for living in the flesh also meant being separated from God.

We see, however, that it was only indirectly, so to speak, that the martyrs brought about conversions: it was admiration, it was horror, it was the revelation of God by them which made conversions, but their intention seems to have been no more than to be witnesses of Christ, witnesses of the victory of God.

Since the revolution, in this world of incessant persecutions which are sometimes terrible and sharp, sometimes secret and hidden, a new mentality has developed. In this connection we can start with a thought that comes not from the Slavic world but from the West. Jean Daniélou says that suffering is the meeting-point of good and evil, of life and death. This is true, because evil is never something absolute, meta-physical and disincarnate: it always expresses itself in human persons, through human persons and to the detriment of human persons.

Evil always slashes, plunges into human flesh or into the human soul. There is always a person-to-person relationship where there is suffering, hate, greed or cowardice. But the victory is decisive: evil falls into the hands of the good, so to speak, because the moment we become victims, we acquire a right which is properly divine, to forgive. And then, just as Christ said, 'Father, forgive them, for they know not what they do,' so can we in our turn say, as one of our bishops did before his death in the course of the Stalinist purges: 'There will come a day when the martyr will be able to stand before the throne of God in defence of his persecutors and say, "Lord, I have forgiven in Thy Name and by Thy example: Thou hast no claim against them any more." '

This represents a new situation, a new mentality in the Church which is also one of the aspects of love, an aspect which surpasses our limits and is often too great for us because we are unable to do it on a small scale. How often are we able to forgive completely the little sufferings that are imposed upon us, the small sorrows inflicted on us? We have here a new upsurge of the love of God in human hearts, a new conquest by God. God manifests Himself once again, and the concept of the suffering Church and the personal martyr becomes at the same time a concept of the salvation of the other.

I hope that these examples will help you to grasp the fact that holiness is never in any way an individual act in the sense in which the word 'individual' signifies the lasts term of a fragmentation, the point beyond which one can no longer divide, and that holiness is always a situation and an act that imply not only the totality of the Church—since we are the living members of a body from which we cannot be separated and which cannot be separated from us—but also that we are members of the created world around us. Holiness is the love of God at work in a concrete, active, deliberate way, which applies itself with rigour and precision to situations that are always fresh and always contemporary with the eternal love of God and with the human presence of men, women and children who are possessed with this love

and, being contemporaneous with their epoch, express it in a way
that only they can choose, discover and put into practice.

The next point I wish to take up is one which, I think, is very
important for the way in which we evaluate the world and our
situation in the world: it is the notion of the *solidarity of God
with the world*. I purposely use the word 'solidarity', which is
neither theological nor pious, in order to avoid using a word,
whatever it might be, that would put us right into an old rut
where we could resolve without effort an extremely sharp and
important problem.

When we come to the subject of prayer in its relationship to
holiness I shall try to give enough emphasis to the aspect of
holiness which is oriented wholly towards God and whose sole
content is God. Before doing that, I think it would be best to
take a brief look at man, who is the object of incarnate holiness,
the one towards whom the instances of human holiness are
directed and with whom they often deal.

Two notions have come to the fore, since the war, perhaps,
more than in the years that preceded it; the notion of the greatness of man, of his significance both for us men and for God, and
the notion of human solidarity. For centuries, it seems, within the
Church we have tried to make our God as great as we could, by
making man small. This can be seen even in works of art in which
the Lord Jesus Christ is represented as great and his creatures as
very small indeed at his feet. The intention was to show how
great God was, and yet it has resulted in the false and almost blas-
phemous view that man is small or, on the other hand, in the
denial of this God who treats men as though they were of no
value. And these two reactions are equally wrong. The one belongs to people who claim to be children of God, God's own chosen people, who are the Church. They have managed by doing
this to make themselves as small as the image they have of men,
and their communities as small and lacking in scope and greatness
as their constitutive parts. The other attitude we find outside the
Church, among the agnostics, the rationalists and the atheists. But
in these reactions we find a common ground—man—who is now
a point of real and extremely fruitful encounter between those who

hold the two most clearly opposed ideologies: faith and atheism. Man is the only object which they have in common. They visualise him and treat him differently, but the fact remains that it is man who is at the centre of both schools of thought. One could almost say that the modern interpretation of St Paul's encounter with that altar 'to the unknown God' would be to say that the unknown god is man, whom everyone is placing on the altar now. The atheist world sets up the empirical man and the collective man. The Christian world also places a man on the altar: the man Jesus Christ. The fact that the breadth of the vision of man in Christianity exceeds all the bounds of the created does not keep Jesus, the Son of God, the Word Incarnate, from being fully man in the total sense of the word 'fully'.

I repeat a point already made. Marx says that the proletariat has no need of a god because man has become his god. And St John Chrysostom: 'If you want to measure the greatness of man, raise your eyes towards the throne of God and you will see the Word Incarnate, the bearer of our humanity, seated at the right hand of the glory.' Here are the two clearest expressions of the modern situation. And yet in both cases it is man who is at the centre of everything.

For the atheist world—I mean the atheist world that has an ideology, not the atheist world of the stomach which one might call 'gastric' atheism, about whom St Paul is speaking when he tells us, 'These men's god is their belly'—for the ideological atheist who bases himself on a conception of the world, theoretical man is truly a god. One might even ask what is the extent of this reality of the man-god for the atheist. The striking thing is that, on the one hand, the theoretical man is a god; at the same time the empirical man is a victim and a slave. This, I think, is explained by the fact that the theoretical man in question who is placed on the altar of atheism is not a personal man, he is not each man considered in his person, which is not only inimitable but also unique, but it is the collective man. And this theoretical-collective man, who is unique, challenges the rights of the individual man. The former is the man of the present and the future, not the concrete man living in the present nor the individual man who will live in the future, but humanity—or the 'class'—and this is always a collectivity which has the right to make absolute demands on each of its members. In the matter of art, literature, civic conduct and conscientious inner conviction, this collectivity has totalitarian claims. And the concrete man, the individual, whose human course proceeds as if made up of little pieces like a mosaic, has only his small place in it: he cannot go beyond the place assigned to him; he only has the right to possess the position and colour that are imposed upon him.

It is necessary to emphasise very strongly the profound difference between the atheist notion of the collective and the notion of the Church, in which we are members of a living body; likewise between the notion of the 'individual' and that of the 'person' which is the condition of man within the Church.

The collective position is that in which an ideological minority becomes a *de facto* majority, having the right to impose its will on each member of the society. In the Church there is nothing of the sort. Even the will and word of God have no authority in the sense of a law which is imposed. It is a voice which reveals to us the reality and truth of things. If we respond to it, we do so because we are sensitive to the truth of what is proclaimed to us and we reach out towards this reality, which is the only means we have of becoming fully free and fully ourselves. The will of God is not a law nor an imprisonment. One of our Russian theologians of the 19th century, Khomyakov, who was one of the most passionate polemicists against Catholicism and Protestantism at the same time—and from this point of view was not exactly a forerunner of ecumenism—tells us that the will of God is a malediction for the demon, it is the law for unregenerate man, and freedom for those who have attained salvation.

In these terms, which are perfectly adequate to the theme, we see that it is not a question of a will imposed from outside, but of a will that appears external to us in the measure in which we ourselves are external to our vocation and to our human reality. On the other hand, in the atheist world of the collectivity it is a will of iron that is imposed on its members: it pours scorn on the convictions and the most categorical imperatives of conscience, because the truth is expressed by the Party, or else by such and such a human group that considers itself to be in possession of the truth and of the right to define it according to needs and convention. In this view man is seen as an individual who has no supra-personal life, no life that transcends him and means that he lives in others and others in him; he forms part of a gear, he is one of the constituent but replaceable elements.

We see the tragic working of this not only in the Russian Revolution in its full scope but even in the story of the members of the Party in the time of the Stalinist purges. One can read the book by Eugenie Ginsburg, who was a member of the Party before the revolution, passionately devoted to her party, and who spent eighteen years in concentration camps simply because she refused to sign a list of statements of confession to crimes that she had never committed but which were useful at the moment to her party's line.

According to Marxist ideology, the individual is an interchangeable being; in contrast, the person is unique and irreplaceable: this is a profound difference that exists within and outside the Church. It is important in the matter of holiness, because each of us is unique, irreplaceable, and only knows God in a unique way that no one else could share. The replaceable individual, towards whom the work of holiness on the part of the Church is directed, should be transformed into that which he really is: a human person. I should like to indicate briefly the difference between these two terms by saying again that an individual is the last term of a fragmentation: it is not possible to divide further than the individual. If you endeavour to go further in your attempt at dissection, you will get a corpse and a soul: you will no longer be in the presence of the whole human being.

The person is altogether different: this can best be defined by the passage from the Book of Revelation in which we are told that in the Kingdom of God each of those who enter will receive a white stone with a name inscribed on it—a name known only to God and to the one who receives it. This name is not the nickname by which we are known in ordinary life—surname, Christian name—it is a name that contains, and defines all that

we are and all that we are called to be. We can imagine it to be
the mysterious word that God uttered in order to call us into
being out of nothingness, out of the radical absence from which
we were drawn by the will of God. This name, which defines us
completely and is known only to God and the one who bears it,
defines the unique, unprecedented and unparalleled relationship
that each of us has with God. In his relationship persons are not
opposable, individuals are indeed: we recognise them by opposing
traits of character, external features, psychological and social
traits; we speak of their colour, stature, weight, nationality. Here
the question does not concern those things: it is a question of
something very profound and unique, such that it is not by contrast nor by opposition nor comparison that we recognise the
human person, but by the fact that he is himself and that no one
has ever been nor ever will be what he is, because if two persons
could be identified with one another, they would be one. Thus
we see clearly that the collective, which deals with individuals,
and the Church, which is composed of members who are living,
unique, irreplaceable and incomparable with one another, are
profoundly different realities. Holiness belongs to the sphere of
the Church as a body and to the sphere of the person, while it
is completely alien to the categories of the individual, who by
definition is contrasted and distinguished, and of the collectivity,
which asserts itself and limits the individual's own possibilities.

So if we as the Church are called to be a human presence of
the kind that can be described in terms of sociology or history,
we must nevertheless remember that this human presence is not
the presence of an ordinary society. It is not only the place of
the presence of God, it is also that of the presence of man, seen,
conceived, lived in a unique way which is unknown to the world.
And in our missionary work, in our enlargement of the limits of
the holiness of the Church and of man in particular, if we lose
sight of this, if we forget that it is God, and man in God, who
is the object of holiness, we have lost sight of the essential. We
can create organisations which are more or less useful—and they
will certainly be replaced some day by more effective social
organisations, because the possibilities of the total *socius* are
greater than those of the particular society that we are—but we

will never attain the goal which is offered to us, to be this revelation of the holiness of God, Who is winning and assimilating the
world to Himself, making us participants in the divine nature and
temples of the Holy Spirit, the really living Body of Christ, and
making our life hidden in God with Jesus Christ.

Thus the element of holiness in the Church is found to be
connected with a two-fold vision of man, but one that is different
from that of the world. In this confrontation, this encounter
between ourselves and the world outside, we must make our contribution to what man is—and we cannot accept the vision of a
secular holiness which knows nothing of the depths of man, of his
bond with God, and which defines holiness in moral and prag-
matic or practical categories.

In the Church we have a two-fold vision of man: empirical
man and the man revealed in Jesus Christ. There is also the
corollary fact that the Church is simultaneously a society in
history and, invisibly yet transparently, a mystery. From the
empirical point of view we are the Church, all of us such as we
are, not only such as we are called to be, but as we are in the
frailty of the individual and in the insufficiency and implenitude
of human becoming. From this point of view the Church can
be defined in the terms used by St Ephraim the Syrian in the
sixth century: 'The Church is not the assembly of saints, it is the
mass of sinners who repent, who, sinners though they are, have
turned towards God and are oriented towards Him.' From this
point of view it is true that the Church is the object of history
and of sociological studies, because from that aspect it belongs
to the world, for it has not yet been liberated by holiness from
the world's grasp. The world is within it through us in so far as
each of us is not freed from the world, in the ascetic sense.

But on the other hand, there is in the Church a vision of man
which is not a theory of man. It is not the ideal man, it is not the
invented man, nor man as we wish he were, and towards which
we aim as a sort of created transcendence. No, it is a real man
really revealed, for it must never be forgotten that among the
people who form the Church of the Living God there is one
such man, Jesus, the incarnate God, true man in the double sense
of the word: he is true in the sense that he is in nothing different

from us, he is not a superman, not a man who appeared in our
midst from outside. He is flesh of our flesh, bone of our bone;
he belongs to us entirely, just as we belong to him entirely. That
is why we can say, even with regard to the human existence of
the Church, that we believe in the Church, for in Christ it is an
object of faith, a vision of man which is not the empirical reality
and which nevertheless already is empirical reality, because it is
an empirical reàlity that we can observe in history. True man, in
the fullness of reality, has appeared to us in the Person of Christ,
the Word Incarnate, a man who is genuine in the fullest sense
of the word. Among Orthodox and Catholics I will also add
that we have a vision of true man in the Holy Virgin, who
attained the fullness of her human vocation, as witnessed by our
common faith in the Assumption, that is to say, in her bodily
resurrection.

Since that time, for the people of the Church, to be a man
has meant seeking this identification with the Christ-Man in the
same way as he accepted his identification with the empirical
man that we had become by our fall and that we are by definition
in the created world. Thus action, service and contemplation
within the Church are correlative and linked necessarily with
one another, for it is only to the extent to which we can see, that
we can grow to the measure of that which we see. Only to the
extent that we can see and hear the God-man in action can we act
in conformity with the divine plan and take our part in the world.

As our holiness can only find its place in the created world
where we are—I do not speak of society, because the anchorites
and hermits are equally a part of the Church and have their
part to play in the created world—it is only as far as we can see
and hear, that we can act, or rather *be*, according to the will of
God, so that our being is a creative and saving act, an act of
holiness that would be our sanctification but is also a sanctification for the entire world. Here is where the notion of wisdom has
its special place. It is a wisdom different from human sagacity.
We see it in the prophets and patriarchs and New Testament
saints: their inner capacity for profound peace, for absolute
stability, for gazing earnestly and patiently at the world in which
they lived in order to discern in it the trace of the passage of

God, the way He followed, in order to follow that way, for it is He alone Who is the Way. And it is on this way that we can find and give the Truth and the Life.

This necessity of looking and seeing is expressed in a way which I find very beautiful in a narrative told by Nathaniel Hawthorne, relating a New World legend. In a village built on a high mountain cut by a stream and facing the little cluster of huts, very high up in the rock, a face has been carved in the rock from time immemorial; it is the face of the god of these villagers. It is a face of transcendent beauty, expressing an ineffable peace and complete harmony. And the villagers hand down a promise from generation to generation that there will come a day when this god will detach himself from the mountain and live among them. They admire this face, they are inspired by it—and they fall back again and again into the cares of their poor community life. However, one day a child is born in the village who, from the moment he was capable of seeing, perceiving and responding, of submitting to external impressions, as soon as he could crawl from the hut where he was born down to the edge of the stream, was struck by the beauty, serenity and majesty of this face. One could always find him sitting beside the stream doing nothing but looking.

The years pass, the baby becomes a little boy and later a young man. A day comes when the inhabitants of the village, seeing him pass by, stop and exclaim, 'Our god is in our midst!' By thrusting his gaze deep into this face he had become inwardly conformed to the whole expression and spiritual content of this other face, by gazing at it he had become imbued with it, he had allowed himself to be penetrated by the serenity, the grandeur, peace and love which radiated from that face of stone. And now his face had become that of the god whom he had venerated and quite simply gazed at.

I believe that there is something essential here in terms of holiness and also in terms of the place which human holiness can have within a complex pluralist society like that in which we live. If only we knew how to gaze with all the depths of our being at the face of Christ, that invisible face which we can see only by turning towards our own depths and which we see emerging from there, then those around us would relive the impact of a serenity, a deepening, a peace, a power both strong and gentle, and they would understand that there is holiness in the Church. And this holiness would have no need to make desperate efforts to manifest itself in order to make others believe that the Church is holy. Everyone would believe—which is so difficult to do when one looks at us!

All holiness is God's holiness in us: it is a holiness that is participation and, in a certain way, more than participation, because as we participate in what we can receive from God, we become a revelation of that which transcends us. Being a limited light, we reveal the Light. But we should also remember that in this life in which we are striving towards holiness, our spirituality should be defined in very objective and precise terms. When we read books on spirituality or engage in studying the subject, we see that spirituality, explicitly or implicitly, is repeatedly defined as an attitude, a state of soul, an inner condition, a type of interiority, and so on. In reality, if you look for the ultimate definition and try to discover the inner core of spirituality, you find that spirituality does not consist of the states of soul that are familiar to us, but that it is the presence and action of the holy spirit in us, by us and through us in the world. It is not fundamentally a matter of the way in which we express it.

There is an absolute objectivity both to holiness and to the spirituality which is expressed in it. Spirituality is that of the Spirit; didn't St Paul tell us that it is the holy Spirit who teaches us to say: 'Abba, Father'? Doesn't he mean that it is the holy Spirit, God Himself, who shapes in us the knowledge of God? And, furthermore, there is no other holiness than that of God; it is as the Body of Christ that we can participate in holiness, in Christ and in the holy Spirit.

If such is the case, a question of tremendous importance arises. In view of our search for holiness, in as much as it is situated, whether we like it or not, within the framework of the created world and the world of men, the tragic, complex world in which we live— if it is the presence of Christ Himself and the inspiration of the Spirit which the holiness of the Church should express in each of its members and in the totality of its body, *where is the limit of this love*? In other words, where is the limit of our sense of solidarity and responsibility? Is there a moment when we should detach ourselves and say: 'I leave you, go your way; if you repent, if you change, we will find one another again, but as you are, I can no longer go with you.' Or are there no limits, not only to God's condescension but also to this tremendous and passionate solidarity of God? Holy Scripture more than once places us in the presence of God's love in terms of 'Eros', that is, a love and attachment that is total and passionate, which embraces everything, leaving nothing outside.

I should like to draw your attention to a quotation which is certainly not scriptural and has no authority in itself, but which seems interesting to me. In the seventeenth century a Russian priest, a man of burning convictions, wrote his autobiography. He wanted to show how a man of faith can remain faithful to what he believes to be the truth in spite of the treachery, or what he considered to be the treachery of the visible Church. A prologue is attached to this *Vita*, written by himself. At one point in it he speaks of the divine Council which preceded the creation of the world and says: 'In the light of what we know of God Incarnate, can we not say that one day the Father said to the Son: "My Son, let us create a visible world and man." And the Son replies: "My Father, let it be according to Thy Will." And the Father adds: "My Son, you know that if I make it through you, there will come a time when man will play us false and in order to bring him back to us you will have to die?" And the Son replies: "Let it be according to Thy Will, my Father!" And the world was created.' This is not apocryphal, in as much as it makes no pretence of expressing a scriptural reality in other terms, but it expresses a profound inner reality: God in His divine Wisdom willed and called the world into being in full awareness of the consequences which this divine call, which made a free world appear out of nothing, would have for God Himself. This is a contest between God and the world, if we may say so, and the tragedy we so often complain about is more tragic for God than for the world!

Throughout the history of the Old and New Testaments we

see how God afterwards takes His full responsibility for His creative act. Step by step he upholds the prophets, declares His will, reveals the depth of His thought. Didn't Amos say that the prophet is he with whom God shares His thoughts? And He remains faithful when creation has become unfaithful—remember Hosea and the images he gives of the faithful husband of a woman who has deserted him. So underlying everything there is a unilateral act of God, but it is an act for which He takes total and final responsibility. This is important because if we are 'in God', we must share with Him, at least take our part of this divine responsibility. Our election to be the Church is not a paradisiac privilege. It is basically an election to share the thought and heart of God, but also to share Christ's work in the Incarnation and the economy of salvation. I want here to insist on the intensity of this solidarity, simply turning your thought to those words of Christ, almost the last ones he uttered on the Cross: 'My God, my God, why hast Thou forsaken me?'

When we speak of the solidarity of Christ with men in the Incarnation, we continually think of the minor and major expressions of this contradiction. We consider the limitations which the divine Word imposed upon Himself in entering time and becoming a prisoner of space: He is hungry, thirsty, tired: On another level, He seeks, He accepts the company of sinners. He lives in the midst of hatred and this hatred kills Him at a certain moment. These last two terms seem very weak to me, and this is their weakness: 'human hatred kills him'. This prevents people from understanding what is special about the death of Christ. If it is in terms of death, all those who have attained mortality die, and He did nothing that each of us will not have to do some day. If it is in terms of suffering, there are millions of people who have suffered infinitely more than He on the cross. Two thieves were crucified at the same time as He, they also died a human death on the cross. If we think of the 11th chapter of the Epistle to the Hebrews, we see that human suffering, human horror, even in terms of holiness, has surpassed all that we can imagine of the physical suffering of Christ. The tragedy of His death is not His ultimate participation in human tragedy and human destiny.

The unique human tragedy, the only one that counts, the one out of which all the others arise, is mortality, and this mortality is linked with sin, with separation from God. And it is here that the death of Christ and his solidarity with us contain something more frightful than we can imagine. St Maximus the Confessor says in his Study of the Incarnation: 'It is unthinkable that human flesh that is united indissolubly for ever with Divinity could, even as human flesh, be mortal.' To be mortal means to be separated. And he stresses the fact that from the moment of the Incarnation Jesus of Nazareth, by reason of the union of divinity with humanity, was immortal, free of the necessity of death. His death is not only a simple acceptance of the human condition; it is conditioned by the ultimate experience of the human tragedy, which consists in losing God and dying because of this. Here we have something extremely important: Christ in his Incarnation accepted not only the limitations but the depth of our tragedy. According to the old saying what Christ has not participated in remains outside the mystery of salvation. If Christ had not participated in our break with God, in our estrangement, in what one of our theologians called a psychological eclipse which made him lose sight of the presence of God, he would not have participated fully in our mortality, and our mortality would have been outside the mystery of the Redemption.

Thus we see how far divine love goes in this solidarity with us: Christ accepts not only being like one of us, not only participating in everything except sin, but in participating even in 'estrangement', in the fact of becoming a stranger, of withdrawing from the Father in order to participate in the unique tragedy of man: atheism.

The same idea is expressed in the Apostles' Creed, when we say, 'He descended into Hell.' Since Dante we have thought of a hell of torments: but the Hell spoken of in the Old Testament is not a hell of torments: it is Sheol, which is simply the place where every human soul is cut off, the place where God is not, because before Christ's Redemption there is a gulf between God and man which only the Redemption, the Christ-mystery can fill. He descends into Hell. Hell opens wide to seize a new prey in whom to press a final victory over God, without knowing

whom it is receiving. And into this Hell which receives a man
God Himself enters. I believe there is a final touch here which
explains what the psalmist has a foreboding of when he
exclaims: 'Whither should I flee before Thy face? To Heaven?
But that is Thy abode! To Hell? But Thou art there also!'
Nothing in the condition of the created, nothing in the condition
of man, except sin, is now outside the experience of Christ, outside the reality of Christ. Everything is contained in him, and
there is not an atheist in the world who has known atheism, the
loss of God, in the way Christ, the Son of Man has, who died on
the cross with that cry of ultimate anguish and agony. Here again
we see the breadth of divine love and the depth of this acceptance
by God of everything which is the human condition. 'Nothing
human is alien to me,' said Tertullian. Perhaps he did not know
how far this acceptance of the human condition went for God.
He died. He died without sin. With what death did he die? With
ours, with a borrowed death. Is not this the divine vocation, to
remain without sin and to die a borrowed death?

I should like now to speak about prayer in connection with
what has been said so far about holiness. Prayer and holiness seem
to me to be rooted in a twofold experience, not in two experiences
but in a twofold, correlative one. On the one hand there is the
amazement that we feel in the short—but real—moments when
we perceive God, when we almost touch the hem of His garment;
these moments of wonder are flashing instants of contemplation,
and they leave us in a contemplative state, in deepening prayer,
meditation and interiority which are on the border of profound
contemplation and life in God. On the other hand, at the other
pole of this twofold reality of prayer and holiness we find despair
and compassion: despair such as we see, for instance, at the end
of the 10th chapter of St Mark, the despair of blind Bartimaeus
at the gate of Jericho, the despair of a man who has been blind
and has suffered from it, who has fought for his sight for years and
finally, crushed by misfortune, has settled into his blindness. And
then suddenly he hears that there is a man living in Galilee in
Judaea who has the power to give sight to a man born blind, to
cure every sickness, to heal every infirmity. And this man is
passing his way. And this moment when the last hope is passing

by is a moment of reawakening of all the feelings of despair that he bears within him as well as all the hope of which he is capable.

We can pray at moments when we become aware of our blindness—and we can include in this term whatever makes us blind to God and to all that surrounds us—and when we sense that the One who can cure us is passing near. Prayer arises at moment when we become deeply aware of our separation and of the fact that our life is suspended over death, that nothingness is within us and lapping round us from all sides, ready to engulf us. And when we turn our gaze towards others, in place of that despair linked to an ultimate hope, which is the hope that Bartimaeus had, it is compassion which awakes in us, the capacity to suffer deeply, intensely, not the suffering of the other—for one can never suffer the suffering of another nor ever understand another —but one can suffer from the fact that he is suffering, and in a mysterious way, beyond all experience, participate within this unity of the Body of Christ, in the common suffering which is his.

There is a link between *contemplation and intercession*, between the contemplation of God and this active, concrete prayer directed to the present and to .the world in which we live. A Russian monk from a monastery which is now in Finland had spent fifty years in his monastery without consenting to make profession, saying: 'I am unworthy, I don't yet know how to love. . .' And when he was asked: 'But what would you say a monk is, after all?' he answered: 'A monk is one who can weep for the whole world'. Here you see a man who had spent fifty years in a completely contemplative life, not oriented towards anything—in the last twenty years of his life he was bedridden because in the course of his work he had lost an arm, had lost a leg, had become blind—and nevertheless he refused the monastic profession because it seemed impossible for him to love and be a monk, that is, to be alone with God, not in a withdrawn solitude but in ardent and active solitude. Thus there is a bond which does not allow a separation between *contemplation in prayer*, the adoration of God, and *action*, the prayer of intercession or physical presence. But it is only to the extent to which our physical presence is the presence of God through us, the presence of Eternity in time through us, that we remain the Church while remaining engaged in action. If our activity in the world becomes a disengagement in relation to God, we fall back into the condition of a human society which has an ideology but no transcendent reality.

If we want to be active and contemplative at the same time, if we want to follow the line of holiness or communion with divine life, in a profound, intense, creative way while being at the same time in the midst of the world, whether in a cloistered order—for the cloister is now more than ever incapable of being radically set apart—or actively engaged in life, we must learn a way of prayer that permits inner stability—not psychological stability (which we lack, but the problem is not in that, nor is the solution to be found on that level), but an inner stability which consists of standing immobile, face to face with the living God. We must attain to a prayer of presence, our presence with God and his presence in the world through us. This is one of the aspects of intercession.

I should like to say a few words about this aspect in order to be able to use it in what follows. I should like to give you the story of the Wedding at Cana as an example of intercessory prayer defined as a presence.

You know the scene: a village wedding, poor and simple, with Christ, the Mother of God and his disciples who have been invited. Long before hearts have been seized with joy, long before they are overflowing with that life, the human conditions for joy begin to run out. No doubt the lights are going dim, the bread has been eaten and the wine is failing. At this moment the Holy Virgin makes an act of presence, not in the vulgar sense in which we speak of putting on an act as distinct from inner involvement,— but she makes the act of being there, fully and completely involved. As you will see, she is involved exactly in that twofold way which makes *contemplation active and action contemplative*. She turns to the Lord and says to Him: 'They have no more wine.' What is Mary asking? Would she really like the Lord to perform an act of magic and multiply the wine until the guests had drunk so much that they fell asleep under the tables? Is this the joy that she wants for them? It is unthinkable. So there is something more in it; there is a premonition, a foreknowledge of the fact that if Christ gives them what the earth is now refusing, the gift will be one that is at the same time of the order of eternal life. Christ then turns to her and asks her a question: 'What have you and I in common? My hour has not come.' I know that there are pious translations which try to avoid a sentence that seems incomprehensible and difficult, that seems to be an insult to the holy Virgin, and they do their best to translate this sentence too briefly to be perfectly clear semantically, by saying: 'What does it matter to you and me?' But 'What does it matter to us' would be an atrocious thing for Christ to say. 'What is it to me that their joy is fading, what is it to me that this party isn't finished and doesn't reach its perfection? Haven't we who are sober had enough to eat?' Is that what he means? Certainly not, for 'My hour has not yet come' is a statement that pertains to eternal life and the coming of the Kingdom, and not simply to the magistery of a miracle-worker. 'What is there in common between you and me?' How are we to understand this sentence? St John Chrysostom comments on it in a way that seems to me more than strange: I believe he is in line with a certain modern psychology which always sees all the faults on the side of the parents. Here, according to him, not even the holy Virgin has escaped this tendency of all mothers to believe that because they have brought a child into the world, they have imprescriptible rights over him until his death. So there she is intruding, giving herself rights. . . and Christ puts her back in her place. Saint though he is, I believe that in this case St John Chrysostom, not through any lack of devotion, has misunderstood the text. Other commentaries seem to me more adequate. 'What have you and I in common? Why is it you who make this request? Is it because you are my mother according to the flesh that you feel you have rights over me?' (We are in line with St John Chrysostom.) Or 'Has everything that you learned from the angel, everything that you kept in your heart and pondered in the course of your life, revealed to you that "I am here", a presence which makes this human marriage unfold to the dimensions of the Wedding of the Lamb? If you are speaking to me because you are my mother according to the flesh, my hour has not yet come.' He leaves the question hanging. The holy Virgin does not answer: 'Am I not your mother? Don't you know how much faith I have in you?' She only answers him with a gesture, but it is much more convincing than all the phrases she could have uttered. She turns to the servants and says to them: 'Whatever he tells you to do, do it.' She makes a total, integral, unlimited act of faith, the faith on which the Annunciation was founded; the faith that she bore witness to in being the mother of the Child-God now comes to light in all its fullness. Because she believed in a perfect way, she established at this instant, in this village wedding, the Kingdom of God. For the Kingdom of God is that in which we offer to God with a pure heart a faith without blemish. There is an old saying of Israel: 'God is everywhere man permits Him to enter.' The holy Virgin, by this act of faith, established the conditions of the Kingdom and opened to God the doors of this village wedding. So it turns out that the hour of the Lord has come: it is the hour of the Kingdom, where everything is in harmony with God because man has believed. He blesses the exhausted waters, the useless waters, the waters soiled by washing, and transforms them into the wine of the Kingdom, into a revelation of something greater, which makes this wedding that had begun as a human event unfold to the measure of the Kingdom of God.

You see what this presence and this holiness can be: the presence of God, because one human person was present to God. When this takes its place in the world of the Church, we find ourselves in the presence of the People of God, which is the very place of the Presence. If we wish to pray within this situation, we must learn to pray in *stability and silence:* stability in the sense that we must find a way of praying while standing face to face in the immobility and deepening of silence, contemplation, wonder and anguish that are due to God's Presence. The reason we so often lose this Presence is that our very prayer, not only our life, keeps moving and shifting. We start with one idea and turn towards another; we continually change our terms of reference. God remains Himself constantly, but we offer Him prayer that is always changing, always expressing the external and internal changes, and even conditions them. If we say discursive prayers, we have to adjust our heart and spirit along a line that is often very complex and greatly lacking in sobriety in certain cases, whether the prayers are our own—often much too rich and ornate —or we find them in the Christianity of the Middle Ages or that of Byzantine rhetoric.

So it is first of all a question of establishing ourselves before God. And this is by no means different from action or incompatible with it, because the sense of internal tension, the sense of haste and of movement are internal states that are not connected with the circumstances of our life. You have surely seen people who are old or infirm loaded with a suitcase and trying with all possible speed to catch a bus that is about to leave. They hurry desperately. And nevertheless, objectively, their movement is slow and heavy, their change of position minimal. You also know how easy it is for us sometimes when we are on holiday, when we are not striving towards any concrete goal, to feel wholly within ourselves, collected. One of the fifth century Fathers said that we must establish ourselves firmly inside our skin with nothing protruding outside. At the same time we are full of vivacity, we move fast and are capable of acting quickly. Why? Because we are not reaching after anything, the aim and content of our life in this situation is to be where we are now, whereas ordinarily, and nearly all the time, we live as if we were trying to catch a bus.

We have an erroneous notion of time. The amazing thing in life, said a seventeenth century Russian philosopher, is that all the necessary things are simple and all the complicated things are useless. In fact, if we could only remember that time does not run away, that at a slow pace or at a gallop it rushes towards us, we should be much less fearful of losing it. Do you think that by going towards the hour of your death as fast as possible you can prevent it from coming, or catch it? Do you think that if you go on placidly, tranquilly listening to me, the hour of your deliverance will not come? In both cases it is time which is coming towards you, you have no need to run after it.

It is coming. . . and you will not escape it any more than it will escape you. Therefore we can establish ourselves quite peacefully where we are, knowing that if the time ahead has a meaning that is necessary for us, it is inevitably coming towards us at a sure and regular pace, sometimes much more quickly than we could run to meet it.

On the other hand, if we establish ourselves peacefully in the present, we are living in a world of realities, whereas if we hurry towards the future, we are moving towards a world of unreality. I think the importance of this is truly essential. We must know how to use time, the time within which we find—at least we can find—all eternity, for eternity and time are incommensurable with one another. Eternity is not an indefinite length of time; eternity is not the presence of time without end. The difference between time and eternity is that time is a category of the created: it appears at the moment when something which did not exist before begins to be and to become, and it exists as long as the becoming continues. Eternity does not answer the question: 'What?' It answers the question 'Who?' Eternity is God, God who is always contemporaneous with each moment of time; He is always there, completely stable, unchanged and unchangeable because He already has in Himself, before the first thing was, all the richness necessary to meet all things and all situations. He does not need to change in order to be contemporaneous.

If we wish to learn this prayer of stability, then, we must first realise that it is useless to look for God within a time. He is in the time in which we are, He is in every instant, every 'twinkling of an eye', to use a formula of Romano Guardini's, who distinguishes the past, the future and, not the present, which seems to him too thick, but the 'twinkling of an eye', the instant which has hardly appeared before it is gone. If we want to draw upon this prayer of stability, we must learn to manage time. We always know how to manage time when it is not a matter of God or of prayer; we do not know how when it concerns eternity! This remarkable, illogical situation is the constant experience of each one of us. Take, for example, what you do when you get on a train: you install yourself as comfortably as possible, you are at ease. From within this repose you look around you, you read, you speak, you think, I suppose you sometimes even pray . . . and you worry about nothing because you know that the train will arrive at the destination no matter what you do.

There are some rather simple and nervous people who sometimes try to go from the last carriage to the first in order to be a little closer to their destination. Those who have a little more sense realise that two hundred meters out of fifteen hundred kilometers make no essential difference and that one can simply allow oneself a few hours' rest. Why do we never do this in prayer? Isn't it remarkable that we should find this the most natural thing in the world when it is a matter of getting to another place, simply because we are sure of what is happening as far as the train is concerned—and yet there are so many possible hazards—and we are never sure of what is going to happen with God! It feels to us as though unless we are quick, mistrustful and active, He will escape us. In fact, in a certain way He does escape us. And that is not because we do not look for Him but because we look for Him everywhere where He is not. From this point of view Bonhoeffer is with us when he says that Christianity is a religion without religion, if we understand by the word 'religion' a system of methods that make it possible to catch God, to take Him captive, to get Him in a trap and keep Him there. Yes, in this case Christianity, and only Christianity, is a religion without religion, gecause God wanted to make Himself interior to our condition, and He wanted us to have no need to try to hold Him captive, Who became flesh in order to be with us. There is no need for us to try to use methods and techniques to make Him our prisoner.

Not only is He in our midst, but He created this Church, which is not just a human society oriented towards God, for it is the place of His Presence, the mystery of the union with God, an organism which is simultaneously and equally human and divine, where the plenitude of God resides with the implenitude of men, leading little by little towards that accomplishment in which God will be all in all and the Church will encompass all things.

Hence it is a necessity for us to learn to master time in this way. For this there are techniques, techniques addressed to our restlessness, to our incapacity to believe in the Word of God Who has promised to be with us until the end of the ages.

The first thing we could do is to compel ourselves to place ourselves in the Presence of God and to remain there a few moments without trying to escape—and without trying to give to this presence a discursive content, whether of emotions or of thoughts. If you sit down in a room and say to yourself: 'I am in the presence of God', you will see that at the end of a moment you will be wondering how to fill this presence with an activity that will suppress your restlessness. For the first few moments you will feel fine because you are tired and it is a rest to be sitting comfortably in an armchair, and the silence of your room gives you a feeling of quietude. All this is true. But if you have to go beyond this moment of natural rest, and you remain in the presence of God when you have already received from physical nature all that you can get from it, you will see that it is very difficult not to wonder: 'And now what shall I do? What should I say to God? How shall I address Him? He is silent. Is He there? How can I make a bridge between that mute absence and my restless presence?'

So one of the first things to understand is the importance of sitting and doing nothing in front of God. This does not seem very pious, and yet if you arrive at that repose which the mystical Greek Fathers at Mt Athos called 'Hesychia', a word that has given rise to a whole tradition, hesychasm, the tradition of the Jesus Prayer, a tradition of silent and contemplative prayer—if you reach that, then within that silence and immobility you will be able to do something.

But this immobility and silence, this presence with God must be learned. If you have learned it, you can try to do more difficult exercises: 1) make your presence with God a little longer; 2) learn to manage time, not when it is moving in a sluggish, meandering way, but at the moment when it is trying to rush like water from a burst pipe. It is simply a matter of saying at the moment when you are busy with something useful which must be done: 'I stop doing this, I'll keep still an instant and remain alone with God! All that I am doing can wait!' The Russians, who are not oppressively active people when they can avoid it, have a point of view which I think has spiritual value. One said to me: 'It is so wonderful: I can always be unhurried because if I do not die immediately I shall have time to do it, and if I die, it is useless for me to do it!'

Ask this question: Does the salvation of the world truly depend on the letter that you are writing, the copper you are cleaning, the sentence full of wisdom that you are in the midst of pronouncing? Did the world not exist for millions of years before you said or did this or that? Will it not still live millions of years without your continuing to be a useful presence? So give it a chance now to enjoy your absence. Settle peacefully and say: 'Whatever happens, I will not budge.' Say to all those, visible and invisible, who come to disturb you: 'I am very sorry; I am here, but not for you! . . .' This is what we are always doing: suppose we are in conversation with someone and another person knocks on the door, you answer: 'I am sorry, I am busy.' If you are busy with God, you do not say: 'I am sorry, go away.' What logic, what common sense is there in this? It is not even a matter of contemplation, it is a matter of being polite!

Learn to remain in interior repose, peacefully and tranquilly, in spite of the telephone, in spite of someone's knocking at the door, in spite of the demon's saying to you: 'And you have forgotten this. . .; you still have to get this done by such-and-such an hour. . .; and the brass is not shiny enough, the sun is brighter than it. . . and if you added this sentence to your letter, you would be doing something worthy of the Fathers and Mothers of the Church.' But you answer him: 'If this comes from God, He will be quite able to remind me at an appropriate time, if it comes from you, I mistrust it. . .'

If you learn to stop time, to manage it in this way one, two, three, ten times a day, for longer and longer moments, you will come to the time when you can do it at any time, no matter what your activity, no matter what the word or thought, whether in the liturgy or in everyday life. . . Thus you will be able to be interior to yourself, constantly face to face with God, asking Him unceasingly what you must do, what you must listen to. You will be fundamentally in the position of a monk or a nun: obedience, which consists of *ob-audire*, listening, listening with the intention of hearing—which is not always what we intend when we listen to our neighbour—of understanding what he says, of grasping what he wanted to say and of perceiving the depths from which this word came and what it is meant to make us discover.

I remember something my grandmother told me when I was a child. She was talking to me about the Greek war of independence against Turkey. . . and she told the case of a soldier who, after the battle, in the dark night, called his lieutenant and cried: 'Lieutenant, lieutenant, I have taken a prisoner!'—'Bring him here,' answered the lieutenant.—'I can't, he is holding me so tight,' replied the soldier. This seems absurd. . . and yet I have the impression that very often it is the situation in which we find ourselves with respect to the world when we who are prisoners of this world in a thousand ways—not so much outwardly as inwardly—think that we can transform it, and we are aware that we can only begin to do it when we try to change our place and pull the world in our direction instead of staying in the midst of it where it is and imagining that our presence is enough to be a miracle of transfiguration. There is something very important here, I believe, for the way in which we will appraise *active holiness*, in the world in which we are.

In the Gospel there is a commandment which seems to me absolute, to disengage in order to engage ourselves in a new way: we are called to be 'in the world' and not 'of the world'. Not to be of the world is a radical disengagement. To be in the world is a total engagement, which has the same radical sense of totality as the Incarnation, which made of the Word of God, of the eternal Word, a human Name and a Presence of God in the flesh for ever. And there is that Gospel about rejecting those who are closest to us at the same time as there is the Gospel call to love the entire world with complete love, with sacrificial charity, totally engaged. In this there is, if not a paradox, at least a tension that often seems irreducible to certainties. The fact is that it is only to the extent to which we are disengaged that we can engage ourselves in a fruitful way. You know that if someone is drowning, you must jump in to rescue him but not let yourself be grabbed, because otherwise you both will drown . . . and you will get a posthumous medal for heroism, but that is useless. This is exactly the image of the Incarnation of the Son of God and of the incarnate way in which we must act in the world. We must *be in the world* without letting ourselves be caught hold of, we must be free of its grip. In terms of the theology of the Incarnation, this is called 'without sin'. In terms of our life it would be an exaggeration to say so even in the sense of an intention or a hope. But one must be sufficiently disengaged not to be an integral part of the sin of the world, even if we do not succeed in freeing ourselves entirely from this imprisonment. We are called to disengage ourselves from the bonds which hold us prisoners, in order to give ourselves freely as Christ did: 'Nobody is taking my life from me, I give it freely.' Thus we shall be able to live and die, but in Christ's way, in the way of a Christian: to die freely and not by suffocation. Christ became fully man but *without sin*. He lived our life and He died our death, without, however, participating in the evil which limits our life and provokes our death. As for ourselves, we must be *in the world* and not *of the world*. It is only under those conditions that we become capable of loving, not with a passionate love that imprisons us and imprisons others, but with a love that is free with the freedom of the children of God and that gives freedom.

In this *disengagement-engagement* there are two points to be raised. First, the necessity of disengaging from oneself, getting free from oneself. We have an exaggerated tendency to think that we are prisoners of other people. In reality we are prisoners of ourselves, for if we could only release ourselves from the grip of our ego, other people would have no power over us. They have power over us only by reason of our covetous desires and our fears and dreads. In this liberation from oneself there are several points which I would like to make you understand through images.

An English author whom I like very much and who has taught me a great deal, Charles Williams, in a book entitled: *All-Hallows Eve*, gives two images which, I think, are very illuminating. The story takes place in the city of London. A young woman has been killed in an accident. . . She is dead, but her soul still remains unmoving at the place on the bridge where death overtook her. . . She is dead, but her soul is not yet engaged in the invisible world nor disengaged from the visible world, because there is nothing in the invisible world that is familiar to her and to which she could attach herself. She is still engaged in the visible world because it is the only one which she knows. And nevertheless we see her standing there surrounded by a world of dead forms. She sees around her the banks of the Thames and the houses which line them. Sometimes they are dead blocks with black windows. . . sometimes those windows are lighted. But she sees nothing besides this, because in the course of her whole life she has never loved anything but herself. She is not connected with any of the objects around her by the values of eternity, values that can survive the death of the body. She perceives the bridge on which her spiritual feet are weighing, and she sees as cadaveric effects everything around her: nothing has life, for nothing is joined to life either within her or outside her, as far as she is concerned. . . At a certain moment something happens: her husband crosses the bridge and she sees him. He is the only person that she has ever loved—with an unstable love that had no great depth, was often possessive and selfish—but this is nevertheless a reality of fondness and love outside herself. From the moment she perceives him a whole set of relations awakens in her: through this fondness, this love that she has for her husband she begins to rediscover things, human names which suddenly acquire significance in eternity, places, situations. . . I shall not tell you the story. What is important is to understand that the perspicacity of this soul detached from the body and no longer able to be connected to visible things through the body and not yet linked to invisible things through an interior light, this clearsightedness of the soul is awakened only at the moment when love unites it to someone or something.

Here we have a beginning of liberation from the self: the moment we become capable of loving we begin to disengage ourselves from this prison which we are in relation to our person. There is in fact a complete connection between 'loving' and 'dying'. To love means to disengage little by little from the exclusive interest that one has in oneself and to transfer that interest and that concern to someone. The deeper our love is and the more all-embracing it is and the more it is disengaged from the large categories of lust and fear, the more it frees itself from that aspect which C. S. Lewis so well describes as a diabolic love that consists in the wish to devour and assimilate the loved one, making of him a total prisoner. Ultimately, the more this happens, and the more the egoistic self gets free, the more free we are. Subjectively speaking, perfect love corresponds to death, that is, to a disappearance of our self-assertion, our affirmation of ourself by contrasts and opposition in terms of aggression and rejection. And the woman of Charles Williams' novel makes her first discovery: it is only to the extent to which we become capable of loving that we become capable of seeing and perceiving. To *see and perceive*, whether it be God or the world around us, whether it be the individual neighbour or the more or less complex situations that include our neighbours, all this is possible only insofar as we love them and accept dying in order to be able to see, live and participate.

There is a second passage in the same novel by Charles Williams that permits me to take up another aspect of these matters. We are surrounded by opacity, density: the world is not transparent to our gaze—and when I speak of the world I do not refer only to the cosmic world that surrounds us and that we may sometimes grasp in the light of God, because it does not present a danger to us: we can consider it in its natural beauty and its harmony, that is created or structured by man, without fear of being devoured or destroyed ourselves. But when we go back to our neighbour, whether in his individual aspect or in a wider collectivity as a social group, a society, he becomes more and more opaque because all the judgements that we pass, all the reactions that we have are defined by a 'How?': How does this person, this group affect *my* security, *my* integrity? To what extent is it a danger or a possibility for expansion? When it is a possibility for expansion it is almost always in a very mitigated, and especially Christianly mitigated, form, of an aggression. We make progress with our neighbour, in our group. We feel secure because we have increasingly put our hand on something. Or we ask: To what extent are we secure because the group is not attacking us? So we have a collection of opacities surrounding us. How are we to get through these opacities?

In the story by Charles Williams we find a further passage in which this girl, who is called Lester is beside the Thames. She sees it with her disincarnate eyes for the first time! For the first time she has no repulsion towards the sight of this Thames. Previously when she had looked at the river's edge she had always had a feeling of disgust: those thick lead-coloured, greasy, heavy waters, which transport all the city's refuse, had been repulsive to her because, having a body, she could only see them insofar as she imagined or thought of being able to drink them or jump in! But now Lester is free of her body: she has no body, she is a soul; so she has no fear of contact with those repulsive waters and as soon as she no longer fears contact, these waters no longer repel her. As the author says, she sees them as a 'fact', but as a fact which in itself has complete harmony. It is a harmonious fact because these oily, thick waters that are carrying all the city's refuse are exactly what the waters of this great river that goes through this big city should be. They correspond exactly to their own nature and their vocation. The moment she sees them as a legitimate fact which she can consider outside herself, she begins to discern what she had never seen before. Through this initial opacity she begins to distinguish a series of brighter and brighter patches of light. The deeper her gaze goes, passing through a greater opacity in order to reach a lesser opacity, the more she becomes aware that farther and farther away, closer to the bottom of the river, there is a light. And in fact, after first passing through opacities that diminish and then clear places that increase, at the heart of this river she succeeds in recognising, with the eyes that death has given her, the primordial waters, the waters as God created them in the first chapter of Genesis. And more deeply still, giving them their brightness and revealing their ultimate vocation, that water of which Christ spoke to the Samaritan woman.

This process is exactly the reverse of what often happens to us. We go from clarity to opacity. A first meeting can reveal a person to us in the light. And then with the bad clairvoyance, or rather the progressive blindness given us by selfishness, coldness, calculation, the fact that we think of everything in terms of ourself, we begin to discern greater and greater opacities. It is only by an act of faith that we manage to say: 'Yes! this is a child of light!' We say it, but very often we do not see it. And this is why it is so often almost impossible for us—and when I say 'almost' it is a polite exaggeration—it is almost impossible for us to see the face of Christ in the faces round about us. This is important because it is fashionable now to look for God in one's neighbour; it is not a new fashion: the desert saints of the third and fourth centuries told us: 'If you have seen your neighbour, you have seen your God.' But they saw him, whereas we most often only say it! The fact is that in order to see the features of Christ on our neighbour's face, which is sometimes very difficult to read, we have to have in us the vision of Christ so as to be able to project it on them. Then we see, in the light of those divine features, that even in this portrait that sometimes has become so hideous, we can recapture the features of *His image*. I am not referring to momentary uglinesses, superficial evil, but to a profound evil more important than what one does, the evil that corrodes and causes the doer to lose the sense of the good— and the sense of what is luminous in himself—such people as one finds in prisons, everywhere, even in the Churches.

And so, at this moment, it is absolutely necessary to be able to recognise the light places through the opacities and to recognise in the features of the portrait, retouched from generation to generation by the whole heredity of man, the conformity that we have with God, His image. It is a question of recognising, beyond the heavy materiality which leaps to our eyes, that which transcends it. The world around us, including our neighbour, to the extent that we lack this clairvoyance, this insight into the depth, appears to us as an opaque mass. This mass, these volumes that surround us, which we collide with and almost never meet— for meeting somone is looking at him face to face, in depth— these opaque masses belong to a material world to which we implicitly deny depth. The material world has thickness: it has no interiority. I think I am not being too complicated, in saying that if you are in the presence of a glass sphere and you try to penetrate it with your gaze, the farthest you can reach is its centre: it is the ultimate point which cannot be transcended, there is no other depth beyond. If you go further, you come out again to the farthest surface. But all objects, even our neighbour, have only one density, one thickness, one heavy presence if we do not discover something more, that which is revealed concerning them by Holy Scripture, in which the psalm tells us: 'The heart of man is deep.' It is not a matter of the heart of flesh nor of a measurable depth, it is a matter of infinity, that is to say, of the fact that the heart of man cannot be measured, for it opens into the depths of God.

This is why, in all our inquiries into prayer, it is an interiority that we must seek, not the interiority of the psychologists, of a depth psychology that belongs to the realm of the created and at a certain point permits us to touch bottom, like the final and ultimate point that is the centre of a sphere. No, the depth we are concerned with is correlative with the fact that we are a will of God become tangible and visible. At the heart of our reality is the creative word of God. And the Word is the divine reality onto which we open in the depth. There is no use in looking for God round about. If we have not found Him within us, we shall never recognise Him in our neighbour, in historical events, in the heights.

If we have made the discovery of our neighbour in this way, if we have discovered that we have a depth that opens upon God, then we shall discover that very often our relationship with our neighbour can only be realised in silence. We all know in our everyday life those indescribable instants when at the most unexpected moment silence and peace descend upon us. When we are two who perceive this silence, when it envelops and lays hold of both of us, the words die on our lips and every gesture becomes a breaking of a relationship more important than anything one could express. If we let this silence penetrate us more and more deeply, there comes a moment when we can no longer express anything, when we feel that we are more and more close to a depth that we would never have known how to reach without the gift of God. When this silence has reached maturity, we shall discover that at the bottom of the silence there is a security and certainty that make us able to begin to speak. And then the words are sober: we search for them carefully before offering them; we utter them in a way that will not break this silence given by God.

There must always be, between us and God, a depth that we can reach—and I insist on this fact—that we should be able to reach. We should learn by the practice of the presence of God, by stopping time, by letting our being go deeper, to reach it almost at will, for it is our vocation to remain in the presence of the Lord. We should learn how to descend into ourselves when we are in the presence of our neighbour, whoever he is—not the pious one, the easy one, of whom we are ready to write in large letters: 'This is an image of God!' but the difficult neighbour, the unacceptable neighbour, the one who is an insult to all that we think of God and His Incarnation—we can then meet that neighbour in the place which no means of communication would enable us to reach, because we refrain from communicating on the level of words, gestures, external relations: we are not up to that, we are too small, too weak and friable for that.

If we take on our neighbour in this way, if we accept him in silence, we are making an initial act of essential importance: it is the act of justice—not an act of social justice, which is distributive, egalitarian—but a dangerous act of justice which consists, in the first place, of accepting our neighbour just as he is and giving him the right to be as he is, even if his way means our death and our destruction. It is an act of radical justice such as we see in God, who accepted fallen man instead of rejecting and destroying him; who accepted man in his downfall, knowing that the downfall of man meant the crucifixion of the Son of God. That is the act of Christian justice; it is there that justice begins, and not when we distribute the spiritual or material wealth equally or selectively. It is the moment when we allow the other person to be himself, whatever the consequences. It is only at this price that we can look and see in the features of the other person a living and glorifying projection of the face of the Lord.

This implies something I have already spoken of: *solidarity*, such as we see in Christ. This solidarity within fallen man, man in his final agony, in his radical godlessness, or rather his relative godlessness—for only Christ's is radical—this enables us to take up our responsibility. But here I must point out that Christian responsibility and solidarity have a quality that makes them inacceptable and impossible on a certain level, because they embrace both parties in conflict. A Christian can, in fact, support one human group against another, but he cannot undo his solidarity with the other in favour of the first. In a conflict, whether it be armed, social, economic or psychological, the Christian should be present at the point of rupture and accept in a total way the responsibility for both sides.

I shall first give you an example in terms of common law, from Church history. St Basil established a canonical rule which has never been applied—like so many canonical rules—which says that in case of armed conflict the Christian is called upon to take part in it, 'because' it says, 'if he had been a Christian worthy of the name, he would have been able to convert those around him to mutual love, and there would have been no armed conflict. But as it is he who bears the responsibility for the bloodshed, he should take part in this conflict. However, all the time the conflict is going on and for three years afterwards he must be excommunicated.' Here is a situation that is clear, precise, perfectly tenable theologically and of very great interest, which has never been applied because it implies at the same time the radical sense of bipolar solidarity and responsibility which is essentially identical to the Incarnation.

This is very important and I should like to say a few words about it. Remember the passage from the Book of Job I mentioned earlier. Towards the end of the ninth chapter Job in his despair turns to the empty, silent, cruel heaven and says: 'Where is the man who will stand between me and my Judge and put his hand on the shoulder of each of us?' Where is the one who will make an act of intercession?—for to intercede does not mean: to remind the Lord of what He has forgotten, as we so often do: 'Lord, this man is hungry, this one is thirsty; there is the war in Vietnam, tensions in America; there is this and that, do what is necessary?' No, intercession does not consist in simply telling God what He has forgotten to do and leaving Him in charge of the situation. According to the Latin word, to intercede means to take a step which brings us to the heart of a situation of tension, violence or conflict, and to stay there once and for all. What Job had sensed is that in this contestation between him and God, the only one who could place himself between the two would be someone who was the equal of each of the two, who could put his hand on the shoulder of the living God without sacrilege and on the shoulder of the man, in his agony, without destroying him. Here is a first vision of that which Christ will be, true God and true man, fully God and fully man, the One in whom and by whom the plenitude of Divinity has lived in the flesh, in our midst. And this act of Intercession by Christ which is the Incarnation—is a definitive act. Christ has not become man for a time: the Word of God is incarnated for all time.

This is what intercession is: at one and the same time an act which precedes prayer, a complete engagement which makes us simultaneously engaged and disengaged from the two sides, in solidarity with one side as well as with the other and, because of this, rejected by one as well as by the other. The Incarnate Word was killed by men because He was God; He was consigned to the cross because He was a man. He died a borrowed death which is a man's death. He was not accepted, because His witness was one that favoured God, from whom the people of Israel had already turned away. 'We want to be like all the nations!' they had said to Samuel when they asked for a king, and God answered Samuel: 'It is not you, it is I Whom they have rejected!' And the final rejection comes in these words of the people before Pilate: 'We have no other king than Caesar!'

The act of intercession is a prayer that is itself an act, and an act that is a prayer. Thus the action appears to us as a lived faith, something in which prayer becomes life. And if prayer and life are not the two faces of one same reality, one coin, neither one has authenticity.

Amos said that a prophet is one with whom God shares His thoughts and who not only receives the thoughts of God but, like a true prophet, proclaims them, lives them, witnesses to them, becomes an act of God. And it is to this that we are called in the Church, to be an act of God in the midst of the world. This is the special activity of the Church, which means that in all domains, political, social, economic, educative, the Christian's role has a peculiarity that makes it different from all the other functions in the world: it is an act of God and as such it can be

in harmony with everything that goes on. One of the Christian
obligations is precisely that of being not only the leaven in the
dough but also the sword that divides the darkness from the
light, truth from error, death from life, God from Satan, of being
the stumbling-block, the scandal, the constant provocation, the
constant affirmation that we are not seeking the kingdom of the
Beast, that we do not accept a harmony based on apostasy, that
we do not want a justice that is a denial of divine justice, a truth
that is a refusal of the personal truth: 'I am the Truth!' and so on.

We are called to be that divine act by which God reveals Himself to the world, and, as such, our destiny can only be that of
Christ. Yes, Christ did say to us: 'You will do greater works
than mine. . .' and it is true: in His power and that of the Spirit
we are called to complete a work in which His action was
decisive but not final.

We must be a witness to the world of the Presence, of the
transcendence, of the fact that the Eternal has become immanent
and is in our midst: God is in us and through us, God Who has
no common measure with man, the divine mystery. At the same
time this God reveals Himself in an incredible way which man
could not invent, in Christ, who appears to us defenseless, vulnerable, abandoned to the discordant wills of men, surrounded by
hate, rejected, Who dies because of this and whose victory is in
His humiliation.

I believe that what I have said can be referred back to the
image that Chist gave us when he said: 'I consecrate myself, I
sacrifice myself for them.' I don't know which of the terms
should be used, because the Greek word is too rich to be translated by only one of them. It concerns a prime act of consecra-
tion: it belongs to God without limitations. *It is God*, and not
only that but in its very humanity it has only one will, a life with
God, and this in a free act in which the two wills find themselves
united in a perfect way, in which the two natures are inseparable,
in which the Word of God listens in on the will of God
and watches in the depth what the Father is doing, then continues
to act and work in the world, to accomplish now what the Father
wills in the mystery of divine thought.

He sacrifices Himself. To sacrifice oneself now means to shed

one's blood or to impose limitations on oneself in favour of someone—this is the way we are always sacrificing ourselves, doing a
very little bit for our neighbour—but 'to sacrifice oneself' means
'to make oneself sacred, to consecrate oneself', and also to offer
oneself or be given in sacrifice. Did not Christ say: 'Nobody is
taking my life, I give it.' He gives himself up, He dies.

What is our attitude in such a situation? Is it not this combina-
tion of successive and disordered images that I have tried to give
you in the course of these talks? Is it not these images which
should permit us to feel our way, in the oneness of the ever contemporaneous Presence of God, into the multiplicity of ways in
which this total Presence brings itself to bear, expresses itself,
integrates itself into the variety of situations? But then our role
also consists in being perfectly obedient, not in the sense of
mechanical obedience, which would mean hearing orders and
carrying them out, but in the sense of an obedience in depth
which wants to listen in with vigilance, tension, alert vitality, in
order to hear and express what it perceives.

And this can be harmonious with what the world is seeking,
because the holy Spirit is not at work solely in the Church but
everywhere, with a power and a force that are sometimes impres-
sive. It is God who judges the Church at this moment by all that
goes on around it, by the persecution, by the protestation, by the
atheism, by the rejection of the caricature of God which we offer
for man's worship. And we most certainly must learn to assume
our responsibility for the sins of the past, and not to bewail ourselves as we recognise them but to see in them the judgement of
God as we endeavour to realise that which is the eternal truth
of God in the present situation.

I cannot give you recipes, I can only indicate *three elements*
as a conclusion to these considerations.

Interior contemplation, which is not a form of life but a
position vis-à-vis God, a standing before Him in a deepened
silence; the double and reciprocal presence of God with man and
man with God.

Prayer, in its active, human aspect, in its tension towards God,
with the resulting inward state of orientation towards God and
being present to God, and, lastly, its final state which is a position

in the world where we are: the prayer of the world to God, the articulation of the cry of the entire world to the living God. And this is obviously an ascetic exercise to the extent to which we are under our human vocation.

Finally, there is *action*, but as I said before, this action must be an act of God, by our instrumentality. Let us first learn to listen, hear, see and understand God, the world and our neighbour. And then to act not solely according to human wisdom but, above all, primarily on the basis of the divine wisdom which is revealed to us in Scripture, in life and in the sacraments—for the early Church strongly emphasised that these form the gateway to the knowledge of God and to action in the name of God. And if in all honesty we try to live in God and to live His presence in the world, I trust that in every situation God will teach us how to do His will: the ways may be different, opposed, incompatible. . . For if you read the Old or New Testament, you will see that there are no rules, no precepts—still less, recipes. There are divine responses which are mutually contradictory, because when God confronts this fragment of time that asks Him a question, He faces each situation with the whole of Eternity.

CHAPTER FIVE

JOHN THE BAPTIST

JOHN THE BAPTIST was the forerunner of Christ. He was the
one who came before Him to make the pathway smooth, to
make the crooked way straight. I believe this is exactly what all of
us are called to do now with regard to other people, to make it
smooth for them to find their way, and to help them to find a
way which is straight, to the Lord.

I would like to single out a certain number of features in the
person of St John the Baptist which I feel could teach us something about our situation, and what we should do, and what
disposition of mind we should be in.

First of all, when you open St Mark's Gospel you find that he
is defined as a voice that shouts in the wilderness. He is not even
defined as a prophet or a messenger of God. He has got so
identified with the message, he has become so one with God's own
word which he has got to proclaim and to bring to people that
one can no longer see him behind the message, hear the tune
of his voice behind the thundering witness of God's own spirit
speaking through him.

This is one thing which we should learn. Too often when we
bring a message, people can perceive us and a message which
perhaps comes through us, because we are not sufficiently
identified with what we have got to say. In order to be identified
we must so read the Gospel, make it so much ourselves, and ourselves so much the Gospel, that when we speak from within it,
in its name, it should be simply—whatever words we use and
I am not speaking of quotations—it should be simply the Gospel
that speaks and we should be like a voice—God's voice. The
second thing is that to attain to that state in which he could

speak and not be noticed, in which all that people could perceive of him was a man who had been completely transformed into a message, into a vision, into a proclamation, meant he was a man who accepted to lay aside all that was selfish, grasping, all that was delighting selfishly in whatever he wanted to have. He had a pure heart, a clear mind, an unwavering will, a trained body, a complete mastery of self, so that when the message came, fear would not defeat him and make him silent; promises would not beguile him and make him silent, or simply the heaviness of the flesh, the heaviness of the mind, the heaviness of the heart, should not overcome the lightness and the lightening power of the spirit. This is something that is also our task.

I do not speak now of the forms of asceticism or the way in which one does it, but we must learn to be free, and to be free, we must acquire mastery over ourselves. This is terribly important, and to achieve that, we must learn to look and learn, but not only to look at people and situations—look at God and learn and hear. Obedience is vital. To obey the will of God requires a training. The will of God is madness, the will of God is paradoxical. You cannot adhere to the will of God for good reasons. More often what He often asks is an act of folly which we would not otherwise dare to commit. Remember Abraham: God promised him a son, and the son was born. He promised that the son would be a beginning of a generation of people more numerous than the sands of the shores; and Abraham believed Him. And then God commanded him to take his son and to bring him, a blood offering, to Him, and Abraham did it. He did not tell Him. 'That contradicts your previous injunction; this is contrary to your promise.' He trusted the Lord and did what the Lord said at that moment, leaving the Lord to fulfil his promises the way He knows.

This happens to us also. We are called to act day after day, moment after moment, according to the will of God revealed within that moment when the difference between Christian action and just action resides in the fact that action must be planned, action must not contradict action. There are no returns and moves back and sideways; it must be a straight course. If we want to act within the will of God, we must be like Christ who listens and proclaims the word, who gazes attentively at God who is at work, and when he has seen, performs the action which is implied in the willing, in the thinking, in the rich creative imaginings of God. This we must learn, but to do this, we must learn to master ourselves and become capable of acting not only when we agree, not only when we understand, but when we disagree somewhere within the old Adam in us, or when we cannot understand but say 'I trust you, I will act with folly.'

The forerunner has another quality. Remember what he said: 'I must decrease in order that you should increase.' Our role is to cut straightways; our role is to make rough ways smooth, but when we have done this, we must step aside, and allow the Lord of life, Him for whom we are preparing the way, to come in a lordly manner, or with the humility of Christ come with the simplicity of His entry into Jerusalem. And we must be forgotten because as long as we loom large, people will not see Christ.

There is a way in which our absence is as necessary to the glory and action of God as our presence is at another moment.

Remember the other way in which the forerunner is defined. When speaking about himself he says that he is the friend of the bridegroom—the one who so loves the bride and the bridegroom that he brings them together, so loves them that he is the protector of their love, of their intimacy, of their peace, of their meeting, and whose vocation is to bring together bride and bridegroom— the living God and the living soul, and then stand guard to protect this meeting against any intrusion, but not to be party in this meeting, to be outside; that is his particular form of love and service. At the same time, we must be prepared also to face, in the name of the bride and groom whom we serve, in the name of this mystery of love, the coming of the kingdom; the conquest by God of all that is death, evil, sin, separation, meanness which is to small for the measure and the stature of man. We must be prepared to speak to man the truth, God's own truth, not our own.

Remember the way in which the forerunner spoke to Herod, the way in which he spoke to the multitudes. To do this we must have authority, and authority is not gained either by rank or by social standing. Authority is gained by this fusion between our own will and God's own will; our own word and God's own word, our own life and God's own life, us and Him; then we can speak, and then our words, however hard, however sharp, however truthful, however deep they will go down, however much they separate body and soul, our words then will also be words of love, because God's word is always the word that gives truth and light, love and life. And then we must be prepared not to see the results of what we have done. The forerunner died before he had seen Christ; coming to the end of his mission and fulfilling the promises of his vocation, he died. He died of his message, he died of the truth of God, he died because he had become identified with the message and the truth, because he was a friend of the bridegroom that had to decrease so that the bridegroom should have all the field.

We must be prepared for that. In every case, with regard to every soul, to every group, to every event, to every situation, there is this time for the forerunner and there is the time for him to decrease and die out—perhaps not physically, but in the memory of people, in their hearts, in their relationships. We must be prepared never to be remembered because what has been sown by the word is so rich, so overwhelming, that the forerunner, the one that has prepared the way, the one that has ploughed, the one that has sown, can be forgotten. This is joy. It is joy to see Christ, the Lord, grow to his full stature, to occupy his real position, to be the king and the lord and master, and the brother and the saviour and the joy and the freedom of those to whom we have come and said 'He is coming, open yourself to him.' This is what the scriptures call repentence or conversion.

Now I will tell you what a priest at the end of a Roman Mass says to the people—'Go'—it is a dismissal; but what is a dismissal? Does it simply say the service is over, out of the chapel, while the congregation in a rather ambiguous way says: 'Thanks be to God.'

No, it is not that. The dismissal means this: You have been on the Mount of Transfiguration, you have seen the glory of God, you have been on the road to Damascus, you have faced the living God, you have been in the upper chamber, you have been here and there in Galilee and Judaea, all the mysterious places where one meets God, and now having spent several days with him, he says now that so much has been given—go, your joy will never abandon you. What you have acquired, you will never lose as long as you remain faithful. Go now, and if truly you have discovered joy, how can you not give joy to others? If truly you have come nearer to truth, how can you keep it for yourself? If truly something has been kindled in you which is life, are you going to allow anyone not to have a spark of this life? It does not mean go round and tell everyone specifically religious things or use clerical phrases. It means that you should go into the world which is yours with a radiance, with a joy, with an intensity that will make everyone look at you and say 'He has something he hadn't before. Is it that truly God has come near? He has something he never had before and which I do not possess—joy, life, certainty, a new courage, a new daring a vision, where can I get it?'

People will also say to you, 'Mad you are'. I answer in those cases, and they are many, I say 'I am mad, but one thing I find strange. You who are wise call to the mad man, and the mad man is happy, alive and you feel dead; let us share my folly, it is God's folly.'

You are now going to start. With God you go now, with him on all the ways, on all the roads; you can dance on the Mount of Transfiguration, you can bring concreteness of life for others. May God bless you in it with joy. I don't know any other words than 'with joy'—go with joy, bring joy, and then you will have brought everything else, because God is joy, he is life, he is intensity.

And may God bless you, and not only you but everyone, your family, you friends, those who have been, those who have not been here, those whom you will meet throughout your lives—bring them a spark.

METROPOLITAN ANTHONY
OF SOUROZH
and
GEORGES LEFEBVRE OSB

Courage to Pray

Translated by
Dinah Livingstone

Part I

Courage to Pray

by

Metropolitan Anthony

CONTENTS

A DISCOVERY

PRAYER IS THE search for God, encounter with God, and going beyond this encounter in communion. Thus it is an activity, a state and also a situation; a situation both with respect to God and to the created world. It arises from the awareness that the world in which we live is not simply two dimensional, imprisoned in the categories of time and space, a flat world in which we meet only the surface of things, an opaque surface covering emptiness. Prayer is born of the discovery that the world has depths; that we are not only surrounded by visible things but that we are also immersed in and penetrated by invisible things. And this invisible world is both the presence of God, the supreme, sublime reality, and our own deepest truth. Visible and invisible are not in opposition neither can they be juxtaposed like in an addition sum. They are present simultaneously, as fire is present in red hot iron. They complete each other in a mysterious way which the English writer Charles Williams describes as 'co-inherence': the presence of eternity in time and the future in the present, and also the presence of each temporal moment in eternity, past present and future all-at-once eschatologically, the one in the other as the tree is in the seed. Living only in the visible world is living on the surface; it ignores or sets aside not only the existence of God but the depths of created being. It is condemning ourselves to perceiving only the world's surface. But if we look deeper we discover at the heart of things a point of balance which is their finality. There is no inwardness to geometric volume. Its finiteness is complete. The world of such forms is capable of being extended but cannot be deepened. But the heart of man is deep. When we have reached the fountainhead of life in him we discover that this itself springs from beyond. The heart of man is open to the invisible. Not the invisible of depth psychology but the invisible infinite, God's creative word, God himself. Returning to ourselves is thus not a synonym for introversion but for emerging beyond the limits of our limited selves. Saint John Chrysostom said 'When you discover the door of your heart you discover the gate of heaven.' This discovery of our own depths goes together with the recognition of the depths in others. Each has his own immensity. I use the word 'immensity' on purpose. It means that the depth cannot be measured, not because it is too great for our measurements to reach it, but because its quality is not subject to measurement at all. The immensity of our vocation is to share the divine nature, and in discovering our own depths we discover God, whom we could call our invisible neighbour, the Spirit, Christ, the Father. We also discover God's immensity and eternity in the world about us. And this is the beginning of prayer, the recognition of a three-dimensional world of time, space and a stable but ever changing depth.

A TRIPLE RELATIONSHIP

Prayer is the relationship between man the visible and the invisible x. This is why I said that prayer is a search, an exploration of this invisible world of our own depths which God alone knows and he alone can reveal to us.

And it is by prayer, gropingly at first, in the dawn of a new vision, that we seek and find God and ourselves in a co-relative way. Then later, when a clearer light has shown us what we can see of the invisible and the visible transfigured in the light of its own immensity and the eternity in God, prayer becomes a state. It also constantly remains a situation, as I said at the beginning. While we are seeking, part blind with partly restored sight, our first steps in prayer take the form of astonishment, reverent fear and a sense of sadness. We are astonished at the discovery of ourselves which is also the beginnings of knowledge of God; we are astonished to see the world open out towards God's infinity. We are afraid, glad and terrified when we come into the presence of God's holiness and beauty. We are also sad, both for ourselves and the world. It is sad to be blind, it is sad to be unable to live the fulness of our vocation, to be trapped again and again in our own limitations. It is sad to see our world without God, vacillating between life and death and unable to choose life once and for all or to escape once and for all from death. Wonder and sadness are thus the two sources of our prayer. Both arise from our encounter with the world's depths, which have begun to be revealed to us in their totality. Without this encounter, our world and the forces at work in it are incomprehensible and often monstrous; we are bewildered and afraid.

ENCOUNTER

Thus encounter is central to prayer. It is the basic category of revelation, because revelation itself is an encounter with God who gives us a new vision of the world. Everything is encounter, in scripture as in life. It is both personal and universal, unique and exemplary. It always has two poles: encounter with God and in him with creation, an encounter with man in his depths rooted in God's creative will, straining towards fulfil-

ment when God will be all in all. This encounter is personal because each of us must experience it for himself,
we cannot have it second-hand. It is our own, but it also
has a universal significance because it goes beyond our
superficial and limited ego. This encounter is unique because for God as for one another when we truly see,
each of us is irreplaceable and unique. Each creature
knows God in his own way. Each one of us knows God in
our own way which no one else will ever know unless
we tell them. And at the same time because human
nature is universal, each encounter is exemplary. It is a
revelation to all of what is known personally by each.

AS THROUGH A GLASS DARKLY

We should try and analyse this encounter carefully, because if we do not know the laws it follows we may let it
slip away. It is always a mutual encounter. It is always
a discovery not only of the other but of ourselves. It is
always a relationship. Perhaps the best image for it is a
stained glass window. The light shining through it shows
up its design, its colours, its beauty and its meaning. But
at the same time the window itself by its design,
colours, beauty and meaning reveals for us the invisible
light beyond it. Thus the window and the light are discovered in relationship to one another. Discovering God
in his serene eternity and in the man of sorrows who was
the incarnate word, is also a discovery of the greatness of
man. When we discover the depths in man, we go
beyond the front he presents to us and discover his
destiny which is not individual but personal. This destiny
makes him more than an example of humankind; it
makes him the member of a mysterious body, the whole
of mankind, which is where God's presence is.

THE NATURE OF THIS ENCOUNTER

However at the start any man seeking this encounter is

alone and must learn to recognise the existence of the
other. And this recognition must take place in a relationship and not in isolation. This is important. We know
nothing and nobody except through a relationship. If
we are disconnected nothing exists for us. But there is a
danger in not knowing anything or anybody except in
relation to ourselves. This is to de-centre the universe. In
referring everything to ourselves we deform it and make
it as small and mean as we are, with our small mean
cravings. So when we begin to recognise the existence of
the other, we must be prepared to set ourselves aside to
some extent, to go beyond ourselves and to admit the
other's needs and his rights to independence and freedom, outside us. We must accept his irreducible *otherness*. Whatever we do, however well we know him,
however close we are, and this is even truer of man and
God than man and man, there remains a central mystery
which we can never solve. In the Book of Revelation
there is the marvellous passage where John says that
those who go into the Kingdom are given a white stone
with a name written on it which only they and God know.
This name is not the label we are given and called
by in this world. Our true name, our eternal name
exactly fits us, our whole being ... It defines and expresses us perfectly. It is known by God alone and he
tells us what it is. No one else can know it because it
expresses our unique relationship with our creator. How
often human relationships come to grief because one
person wants to reveal himself beyond what is possible
or the other person wants to probe into a territory which
is sacred to God alone. It is a vain wish and cannot be
fulfilled. It is like a child trying to find the source of a
spring, the point where the water begins, that point just
before which there is no water. In this case it is only
possible to destroy, not to discover.

But it is not enough to recognise the other's right to

exist, to accept his irreducible otherness. We must be able to see, hear and judge. Otherwise the encounter cannot be fruitful.

SEEING

Christ speaks of the clear vision we need to see things as they are. If there is something wrong with our eyes we project shadows onto things or see instead the distorted shapes which our poor eyes form in our imagination. But clear vision is not enough. We must choose the right standpoint. We must find the right distance, from which we can see an object whole. Isn't this essential when we are looking at a work of art? A painting or a statue needs to be seen from not too close and not too far away. There is the best standpoint, from which we see it as the artist intended, from which we can see the whole and are not overwhelmed by its parts. The same is true of human relationships. We must find the right distance, not in time and space but in inner freedom; freedom which is a bond but not a chain.

An example I have used in a previous book will perhaps make the point better than a long discussion. In a remarkable book the English author Charles Williams shows us a girl who has just been killed in a plane crash. Her soul released from her body discovers a new world which she never saw before, she has just entered the invisible world which is now the only reality to her. She cannot see the visible world with the eyes of her soul. At one point she finds herself beside the Thames. She had seen it before as a foul stretch of filthy water, a refuse dump for London. But because she is now out of her body and does not relate everything to herself, she *sees* the Thames for the first time. She discovers it as a fact, a great river flowing through a great city. Its waters are dirty and opaque, they carry London's refuse to the sea. But this is as it should be, this is their proper role and they are authentic. And when she sees them as they are and accepts them, without emotion or physical repulsion because she can no longer feel disgust for them no longer having a body, to bathe in them or lips to drink from them, she sees the depths of the waters. They become less and less opaque. And at last they become transparent. This transparency increases until at the heart of the waters she sees a luminous thread which is the primordial water, as God created it, and at the heart of this primordial water, a yet more luminous thread, which is the marvellous water that Christ offered the Samaritan woman.

Through her disembodiment, the dead girl has been able to see things she was formerly blind to. The same is true of us. If we could become detached from ourselves and gain the inner freedom which the Fathers called 'apathy', that is to say the absence of passion, we could see things more and more luminously. We could also see the splendour of God's presence in this dark and opaque world. We could see grace active everywhere and in all things.

HEARING

I said before that seeing is not enough. We must also hear. Hearing is an act of sustained attention. In order to hear, we must not only lend our ears, but also try and understand the meaning and intention of the words. Hearing means bowing our heads in humility which is capable of accepting what the other person is sowing on the ground of our mind and heart. This is the true meaning of the word 'humility'. The word comes from the Latin 'humus', fertile soil, that soil which we no longer notice because we are so used to it, dumb and dark, capable of making good use of the rubbish we tip onto it, capable of transforming our refuse into wealth, of accepting every seed, giving it body, life, growth, to become fully itself, without ever denaturing it. Our own power of hearing begins with humility. Like the rich silent, creative earth, we should offer ourselves to the Other.

HUMILITY AND OBEDIENCE

But this humility is also obedience. The Latin word *obaudire* means both to listen and obey. We must listen in order to hear and profit by what we hear. This is the proper attitude to God, total attention because we must hear him, and the desire, determination to receive his message and profit by it, that is to say be transformed, changed, to stop being what we are and become what we are called to be. This fundamental attitude of prayer is a bit like a bird watcher. He gets up early in the morning because he must reach the fields and woods before the birds wake up, so that they will not see him coming. He is silent and keeps quite still. He is all eyes and ears. He is receptive to every sound and every movement. He listens and he watches but he will not see what is happening around him unless he is free of prejudices, ready to hear what God speaks. It is an attitude of self surrender which is at the same time extremely active. Self surrender because like the earth, *humus* he offers himself without reserve. Active because he is ready to respond to God's every suggestion, every call. It follows that if we want to have a real encounter with God, we need more than mere organs of hearing and vision. We must have the enthusiasm, the desire, we must want to hear and see.

OBEDIENCE AND LOVE

And for this we must love. However little, we must love. Charles Williams in the same book *All Hallows Eve* which I quoted above, describes on the first page the soul of his dead heroine on one of the bridges of London where she died. She sees nothing but herself, the point at which her feet touch the ground and the aeroplane which crashed and killed her. She sees nothing because her heart is attached to nothing. She sees an empty bridge when in fact it is crowded with pedestrians, all the time. On either bank of the Thames she sees houses, but as walls with gloomy eyes, windows which light up and go dark again but meaninglessly. She has no key to the world around her because she has never loved anything and is a stranger here. Suddenly her husband, now her widower walks over the bridge. They see each other, he because he loves her and he bears her in his heart, weeps for her and seeks her in the invisible world, she because he is the only person she ever loved in her poor selfish way. He is the only person she can see. She sees him. He goes on. But her heart has stirred and through her husband she remembers her world, husband, their home and friends. And gradually, through this love she begins to discover the world she lived in without knowing it and at the same time the new vast world she has just entered. These two worlds interpenetrate in the co-inherence which is Charles Williams particular philosophical theory. For we only see what we love. We think we see what we hate, but really in our hatred we see only deformed images, caricatures. And indifference and luke-warmness are blind.

AN EYE PURIFIED TO JUDGE

But to know truly, to see reality in an adequate manner, it is not enough to look, listen or even to love. We must also have a pure heart capable of finding God beyond the darkness which hides him. Just as an unclear eye projects its own shadow on all it sees, so an impure heart cannot judge or see things in the way that God sees them.

A story about the desert fathers illustrates this clearly. One of them followed by his disciples comes to the gates of Alexandria. He sees a very beautiful woman coming along the road. The disciples cover their heads with their cloaks so as not to fall into temptation. Perhaps they escape from the temptation of the flesh, but not from the temptation of curiosity. From underneath their cloaks they see their master and are scandalised to find that he is looking straight at the approaching woman. After she has gone into the town, they remove their cloaks and ask him, 'How could you succumb to the temptation to look at this woman?' He replied sadly, 'How impure are your hearts. You saw her only as a temptation. I saw her as one of God's wonders.'

THE EXPERIENCE OF A STARETZ

So every encounter with God or man has more than technical requirements. When we seek God we must love our neighbours and when we seek our neighbours we must love God. In one of his letters a Russian *staretz* describes how one day he was asked a question: 'Why is it that the workers under your charge work so hard and so well when you do not watch over them and those that we watch over are always trying to deceive us.' The holy man replied: 'When I come in the morning to give them their work, I am overcome with pity for them. They have left their village and their family for a tiny wage, how poor they must be. And when I have given them their work I go back into my cell and pray for each one of them I say to the Lord: "Lord, remember Nicholas he is so young, he has left his new-born child to find work because they are so poor he has no other means of supporting it. Think of him and protect him from evil thoughts. Think of her and be her defender." Thus I pray but as I feel the presence of God more and more strongly, I reach a point when I can no longer take notice of anything on earth. The earth vanishes, God alone remains. Then I forget Nicholas, his wife, his child, his village, his poverty and am carried away in God. Then deep in God I find the divine love which contains Nicholas, his wife, his child, their poverty, their needs and this divine love is a torrent which carries me back to earth and to praying for them. And the same thing happens again. God's presence becomes stronger, earth recedes. I am carried again into the depths where I find the world that God so greatly loves.' Encounter with God, encounter with man. They are only possible when both are so greatly loved that the one who prays can forget himself, become detached from himself, and become only an 'orientation' towards them, for them. This the fundamental character of intercession.

I should now like to explore this theme of encounter a bit further. First I should like to stress that encounter with God and man is *dangerous*. It is not without reason that the eastern tradition of Zen calls the place where we find him whom we seek the tiger's lair. Seeking God is an act of boldness, unless it is an act of complete humility. Encountering God is always a *crisis* and the Greek word crisis means *judgment*. This encounter can take place in wonder and humility. It can also take place in terror and condemnation. So it is not surprising that orthodox manuals on prayer give very little space to questions of technique and method but endless advice on the necessary moral and spiritual conditions for prayer. Let us recall some of these. First the gospel commandment: 'If you come to the temple and you remember that your brother has something against you, leave your gift, return to him you have offended and make your peace with him, then come back and offer your gift'. This commandment is taken up in an excellent manner by Simeon the New Theologian, who tells us that if we want to pray with a free heart, we must make our peace with God, our conscience, our neighbour and even the things about us. That is to say that the condition of a life

of prayer is a life in accordance with the gospel. A life
which makes the commandments and counsels given us
by the gospel second nature.

It is not enough to obey them as a slave obeys his
master's will. We must want to obey with all our heart,
like a son, like children of the kingdom who truly want
what they pray when they say 'Hallowed be thy name,
thy kingdom come, thy will be done'.

Let us now consider an encounter with the Lord in a
number of particular situations, in humility, in truth, in
despair, in tumult, in life, in silence, in the liturgy.

IT IS TERRIBLE TO FALL INTO THE HANDS OF THE LIVING GOD

If we remembered that every encounter with God and
every deep encounter with man is a judgment, a crisis,
we would seek God both more whole-heartedly and more
cautiously. We would not be bitter if this encounter did
not immediately take place. We would approach God
with a trembling heart. In this way we would avoid many
disappointments, many useless efforts, because God
would not give himself to us if we could not bear the
encounter. He prepares us for it, and sometimes by a
long wait. The Gospel gives us examples of the attitude
we should imitate. Luke shows us ten lepers seeking to
be cured. They come towards Christ and stop a little
way off because they know they are impure. And in their
misery they cry to the Lord with all the faith and hope
they are capable of but without going up to him. And
the Lord does not take one step towards them. He simply
commands them to go and show themselves to the
priests. He promises them nothing. He sends them to
their cure. And this cure is granted them in their faith,
hope and humble obedience. How different is their
humility from our prayer of 'humble access' when we
should be trembling but are often arrogant.

We may also remember the example of St Peter who
realised his master's godhead through his words and the
miraculous draught of fishes, and fell at his feet crying,
'depart from me for I am a sinful man, O Lord'. The
vision of the holiness and glory of God did not lead
him to seek an intimacy with it which he could not
bear. He asked the Lord to go away. But the Lord
decided to stay.

We have also in the gospel the story of the centurion
who asks the Lord to cure his servant and when the Lord
says he will come, the centurion replies, 'Lord I am not
worthy that you should enter under my roof, say but the
word.' A total faith and perfect trust, such great humility
which should shame us because we do not feel our own
sinfulness enough, we do not feel ourselves unworthy
enough to ask the Lord not to trouble himself at the
same time believing that he can do everything for us.

But this is a basic attitude. Unless we give up seeking
a tangible shining presence of the Lord, we are going
towards our own judgment. If the Lord comes to us, we
should receive him with great joy and humility. But let
us be careful not to seek mystical experience when we
should be seeking repentance and conversion. That is the
beginning of our cry to God. 'Lord make me what I
should be, change me whatever the cost.' And when we
have said these dangerous words, we should be prepared
for God to hear them. And these words of God are
dangerous because God's love is remorseless. God wants
our salvation with the determination due to its importance. And God, as the Shepherd of Hermas says 'does
not leave us till he has broken our heart and bones'.

LET ME KNOW MYSELF

A second form of encounter is the encounter in the
truth. An encounter is only true when the two persons
meeting are true. And from this point of view, we are

Image of God ————→

continually falsifying this encounter. Not only in ourselves but in our image of God, it is very difficult for us to be true. Throughout the day we are a succession of social personalities, sometimes unrecognisable to others or even to ourselves. And when the time comes to pray and we want to present ourselves to God we often feel lost because we do not know which of these social personalities is the true human person, and have no sense of our own true identity. The several successive persons that we present to God are not ourselves. There is something of us in each of them but the whole person is missing. And that is why a prayer which could rise powerfully from the heart of the true person cannot find its way between the successive men of straw we offer to God. Each of these speaks a word which is true in its own partial way, but does not express the other partial personalities we have been during the day. It is extremely important that we find our unity, our fundamental identity. Otherwise we cannot encounter the Lord in truth. The search for this unity may take time. We should be on the watch all the time to see that none of our words and actions are incompatible with the fundamental integrity we are seeking. We must try and discover the real person we are, the secret person, the core of the person to come and the only eternal reality which is already in us. This discovery is difficult because we have to cast aside all the men of straw. From time to time something authentic shows through, when we forget ourselves our deep reality may take over, in moments when we are carried away by joy so that we forget who might be looking at us, forget to stand aside and look at ourselves, or when we are unselfconscious in moments of extreme pain, moments when we have a deep sense of sadness or of wonder. At these moments we see something of the true person that we are. But no sooner have we seen, than we often turn away because we do not

want to confront this person face to face. We are afraid
of him, he puts us off.

Nevertheless this is the only real person there is in
us. And God can save this person, however repellent he
may be, because it is a true person. God cannot save the
imaginary person that we try to present to him, or to
others or ourselves. As well as seeking the real person in
us, through these chance manifestations, we must also
seek constantly the person we are to God. We must seek
for God in us and ourselves in God. This is a work of
meditation which we should engage in every day all
through our lives.

We can begin simply. When we read the scriptures
honestly we can admit that certain passages mean little
to us. We are ready to agree with God because we have
no reason to disagree with him. We can approve of this
or that commandment or divine action because it does
not touch us personally, we do not yet see the demands
it makes on us personally. Other passages frankly,
repel us. If we had the courage we would say 'no' to the
Lord. We should note these passages carefully. They are
a measure of the distance between God and us and also,
perhaps more importantly for our present point, they are
a measure of the distance between ourselves as we are
now and our potential definitive selves. For the gospel is
not a succession of external commandments, it is a whole
gallery of internal portraits. And every time we say 'no'
to the Gospel we are refusing to be a person in the full
sense of the word.

There are also passages of the gospel which make our
hearts burn, which give light to our intelligence and
shake up our will. They give life and strength to our
whole physical and moral being. These passages reveal
the points where God and his image in us already coincide, the stage we have already reached, perhaps only
momentarily, fleetingly, in becoming what we are called

to be. We should note these passages even more carefully than the passages mentioned above. They are the
points at which God's image is already present in us
fallen men. And from these beginnings we can strive to
continue our transformation into the person we feel we
want and ought to be. We must be faithful to these
revelations. In this at least we must always be faithful.
If we do this these passages increase in number, the
demands of the gospel become fuller and more precise,
slowly the fogs disperse and we see the image of the
person we should be. Then we can begin standing before
God in truth. However as well as this essential, fundamental truth, there is also the partial truth of the
moment.

How often our prayer is false because we try to present
ourselves to God not as we are, but as we imagine he
wants us to be. We come to him in our Sunday best or
in borrowed finery. It is important that before we start
to pray we should take time to recollect ourselves, to
reflect and become aware of the real state in which we
present ourselves to the Lord. 'My heart is ready, Lord.
my heart is ready,' we can say. 'As pants the hart for
cooling streams, so longs my soul for Thee O God.' But
too often we drag ourselves into God's presence by a
dour effort of will. We are doing a duty with no heart
in it. We force ourselves to appear to be what we know
we are deep down but do not at the moment feel. The
living waters have sunk in dry sands. We should tell
this to God who is the truth. 'Lord I come to you with a
dry heart, but I am forcing myself to stand before you
because of a deep conviction. I love and worship you with
my deepest being, but today this deepest being has failed
to surface.' Sometimes we find that we do not even
present ourselves to God out of deep conviction, but out
of an almost superstitious fear. 'If I do not pray perhaps
God will withdraw his protection from me.' We should

confess this distrust and lack of faith and hope in God's love and faithfulness. There are many other ways in which we present ourselves to God. We have to become aware of these different states in which we pray. Otherwise our prayer will not even contain the truth of the moment. It will be an absolute lie, a betrayal of both the old and the new Adam in us. It will neither be true to what is stable and eternal in us nor to passing moods.

LET ME KNOW YOU

But an encounter does not depend on the truth of only one of the parties to it. The Other is equally important. The God we encounter must be as true as we who seek him. But is not God always true? Is he not always himself, unchanging? Of course. But it is not only God as he is in himself who is involved in our prayers. It is also the image we have of him, for our attitude depends not only on what he is in himself but also on what we believe him to be. If we have a false image of God, our attitude towards him and our prayer will alter accordingly. It is important that throughout our life, from day to day we learn to know God as he is. Not in the fragmented way which makes us see him sometimes as a ruthless judge and sometimes as a loving saviour, but in all his complexity. We must also beware of thinking that even the sum total of human knowledge of God constitutes an authentic image of the living God. God, even as he reveals himself in scripture, does not reveal himself in a total and final manner. If we try and place ourselves before an image of God made up of all that we know of him through revelation, through the experience of the church, our own experience, we are in danger of standing before a false image, because it pretends to be a total image, when it can only ever be a poor approximation. As Gregory of Nazianzus says, this is worship-

Prayer without or images (handwritten annotation)

ping an idol. This is why the Eastern Church Fathers continually stress the necessity of presenting ourselves to God without images or imaginings of him. Everything that we know about God should lead us to God, but when we stand before him, we should leave all this knowledge of him behind, however true and rich it may be. We should stand before the unknown God, the mystery, the divine darkness, we should be ready to meet God as he wishes to reveal himself to us today. Otherwise it will always be the God of yesterday, and not the true God himself. But the true God is the only object of our seeking, the only partner in authentic prayer. This encounter in the truth cannot happen with an artificial presence, because in our encounter we are not seeking merely emotions of joy, ecstasy etc. but God himself.

THE ABSENCE OF GOD

And in this context of truth we must recognise the fact that God may be absent. This absence is of course subjective, in so far as God is always present to us. But he may remain invisible and intangible. He escapes us. What we said above about humility should help us here. When God does not give himself to us, when we cannot feel his presence, we must be able to wait with awe and reverence. But there is also another element in this subjective absence of God. A relationship can only be true if it takes place in mutual freedom. We too often feel that we have only to start praying for God to be obliged to offer himself to us, to listen to us, to let us feel his presence, to assure us that he hears us. If this were so, it would not be a free relationship, it would be mechanical and could have no joy and spontaneity. It would also suppose that we were always in a fit state to see God. Alphonse de Chateaubriand in a remarkable book on prayer called *La Réponse du Seigneur*, tells us that God's apparent absence is usually caused by our own blindness.

I should like to illustrate this phrase by an example.

One day a man came to see me, a man who had been searching for God for many years. He told me in tears: 'Father I cannot live without God. Show me God.' I told him that I was unable to show him God, but I did not think that he was in a fit state to see him anyway. Astonished, he asked me why. Then I asked him a question which I often ask those who come to see me. 'Is there a passage in the scripture which goes straight to your heart, the most precious passage you have found?' 'Yes,' he replied, 'the story of the adulterous woman in John chapter eight.' Then I asked him, 'Where do you see yourself in this scene?' Are you the woman who has become conscious of her sin and stands to be judged, knowing that it will be a judgment of life or death? Or do you identify with Christ who understands everything and will forgive her, so that she can live with a new life henceforth? Are you waiting for a reply and hoping it will be merciful, as the apostles must have been? Are you one of the crowd, one of the old men who knew they had sinned themselves and were the first to withdraw, or one of the young men who gradually realised they too were sinners and dropped the stones they had picked up to throw? Who are you in this dramatic scene? And after a moment's reflection this man replied, 'I am the only Jew who would not have withdrawn without stoning the woman.' So I said, 'You have your reply. You cannot see God who is a total stranger to you.'

Isn't there something similiar in the experience of each one of us? Isn't there in each one of us a resistance to God, a denial of God? When we seek him, do we not seek a God in our own image, a God who is convenient to us? Are we not prepared to reject the true God if we find him? Are we prepared to find God as he is, even if this encounter condemns us and upsets all the values which have hitherto been dear to us? Isn't the absence

of God in our life and in our prayers often due to the
fact that we are strangers to him and that if we did come
face to face with him we would not see him, or recognise
him? Isn't this what happened when Christ was on the
roads of Judea and Galilee? How many of his contemporaries met him, passed him by, without recognising or
even suspecting that there was something special about
him? Wasn't this the way he was seen by the crowds on
the road to Calvary? A criminal, a man who had caused a
breach of the peace – nothing else. Isn't this often the
way we think of God, even when we are able to feel
something of his presence? Don't we turn away from
him, because we sense that he will cause a breach of the
peace in our lives, upset its values? In this case we
cannot rely on encountering him in our prayer. I would
put it even more strongly, we should thank God with
all our hearts that he does not offer himself to us at this
moment, because we doubt him not like Job, but like
the bad thief on the cross. An encounter would be judgment and condemnation on us. We should learn to
understand this absence and judge ourselves because we
are not judged by God.

Another aspect of God's absence can be illustrated by
another story. A few years ago a young woman with an
incurable disease wrote to me. 'How grateful I am to God
for my illness. As my body weakens, I feel it becoming
more and more transparent to God's action.' I replied,
'Thank God for what he has given you, but do not expect
this state to last. The time will come when this natural
weakening will not continue to make you feel more
spiritual. Then you must rely on grace alone.' Some
months later she wrote to me again, 'I have become so
weak that I no longer have the strength to throw myself
on God. All I can do is to keep silent, surrender myself
hoping that God will come to me.' She added what is
the point of the story for us, 'Pray the Lord to give me

courage never to try and construct a false presence to fill the frightening void of his absence.'

I think these two stories need no comment. It is important that we rely on God. We must not rely on our own strength, neither must we rely on our own weakness. An encounter with God is a free act where God is in control and it is only when we are humble, as well as beginning to love God, that we are able to support his absence, to be enriched even by his absence.

BARTIMAEUS

Despairing hope is also one of the ways in which we can encounter God. We have several examples in the gospels and the lives of the saints. In the Gospel of St Mark, chapter 10 we have the story of Bartimaeus the blind beggar who sat at the gates of Jericho. The gospel story of his cure gives us certain crucial facts for the understanding of prayer. We are too often astonished that our prayer is not heard. We think we have only to offer a prayer for God to be obliged to answer it. In fact, if we strictly examine our motives for praying, and our needs, we see that we often do not pray for what is necessary to us but for what is superfluous. The ease with which we abandon our prayer when we are not heard proves that even when we are praying for something without which we ought not to be able to live, we have neither the patience nor the perseverance to insist on it. In the last resort we prefer to live without this necessity rather than fight desperately for it. A Father of the Church tells us that prayer is like an arrow. It is always capable of flying, of reaching its target, of piercing through resistance, but it only flies if it is shot from a good bow by a strong hand. It only hits the bull's eye if the archer's aim is steady and accurate. And what our prayer lacks is often this strength of spirit, the sense of the seriousness of our situation.

Bartimaeus is blind. We do not know if his eyes went slowly dim, the dear familiar world faded from his sight little by little, or whether he was born blind. But what we do see clearly is a grown man sitting by the dusty road begging. How many times in his life of perhaps thirty years must he have tried to regain his sight? How often must he have visited doctors, priests, healers, asked for prayers and help from whoever could give them? How often he must have hoped, with a hope that depends on men, reason and experience, but also on faith in mercy and compassion in the goodness and brotherhood of men? How often must this hope have sprung up only to wither unfulfilled? And now we find him by the roadside at the city gates, defeated by life, no longer seeking to recover his sight but trying merely to survive through the charity of the passers by. Not the burning charity which cherishes, but the cold charity which gives without compassion – money thrown anonymously to a hungry beggar, without even looking at him. The passerby is as blind as the beggar by the roadside, and his blindness is perhaps the greater because it is blindness of heart and conscience, he no longer has any part in human brotherhood. But this story takes place in the time of Christ. This blind beggar must have heard of this teacher who first appeared in Galilee and is now travelling throughout Judea and all the Holy Land, working miracles. A man who is said to cure the blind, to have given sight to a man born blind.

How this far off presence of a healing God must have revived his faith and hope but also his despair; hope because everything is possible to God, despair because nothing is possible to man. If God came to him, he could be cured. But how could he who was blind find this elusive miracle worker in Galilee or Judea, for he moved about continually and often appeared only to disappear almost at once? This way in which God's approach

arouses both a last hope and an even deeper despair is
true not only of Bartimaeus. It is also our own situation.
God's presence like a sword separates the light from the
darkness, but so often throws us back into the darkness
because his presence dazzles us. It is because God is
there, it is because eternal life is possible that it is so
desperately urgent not to vegetate in a life which
passes.

One day Bartimaeus sitting by the roadside hears a
group of people go by. His practised ear discerns something particular about their walk, their conversation,
their atmosphere. It is not a noisy crowd or caravan, this
group has a centre. He asks the people passing, Who is
it? They reply, Jesus of Nazareth. In a moment all the
hope and despair of his life reach their climax. He is in
deepest darkness and brightest light. He may be cured
because God is walking by him. But he must seize the
passing moment which will be gone in a twinkling. Jesus
will only be within his reach for a few paces. Beforehand
he will be too far away engrossed in conversation with
others. Afterwards he will have passed beyond him for
ever. Bartimaeus cries out his desperate hope. 'Jesus son
of David have mercy on me.' This is in itself a profession
of faith. The blind man must have thought it out in the
months before when he heard all the stories of the cures
worked by the Lord. For him, Jesus is not a wandering
prophet. He is the son of David. Thus he calls him, begs
him. And all around him voices are raised ordering to
keep silence. How dare he interrupt the Master's conversation with his disciples? How dare he make such an
unimportant request to the Master who is talking about
the things of heaven? But he knows that his whole life,
all the joy and despair of his life is in his blindness and
the possibility of its cure. So he cries out and the more
they try to silence him the louder he cries. And because
he prays insistently for the one vitally important thing

to him, he is heard, the Lord hears him, God cures him and opens a new life to him.

This is a very difficult lesson for us. How serious we must be about praying if we want our prayer to be worthy of the greatness of our destiny and of him who in all humility is willing to hear us. Despair, hunger for God, the vital necessity to us of what we ask, these are the conditions to make the arrow of our prayer fly sure to its target, aimed from a taut bow by a strong hand and a steady eye.

There is something special in this story which I should like to dwell on a little longer. It is the tumult surrounding this prayer as it reaches the Lord. For this encounter between the Lord and Bartimaeus took place in a double tumult. The inner tumult of his conflicting feelings of hope, despair, fear, excitement, and the tumult outside him, all the voices ordering him to silence because the Lord was busy with things worthier of his dignity and holiness. Bartimaeus is not the only one to encounter the Lord in tumult. Our whole life is an incessant tumult. It is a succession of situations demanding our presence, feelings, thoughts, heart and will in harmony, in contradiction and so on. And in this tumult our soul turns to the Lord, cries to him, and seeks rest in him. How often we think it would be so easy to pray if there was nothing to prevent us and how often this very tumult helps us to pray.

PRAYER IN TUMULT

But how can we pray in a state of turmoil? I should like to give a few examples to show how this is possible. I might almost call this turmoil an advantage, because like rugged rocks it helps us climb upwards when we cannot fly. The first story is taken from the *Lives of the Church Fathers*. An anonymous ascetic meets another ascetic, a man of prayer, in the mountains. They start a

conversation during which the visitor who is struck by
his companion's state of prayer, asks, 'Father who
taught you to pray without ceasing?' And his host, who
realises that his companion is a man of spiritual experience replies, 'I would not say this to everyone, but I will
tell you truly, that it was the demons.' The visitor says, 'I
think I understand you Father, but could you explain
in greater detail, how they taught you, so that I don't
misunderstand you.' And the other tells him the
following story: 'When I was young, I was illiterate and
I lived in a small village on the plain. One day I went
into church and heard the deacon reading the epistle of
St Paul which commands us to pray without ceasing.
When I heard these words, I was warmed with joy and
illuminated. At the end of the service I left the village
in great joy and retired to the mountains to live by
prayer alone. This state persisted in me for several hours.
Then night began to fall, it became colder and I began to
hear strange noises, footsteps and howls. Gleaming eyes
appeared. The wild beasts had come out of their lairs to
hunt the food that God had appointed them. I became
afraid, more and more afraid as the shadows deepened.
I spent the whole night in terror of the footsteps,
crackling sounds, shadows, gleaming eyes, the sense
of my own weakness knowing nowhere to turn for help.
Then I began to cry to God the only words that came to
my mind, words born of my fear, "Jesus, Son of David,
have mercy on me, sinner though I am." Thus the first
night passed. In the morning my fears vanished but I
began to be hungry. I looked for my food in bushes and
in the fields and it was hard to satisfy my hunger. And
as the sun was setting and I felt the terrors of the night
returning, I began to cry to God my fear and my hope.
Thus days passed and then months. I became accustomed
to the terrors of nature, but even as I prayed from moment to moment, new temptations and trials appeared.

The demons, the passions began to attack me on all sides, and just as the night beasts ceased to frighten me, the powers of darkness raged against my soul. I cried even more than before the same words to the Lord, "Lord, Jesus Christ, have mercy on me." This struggle went on for years. One day I reached the limits of my endurance. I had cried unceasingly to God in my agony and distress and I received no reply. God appeared to me implacable and then when the shred fibre of hope was breaking in my soul, I surrendered myself to the Lord saying, "You are silent, you don't care what becomes of me, but you are still my God and my Master and I will die here where I stand rather than abandon my quest." Suddenly the Lord appeared to me and peace came upon me and everything round me. The whole world had seemed to me in darkness and now I saw it bathed in divine light, shining with the grace of God's presence which sustains all that he has created. Then in a burst of love and gratitude, I cried to the Lord the only prayer that expressed all that was in me, "Lord Jesus Christ, have mercy on me, a sinner." And ever since, in joy, in suffering, in temptation and struggle or at the moment when peace comes to me, these words always spring from my heart. They are a song of joy, they are a cry to God, they are my prayer and my repentance.'

This example of the unknown ascetetic shows how suffering, despair and turmoil bring these words out of us; this desperate cry, born of a hope that is stronger than despair itself, fed by despair and transcending it.

THE STILLING OF THE STORM

Often we are in tumult, perhaps less of a tumult than the young ascete, but we surrender to it and are defeated. That is why our prayer is trembling and hesitant, a prayer of tumult, uncertainty and incoherence. Isn't this the story of the storm on the lake of Galilee? The Lord

and his disciples are on the lake. A tempest comes up
when they are out to sea. Death threatens them, the
waves are huge, the winds beat against them. They fight
for their lives as hard as they can, and all this while the
Lord is asleep on a cushion at the prow. He looks comfortable to them. They can't bear him looking so comfortable, his indifference. In their wretchedness they turn
to him, wake him up, try to force him to realise what is
happening. 'Lord, do you not see that we perish?' But
what are they doing by asking this question? Are they
appealing to the Lord to control the storm? Yes and no.
First of all they want him to share their suffering. They
want him to be as anxious as they are. They think he
will not help them unless he shares their anxiety. The
Lord gets up, he refuses to share their panic. He keeps
his own serenity. First he turns to them, 'How long must
I be with you, men of little faith?' And then he turns
towards the storm, and casts his own serenity onto it. He
orders the waves to be still and the wind to be silent, and
his own peace to come down on everything about him.
The storm is still and the disciples fall at his feet. Who is
he? They are still doubtful. We often make the same mistake. Instead of seeking to share God's serenity, we ask
God to share our tumult. Of course he does share it, but
with his own serenity. This turmoil, disorder, disharmony,
discord often enter our lives both in us and around us.
They are caused by events we do not understand and
human actions which are also tormented. And this is
the essential problem, the link between the turmoil of
life and our prayer, disturbance and serenity. We must
realise in advance that in every confrontation between
our inner peace and the hurly-burly of life, victory will
go to the turmoil, because our prayer is weak and life is
hard. Life is ruthless whereas our prayer, our inner
peace and serenity is fragile. If we want to keep it and
gain the victory over life, this must not be by open con-

frontation but as water waters the earth. The Fathers said that water is an image of humility. It goes to the bottom. This is quite true, but water is also invincible. When through its weight it reaches the bottom, it begins to rise and nothing can stop it. This is what our prayer should do.

CONSTANT PRAYER

It is difficult to pray for a whole day. Sometimes we try and imagine what it would be like. We think either of the liturgical life of contemplative monks or else the anchorite's life of prayer. We don't so often think of a life of prayer taking place in ordinary life, when everything becomes prayer or an occasion for prayer. But this is an easy way to pray, although it is of course very demanding. Let us rise in the morning and offer ourselves to God. We have woken from a sleep which divides us from yesterday. Waking up offers us a new reality, a day which has never existed before, an unknown time and space stretching before us like a field of untrodden snow. Let us ask the Lord to bless this day and bless us in it. And when we have done this, let us take our request seriously and also the silent answer we have been given. We are blessed by God, his blessing will be with us always in everything we do which is capable of receiving this blessing. We will only lose it when we turn away from God. And God will stay near us even then, ready to come to our aid, ready to give us back the grace we have rejected. We have put on the armour of God, as St Paul says in Ephesians chapter 6. Faith, hope and charity is our armour and also our cry to God. And we begin this day in grace and glory, with the Lord's cross and the Lord's death in us.

But the day itself is also blessed by God. Doesn't this mean that everything that it contains, everything that happens to us during it is within the will of God? Believing that things happen merely by chance is not believing in God. And if we receive everything that happens and everyone that comes to us in this spirit, we shall see that we are called to do the work of christians in everything. Every encounter is an encounter in God and in his sight. We are sent to everyone we meet on our way, either to give or to receive, sometimes without even knowing it. Sometimes we experience the wonder of giving what we did not possess, sometimes we have to pay with our own blood for what we give. We must also know how to receive. We must be able to encounter our neighbour in the way we tried to describe at the beginning of this essay. We must be able to look at him, hear him, keep silence, pay attention, be able to love and to respond wholeheartedly to what is offered, whether it be bitterness or joy, sad or wonderful. We should be completely open and like putty in God's hands. The things that happen in our life, accepted as God's gifts, will thus give us the opportunity to be continually creative, doing the work of a christian.

Too often christians have the habit whenever a problem or danger arises of turning to the Lord and crying, 'Lord protect us, save us, fight for us.' How often the Lord must look at us sadly and say to us in the silent language which we could understand if only our hearts were not so deafened by their fear, 'But I sent you into this situation to fight for me, are you not part of the army, the avant-garde of the kingdom which I have sent out to fight for me on earth? Did I not tell my apostles, "As my Father sent me, so I send you to live and die?" Have you forgotten the examples and counsels of the apostles?' It is for us to be Christ's presence on earth, sometimes victorious sometimes crucified. We must give ourselves always, and never run away. Everything is possible to us in the power of Christ, but it is for us to shed our blood, now it is for us to struggle and sweat. It is not for him

to come down and go through it all over again. Isn't this
the meaning of the conversation between Christ and
Peter whom he met at the gates of Rome trying to escape
from persecution, 'Where are you going Lord? Quo vadis
Domine?' 'I am going to Rome to be crucified again.'
Our job is to be present, not to be safe and sound. In
this day undertaken in God's name, we will have many
opportunities of asking what it means, what the successive things that happen mean. We must be able to
be quiet and meditative, look calmly at all the things that
puzzle us, for we will not be able to understand everything until we see God's whole plan. Our mistake is
nearly always supposing that human wisdom together
with plaintive prayer will be enough to solve the problems of eternal destiny. For everything, even the most
insignificant detail, is part of this eternal destiny, this
future of the world to which we belong. Human wisdom
must give way to the capacity to contemplate the mystery
before us, to try and discern the invisible hand of God,
whose wisdom is so different from human wisdom. But
his wisdom is also in the human heart. We must try and
be a silent balancing point in the tumult of life. We must
learn to wait till we understand. An English writer com-
pares the perfect christian to a sheepdog. A sheepdog,
says Evelyn Underhill, stops still when it hears its
master's voice, looks at its master and listens to its voice
to try and find out what he wants. The moment he understands he dashes off to do what its master wants. And,
Evelyn Underhill adds, the dog has a quality possessed
by very few christians – it never stops wagging its tail.

   In our lives with all their turmoil and apparent disorder, we must try and discern God's plan by attentive
prayer and silent meditation. We should be able to find
courage, strength, inspiration and the advice we need in
our prayer. But this is an ideal situation; we cannot
venture into it immediately, because we are not yet ac-

customed to praying without cease, of being always
aware of ourselves and the life going on about us. We
must try to do this gradually, starting with a few hours
or less, because if we force ourselves too strenuously and
for too long to pay attention in this way, we will find it
beyond our strength and we will collapse. Not because
grace will fail us but because of our human weakness.
Then we will be disgusted and exhausted by prayer. The
most vital words will be like ashes in our mouths and we
will not feel we are living the day in and for God. In
these moments we must humbly accept defeat and realise that we are not yet strong enough to live constantly
in God's presence. Then we must fast spiritually, limit
our burst of prayer, particular prayer in words and know
that if we try and live through the day which we com-
mended to God in the morning, this is a prayerful situation in itself. Then gradually, as our will becomes
trained and the concentration of our heart and mind
improves, we will be able to spend whole days in prayer.
This prayer will not be merely the prayer of daily
life which cannot yet transform it, but a much more
conscious, deeper prayer, of which we will speak
again.

THE ROLE OF ASCESIS

What we have just said brings us to a problem which is
difficult for beginners to solve. This is the problem of
effortful prayer, ascesis. It is easy to pray in wonder or in
pain. It is much harder to pray on drab ordinary days,
when there is nothing within or without us to help us
pray. Then we must be able to force ourselves. Why?
Because our life of prayer should not only be our spontaneity, but also our firm unalterable conviction. This is
true of all our feelings, as well as our feelings about
praying. Are there not moments when we feel tired out
and if we were asked about our affection for those most

dear to us, we should have to say that we were incapable
of feeling it at the moment but that we were quite certain we had a very strong affection for them. But our
tiredness dominates our feelings. We can be spontaneous, but sometimes we are too tired and feel we
cannot feel. Then our affection resides in the will. But the
will together with firm conviction is the essential lever
in our life. If we force ourselves to do something purely
out of social convention, this constraint has a deadly
rather than a life-giving effect. Constraint need not be
sheer force, we can also add self-knowledge, knowledge
of others and kindness. When spontaneity and enthusiasm are lacking, we force ourselves to pray. Then we
must stand in God's presence by a pure act of faith; we
know that he exists and who he is. We approach him in
worship, in the reverent fear due to all that is holy. We
make a firm effort to pay the attention due to him. We
force ourselves to do this because we want to encounter
God not just for the immediate joy but for the longer-
lasting joy which will come to us when we have been
transformed by this contact with him and we live with
God's life. What we must do, without deceiving ourselves
or trying to deceive God, is to stand in his presence and
offer him even this unspontaneous prayer with firm
intellectual conviction and a determined will.

This means two things. First that we are not primarily
seeking the joy of an encounter with God but the deep
transformation that God alone can work in us, that we
are prepared, as the Church Fathers said, to give our
blood in order to receive the Spirit. And secondly it
means that our prayer must be the most accurate possible
expression of our true convictions. When we pray in
our own words our prayer should be sober, attentive and
humble. It should express the reality of its own poverty
as well as our firm convictions and desire. This requires
a strong effort of detachment. But such detachment is

one of the elements necessary to any encounter. If we use 'ready made' prayers (prayers made by others in suffering or in spontaneous enthusiasm) we must be careful not to lie to God under the pretext of offering prayers worthy of him.

THE CONSOLATION OF THE SCRIPTURES

For periods of dryness we also need some prayers in reserve, which have meant a lot to us at other times. These prayers which have expressed our minds and hearts can be offered to God when we feel we have little to express. But sometimes we need to qualify them. There are prayers suitable to luminous moments in our lives which cannot be simply repeated as an act of faith in ourselves. When we are full of doubt, we cannot say to the Lord, 'Lord my heart is ready, my heart is ready.' And there are many other prayers the same. We must alter them a bit, so that we tell God the truth. We must find a balance between expressing our firm conviction and distorting our present reality. It is important to be able to use these prayers to wake ourselves up or bring ourselves back to life. For life comes from the Word of God. In dreary times we can recommend two things. We can start from a scripture text. When we feel low and sad, we can still sow the word, and perhaps we are more capable than we think of receiving it and bearing fruit. We should choose scriptural texts which we usually find moving, texts we have often thought about and responded to, which mean something in our lives and have permeated it like the leaven the woman added to the dough. We should re-read them when we feel unenthusiastic. And from them we can offer a prayer which may seem cold and dead to us, but which is at least truthful. We should not of course only pray from the scriptures in moments when we have to force ourselves to pray. It is always a good way of praying. But we need it paricu-

larly in bad moments, because the word of God is powerfully creative, it reaches beyond the depths of our souls,
it is life and can give us life, because it is God himself
speaking.

BEARING WITH OURSELVES

If we use prayers made by the saints (as I have said they
are useful to have in reserve) when we cannot think up
our own, it is difficult in these times when we feel dead
to know who to pray to. God seems to be absent, the
heavens are empty and we feel as if we are crying out in
despair with no one to hear us. Do you know these
passages from Emile Verhaeren:

Worshipfully
the winter night offers its pure cup to heaven.
And I raise my heart, my benighted heart.
Lord my heart, to your emptiness.
But I know you will not answer.
You do not exist, my heart's desire.
I know you are a lie and my lips pray
and my knees. Your large hands are shut,
your large eyes withdrawn from my despair.
I know you are my imagination.
Lord have pity on my hopelessness.
To your silence I must cry.
The winter night offers its pure cup to heaven.

Darkness.
I am here, the other is elsewhere, the silence doesn't
    give
We are unhappy. Satan passes us through his sieve.

We both suffer and there is no road
between us, neither hand nor word.

Only the common night incommunicable
when we cannot work and love is not possible.

I listen, I am alone and it frightens me.
I hear the sound of her voice, I hear a cry.

I feel a slight wind ruffle my hair.
From the jaws of the beast, from death, save her.

Again I feel death between my teeth.
My stomach turns, I catch my breath.

Alone in the winepress I trod grapes deliriously
all night from wall to wall, laughing wildly.

Will he who made our eyes not see me?
And he who made our ears not hear me?

I know that where sin is great, your mercy is greater
still.
In the hour of the Prince of this world, deliver us
from evil.

When God seems absent, the heavens empty and the
void immense, we should direct our prayer not to him
but talk to ourselves. We should address each word of
our prayer to our own depressed and dormant soul. We
must treat our soul like a mother taking a naughty child
onto her lap and telling him a story. At first the child
ignores her then he begins to pay attention. In the same
way we should begin by saying each word only for its
bare meaning, without reflecting on its weight. First we
say the words and simply understand them with our
mind, then we offer them to our heart, repeat a phrase
or part of a phrase perhaps once, twice, three times, to
try and kindle what is still alive in us, under the ashes.
We must not straitjacket our will, but let it lie comfortably at rest. For rest is part of ascesis. We should be
able to let ourselves go, be supple, not passive but in an
attitude of surrender. We should listen intelligently and
respond with all that is still alive in us to the familiar
words, to words spoken in deserts, by heroes in prayer

and the life in God. If we simply listen to these words, without effort, without adding to our weariness and exhaustion, then repeat them, try to savour them and feel their weight, often after a while, perhaps a long while, these words restore us to life, first our heart, then our will, and make us active again, capable of the sublime action of prayer.

In this situation our body, which is so often a nuisance to us in our life of prayer, can be immensely valuable. This body which is a member of the body of Christ and fed by the sacraments, can restore our soul. For the body plays an active part in our inner life. It has a part, felt or unfelt, in every movement of the soul, every feeling, thought, act of will or transcendent experience. The body's response is two-fold. It plays its part in our effort of concentration and it adapts to the object of that concentration. This does not happen just anyhow. Different parts of the body are involved in different objects of concentration, and thinking or feeling about the same object, with greater or lesser purity, in a more active or more passive way, also involves different parts of the body. Only daydreams cannot fix themselves, they wander at will like, according to Theophanos the Recluse 'a disorderly swarm of flies' or, according to Ramakrishna 'monkeys jumping from branch to branch'. As soon as a commanding thought or feeling engages us, all our physical activity groups round it, acquires a greater simplicity and cohesion. The field of consciousness narrows and defines a physical space of attention with its accompanying somato-psychic characteristics.

The ascesis of constraint, corporal ascesis is the only way of establishing prayer in complete stability. Spontaneous prayer, born of wonder or suffering is too dependent on incident. Only prayer born of conviction and a steady will can establish us face to face with God. The supreme prayer of stability in the orthodox church, called the prayer of Jesus is : 'Lord Jesus Christ, son of God, have mercy on me'.

GOD'S SILENCE AND MAN'S SILENCE

This encounter between God and us in stable prayer always leads to silence. We have to learn to distinguish two sorts of silence. God's silence and our own inner silence. First the silence of God, often harder to bear than his refusal, the absent silence we spoke of earlier. Second, the silence of man, deeper than speech, in closer communion with God than any words. God's silence to our prayer can last only a short time or it may seem to go on for ever. Christ was silent to the prayers of the Canaanite woman and this led her to gather up all her faith and hope and human love to offer to God so that he might extend the conditions of his kingdom beyond the chosen people. The silence of Christ provoked her to respond, to grow to her capacity. And God may do the same to us with shorter or longer silences to summon our strength and faithfulness and lead us to a deeper relationship with him than would have been possible had it been easy. But sometimes the silence seems frighteningly final to us. Do you know the words of Alfred de Vigny :

If, as we read, the Son of man
cried in the sacred Garden
and was not heard,
if heaven abandons us for dead,
we should spurn God's unjust absence
and render silence for silence.

Isn't this the impression that many christians are left with after reading the account of the agony in the Garden? And this silence is a problem for us which we have to solve, the problem of prayer which apparently receives no answer at all. If we read the gospel we find that the only prayer to God which is not heard is the prayer of Christ in Gethsemane. We should remember this because all too often we try and interpret God's silence as man's or God's insufficiency. When we are trying to defend God's honour we say my faith or your faith was not great enough for God to reply with a miracle. When our faith is weak we say, perhaps God could not reply, through impotence or indifference. But we have nothing to say to Christ's own prayer remaining unanswered. The faith of Christ the Son of God must be perfect. We cannot doubt God's love for him and does not Christ himself say that his Father could send twelve legions of angels to deliver him? If Christ is abandoned, that is because God has foreseen something better will come of it for us, at the price of his life. In this and other prayers in the gospel we see that a prayer remains fruitless if it is not supported by faith. Do you remember the passage where Christ was unable to work any miracles in Nazareth because of their unbelief? As soon as there is faith, then the conditions are present for a miracle, that is the kingdom of God come in power. And without intrusion, simply because he is the Lord of his kingdom, Christ acts with sovereign power, answers our prayers, helps us and saves us. But when our faith is firmly anchored in him we become capable of sharing his care for the world; we share in his solitude in the face of God's silence. We should realise that God's silence is either an appeal to forces dormant in us, or else has already taken their measure, and offers us a share in Christ's redemptive work.

God's silence and absence, but also man's silence and absence. An encounter does not become deep and full until the two parties to it are capable of being silent with one another. As long as we need words and actions, tangible proof, this means we have not reached the depth and fulness we seek. We have not experienced the silence which enfolds two people in common intimacy. It goes deep down, deeper than we knew we were, an inner silence where we encounter God, and with God and in God our neighbour.

In this state of silence we do not need words to feel close to our companion, to communicate with him in our deepest being, beyond ourselves to something which unites us. And when the silence is deep enough, we can begin to speak from its depths, but carefully and cautiously so as not to break it by the noisy disorder of our words. Then our thought is contemplative. Our mind instead of trying to make distinctions between many forms, as it usually does, tries to elicit simple luminous forms from the depths of the heart. The mind does its true work. It serves him who expresses something greater than it. We look into depths beyond ourselves and try to express something of what we find with awe and reverence. Such words, if they do not try to trivialise or intellectualise the total experience, do not break the silence, but express it. There is a remarkable passage by a medieval carthusian writer which says that if Christ is the Word of God, the Father is the creative silence which can only produce a word adequate to itself, a perfect expression of it.

We feel something of this in our moments of silence. Sometimes this silence comes upon us like a miracle, like a gift of God. More often we have to learn to make room for it in ourselves. We must have faith, endurance and hope and also that inner peace which the Greek fathers call *hesychia*. Contemplation requires this silence, which cannot be defined as either activity or passivity. It is a serene watchfulness. But we must also learn through bodily and spiritual ascesis to attain this perfect prayer of inner silence. I will not dwell on this point here. There is more about it in the books listed at the end of this essay.

THE SEARCH FOR SILENCE

We seek for silence in both a human and a divine way.
We must both seek it ourselves and hope for it as a gift.
The human search is described for us in a remarkable
manner in the medieval writings of Fr. Laurence on the
Practice of the Presence of God. In a much humbler
fashion I should like to tell the story of an old woman
who had prayed for many years without ever perceiving
the presence of God but who finally found it in silence.
Shortly after my ordination to the priesthood I was sent
into an old people's home to celebrate Christmas
with them. A very old woman came to me. She told me
that she had constantly recited the prayer of Jesus for
many years but she had never been given the experience of the presence of God. Young as I was, I found a
simple answer to her problem, 'How can God get a word
in edgeways if you never stop talking. Give him a
chance. Keep quiet'. 'How can I do that?' she said. I
then gave her some advice which I have since given to
others because it worked on that occasion. I advised her
after breakfast to tidy her room and make it as pleasant
as possible and sit down in a position where she could
see the whole room, the window onto the garden, the
icons with their little oil lamps. 'When you have sat
down, rest for a quarter of an hour in the presence of
God, but take care not to pray. Be as quiet as you can
and as you obviously can't do nothing, knit before the
Lord and tell me what happens.' After a few days she
came back happily. She had felt the presence of God. I
asked her curiously what had happened. She said she
had done exactly what I had suggested. She sat down and
looked about her quietly and peacefully feeling she had
the right to be inactive and not praying and for the first
time for years, she said, she noticed that the room was
peaceful and pleasant to be in. She looked at it and saw

it for the first time. There was an encounter between her
and the place she had lived in for many years without
ever seeing. Then she became aware of the peace and
silence round her, a peace and silence accentuated by the
ticking of her clock and the clicking of her needles on the
arms of her chair. Gradually this silence which had been
outside her came within her and enveloped her. The
silence took her out of herself into a richer silence which
was not just the absence of noise but rich in itself and
at its centre she found a presence. And when she felt
this presence she was moved to pray but from the depths
of this silence, not in floods of words and a whirl of
thoughts, but gently and quietly taking each word from
the silence and offering it to God. Of its own accord her
prayer had become the expression of her inner silence
and part of the silence of God which she had felt. This
is a method easy for everyone to try. It means of course
contending with the whirl of thoughts, the heart's hesi-
tations, the body's restlessness and the giddiness of the
will. There are many exercises based on ascesis and
psychology But even without these, simply letting go of
ourselves before God into the depth of silence we are
capable of, will help us make great progress.

Sometimes this silence comes to us from God even
more plainly. Without any warning we suddenly find
ourselves silently at rest in God. Praying for others is
shedding our blood, spending ourselves to the limit in
sympathy and compassion. But praying for others is also
going the way of Christ, becoming an expression of his
intercession, uniting ourselves with him in his prayer
and his incarnation. We experience the unutterable
groans of the Spirit in our own hearts. And the greater
our sympathy and the more closely we identify through
compassion with those for whom we pray, the more perfect is our communion with the merciful God. Our prayer
rising out of human suffering leads us to the heart of

God's mystery. First we are achingly aware of earthly suffering, then as our prayer continues we become more aware of the presence of God and a moment comes when we lose sight of the earth and are carried away into the depths of God. Rest, silence, peace and then at the heart of the mystery of love we find again those for whom we felt such compassion. The Spirit of love, the Spirit of God comes into us and leads us back to earth. But now our earthly involvement is bound together with the contemplation of the living God, the God of love.

This silence leads us to an encounter with God in serene and simple faith, to what is sometimes called the 'prayer of simple regard', expressed so beautifully by the peasant of Ars who when asked by his saintly priest what he did when he sat hour after hour in church without even fingering his rosary, 'I look at him and he looks at me and we are happy together'. But this prayer of simple regard is not just prayer it is also a transforming power. In a remarkable book which I have already mentioned, *La Réponse du Seigneur* by Alphonse de Chateaubriand, we find the following passage describing how the contemplative prayer of simple regard transformed a child who prayed thus of his own accord, not only inside but also outside.

'It was in a small remote mountain village nestling under a huge granite rock which had, by an accident of nature, a large human figure carved on it. This face dominated the country round it both because it was so big and because of its majestic expression. Beneath it the village looked like a small kite or merlin's nest. The people of the village believed that one day a very good man who looked exactly like the figure on the mountainside would come to their hamlet to practice his virtue and to do great good.

This is what they said during the long evenings, to

instruct their children, to reawaken happy memories in the old, to give hope to the sick. There was one little boy who had also heard the story and retained such a deep impression of it that he never stopped thinking about it and looking at the figure on the rock. He often sat on his doorstep with his finger in the corner of his mouth and looked up to the huge giant towering over the people below. He would stop in the middle of his games and think about the wonderful promise. What treasures would the hero bring? He became more and more attached to the carved figure and gradually grew to look like him.

This lasted throughout his childhood ... Until one day he was walking through the village square and his friends and neighbours looked at him with amazement and saw that he of whom the ancient tradition spoke was among them.'

The example of the monk Sylvanus shows us that prayer gives us both God and man, man and God. As we said at the beginning, this vision of things in depth gives us knowledge of all reality, our visible neighbours and our invisible Neighbour.

PRAYER AND OUR NEIGHBOUR

This leads us to our final point in our consideration of this encounter, encounter with the human community. This human community comes to us in two very different ways. On the one hand it is a secular community, the total human world about us, which we are part of. On the other hand it is the community of the church which we are also part of. In the secular community the christian has to be the presence of Christ. This means a total commitment. The central action of the economy of salvation is the incarnation of the word of God, an act by which the free transcendent God becomes one of us, involved with us, forever. The christian must be involved in the same way. Did not Christ say, 'As my Father sent me, so I send you'. Did he not add that he was sending us out as sheep among wolves. Did he not say that we must be in the world but not of the world? This gives us the obligation to meet the world as a whole, each member of the human community personally, but in a new way, in God's sight and in God. And also to judge everything in a new way, in God's way, who did not come to judge the world but to save it, God who so loved the world that he gave his only son for its salvation. In the gospel there is a radical change of values in the encounter between God and man. Not that good and evil lose their meaning, but evil is seen as a wound, as a sickness troubling our neighbour and from which we also suffer. We can hate evil and love our neighbour very much, to the death. A Russian martyr bishop said that it is a privilege for a christian to die as a martyr because only a martyr can stand before God on the day of judgment and defend his persecutors. 'Lord in your name and following your example, I forgive them. Ask nothing further of them.' And this upsetting of values is ruled by the mystery of the cross, the innocent dying for the guilty. We see three crosses on Calvary. Two thieves and the Son of God made man. The thief on Jesus's left judges by human values – if human justice has committed the crime of crucifying the innocent, it loses the right to be called justice. The criminal can appeal against it, curse it, reject it, deny it. He dies in a state of rebellion. The thief on Jesus's right sees that human justice can act unjustly and condemn the innocent, but also the guilty. He accepts his own suffering and condemnation because an innocent man is suffering with him. He finds peace and goes to paradise. Since the passion of our Lord Jesus Christ, since God made man appeared as a criminal, we can no longer judge the criminal in the same way as the

ancient world, we can no longer trust completely the
evidence of our reason and our senses.

In God's sight we see the actions we condemn and
should be ready to give our lives for the person who did
the wrong. When we are the victims of these actions,
we receive an extra power, the divine power of forgiving
these wrongs now and for eternity. This means that our
prayer is a situation in which we present to God all the
things that happen in a world that is estranged from him.
Our prayer has a priestly function. We should sacrifice
our own ego. We are a royal priesthood called to make
all things holy. We condemn the evil we see done, but
the doer is our brother and we must pray and live and
die for him. This is the meaning of intercession which we
discuss later on.

We discover God in Christ in the community of the
church. True christian encounter includes the visible
world with both its outward and inward face, and the
God of this world with all his invisible reality. Christian
encounter should include the whole universe. The unbeliever does not see the invisible world. Unfortunately
the christian is sometimes also blind to the visible world
and thinks this a virtue. The whole human community
with all its problems, all its future both temporal and
eternal should be of interest to the christian. Christian
prayer should be wide enough to contain it all. If we
remembered more often that everything is important,
nothing is profane except when we make it so by deny-
ing its holiness, we would have fewer distractions in our
prayers. The world can distract us from God in our
prayers. But when we are worried about something and
unable to encounter God in silence, we often try mis-
takenly to put our worry out of our mind, as if it were a
barrier between us and God. We think it wrong that
anything else could claim our attention when we are in
the presence of God. I think that often we could en-

counter God by sharing our worry with him instead of trying to push it aside. We ought to present it to God in detail but with precision and sobriety. We should present it as a mother brings a child to a doctor she trusts. We should say to God, 'This is all I can talk about to you at the moment. You who know everything look at my problem, understand it with your own understanding.'

When we have thus offered a person or a situation to God, we should be able to become detached from it. This requires faith and the ease with which we can detach ourselves from a care, is the measure of our faith. If we can say, 'Lord now I have told you everything, my heart is peaceful and I can rest in you.' If our heart is really at peace, if our mind is really freed from worrying, then our faith is complete. We have laid our burden at God's feet and now he is carrying it on his broad shoulders. Let us be encouraged by the story of the monk who was praying for his neighbours and who gradually lost consciousness of the earth because he became so wrapped up in God and who then found all his neighbours again in God. It should show us how easy it is to encounter God when we are troubled, if we offer him our troubles in true charity, not in selfishness. For he is the God of history, he created us, he became man in the fullest and most painful, richest and poorest sense of the word to save us and bring us to him. By our prayer of compassion we should be as involved in the human situation, as Christ was by his incarnation. We should engage in action which supports our prayer and makes it truthful. Prayer without action is a lie. This is the fundamental nature of intercession.

INTERCESSION

Interceding does not mean reminding God of things he has forgotten to do. It is placing ourselves at the heart of a troubled situation. Here is an example from the time of the Great War and the civil war in Russia, when the country was engaged in war abroad and at home. In a small provincial village which had just changed hands, a young woman of twenty-seven or so was trapped with her two small children. Her husband belonged to the opposite side. She had been unable to escape in time and she was in hiding, trying to save her own and her children's lives. She spent a day and a night in great fear and the following evening the door of her hiding place opened and a young woman, a neighbour of her own age, came in. She was a simple woman with nothing extraordinary about her. She said, 'Is So and So your name?' The mother replied 'Yes' in great fear. The neighbour said, 'You have been discovered, they are coming for you tonight to shoot you. You must leave.' The mother looked at her children and said, 'Where shall I go? How can I get away with these children. They could not walk fast enough or far enough for us not to be caught.' And this neighbour suddenly became a neighbour in the full sense of the gospel. She approached the mother and said with a smile, 'They will not go after you, because I will stay here in your place.' The mother must have said, 'They will shoot you.' She replied, 'Yes but I have no children. You *must* leave.' And the mother went. I do not tell this simply as a story of sacrifice. I should like to dwell on certain points which gives it a particular significance in Christ and, through the cross, lead us to the idea of the resurrection and the life of him who is greater than us in those who are smaller.

NATHALIE IN CHRIST

The mother went out and the young woman stayed behind. Her name was Nathalie. I do not want to try and imagine what happened that night. I should simply like to point out a few parallels. Night fell, an autumn night, which became colder and wetter and darker. This young woman, alone, expecting nothing from anyone except death, faced this death she was about to suffer for no reason – she was young and healthy and they were not after her. Remember the Garden of Olives. In the darkening there was a man, also young, in his thirties, whose friends were all asleep, waiting for death, waiting for them to come for him, because he had accepted death in our place. And we know the story in the gospel, his anguish, his cry to his Father, his sweat of blood. We know that when he could no longer bear his loneliness he went to see if his disciples were awake and then went back to face his death alone, a death for others, impossible, absurd. This is the first image, Nathalie in Christ.

Nathalie must have gone to the door more than once and thought to herself. 'I have only to push it open and I am no longer N.. I'll be Nathalie again and not condemned to death.' But she did not go out. We can imagine what her terror must have been like when we remember the courtyard of the house of Caiphas. Peter the rock, the strong one who had said to Christ that if the whole world denied him, he would not deny him, that he would die for him. Peter met a servant girl who had only to say, 'You also were with him' for Peter to answer 'I do not know the man', for Peter to deny Christ twice more and for Christ to turn and look at him. Nathalie could have surrendered too and said, 'I shall not die, I'll escape.' But she did not. This young woman of about thirty resisted in Christ, when Peter failed him.

And this young woman must also have wondered whether her death might not be in vain. All very well to die to save a woman and her children, but what if the woman were caught and also killed. Remember the man who was the greatest among those born of woman – John the Baptist. At the end of his life, when his death

was also near, St John the Baptist sent two of his
disciples to ask Christ, 'Are you the one who is to come
or must we wait for another?' What a weight of suffering
there is in this question which sounds so simple. He was
about to die for being the fore-runner, the prophet and
baptiser of Christ and just before his death, doubt
entered. 'What if I made a mistake, what if he whom I
prophesied is still to come, and he to whom I bore witness is the wrong man?' Then his hard life in the desert
would have been in vain. He was called a voice crying in
the wilderness, not a prophet speaking in God's name,
but the voice of God speaking through him because he
was totally identified with that voice. And now he was
near death if Jesus of Nazareth is really the one, then it
was all worth it, but if he is not, then God himself has
deceived him. And like Nathalie in her hiding place,
the prophet received no answer, or rather he received
a prophet's answer: 'Go and tell John what you have
seen, the blind see, the lame walk and the poor have the
gospel preached to them. Blessed is he who is not
offended by me.' In his prison he had to confront his
past, his present and his death, alone. And Nathalie also
received no reply. I could have told her now that N.. was
saved, that her children are now more than fifty years
old. I could have told her other things too, but she
never knew. She was shot in the night.

But there is something else to intercession besides
sacrifice. As well as the cross and Gethsemane there is
also the resurrection, a resurrection conformed to our
share in the mystery of Christ but also to our human
littleness. You remember the passage in St Paul where
he says, 'I live, not I, Christ lives in me.' Sometimes we
might wonder what these words mean exactly. N.. and
her children know one thing, theirs are henceforth borrowed lives. Their own lives died with Nathalie, she goes
on living through them. They live because she died. She

took their death on her, gave them her life. They live with a life that belongs to her.

THE INTERCESSION OF CHRIST

This human story illustrates something very important about salvation. It shows us the hard reality of intercession. We often intercede. We pray to God to be merciful and kind to those in need. But intercession is more than this. The word in Latin means to take a step which puts us at the heart of a situation, like a man who stands between two people about to fight. The first image that comes to mind is from Job chapter nine, where this man who has suffered so greatly says 'Where is there a man who will stand between me and my judge?' Where is the man with the courage to stand between God and his poor creature, in order to separate and unite them. To separate them from the opposition which makes each a prisoner of the other and to unite them in the freedom of harmony restored. And this man is Christ, Christ who is God the Word Incarnate, he takes the step, to stand between fallen man and God. He is God's equal and man's equal, one with God because he is God, one with man because he is man and prepared to take the consequences of his divine love upon his human flesh. This is intercession, this is what it means to take that step into the heart of a situation for ever, for all eternity, because Christ born of the Virgin is both he who died on the cross and he who rose from the dead and carried his human flesh to the heart of the mystery of the Trinity in his Ascension.

We see through the example of Nathalie that Christ is really the Way, the way to live, the very being of the christian, the sole human and divine reality. He is the way to life, life so full and overflowing that it gives eternity both to him who lives it and those near him, at the price of the cross. It is the martyr's victory, the victory of the weak over the strong, the victory of the vulnerable, human and divine love over what appears invincible, hatred which exhausts itself and has only one time.

THE IMAGE OF THE MOTHER OF JESUS

Besides Nathalie's heroic sacrifice, we are committed to the world in another way, simply by our presence. 'You are in the world but not of the world,' Christ said. I think the best illustration is the story of Mary the mother of Jesus at Cana of Galilee. Some humble people are celebrating a wedding. They are good and upright people who have invited Christ to their wedding and he has not refused to come. His mother is also there and his disciples. The moment comes in the midst of the feast when the wine runs out. There follows a disjointed sounding conversation. Mary says, 'They have no more wine'. 'Woman, what is there between you and me?' Christ answers, 'my hour has not yet come'. Instead of telling her son that she is his mother and the hour for kindness and compassion is always come, Mary says nothing. She simply turns to the servants and says, 'Whatever he tells you, do it'. And Christ contrary to what he has just said, blesses the washing water and it becomes the wine of the kingdom. How can we understand this conversation and the contradiction between Christ's words and actions? Doesn't Christ's question to his mother mean something like this? 'What relationship gives you the right to approach me thus? Is it because you are my natural mother who gave me birth, is it because you are my closest natural relation? If this is why, I can do nothing, because the kingdom has not yet come.' And Mary instead of answering him, brings the kingdom by showing that she has perfect faith in him, that the words she has pondered in her heart from the beginning have been fruitful and she sees him for what he is, the word of God. But then conditions are right for the kingdom. God is present because she has given herself to him completely, with total faith. He can act freely, without forcing nature, because he is in his own domain. So he works the first miracle of the gospel.

We too can be in the same situation as Mary. We too can make God's kingdom come, wherever we are, in spite of the unbelief of the people we are with. Simply by having complete faith in the Lord and thus showing ourselves to be children of the kingdom. This is a crucially important act of intercession. The fact that we are present in a situation alters it profoundly because God is then present with us through our faith. Wherever we are, at home with our family, with friends when a quarrel is about to begin, at work or even simply in the underground, the street, the train, we can recollect ourselves and say, 'Lord I believe in you, come and be among us'. And by this act of faith, in a contemplative prayer which does not ask to see, we can intercede with God who has promised his presence when we ask for it. Sometimes we have no words, sometimes we do not know how to act wisely, but we can always ask God to come and be present. And we shall see how often the atmosphere changes, quarrels stop, peace comes. This is not a minor mode of intercession, although it is less spectacular than a great sacrifice. We see in it again how contemplation and action are inseparable, that christian action is impossible without contemplation. We see also how such contemplation is not a vision of God alone, but a deep vision of everything enabling us to see its eternal meaning. Contemplation is a vision not of God alone, but of the world in God.

THE CHURCH IS A MYSTERY OF ENCOUNTER

Within the total human community, there is a community which alone is capable of grasping our transcendent vocation. This is the church, a chosen community, whose members are not chosen for privilege but for duty. Christ told us he was sending us out as sheep among wolves. He ordered us to go. On the eve of his resurrection he told us that as his Father had sent him, he sent us. He told us we were like a heavenly colony on earth, an avant-garde of the kingdom of God, fellow soldiers with the Lord in the battle to free the world from the powers of evil and death. The Church can only be defined from the outside. Within it is the mystery of being in God, the mystery of encounter, presence and communion. It is not a human community turned towards God, obedient to God, centred on God. It is a living body and this body is both human and divine. It has a visible aspect, us, and an invisible, God, and us in God and God in us. In one respect the church, as St Ephraem the Syrian defines it is not the assembly of the just, but of sinners on the way to repentance. It cries to God in its suffering and needs his salvation. In its other aspect, it is not simply on the way, it has arrived. God is with it and it has his peace. Its nature is complex and is revealed both in the sinner needing salvation and in the incarnate word, true God and true man. He gives the full measure of humanity which is the temple of the Holy Spirit. The Holy Spirit makes us members of Christ's body, the whole Christ we shall one day become, in the daring phrase of one Father of the Church 'only son in the only son'. The Holy Spirit is the Spirit of God who teaches us to call the Father of the word, our Father.

The church is a mysterious body in which we become through the Spirit what Christ is, just as he became what we are. In the church our lives are hidden with Christ in God. The dimension of the church which makes it essentially different from the world is the eschatological dimension. It already belongs to the age to come.

That is why the Spirit of God is present in the church's life. That is why we address him in the eucharistic prayers. The kingdom is already present, in which all will be fulfilled. God is already all in all, just as he is already in the bread and wine. And it is because the church knows things not only in their present sadness but in their final fulfilment, that it can give thanks from this sad and often bestial world for all things. She gives thanks for their ultimate fulfilment, not for their present state which would be unforgivable by the world and by God. We should be able to turn to the Lord from our own experience and say, 'Lord you are just in all your doings, you are right'. And the Church can only do this because of her vision of the end. She sees not only the world darkened by sin but the world transfigured, in which the resurrection and eternal life are already present.

And that is why the church makes no distinction between the living and the dead. God is not the God of the dead, he is the God of the living. For him all men are alive, and so they are for the church. Within this eschatological perspective we can see death as the great hope and joyfully await the judgment and the coming of Christ. We can say with the Spirit of the church 'Come soon, Lord Jesus'. History and eternity are one eschatologically and eucharistically. The prayer of the church includes not only the members of the church but through them and because of them, the whole world. She sees the whole world as the potential church, the total church for which she hopes. And in the church, within this eschatology, all things are already accomplished as well as being in process. We have a living relationship in the communion of saints and sinners with all the living and the dead.

There is something here which the reformed church has lost. — difficult to define — for us the church is the people — but here the church is a spiritual community

THE LIVING AND THE DEAD

What does it mean to pray for the dead? Are we asking the Lord to act unjustly? Certainly not. By our prayer, we bear witness that the dead have not lived in vain. We show that as well as the many worthless things they did in their lives, they also sowed the seed of charity. We pray for them with love and gratitude, we remember their presence among us. And our prayer for them must be supported by our lives. If we do not bear fruit in our lives of what the dead have taught us, our prayer for them will be feeble indeed. We must be able to say, 'Look Lord, this man lived and made me love him, he gave me examples to follow and I follow them'. The day will come when we shall be able to say, 'The good that you see in my life is not mine; he gave me it, take it and let it be this for his glory, perhaps for his forgiveness'. Do you know the prayer that was reported in the *Sud Deutsche Zeitung* of the man who died in a concentration camp:

'Peace to all men of evil will. Let vengeance cease and punishment and retribution. The crimes have gone beyond measure, our minds can no longer take them in. There are too many martyrs ... Lord do not weigh their sufferings on your scales of justice, and let them not be written in their act of accusation and demand redress. Pay them otherwise. Credit the torturers, the informers and traitors with their courage and strength of spirit, their dignity and endurance, their smile, their love, their broken hearts which did not give in even in the face of death, even in times of greatest weakness ... take all this into account Lord for the remission of the sins of their enemies, as the price of the triumph of justice. Take good and not evil into account. And let us remain in our enemies' thoughts not as their victims, not as a nightmare, but as those who helped them overcome their crimes. This is all we ask for them.'

The life of each one of us does not end at death on this earth and birth into heaven. We place a seal on everyone we meet. This responsibility continues after death, and the living are related to the dead for whom they pray. In the dead we no longer belong completely to this world, in us the dead still belong to history. Prayer for the dead is vital, it expresses the totality of our common life.

THE SAINTS

We also pray not only for certain people but to certain people. We pray to Mary and the saints. But we do not pray to them to turn away God's strict justice by their gentleness. We know that their will and God's are one and this harmony includes in charity all the living and the dead. If it is true that our God is not the God of the dead but of the living, isn't it natural that we should pray to those who are particularly shining examples for us. We can each find among the saints one that particularly attracts us. We do not make a radical distinction between those who are saints and those who are not. Certain saints were set apart by God as examples for all christians. This does not mean that others were not. And it is quite proper for us to pray to our dead parents and friends without this being blasphemy.

Our prayers to Mary are particularly important. She is closest to Christ of any human being. Not because she gave birth to him, but because she was truly his mother not only physically but also spiritually. When we pray to her we should remember that our sins caused the death of Christ on the cross and she is his mother. We can pray to her as follows: 'Mother, I killed your son, if you forgive me, no one will dare condemn me'. This expresses our faith in her charity.

LITURGICAL PRAYER

We must now say a few words about liturgical prayer. This prayer which is always going on in the church, may seem to lack spontaneity. It is indeed rigidly structured, because its aim is not only to express collective human spontaneity, but also to educate it. It is also an expression of beauty, but not just of the beauty which is present but of what the world could be, what God wishes it to be. We could discuss many details of the liturgy of the orthodox church, the actions, the icons, the bible readings. The liturgy is a school for spirituality, it is a situation and an encounter with God and the world in God. It has its own spontaneity which goes beyond the actual spontaneity of each of its members. It is the holy spontaneity of the community already fulfilled and in God. In the sacraments we come face to face with God not only through the word and its invisible grace but also through visible things. The waters of baptism become the primordial waters of life and also the water promised by Christ to the Samaritan woman. In the bread and wine which have already become the body and blood of Christ, we prefigure the day when God will be all in all. In the church we encounter God and the world in God. The christian must also meet the world, in all its sadness and serve it like the son of God made man. He must be totally involved in this incarnation, it is part of being human and in it his prayer becomes intercession and intercession becomes the sacrifice of Calvary.

There is a tension between ecstatic encounter with God and our presence in the world. It is impossible to live God's life to the full without losing contact with earthly life. 'This,' says Symeon the new theologian, 'happens not to the perfect but to novices.' The ideal is a perfect union between the two, in which the whole man takes part, body, soul and spirit, like our Lord Jesus Christ, and some of the saints. Detached from the world and free from struggle and uncertainty, the soul gains a clarity and power before unknown to it. The feeling is keen, fervent and very pure. Detached from emotion and passion, the soul has power and light. The emotions obscure thought, but in this state thought is very clear. It is fully conscious and free – for the soul is never passive although it is freed from self engrossment and surrendered to God – it is in complete control and can either keep quite silent or pray actively. Sometimes the words of this prayer arise spontaneously from the heart and mind; sometimes there is deep silence. He contemplates with his whole self the divine uncreated light, the mysteries of the world and his own soul and body (St Isaac the Syrian quoted by Nil Skorski, *Testament spirituel sur la vie des Skits*).

All true prayer, that is prayer made in humility and surrender to God, is sooner or later quickened by the grace of the Holy Spirit. This grace becomes the force behind every action and thus everything in life. It ceases to be an activity and becomes our very being, the presence in us of him who fills all things and leads them to their own fulness.

BIBLIOGRAPHY

La Petite Philocalie du coeur translated and edited by J. Gouillard. Published in the series 'Le Livre de Vie', Editions du Seuil, Paris.

The Mystical Theology of the Eastern Church by Vladimir Lossky. Published by James Clarke, London and Allenson, Napierville, Illinois.

Living Prayer by Metropolitan Anthony. Published by Darton, Longman and Todd, London and Templegate, Springfield, Illinois.

School for Prayer (published in USA as *Beginning to Pray*) by Metropolitan Anthony. Published by Darton, Longman and Todd, London and The Paulist Newman Press, New York.

God and Man by Metropolitan Anthony. Published by Darton, Longman and Todd, London and the Paulist Newman Press, New York.

Techniques et Contemplation by A. Blum. Published in *Etudes Carmélitaines*, 1948 pp. 49-67.

The way of a Pilgrim translated by R. M. French. Revised edition published by SPCK, London with a foreword by Metropolitan Anthony.

Part II

Lord Stay With Us

by

Georges LeFebvre OSB

CONTENTS

Introduction

LORD STAY WITH US

'He was probably right, the teacher who once told me that everyone has a mysterious prayer within him and does not know where it comes from, but that it presses everyone to pray however he can and in the way he knows.' Russian pilgrim.

TODAY PEOPLE ARE sometimes uneasy about the traditional forms of piety because they consider them too 'individualistic'. Is the ambiguity of the word partly responsible? What turns us in on ourselves is individualistic and shuts us off from other people. This is an essential contradiction to the christian mystery, the mystery of that union beginning in the Trinity and expressed in the one body of Christ whose members we all are, and of one another. So Mgr Elchinger could tell the Vatican Council: 'Individualism is a heresy.'

In the image of the Persons of the Trinity, each of whom is all that he is in relationship with the other two, a person is made for relationship with others and this is the only way he or she can develop. Turning inwards individualistically is isolation; we become persons in relationship with others.

But we can only truly turn to others by turning to God. In him alone can our relationships with others reach their proper depth.

To love others, and to respect them as that love requires, we must recognise their special relationship with God. God calls each single person and puts desire in his heart, that desire for God which is each man's truth and proper stature. But before we can see this in others, we must find it in ourselves.

To believe in this presence of God in all human life without being put off by appearances we must have experienced with amazement the faithfulness of God's love for us, however unfaithful we have been. We must have learnt how steadfast is God's love to us in our poverty, the love for humanity to whom he gave his Son.

If we wish to see our neighbour as we should, we must see him as he is in the eyes of God. Only then can we love him. This is why it is necessary to see ourselves in the eyes of God.

Then we can love with that love which comes from Christ. A love which is 'different' from all human goodwill, because we respect our neighbour for his relationship with Christ, even if he does not know it, because Christ knows every man. He is present in all our lives.

Thus we can be witnesses to the love of Christ by recognising his presence in our love. We are witnesses to the love of Christ and must bear witness to the joy he brings us: the joyful freedom of believing in this love and following where it leads untroubled by any care for self, free of self. A joy and a freedom making us available to others.

'We must have in us the almost careless spontaneity of a man dazzled by God,' which requires a living faith, 'and such faith requires the habit of recollection and paying attention to God' (François Stoop, Taizé Brother).

To bear witness to Christ and help others to recognise him and come to him, we need above all to live with him and stay with him. This is what we call prayer. What is prayer and how do we pray?

Christians who want to make prayer the centre of their lives often say they want texts not only explaining what prayer is, but texts to pray with. This is what the following pages try to be. They suggest certain prayerful attitudes in the presence of God. This is why they are often repetitive, returning to the same thoughts under different aspects, to try and come closer to God's mystery and live by it.

I

Never Alone

LOSING ONESELF

PRAYER IS AN end to isolation. It is living our daily
life with someone. With him who alone can deliver us
from solitude. For he is the only one we can find in our
own heart, the only one to whom we can tell everything
that is in us. He is ever present. Intimately. Prayer
makes us aware of his presence, which we might not
realise if we did not pay attention.

It is a living presence. The presence of him from whom
we receive everything. We depend on him fundamentally. We discover his presence within us as we become
aware of our total dependence on him. That is why
prayer must be an attitude of humility. Not self regard-
ing humility intent on considering our poverty and weakness. But a God-regarding humility joyful because of his
closeness.

St Teresa of Avila writes in her 8th Spiritual discourse
that she feels she has 'partly lost herself'. Doesn't anyone feel this who truly prays? He who does not pray
belongs to himself. He is his own territory. He enjoys his
independence. He is responsible for himself and he tries
to reach his goal by his own efforts. He who prays knows
that he needs another. Gradually he realises how much
he needs this other to whom he turns in prayer, how he

cannot live without him, how he can belong to none
other but him who is his whole life. He is radically
dispossessed of himself. He feels he has 'partly lost himself', he is not his own as he used to be, his treasure
belongs to someone else.

Everything in him is now open to another, available
to another and waiting on him. And in this openness to
another, he gives up his independence, only to find true
freedom: freedom of believing in a love which expects
everything and to which he admits he owes everything.
At the centre of prayer there must be faith in that love
which created us for itself and which does its own work
in us, which satisfies the desire it has given us. So our
prayer does not belong to us. We have only our faith in
that love which will not disappoint us however badly we
serve. However poor and weak we are, our faith remains.
It does not matter that we have nothing because this
love is a love which can give us everything. It is present
and at work in our secret hearts. We look towards it. It
is the reason for our hope. We cannot even desire without it, our desires are so poor and weak. We can only
wait for the Lord to work in us. 'Come and help me,
because I am alone and I have only you O Lord' (Esther's
prayer).

A COMMUNION

Praying is living our whole life as a communion with the
Lord. Do we really understand what this means? For
the other remains other to us, how ever close we are. In
a true communion we come so close to the other that we
are identified; it is more important for us for him to be
what he is than for us to be what we are. We need him
more than ourselves in order to be ourselves. A true
relationship between persons cannot be an external bond
which does not change them. A true personal relation-

ship enables two people to enter into each other without losing their identity.

This can help us understand the communion between the three persons of the Trinity. And it shows us that there can be no true personal relationships without God or without reference to God, the awareness of being in him and through him. Personal relationships are such a deep reality that they can only come from God. We know a spiritual being by communion with it, by being in one another. We know God by being aware of him in ourselves. This is why prayer is essentially personal. Grace cannot be impersonal. It is the acceptance of someone. Someone with whom we live, who has a plan for us and who himself fulfils it patiently, perseveringly and with faithful love.

God exists before us. Prayer does not create his presence, it makes us aware of it. How freely we live in this presence if we truly believe in it. It makes itself felt in little ways, which are not proof but rather an invitation to turn towards it. We must believe, and be led to believe more and more simply and express this belief by an attitude of submission.

It is less important to become aware of this presence than to accept it. We have to accept that it holds us and we no longer belong to ourselves. This is the free consent of love. We consent to be in and through another.

IN OUR HUMBLE CONDITION

God came to us in the Incarnation by coming to share our condition. It is in this human condition that he is present to us and that we live with him. We have to learn to recognise the divine mystery which he shares with us in the human form it takes in us. We must not seek 'beyond' ourselves. It is *in* ourselves that the change has happened through the presence of the Lord, our belief in this presence and attention to it. We are reconciled, freed. Everything acquires a profounder meaning, a density. We cry to God with all that is deepest and truest in us. That is why this aspiration is different from all our other ones. We encounter God in all that is deepest in ourselves. We are not astonished by the darkness of God's mystery, we simply accept it, although we do not see plain. We do not know what power of love we are opening to when we do this. If we saw clearly we would be aware of the presence of God simply by being aware of ourselves, because in his presence we are all that we are. Nothing in us, nothing in the very depths of our hearts can live without him. Our awareness of his presence makes us naturally obedient to it.

We must live our whole lives in his presence, realising that we do not belong to ourselves but to his love. We are in his hands, confidently. Simply and with spontaneous joy. However little we know of our own hearts, there is something in us which looks towards God and his grace. We must simply offer it to him. We must know that he holds us in his hands. We must do what he wants. We must let him lead us, form us, make us do his will. He does not manifest his presence by any clear sign, but we know that we cannot live without him. Our bond with him always remains. However empty, wretched and dull we feel, the Lord is present in us and at work. We must believe in his presence and trust him. We must let him take over.

We must let the Lord accomplish his work in us in the way he chooses, for he alone can do it. We must accept everything as coming from him. We must believe simply and joyfully in his presence, for we cannot doubt his love. We must let the joy of his presence calm us. For his love cannot fail.

2

Humble Love

IN FAITH

OUR PRAYER EXPRESSES much more than we are
conscious of. It is an attachment and consent to be what
we are in Christ. Our whole being is involved. Our true
being is a gift of God in Christ, in communion with
him. We should accept it as a gift. We should live in that
freedom which is the recognition of that gift of love by
which we are all that we are. We should see everything
that happens to us in the light of our life in Christ,
then we will understand it properly. We should accept it
meekly, believing and accepting the mystery. What we
are in Christ is hidden from us, but we come to it by an
act of faith, which is contained in the faith of the Church.
We find our unfailing support in the faith of the church,
with which we are in communion.

In the light of this faith we can grasp what our heart
guesses at, and live by it through all manner of
adversity. We should bear. humble witness to what the
Lord works in us. He allows us to guess and glimpse his
will. This affirmation of faith makes it a support, a comfort and a joy, something deep within us which remains
the first essential even when everything seems empty.
This firm faith in God gives us a freedom towards everything else; in his presence it seems essentially relative.
A joyful freedom. Even when everything seems empty

we can be certain that the Lord is there. He cannot fail us, however badly we fail. We must live simply with this certainty. And we will realise more and more the truth of his presence. We will feel the joy of his presence.

We know that someone is there and we know what that someone means to us. Christ is present in peace – he fulfils our deepest wish – and that peace is our faith in him. This is where we must seek him. This is where we may abide with him. In difficulty we do not have to accept 'something' which costs us dearly, but to let ourselves be led by 'someone' in love and trust. We must follow obediently where he leads.

BE HUMBLE 'WITH' GOD

Faith is recognition of the mystery, surrendering ourselves to its fulness. Faith is humility. The Lord is present at the heart of all humility. We can feel the truth of this by living it. With the silence of humble attention, respect, and a sense of the infinite fulness of God. Humility feels itself in deep harmony with this fulness. And in this harmony it slowly finds that the fulness is also a mystery of humility, a loving God.

We must not only be humble 'before' God. But more fundamentally, we must be humble 'with' God who comes to us in a mystery which is a mystery of humility. We have no other God but Christ. Everything that we know about God through revelation, we know in and through the humanity of Christ. 'He who has seen me has seen the father' (Jn. 14.9.).

Christ in all his words and deeds is our God living and doing, fully himself. Our God is he who is humble merciful, weak among men, suffering with them. He is Christ among us, with us. He is the God whose omnipotence is expressed in the mystery of the Cross, the mystery of humility, poverty, weakness by which he shows the fulness of his love which is stronger than us, defeats our resistance and overcomes our sin. He is personally involved in a loving relationship with us. He lives with us, in our condition.

As he once shared our human condition on earth, now he still shares it in each of us. Through his love he truly shares our life. In love it is impossible to stay apart, love demands life together, involvement, solidarity. He lives with our poverty and wretchedness in this solidarity of love. He does not cast a merciful glance at us from afar. He joins us on our way and his mercy shares our poverty and our whole life.

We should also see others as living thus with Christ. We should respect the presence of Christ in their everyday life. We should love even their failings, for Christ is also present in them. This is the source of that patience which is also love. Humility is the ultimate secret of God's perfection, because it is the fulness and delicacy of his love. A humble God, infinitely close. In the sight of God's humility, only humility makes sense. A humble God, found simply but very close in our secret prayer.

The Lord is infinitely beyond us, but also infinitely close. That is why his presence can be both secret and intimate. We must be content with nothing less than God, but we must find him in our simplest, humblest and most unassuming prayer. We must be humble before God who calms and satisfies all our desire. We can look to God quite simply, but we put our whole self into this relation. We only exist through it.

NEEDING ANOTHER

Loving is not just looking at someone, it is living with him. It is sharing our life and all our reasons for living with another, sharing even our self awareness. It is becoming inseparable. Loving is forming a bond so close, that our inmost being would change if the other ceased to exist. We can no longer see ourselves except in terms of this other. So we truly no longer belong to ourselves. We are radically stripped bare of our self possession because we know that everything we are is in relation to another, in communion with him. There is nothing left but this presence.

This presence can be obscure but it must either remain our deepest truth or we perish. We cannot live otherwise. Our poverty is so radical that it must be a cry to God. God cannot be purely and simply absent. Our poverty itself speaks of him and he dwells in it.

Praying is keeping away from all those things where we do not find what we seek. We are waiting, appealing for him who can satisfy us. We turn towards him. We live in vital need of him. We are open to him. We cry for what will one day satisfy our heart and is already present in hope. We can now only guess at the fulness for which we are made, and our desire for it. Our openness to God is a grace, a gift. We should accept it as such and live with it, in simplicity. We are barely aware of it, we wait. However it is by this gift that we are all that we are. It is our one deep truth. The gift of living in prayer is one with the gift we shall receive of living in heaven. It is the same living reality and the seed contains the fruit. So our humble prayer contains within it a hidden fulness. The only worthy praise of God is our whole being involved in communion with him and only living in and through this loving communion. This is the joy of being filled by God, turned towards God.

3

Learning to Believe

HE WHO LOVES US

THE MEANING OF our time of trial here below is not
to give us the chance to earn a reward but to teach us
how to love, to enable us to enter into a true loving
relationship with God, in which our response to him is
a truly personal free response. If God keeps us in the
dark, this is not because he wishes to keep his distance
from us, it is in order to lead us to a deeper communion
with himself through humility.

We must trust in the Lord. Let him act. He can use
the darkness to lead us further into the mystery of his
presence. All that his presence is for us can be expressed
in a simple attitude of waiting. We cry to someone, who
is not far off, but is himself present in our cry. He is
there and he holds us. His presence is more powerful
than the darkness. Praying is to live in the sight of him
who by his love makes us what we are. We must be
obedient to him. We cry to the Lord who lives in the
depths of our heart and who is one with our deepest
being. We have only to listen to him. It is like listening
to silence. A silent cry, simple, peaceful, an act of faith.

This cry is not only the deepest desire of our heart but
an answer to the gift of God which is beyond the
imagination of our heart. Everything we find at the
depths of our heart shows us how we are loved. We must

have faith in this cry and live by it, through all the silences. Our peace and our confidence are supported by our faith in the love of Christ. We must truly believe in it. Our one deep need, without which we cannot live must be to feel ourselves in harmony with Christ.

We must be everything that we are in an act of faith – which is putting our whole self into the hands of him who is our sole reason for living. Prayer is what makes all the difference. We would not be the same if we did not have in our heart the awareness of being in the hands of God. We must pay attention to God, not just in thought, but more deeply, with our whole self. This attitude is quite simple and the Lord will see our deep desire to be available to him, our turning to him, our humble hope. We must believe in the power of the mystery of grace which holds us and only care about giving ourselves and opening ourselves as much as we can. We should feel close to anyone who has not yet received the gift of faith but is still in the hands of God whom he seeks without knowing it. The mystery is a living reality. It is present and manifest in human history, in the lives of our neighbours and our own. It is Christ present and active in the power of his Spirit in all humanity and all time. Everything subsists in him and through him. He surrounds us.

THE HUMILITY OF FAITH

The humility of faith is true humility, a simple poverty. It is an ordinary poverty. Humility is the only way we can express our littleness, our powerlessness in the sight of God. The sign that we are in the presence of God may be a deep peace, but also a deep humility. And perhaps the humility will lead us to the peace.

When we no longer even desire, it is enough that we know that someone has a plan for us and to agree to this plan. We can only live by an act of trust which we con-

stantly renew and this makes us realise our closeness
to him who is our only hope. Living in this state of trust
and radical dependence makes us lose ourselves. Everything in our lives belongs to God and God alone. Nothing
belongs to us any more. The work he gives us to do, he
does through us. We must let him do everything he
pleases. We must belong wholly to the Lord and we will
become more and more aware of him the more we trust
him and understand the meaning of our act of faith
by which we give ourselves to him. Our act of faith
brings us into closer and closer communion with Christ.
We discover the meaning of our faith by living it in self
surrender. We discover what Christ means to us and
what it means to put our hope in him.

Life is given to us to learn to believe. Everything
that happens, however upsetting, should lead us further
in our faith. Whatever our difficulties and our fears of
going astray, we can be sure that we are on the right
road if we understand more and more clearly what faith
means. The Lord does his work in us. Awareness of our
poverty is a taste of the infinite fulness whose presence
makes us feel our poverty. And even in our poverty we
can put complete trust in this fulness. Our trust in God's
love must also be trust in his mercy. We must accept his
plan which is his mercy. We must see our poverty in the
sight of his mercy. And we must also judge others
in this mercy's sight. Then nothing can prevent us loving.
This is the true christian attitude. This is the only way we
can look to God with confidence and live simply and
freely in that confidence.

WITH CHRIST

We must have faith in the mystery of our life in Christ,
that communion with him constantly renewed in the
eucharist which can become a familiar and ever present
reality in our lives. What was Christ's own consciousness

of his sonship? Did he not also in this share to some extent in our human weakness? We have only an imperfect knowledge, proper to our earthly state, of our own deep truth, what we are through our communion with Christ. Didn't he come close enough to us for us to be able to feel that in this imperfection he is also with us? That this also makes us members of him and we can live it in him?

We become aware of what we are in Christ by sharing his trusting submission to the Father's will: 'My food is to do the will of him that sent me and to accomplish his work' (Jn. 4.34.). Our human condition is essentially a conditon of distress. We must accept this. But we are given someone to hope in. We are given Christ.

4

Knowing We Are Loved

AN AMAZING LOVE

OUR PRAYER BECOMES truly simple, the more we understand that God alone does his own work in us. Then simple silence becomes an attitude of faith and humility. We look simply towards him from whom we await everything. We realise the extent of our dependence the more we grow in simplicity. We know how poor we are, we ourselves and all those things that we are incapable of giving up but let us still offer God our sincere desire that he should take what we do not know how to give and let us be peaceful. We belong to God, we are in his hands. This is the ground of our hope. Nothing can destroy this hope because it is beyond earthly hope. We should be amazed that God loves us. How could such an amazing love fail us? We should have the humility to see that our wretchedness, however great, cannot be an obstacle to the power of God.

Everything we have comes from God. He willed us and made us what we are. Our deepest being is an expression of what God means us to be: it is creative grace by which he forms us according to his plan. His loving plan. Everything in us is caught up in this grace. Everything in us comes from this grace and it is present in all things.

Christ takes hold of our desires and takes them up into

his grace. We must learn to recognise him at the heart
of our desires, because he alone can satisfy them. We
must hope, with all simplicity.

LOVING IS BELONGING

We must experience ourselves as belonging to someone
else. We may be poor or sinful but we can remember
quite simply that we belong to God who is our deep
truth. He is our cure. We must accept that we cannot
be sure of ourselves. In this insecurity our one hope is
faith in the love of God whose mercy is infinite. We
must remain 'alone with this God by whom we know we
are loved and forget ourselves' (St Teresa of Avila). We
must believe in the love of God and its reliability. We
know that we are in his hands and that he will not fail
us. However feebly we pray, he will not fail us. To believe
in the love of God is to pray. Our prayer does not rely
on what we are in God's sight but on our faith in what
he is to us, unfailingly. We can become simple in the
spiritual life to the extent that we truly believe in the
love of God – a mystery which is beyond us whose fulness is our boundless hope. God is close to us, he really
shares his life with us in true communion. Isn't this
amazing? How can we understand it except as infinite
love – God's humility which is ready to bring his greatness into a truly loving relationship with our smallness.

THE SIMPLICITY OF FAITH

The great God can only truly reveal himself in simplicity.
We should not be more astonished by the simplicity of
prayer than by the simplicity of bread and wine which
he has given us as signs of his presence. This simplicity
has something essential to teach us about God and about
the relationship he wants to have with us. Very simple
attitudes: humility, a sense of our poverty, confidence,

inner peace, the feeling that we are not alone. They are indeed simple attitudes but they have a density and depth which go beyond themselves, towards something which our heart wants but which is greater than our hearts.

These attitudes have no meaning except in the light of faith and are also the expression of our truest being. To live them is to live the reality of our faith and to become conscious of it as an experienced reality. What God tells us in Christ and what we hear from the Church in our communion with the faith of the church is not merely an answer to the prayer of our heart. Our prayer has become what it is in the light of this faith. It is penetrated by this faith. It enables us to live by this faith. It may be sure or unsure. We may not understand it but we know that it is there.

It lies so deep in us that we may not be aware of it. We live by it. It is a call for God's presence or perhaps, more than we know, the joy of being gladdened by his presence. It is such a deep experience that it remains through all silences and darkness. Silence, our inner silence, just as it is. To remain in it is to remain with him who, we know, is always with us. When we know that someone is there, keeping silence is listening. 'What the soul does then is to practise what has been done in her, that is love continuing the union with God' (John of the Cross).

LOVE WHICH UNITES US

We know that we are loved in a deeply personal way and also in a way that takes complete possession of us. This is why we can believe in it. It is not a privilege setting us apart – or we should feel unworthy of it – it is a love which unites all of us. This love which is personal to each one of us is not confined to one or other of us. It is for others too. It is an aspect of the mystery by which we live together in a communion whereby each of us is all that he is – all that he is given to be – with and for the others We belong to each other in love. This love makes us become an offering.

The Lord is present in the lives of each one of us. He does his work in us with the infinite patience of his grace. To judge our neighbour is to judge not him but his relationship with Christ. It is to judge Christ's work in him. We can be sure of one thing only: someone exists upon whom we can always rely and who will never fail us. No darkness can dismay us because it is merely a sign of our own poverty. And this poverty itself bears witness to him who alone can enrich it. We know that the Lord is there and he can freely do his will in us. He is all our hope, he is the answer, given in advance, to all our prayer. God is faithful. We know that we are in his hands. We must be willing to remain there. He is the real desire of our heart. He is the answer. He shows us his love for us. We do not know everything that is in our hearts by which we live.

LOVE WHICH SATISFIES US

Our heart can only be satisfied by knowing that it lives in a true communion with infinite love. When we know this we feel the peace of knowing the truth. Our heart bears witness to God's presence. However simple, quiet and secret this presence may be, it expresses our certainty in faith and hope. Our desire is deeper than our heart. It comes from further off. But we can guess at God's love for us. Our need to love is also a mystery because it makes us like God. We are created in his image and likeness which is deeper than we know. We have only to give our free consent, so that his measureless love can become the measure of our love for others with whom we are in communion in him. We have found someone who will never disappoint our love. We can always love him more and find him more worthy of love. Our hearts are satisfied.

LOVE WHICH SETS US FREE

God is present. To believe in his presence is to let it become everything to us. A presence which is everything to us and essentially secret. This double nature of his presence shows us the sort of attention we should pay to it. The more it means everything to us, the more there will be something which is always there, whatever the darkness, and we should never doubt it. Someone who means everything to us, more deeply than we know. We experience his presence in freedom and simplicity because it is the presence of someone who loves us. He is with us and he makes us free, simple and without desires. Because we know that we never have enough faith in his love. 'With you I have no desire on earth' (Ps. 72).

This love is candid, like a child's gaze or astonished smile. It accepts the gift it is given without asking how it came to be given. Its simplicity is its freedom. It is free from all the complications and anxieties which would make it turn back in on itself. We should humbly find peace in the thought that it is God who sees us and judges us. We should not think of God as someone who 'forbids' us satisfactions but as a love watching over us and guiding us which we must follow confidently because it leads to that fulness which is our goal. We should live in the sight of his loving kindness and recognise it in all that he asks of us.

We should be docile which is to let the Lord work in us through events, through other people. We should let him take in this way what we are so bad at giving. We should be patient and have confidence in him. Our prayer should express this docility. That is what it means to be in the Lord's hands. That is prayer.

Living the presence of Christ is to want, think and feel everything with him. We can live very imperfect feelings with him if we genuinely want to improve. We learn to know him by meeting him in the Eucharist. He is always with us. He is in our heart and always says yes even when we say no.

5

Simplicity and Freedom

BOUNDLESS LOVE

WE CAN BE certain that a real joy exists and it is already present at the centre of our lives. Loving someone is being happy because of that person. Loving someone is knowing and saying with our whole self that this other person means everything to us. It is recognising that our self lives by another and only exists through that other. It is agreeing to be what we really are: a cry to God, an inability to live except in relation to him, in him, through him, with him. Loving God is not only recognising him as the answer to our prayer. That is a limited sort of love. It is only because God exists that we have this desire for him in us. He is the measure of this desire which is greater than our hearts. It is because God is infinitely lovable that we have an infinite need to love. This is not just a need we have. We are made for another person. Nothing in us makes sense except in relation to him. That is why our cry, our need has an absolute value.

We are grasped by the mystery of love. The only answer we can give is to believe in it, quite simply. We need a real humility to discover the fulness of communion with the love of God. Because this is a truthful attitude to him, it is the only way of recognising him as he really is. This will still be true when we see him in heaven. We must simply accept the poverty of our prayer and be peaceful. This is an act of faith in him who can do what he wants with our poverty. An act of faith – faith in someone – which engages our whole life. It is not our work. It is a gift. We can only see the signs which allow us to think we have received this gift, that we live by it. That is enough to make us grateful. What grace works in us, we live in freedom and simplicity, truly believing in its power upon our hearts. We must be open to this work of grace not try and somehow grab it.

God does not hide. We can always find signs of his presence just beyond us, so that we never cease to seek him. Prayer is the expression of what is deepest and thus most natural and spontaneous in us. It is one with our inmost nature, that by which we are most truly ourselves. That is why we can live by it without noticing. Whatever the ways by which the Lord leads us in prayer, as in all our lives, they are always his ways and the important thing is to know what is the right attitude so that we can do what he wants. This in one form or another is always an attitude of humility. God loves us. He knows us. He knows our weakness. He is moved to see that however keenly we are aware of our poverty and sinfulness, we do not despair or give up seeking him because we need his love too much.

UNITED BY GOD'S LOVE

God loves us quite freely. He does not love in our way and with our limits. He loves in his own divine way, with his fulness, generosity and freedom. He has no limits. Thus we should receive him and let him fill us. We should trust and think no more of our poverty and then we will begin to understand the meaning of his love. His love is not enclosed by our limits and it does not stop at whom I might love 'less' God loves with the same love us. He loves everybody and this unites us. The brother

that he has for me. Our daily relationship must be lived
in the presence of him who loves us both together.

IN THE LIGHT OF FAITH

Humility and trust, humility and joy are all one in our
relationship with God upon whom we depend totally. We
are in the presence of his love. We cannot of course
express this faith properly, it is beyond words. However it is not totally cut off from all that we can express
by words. But what our words say about faith slowly
becomes a living reality. This is our life, and truly our
light. By it we live in the presence of God and become
inseparable from him. So praying is simply living, being
ourselves as grace has formed us. Praying is letting ourselves be drawn to the deepest desire of our hearts, to
what is truest in us, and not being distracted from it.

Faith is a gift which comes from him in whom we
believe. He arouses it in us and puts in our heart something greater than our heart. Faith would not be possible if he in whom we believe did not exist. Faith bears
witness to him. It has its own certainty beyond all our
certainties and all our doubts. The love to which we have
given our faith, he who is our hope and joy, is not an
unknown God, invisible and far away. It is Christ whom
we see speaking and acting in the Gospel and whom we
encounter in the Eucharist. 'He who has seen me has
seen the Father' (Jn. 14.9.).

If we are united with Christ in a personal closeness –
the sign of this is our encounter with him in the
Eucharist – if we live with him in a relationship which
makes us someone to him, this means we want above all
to agree with him in everything. Christ is present. If we
truly believe in him. If he really means everything to us,
we have only to look to his presence, not to ourselves.
Christ is our hope. His presence in our lives is a promise
that none of our desires will remain unsatisfied. He gives

us peace. Whether we feel this peace or not, he has given us the gift of believing in it. Believing is to accept a truth in faith, however little we see what it means. Believing is experience because it involves our deepest being.

6

Lord I Have No One But You

CHRIST IS GOD present to humanity, to all human history. We are as sure of his presence in each of our lives as we are sure of his presence in human history. We should live this certainty in all simplicity, because it is the object of our faith. If we truly believe in the presence of Christ, if it truly means everything to us, we have only to look to him. We should not keep analysing our attitude to God. We should not keep looking at ourselves but should look at him. We should simply remain in his presence. In his presence we are changed as we ought to change. We should offer ourselves to the Lord in all our poverty with nothing but our desire to obey him and to let him work in us.

We are in the presence of him who knows what he wants of us. If we can only stammer in his sight, he can understand what we are trying to say, what we want and how to give it to us. This our utter dependence on him is a great mystery of love. We know that someone is present in our lives and at work in us. We must pay attention to him but his action goes beyond our poor weak attention, which is so easily distracted, so easily disconcerted. Our attention itself is the work of the preceding grace, which arouses it and which is not limited by it.

We should not try and open ourselves more to the love of God by feeling a more intense desire. We should simply offer him our desire, our need for him, just as it is, perhaps barely expressed, as an act of humble trust. Our feelings remain our own simple human feelings. The fact that they are feelings for God is shown simply by a certain depth and peace. Prayer is looking towards God who is inseparable from our lives. In our prayer we express everything in our lives which is a cry for God, a real desire for him. This living reality is the foundation of our prayer. It directs our hearts spontaneously towards God and keeps our inner silence in his presence.

A MERCIFUL LOVE

The sign that prayer leads us deeper into the mystery of God's love is that it gives us a deeper sense of his mercy. First of all our prayer itself has need of mercy. We make our humble efforts in the sight of this mercy for the Lord is always with us. Even when we feel that we are only wretched sinners in God's sight, fit only for reprimand and punishment, this can still be a loving relationship if we accept it humbly. If we get into the habit of seeing our neighbour in the light of the mystery of love and mercy which surrounds us all, this leads us to have a right attitude towards him. We can no longer doubt the mystery. To be patient and merciful is to recognise humbly that we ourselves need mercy.

If our hearts are filled with the presence of Christ so that we really live with his own love, we can at least begin to see how this love is stronger than everything and can never grow weary. So our own hearts will become gentler and more peaceful in the warmth of this love. We must let his grace grow gradually stronger. We must allow it to work and not put obstacles in its way, we must be on the same side as grace and not on the side of our own rebellious feelings however strong these may be and however feeble we may feel our control over them. We must be patient and confident.

With each of our brothers we are in the presence of God's mystery, the mystery of his infinitely patient grace, the mystery of what it can do in each one of us, in spite of all our failings. We must respect this mystery.

We must not judge our neighbour, for our reactions are always so imperfect and even if we cannot see things as Christ sees them, we should at least try and have Christ's attitudes and the joy of agreeing with him. Instead of living with our neighbours immersed in the petty difficulties of daily life we should try to see them in the light of the mystery of love which surrounds us all. Then it will be easy for us to live in our prayers the mystery whose sign is given to us every day in the Eucharist and which is thus always with us. If our act of faith is really an act of love for Christ in complete confidence and humility, this faith will always prevail and we shall see all things in its light, and first of all our neighbour. For it is faith in someone who remains the same through all our changeability, for he does not change.

AN INFINITE LOVE

In our prayer we are really in the presence of a God whose greatness is his love which has infinite resources to draw us to him and bring us close to him. He must be able to love us in our wretchedness in order to be able to cure us. Everything poor and dark in our cry to God pays homage in its own fashion to the mystery of God. We should never be amazed at our poverty in the sight of God. We must accept that we do not even know whether we truly love, that we have only a very halting sort of love to offer him. We must have faith in Christ in whom we find new strength to cope with fresh difficulties and darkness. The more we realise that we are in the Lord's presence and the peace of his presence, the readier we shall be to obey him and let his will rule ours and speak through ours. Believing that someone is holding us in his hands is letting ourselves be guided by him. It does not mean that we feel his presence bodily. It is being drawn to an attitude of obedience. His presence is a mystery. The deeper we penetrate into this mystery the more simply we are able to accept it. We must not be astonished by our own poor response, but open our hearts in faith to what we constantly receive. The deeper we enter into the mystery, the better we understand how it is present in our lives in a simple and unspectacular way. 'My son you are always with me (I am always with you) all that is mine is thine' (Lk. 15.31.). This is the truth by which we live in prayer. The whole fulness and power of God's love for us is present in our cry for him which he himself puts in us. We must trust his love and believe in him. Turning towards God means first of all living in his sight. Living in God's presence and looking to him does not mean we think of him as far away and remain just as we are before him. It is to enter into a communion with him, in which he transforms us in his image and makes us like him.

HE WHO IS EVERYTHING TO US

Loving means that the person we love is everything to us. As Christ becomes our true reason for living we know that we truly love him and we live in the joy of this love. Let this joy enfold all our life and be so strong that nothing can change it or allow us to forget it. It is enough to satisfy us for always and we can lack nothing. We are sure of the love of Christ because he cannot disappoint us and he will give us the grace not to disappoint him.

Our love of God is deeper than our awareness of it. It is a reality of grace which we live in the darkness of faith. We should gratefully recognise this love in our hearts as the gift of the Holy Spirit who cannot be confined to our limitations. All our weakness and meanness does not prevent the Lord from seeing what in us is still a cry for him. He takes it up in his grace and he stays with us. However poor and empty we are, we are not alone. Because it is taken into the grace of his presence our poverty itself is a cry to God. Not something that comes from us, a feeling we feel and on which we can rely, but it is the living certainty of a presence, of him who bears us in his hands. We must believe in this presence and put all our hope in it. We belong to God. We must give our whole hearted consent to this. Perhaps we can never do this perfectly. But we must take great care not to abandon it.

We cannot adequately express our knowledge of a person, what he means to us. We must live our knowledge. It is the same with Christ and his presence in our lives if he is really a person to us, if we 'know' him. He first of all 'knows' us. For he has always been with us and his love has never grown weary. His presence is secret and discreet. We should recognise in his secret presence the sign of his mysterious fulness and see it as an invitation to trust him totally. We should humbly receive the gift of his presence, and accept that it should remain silent and secret. We can expect everything from it if we lose ourselves in its sight. Before him it is impossible not to be simple. The more we feel ourselves to be in his presence, the more transparent we feel. We can be confident and hope for everything from him because we trust in him, expecting nothing from our own poverty.

HUMBLE CONFIDENCE

We should have a simple desire to offer to him who can satisfy it. A desire that is greater than our heart. We can guess at it beyond what we are conscious of. And if we find that we do not know whether we really want what remains so dark, we can be confident in him who calls us to him. We must simply desire what he invites us to hope for in an act of faith in him alone. By turning towards him we will find a remedy for all our ills. We belong to another. We should efface ourselves before him. This attitude is so profoundly true that everything out of harmony with it appears as an illusion. Even if there is only emptiness and silence, we can feel something which is truer than anything which we might be tempted to seek for to fill it. We have a presentiment of God's love for us and call to us. We feel a joy which is a grace we should open our hearts to. We should live by it freely without looking at it too much, without wanting to take 'possession' of it. We should accept it from moment to moment as a gift. We should cling silently to what is at the heart of our self awareness and also beyond it: the living reality of our relationship with God. We must agree with the direction of our will, our whole being, towards God. And we must live this in reality.

BE OBEDIENT

It is an act of humility towards the mystery of the presence of the Lord in our lives to accept trials and difficulties, even upsetting ones, even ones which come from other people. It is letting the Lord follow his plan for us and respecting the mystery of his presence. We must let the Lord be quite free to follow his plan for us. We must accept everything and everybody he uses to fulfil this plan. When it is impossible for us not to be sad, our sadness should be gentle and serene. We must accept suffering and not become bitter.

We must not worry about all that is human and weak in us but we must learn to recognise the Lord's presence in the midst of our difficulties and trials. We must have confidence in him. This confidence is our consent to him, our renunciation of everything which might stand in the way of his grace. When someone makes us suffer, we should not be annoyed for this is always an unworthy attitude, we should try rather to discover how to behave in such a way as to help our tormentor to improve. We must go to God together. The love of God is present in a communion, which we can only enter by loving all who share in it. We should love them as they are, and see God's love in them. We should recognise the Lord who is testing us by this means and we should see both ourselves and the person who hurts us in the mystery of his mercy. This means we must not be hostile. Humility towards God must be part of our deepest being. In our prayer and in our whole life we should not want to achieve something which would be our own work, we should not try and stand alone. We must believe in him who has taken us into his hands and who lovingly does his own work in us. He leads us gradually to become the person he can love, the person who has his own unique place in the communion of love which he invites us to enter. We must believe in his presence and live by the grace of his presence.

We must allow the Lord to make us gentler. We must not become hardened in obstinacy. We must try and find the point where our self love should give way so that we can find peace again. The Lord does what he wants with us. He leads us wherever he wants. We should not try and resist him. Let him form us.

Thy will be done. This is freedom.

THE SILENCE OF FAITH

We must not lose faith in what we cannot see. The silence of faith. Respect for this mystery. The mystery of someone who loves us. He gives us everything. We must remain open to him, in expectation. We feel that we are satisfied. The Lord satisfies us all. Know this. Know that he loves us. Believe because we cannot doubt Christ, his presence in the world and thus in each one of us. His love for the world and so for each one of us. We are taken up in this great mystery. We should simply believe in it. Our faith should be plain faith. Faith is poverty. It accepts certainty as a gift which brings it peace. Emptiness and darkness can always be felt as poverty and become an attitude of confidence. In the most humble prayer we find peace. And we know there is no other way. Anything else would lead to a dead end. God loves us with a love beyond our conception. In the presence of this mystery we can only stammer. But in spite of our poverty, we do have, perhaps more than we realise, a true apprehension of this love. This is expressed by the simplicity of our confidence in God and our meek acceptance of our poverty.

Even when we no longer know it we are loved by a love which never ceases. We must let it work. Let it do what it wants with us. We should sincerely want to be open to the Lord, pliable in his hands. He sees our desire even when we cannot express it. Our desire can only have one object: what God wants of us. We must believe that he wants it with all the strength and power of his love. Let him accomplish his work in our weakness, in spite of our weakness. Expect him peacefully. We can only live in a free consent – the humble wish to be obedient to the Lord's will. Our silence should be an acceptance, the sign of our availability. We should open ourselves to God's love in simplicity, recognising that all we have comes from him, that his omnipotence alone is working in us. This is a truthful attitude towards God's love.

KNOWING WE ARE LOVED

We know we are loved. The only proper reply to this love is to ask it to take all that we do not know how to give. If the Lord is truly our joy and our peace, if we truly cannot live without him, we always feel within us something of that peace that comes from him. The depths of our hearts belong to him. He knows this. Abandoning ourselves in God's hands cannot be a grand gesture. We can only do it simply, like a child. Then it is true confidence. This is the candour and freshness of true confidence, a confidence lived in humility, poverty and detachment. It is the source of serene patience. If we humbly recognise our poverty, the Lord must have pity on us. We must truly believe not in an abstract mercy but in someone whose mercy we know by experience and who will lead us where he wants if we do not absolutely refuse.

Our heart should become one with the love that is its life, so that this is the only love it knows and it sees everyone in the light of this love. Believing in the love of God is being gentle to all those he loves. When God's light reveals to us what our lives have been, we will not be disappointed. We will be cured of the illusion of measuring things according to our own measure, when they are beyond measure.

7

The Gift of God's Presence

IN GOD'S PRESENCE
WE KNOW THAT we are in the presence of God. If we
behave accordingly we gradually become more aware of
God's presence. We remain silent in his presence because
we know that we are not alone. This is an act of faith
in his presence. When everything goes wrong for us, we
should not seek in ourselves something to lean on, but
we should affirm our faith in God's presence. We should
stand quite simply in his prseence; he knows what is in
the depths of our heart. We should simply look towards
God without being self conscious about it. We should
simply be what we are, as God has made us, in his sight.
We are what we are because God's love for us is what it
is. He has made us what we are because of the unique
personal relationship he wishes to have with us. We only
exist in and through this love. It takes hold of our inmost
being. We should give it the freedom to do what it wants
with us.

Our confidence and humble submission is far short of
what it would be if we really knew what God's love for
us was. But we should simply offer ourselves as we are,
knowing all our shortcomings, for this is the only
adequate response to his love. God loves us and does not
ever forget us. He can turn anything in us into a prayer

if it remains turned towards him, even if we are not aware of it. We remain before the Lord in silence. We can be content that he knows that our hearts cannot live without him. In God's eyes, by the very fact that he looks at us we become what he loves. Christ works in us all through our life by the constant presence of his grace and the faithfulness of his love. He puts his mark on us more indelibly than we are aware. He makes our hearts live by him and unable to live without him. He puts a prayer in the depths of our being. We become aware of the work of grace in us by trying to be more faithful to it and to live by it in our behaviour towards our neighbours. We are taken up into the infinite fulness of a mystery of love. It is this love which should pour out of our hearts towards our neighbours. It should overcome all obstacles. Nothing can be for us a reason for loving less.

RESPECT FOR THE MYSTERY

We should have a deep wish to be faithful to God's plan for us and to respond to his love. A desire in faith. A desire which is an act of faith. A desire which comes not from us and which is not limited to our own capacities. We cannot give a full account of it. Faith is firstly the apprehension of a mystery too great for us to understand. We believe in a truth which is beyond all our own truths. The only proper attitude is to remain before it in silence, in humility and adoration. We should truly accept the poverty of our prayer and believe that with the freedom of his grace the Lord works what he wants in our humility. It does not matter if we have little to offer in our prayer, so long as we offer it humbly. However poor our prayer may be, it is still prayer if it stays humble. It is an act of faith in the immense mystery of love in which we are involved, the bowing down of our whole self before it. In our weakness we must live a mystery infinitely beyond us but also intimately present to us.

We want our prayer to be in some way a grasp of God's mystery, recognition of the mystery and of our own littleness before it. We should accept the poverty of our prayer, our emptiness and put our trust in God finding all our support in the mysterious fulness of his love. Prayer is not like a place which belongs to us, where we are at home and at ease. We must accept homelessness and total poverty and learn constantly to receive from moment to moment prayer as a gift. We should have an accepting attitude, open to him who, we know is there even if he gives no sign of his presence. Our situation is always precarious but we can be confident because we know we are loved.

When we receive the Eucharist we cannot doubt that the grace of this mystery is active in our darkness. Can we not then see that our darkness is not unbelief and in no way an obstacle or a refusal of grace? If we really had a sense of God, no darkness would appal us. It would simply lead us to surrender ourselves more completely.

GOD LOOKS ON US WITH LOVE

How can God not love those whom he has made unable to be happy without his love and to whom he has given this bond with him which is unbreakable even if they do not know it or go astray? And we too must love others as God loves them. The way God looks at those who truly seek him through all their weaknesses and errors, is a mystery. The more kindly we look on others, the deeper we enter into this mystery. We will always fall short of its fulness. God will always love more than we do.

God is present. We must believe in his presence and our faith is the result of all our life of grace. Believing that God loves us is to recognise what his love has meant

to us, what we have received from him. It is to believe
in what grace has done in the depths of our hearts, even
if it is not plain to see. The christian mystery is always
expressed in the reality of a history. Our prayer cannot
be reduced to what we feel or do not feel at the present
moment. It is the expression of what we have become
throughout the course of grace in our lives.

Recognising that we have received and continue to
receive everything from God is to recognise his love for
us in the work of grace in our hearts. How then can we
not want to open ourselves wholly to this love of God
and to remove all obstacles from its way? Believing in
God is believing that there is nothing in us which was
not made to be satisfied. It is trusting serenely in the
loving plan which created us.

TOTAL ACCEPTANCE

We must offer total acceptance. God is at work in us and
his action is always a mystery whose very obscurity leads
us to the truth. It leads us to humility which is an
attitude of truth. We should efface ourselves with a
docility which we feel comes not from ourselves. We
cannot deliberately adopt this attitude. We simply cannot be otherwise in the presence of God. That is why our
attitude is a manifestation of his presence. It is also a
manifestation of what this presence means for us. We
can only be thus in the presence of someone who loves
us infinitely. We should offer our weakness to the omnipotence of grace. We should be poor in a manner that
is itself an act of trust. Our poverty should express our
true attitude to God and show what he means for us.
We are not truly poor unless our awareness of our
poverty profoundly modifies our relations with our
neighbours.

We should humbly accept the feebleness of our prayer
even if we see in it the effect of our own lack of true

detachment and generosity. Allowing the Lord to humiliate us in this way, and gently to accept this humiliation is to open ourselves to grace and to allow it to lead us wherever it wants, for grace sees clearly in our darkness. But true humility prevents us from judging others.

HE IN WHOM WE BELIEVE

Here below progress in the knowledge of God is always a progress in faith. It is not changed into vision. The mystery of God remains far above all our conceptions and we can only stand before it in silence. Faith remains dark and the darkness can even increase. But he who is the object of our faith will appear more and more clearly as the one who means everything to us, the one to whom we surrender in faith with total abandonment.

However the God in whom we believe is not completely unknowable, far off and inaccessible. He is present to us – in our lives – in Christ. He whom our hearts apprehend, and everything in us desires, is not a faceless infinite but someone. Offering the Lord a love which we are no longer even very sure of is to put all our trust in him. When we can only say to God, 'I no longer know whether I love you', this is still a way of telling him that we love him, that we cannot stop loving him. We should offer God our love even if we are not sure that we do love him, gently, peacefully, and show that we really trust him. Before God we can never be humble enough. When we know this we know that we will never fully measure what God is to us and what we can expect from him.

TOTAL TRUST

Let the Lord see that we are prepared to let him do what he likes with us. Our cry to God comes from the

depths of our heart and so is part of our simplest self-
knowledge. We should learn to recognise it, not try and
get it up as if it were not already in us as part of ourselves. We must consent to it. Pay attention to it. Not let
ourselves be distracted from it. If our cry to our Father
in heaven is in the depths of our heart, this is because
we are in living communion with Christ. What is deepest in us only lives in and through this communion, it
does not belong to us alone. We should live believing in
Christ who lives in us.

If the Lord is really everything to us, this means he
must be present in our whole life. We should live this
simply trusting in his grace. It is a gift. We must humbly
accept it in peace and trust. Our trust leads us towards
the mystery of God, leads us to live in its light. Our act
of faith brings us a peace which, even if we can hardly
feel it, is like no other peace, because it comes from God.
We look simply towards God but with our whole being
which has become all attention to his presence. When
he whom we love is there, even if we do not see him,
even if he is silent, his presence clothes our silence. It is
not at all like our previous solitude. Our prayer is thus
first and foremost the fruit of God's presence. We receive
our prayer as a gift, from this presence. We should never
doubt his presence. Believing in it is believing in God's
love for us. Paying attention to it is letting ourselves be
penetrated by its meaning.

In communion with the Lord we live all that we are
which is his gift. He is not just someone before whom
we stand. He is not just the one we look towards. He is
in our looking, in our whole being turned to him. If we
were truly open to his grace, if grace could really do
what it wanted with us, we would become all love – for
God and our neighbour. This would be the surest sign
of God's presence. If we see our neighbour as an object of
God's love, we will discover that this love is the primary

reality, enfolding us and revealing the true meaning of everything else.

HE WHO SPEAKS TO OUR HEART

His love foresees all our needs. It is at work in our hearts far more than we are aware. By its very quietness it forms our attitude of humble acceptance, obedience and respect for its mystery. Everything comes from God, even the response to him which he arouses in our hearts. We must let him form us. We should place no limits on our faith in his love. We should express our faith by a humble acquiescence in what remains mysterious to us. We express our sense of God by clinging to God. This is the deepest movement of our heart, in trust, in obedience. Love. We cannot fathom how it works to accomplish its plan for us. We should not form a purely human idea of its influence. We should not judge it by what we feel or do not feel. We must believe in it with a deep and living faith, not expect to feel it at work. We must simply believe, truly, and not demand signs. We should not have more faith in our weakness than in the fulness of this mystery which is all our hope.

Our weakness is not alone in the presence of this love and unable to respond to it. We are taken hold of by this love, carried by it, united to it in a communion which is a mystery of mercy. We should let this love elicit the consent of our heart, given with our whole freedom.

It is joy to say 'yes' to the Lord, through the power of grace at work in our deepest being. We are aware of it as simply and spontaneously as we are aware of our own existence. Our self-awareness is freed at its deepest level from belonging to itself. We henceforth experience it as a gift, the fruit of God's presence.

The simple and gentle acceptance of knowing we are loved. Our weakness should not make us doubt this love. God loves us because he is love. We are unfailingly sure of him, however silent he may be, however poor and weak we are before him. He is there and that is sufficient. God loves us and we know it. Our peace is very simple but at its heart lies a mystery. Our peace is faith in this mystery. It reveals its hidden presence. The mystery of God's love for us. God gives himself to us by giving us the gift of desiring him. He is at the heart of this desire and reveals himself to us in it. What we believe is a cry to God is already an answer to that cry.

Egoism is unlovable. God only loves in us what is or tries to be open to the love of our neighbour. We should love because God loves, because loving is to be in agreement with God. Everything that we receive from the Lord is given to us in a mystery of communion and thus in openness to other people. We progress together, in a solidarity which is also a mystery beyond our conception. Grace works in us by taking us as we are, in the situation we are in. And we should accept each other just as we are and this is the way to live in communion with each other, in grace.

8

A Mystery of Grace

GOD'S CLOSE PRESENCE

IF GOD'S LOVE is primary, it requires our free consent. But these two realities are not of the same order. Our weakness is not alone in God's sight. It is taken up into the mystery of his infinite love. God's love can discern our free consent however we may express it in our limited way. God's love is at the heart of this consent, it enables us to give it. By giving our consent we should become available to God and dispossessed of self. By giving our consent we should see in other people a mystery of grace demanding our respect. If we go no further than their human weaknesses, this is not seeing other people as they are; they too are taken up into the mystery of the love of God.

God is the one we find beyond ourselves but still in us. We can only reach him by going beyond ourselves, which is the only way of being truly ourselves. God is the Other, because from him we receive everything. But he is not other because we are nothing without him. He is present in our whole being which cannot exist without him. We only exist by the incessant creative power of God. God's creative power is at work in us by nature and by grace. God is always at work in us. When we realise this, it gives our prayer great simplicity and freedom.

We know that our least movement towards God is taken up in the mystery of his fulness, carried by it. We know that we are borne by the goodness of our Father in heaven. He is very close to us. He does not look down on us from the height of heaven. He is with us. That is how we can peacefully live our life as a cry to God, through all our weakness and darkness.

As we become aware of the working of grace, we lose ourselves in it and accept our poverty more simply. We have to accept that all we can offer in reply is faith alone. We are led to it by a deeper sense of the hold this mystery has on our whole being, for it is the mystery of God's love for us. We can put out trust in this love. It is our only hope and no shadow of trust in our own strength should detract from it. To have someone in whom we believe with our whole soul, who is all our hope. That is loving. We should allow grace to deepen our sense of God and make us accept our own humility more peacefully. We should lean inwardly towards a basic obedience, which should become a new mode of existence for us. We should no longer be able to live through any happenings as if they arose from ourselves alone.

THE SECRET LANGUAGE OF OUR HEART

It has been formed slowly in our heart because it has been with us all the days of our life, because he has given us to live with him. His own mark is on us and it cannot be wiped out. It lives in the silence of our heart turned towards God. We must try and hear the secret language of our heart. We must recognise the peace and joy which abide in spite of all our troubles, weakness and anxiety. On the most common occasions when we feel most miserably human, the deep intention of our heart does not change and the Lord sees it even if it is hidden from us. We should accept as a grace of which we are unworthy the ability to offer a prayer like the humblest christian's.

If nothing else, there remains the fact that we cannot do without the Lord. We cannot live without him. We should accept this as a grace and offer it to him as the only thing we have left to offer. We need silence and this is our need for God. If we need silence, this is because we find someone in it. It is more than a desire, it is a concentration in which we are all that we are. It is our very life. We should entrust the Lord with our heart's secret. He alone knows it. At the centre of silence let us find the joy of trusting. A sure trust because God is its support. Our hope need have no limits because it is hope in him who is the negation of limits.

The cry to God in our hearts is a grace, a mystery of grace. It is always deeper than we can fathom. We must believe in this mystery of grace which lives in our hearts. We must silently and humbly hold on to it. We should respect it and pay attention to it. Through the attitudes that grace has formed in us, we can glimpse the mystery of God. We live by grace in the presence of his infinite fulness, and our altered mind can sense it. Our sense of God is our peace, our joy, the reason for our hope. He does not change. He is always with us. God is faithful. He is our refuge. He is our ultimate hope. He will never fail us. We should not be astonished at our poverty in God's sight. Our silence in the presence of his mystery should not lead us to discount everything in us that is a cry to God. We must give our consent to what grace has done in our hearts. We should live with this consent which goes further than we realise. We should allow the Lord to open our hearts to the grace of his presence and make us humbler and more aware of our poverty. As soon as there is the tiniest cry to God in our silence, it is like a small flame which is fed by all the oil that is in the lamp. We should let the Lord choose his own way of showing himself. However quiet it is, let us not be dismayed but live in humble trust.

If we cannot do better, it is that the Lord wants us in this deprived situation. We should not stop believing that we are with him. Putting all our trust in God is having no other reason for hope than the fulness of his love; it is remaining in peace because this hope cannot fail us, however poor and weak we are. We have only to recognise it. As we become more aware of the extent of God's love for us, and his hold on our will and our whole being, our response becomes different, not less but greater. It becomes the expression of a more complete self surrender in perfect trust.

A LISTENING HEART

The incarnation is the divine mystery present in our human condition, accepting the lowliness of our condition for itself. We should not be astonished to have to live the divine mystery in this way. We should recognise its presence in the silence of our hearts, a simple human presence. Only the depths of our heart, its most secret depths can remain truly fixed on God without anything distracting it from him without whom it cannot live. Praying is to discover this in our deepest being and to learn to live with it simply in our poverty. When we have been inattentive or distracted and return to ourselves, do we have the impression that we find our heart again in a conversation with the Lord which he cannot interrupt because he is its very existence?

When the Lord tries us, we can see better how it is he who purifies our heart, forms it by his grace, creates new attitudes in us. This should help us to offer him our silence simply, remembering that he knows what is in our hearts, what he has put in them. He also knows what is still very imperfect in us. Entrusting it to him, is a way, perhaps the truest way of ridding ourselves of it.

We should live in agreement with what God does in us. Our real truth is in belonging to God. We belong to him and he wants to make something of us. He has his plan. The thought that he wants to fulfil this plan in our life in his own way, and that nothing can stop him, should make us accept peacefully everything that comes to us. We should simply entrust ourselves to God's plan for us.

A pure act of faith. But what is the object of our faith? We believe that God loves us, that we are caught up in the grace of his love. If we really believe it we can no longer be the same. We have only to believe strongly enough in the mystery of God's love at work in mankind in all its poverty and sin, in order to see the world and the people round us and our own lives in a quite different way. We respect the mystery and recognise its presence without trying to expose it. We see it as the primary reality which nothing can make us doubt; it is the source of our great hope.

It doesn't matter what we can see or feel, so we should not worry about it. What matters is our attitude, which we may or may not feel all the time, which results simply from paying attention to God's presence, consenting to it. This consent is also a prayer. Consenting to God's presence is agreeing that we depend on it for our very existence. It is agreeing no longer to belong to ourselves. It is an attitude of essential humility. It is also an act of absolute gratitude, believing in God's love for us. Thanksgiving is the proper expression of an act of faith which goes far enough beyond itself to reach the whole of God's love. Thanksgiving knows that it can never go far enough, because it can never measure the love of God. It is in thanksgiving that we can best hold on to all that remains hidden from us. It is sure of God's love. It does not need signs or other reassurances. We should offer our heart to God just as it is, as he sees it with his grace at work in it. Prayer in its many forms is the realisation of belonging to God's love. To God's love for us. Prayer is to be no longer ourselves alone. It is to live in communion. It is to be involved with our whole being in the beyond which this communion opens to us. In this communion our assent to the mystery of God's love for us is taken up into this mystery and becomes a part of it.

A COMMUNION OF FAITH AND LOVE

Perhaps our attitude to God is not visible but we can test it in our behaviour to our neighbour. Our behaviour to them must be governed by our faith in God's presence in them. We have recognised his presence and can never ignore it again. Our apprehension of the mystery of the love of God becomes the core of our attitude to our neighbours. We see that this is the only true response we can make to the mystery. If we are tempted to doubt Christ's presence in ourselves, let us live in an act of faith in his presence in others.

This is a profoundly personal experience, but as we cannot contain the mystery within ourselves alone, our experience needs to be expanded by the faith of others. He towards whom we are moving is he who has spoken to us and whose word we have heard in the communion of believers. We would not move towards him if there was not an impulse in the depths of our hearts, we would not know towards whom we were moving if we had not heard the word. Thus we can follow the movement of our heart quite simply. However obscure it may seem to us, we know where it is leading.

9

The Eyes of Faith

'In this life, faith, as in the next life the light of glory, is the way we see God' (Ascent of Carmel, II 24.).

OUR INMOST SELF

WE MUST LET our heart go its own way, towards its own deepest desire, which it knows is different from all others. This desire is different from all others, not necessarily because it is more strongly felt, but because it comes from further off, from what is deepest in us. It is not simply an act of our free will, but something which is in our deepest being and which involves all that we are. It is something quite simple but inseparable fundamentally from our self-awareness and open to a limitless beyond. God reveals himself to us in this awareness that we are essentially a cry for him.

Our inner atmosphere is not made up only of what we are clearly conscious of and can be precisely expressed. It is also composed of all that is living in our inmost depths. This is what makes us realise what we fundamentally are. It is always there. Let everything within us speak of another and surrender itself to him. A fundamental joy. If we doubt it, we need only ask if we would be prepared to exchange it for any other. We should simply believe in this joy which may be very secret but which we cannot doubt. We are sure of our reason for happiness.

A MYSTERY OF GRACE

Everything rests on this mystery which is given to us to live in faith. It is because we believe in this mystery that our cry to God, our desire to live by his mystery is an absolute, a fulness, however feeble our own expression of it may be. Prayer is not complete in itself. Praying is to open ourselves. This only makes sense when we believe in the hidden mystery which requires that we open the doors of our hearts. Our prayer is secretly taken up in the grace of God's presence. We would not be surprised by the obscurity of this presence if we truly believed in the fulness of its mystery. An inner poverty which is content to be nothing but hope. Let the depths of our hearts become all attention.

Believing in God is to offer him in our poverty an act of faith which can secretly receive from him alone life and enlightenment. Believing in God is to live with his presence at the core of our act of faith. Faith is measured not by the believer but by the object of belief. In him and through him faith becomes all that it is. He is present in it. He lives in it and gives it life. Faith is taken up into his fulness. At the heart of our faith we already apprehend his presence and know that we should believe in him totally. Our faith is stronger than all things because it is of another order.

A CLOSE PRESENCE

Our absolute trust is expressed in absolute simplicity in our prayer. Putting all our trust in the love of God is first of all to offer him simply our poor little act of faith just as it is. The more simply we accept God the more humbly we trust in him, the closer we feel him taking hold of us by the grace of his presence. Our faith is a thin veil which is transparent to the Lord's presence. We know that we receive everything from his presence and this means that the simplest act of faith can open our hearts to him and know that he is close within our reach. In this knowledge we can live with his presence, joyfully, through all the silences. Nothing can stop us believing in it, expecting everything from it, because our faith and hope rely on it. Our faith may seem a little thing to us. We do not put our trust in our own faith, but in God in whom we believe. The humbler our faith, the truer it is.

Christ is always with us. His presence and atmosphere is the continuity of our prayer through all the acts of faith which renew our contact with him. We have a relationship by faith with Christ who identifies with us. This relationship is at the centre of what is most personal in us. We should turn every difficulty into an increase of trust. Believing in God means knowing that we can never trust him too much. We should entrust ourselves to God's love which he has for us personally. We should learn to discern his presence in our lives.

Even when we no longer know it, can no longer say we believe it, God loves us and keeps us in his hands. The Lord sees our hearts, our true deep desires. He sees us already as what we should like to be. His grace is always active, freely going before. If it meets with obstacles in us this does not hinder it. It only asks us to allow these obstacles to give way bit by bit, to let it work. It will gradually make our hearts gentler and more peaceful. Grace alone can do this.

THE FREEDOM OF LOVE

Faith gives us a glimpse of God's fulness of charity for all things. People who hurt us and, we feel, do us wrong are also in this order and harmony of charity. God knows his secret ways. We should have enough faith in

God's love to follow him peacefully along his own ways. This is the freedom of entrusting everything to the Lord and putting all our trust in him. It is a freedom lived in gratitude. We should look at things simply, that is to say freed from all the complications of self-attachment.

We apprehend the fulness of God's love as a mystery in which we are involved, which lives in us. Let us also recognise it in our neighbours. We should at least respect our neighbour's secret self in the eyes of God. We should try not to look at him with our eyes alone. There is always a beyond which eludes us. A beyond where a person's deepest truth only exists in God's sight. We receive everything from God's love in the communion with him he has granted us. In him may we become nothing but love. Let us become incapable of not loving.

ALIVE WITH CHRIST

We tremble before the mystery. We hardly dare credit the fulness of communion in which Christ in his all prevailing love has made us so truly at one with himself. In the ever present grace of his Eucharist where we get an inkling of the mystery, we are completely united with him. In us he lives his sonship to the Father. We enter into it with him, in him. Prayer cannot be thought of as a precise operation which can be rigorously defined. Prayer is being ready and open for an unforeseeable exchange, a lived communion in which we gradually discover the Other by learning to be truly ourselves in his presence. We should live in freedom what God's ever present love brings to life in our hearts. We receive it from God. Let us receive it in simple trust. Let us acquiesce. Give our consent. Let our consent pay attention.

Let us believe in God's love, in his faithfulness. He is always at work in our hearts, making our prayer fruitful by taking it up into his fulness. He turns it into a mystery which goes beyond us and whose secret we must respect. We can be certain that our faintest cry opens our heart to God's love. May the simplicity of our hope bear witness to him in whom we have put our trust. A simplicity which is confidence. Let us simply keep close to him who is our only hope. We need nothing but his presence. The presence of the Lord apprehended by perfect trust. He is the one who cannot fail us. The fulness of the mystery in which our hope rests, recognised by the very simplicity of our trust. The way we trust him expresses what we have glimpsed of his fulness. A silence filled with the sense of God's infinite fulness, infinitely beyond us but also infinitely close.

Let us really look to the Lord, to him alone. Let our prayer be a total act of faith in his active presence whose grace takes hold of every heart that really desires it, however poor and weak that heart may feel. Let us be completely docile, at the Lord's disposal and he will see our hearts.

Praying is being open to God's mystery, being taken up into this mystery. It is to enter into a communion with an infinite which wants to come close to us. We cannot see God but we can welcome the gift of his presence. We can pay attention to this presence. His presence begins our awareness and opens the way to his love. And we know that it remains even when we cannot feel it. In dark times we could have doubts about what is in our hearts, if what was there belonged to us alone. But what is in our hearts comes from beyond us. God gives it life and him we cannot doubt. We are sure of his love's faithfulness whose ultimate expression is his mercy. Doubting our own love in dark and difficult times would be to doubt God's love for us. We should pray with confident abandonment and also live.

Conclusion

QUITE SIMPLY LET our behaviour conform with our
deepest truth, with what we are. Let it express our
awareness that we are children of God. Our self awareness is then bound to be a prayer. We only have a full
awareness of what we are in prayer. Praying is being. It
is not something added on, it is being aware of what we
are. It is and remains our deepest truth even when we
walk in darkness.[1]

1. Prayer, in the full sense can only be addressed to God.
It is an attitude appropriate only before God. This should
have been made clear by all that we have said above. What
we call prayer to the saints – perhaps to call it recourse to their
intercession – poses an ecumenical problem which appears to us
to be a problem not about prayer, but about the communion
of saints. That is why we have not discussed it. What we wish
to stress here is that prayer, in the strong sense, can only be
addresses to God. Catholic theology makes this plain by using
two different words for worship of God and honour of the
saints.